CHILDHOOD'S
THIEF

CHILDHOOD'S THIEF

ONE WOMAN'S JOURNEY OF HEALING FROM SEXUAL ABUSE

ROSE MARY EVANS, M.S.W.

BANTAM BOOKS

New York   Toronto   London   Sydney   Auckland

This edition contains the complete text
of the original hardcover edition.
NOT ONE WORD HAS BEEN OMITTED.

CHILDHOOD'S THIEF

A Bantam Book / Published by arrangement with Scribner

PUBLISHING HISTORY
Macmillan edition published 1994
Bantam edition / August 1995

Book design by Donna Sinisgalli

Library of Congress Cataloging-in-Publication Data

Evans, Rose Mary.
Childhood's thief : one woman's journey of
healing from sexual abuse / Rose Mary Evans.
p.   cm.
Originally published: New York : Macmillan,
1994.
ISBN 0-553-37546-6
1. Adult child sexual abuse victims—Case studies.
2. Psychotherapy—Case studies.   I. Title.
RC569.5.A28E94   1995
616.85'82239'0092—dc20
[B]   95-1654
                                           CIP

Published simultaneously in the United States and Canada

Bantam Books are published by Bantam Books, a division of Bantam
Doubleday Dell Publishing Group, Inc. Its trademark, consisting of
the words "Bantam Books" and the portrayal of a rooster, is
Registered in U.S. Patent and Trademark Office and in other
countries. Marca Registrada. Bantam Books, 1540 Broadway,
New York, New York 10036.

PRINTED IN THE UNITED STATES OF AMERICA
FFG   10 9 8 7 6 5 4 3 2 1

ACKNOWLEDGMENTS

This book is an accretion of help, love, serendipity, and a belief in me from many sources:

I'm especially grateful to Donna Lee Graham, whose love, support, and enthusiasm have never wavered; also for the beauty and energy of Dragonback Ranch—her retreat center in southwestern Colorado—which provided the restorative boost I needed to finish the manuscript.

My enormous respect and appreciation go out to the dedicated and overworked staff of the Community Mental Health Center where this story unfolded. Fiscal forces no longer allow public health agencies to deliver the kind of therapy described here.

I feel boundless gratitude to my brother, Carl Evans, who has always been there for me. Always. He's the closest I'll ever come to having a twin.

To Madeleine Krebs, Judy Lazarus, Joan Scott, and Marcia Warrant, dear and faithful members (along with Donna) of a long-standing women's group that nourishes my soul as well as palate.

Thanks to Marilyn Lerch, ever supportive, whose poet's eye and teacher's ear provided an invaluable perspective when I was too close to see.

Dolores LaChapelle, leading an Autumn Equinox Celebration in Silverton, Colorado, in 1985, encouraged me to give voice to the bard housed within my Welsh heritage. I didn't know what she was talking about.

Just before the Spring Equinox in 1988, synchronicity offered separate conversations on two successive days with Milton Kidd and Jeanne Mozier. That's when I finally heard my own enthusiasm for telling this story.

In the early days, keen ears were lent to my fledgling effort by Marcie Telander. Her generous attention validated my direction.

Celia Coates, MSW, was there during a difficult transition, tending that ancient, comforting fire while I talked out my heartache in her office.

I'm thankful to Ann Horton, who, after reading a few pages from a primitive draft, was convinced long before I was that *my* part of the process needed to be included in the telling.

I have great affection for Wilma Dykeman, my mentor over these last several years. At the same time, I've also felt an appreciation for the late Alex Haley, who was her friend and neighbor; I often imagined his spirit was overseeing the progress of this project. Jointly, they led the way to Lisa Drew, my editor, who understood my vision from our first contact.

Thanks to Mark McClure, Trysh Swift, and Laura Goodin for their perspectives.

My deep gratitude, of course, extends to JoAnn and a host of other clients from whom I've learned so much. I hope they'll recognize that many of their teachings have shown up on these pages.

To Ellen Best Evans and Wilson A. Evans
my parents and guides

And to every Honey and the Man
who ever befriended a stray child

The beauty is in the walking. We are betrayed by the destinations.

GWYN THOMAS

CONTENTS

AUTHOR'S NOTE

"JoAnn," who has no fear of the truth, gave me permission to use the names of people and places from her life. However, the part of my training which accepts confidentiality as a cornerstone of pyschotherapy leaves me uncomfortable in doing that. If she should later choose to waive an entitlement to privacy, that will be up to her. Names have been changed, therefore, and identifying information altered in order to protect her anonymity. The gentleman from her hometown, for example, who is described in the last chapter, illustrates this effort to disguise someone's identity while holding to the essence of the event.

INTRODUCTION

It's an old theme: the teacher becomes the student, the patient becomes the healer. The shift may be subtle but it is always profound. In this passage each person realizes a potential not foreseen at the outset when their roles seemed clear.

Undeniably there are those individuals who come to us for instruction, for help, or to be mended who change our lives immeasurably. "JoAnn" was such a person in my life. She was referred to me for psychotherapy, and I'm convinced there was no coincidence to our paths intersecting when they did. While she knew from our first meeting that she needed help, I had no idea I needed what *she* had to offer.

Suffering with a debilitating depression, JoAnn was a forty-seven-year-old woman with no past. At least no distant past, no remembered "childhood" past. Early in our work together I was impressed with her drive to search out the truth. She seemed fearless in this area; she simply had to know all she could know. Displaying little emotion, she clearly was used to being in control. This struck me as curious. How could someone with such a need to control, who had blotted out an entire childhood, be truly unafraid? Or if she *was* frightened beneath the controlled exterior, where did the courage to investigate the unknown come from? I was puzzled and intrigued. After we dealt with the crisis which brought her in, I commented that I knew nothing about her background, the fabric from which she was cut. She'd spoken minimally about her mother, not at all of anyone else. I remember asking the simplest of questions: "Who is your father?" It seemed to be the only thing needed to set things in motion. *My* interest had touched *her* interest.

Thus began JoAnn's search for her past. Her curiosity, already evident in other areas, was touched by the smallest of sparks and fanned by her relentless desire to know. The next three years she spent remembering, directing her considerable energies to uncovering those lost years with an intensity and abandon that belied the tight hold on the reins of her life. She didn't just remember, she remembered everything. I've never known anyone who possessed such sweeping recall as JoAnn had. I think the force she finally brought to the reclaiming of her life was similar to that used long ago to repress those early events she couldn't assimilate at the time.

I feel privileged to have been the therapist in the right place at that right time, invited to travel alongside as JoAnn took her light back into the hidden shadows of a childhood no child should ever have had to suffer. She was remarkably courageous in recalling the horrors of her youth. In doing so she also remembered a very brief, bright period, and the profound influence of two unlikely people who provided a life-sustaining oasis amid the desert of inhumanity that made up the first fifteen years of her life.

It is this story I want to tell.

I think it bears telling because these times are so focused on the cynicism and self-absorption at our collective center stage that we need all the reminders we can get of the potent force love exerts. We need reminding that, yes, there are even miracles in the hell we ourselves construct.

JoAnn's story is a testament to the amazing ability of the psyche to protect the core of life, the human spirit, when the environment is an unsafe place. Then, when circumstances are recognized as finally hospitable and nourishing, that spirit can recover and be regenerated. There is no wonder she had to disremember a traumatic youth. What *is* a wonder is that she chose to venture back into that dark abyss at all. Having the courage to open the door of memory permitted the good which was also buried there to return like soaking rains after a drought. And it was this oh-so-brief moment of love and goodness, I think, that saved her life.

At the entrance of the 1970s, at the threshold of my professional life as a psychotherapist, I frequently marveled at the struggles faced by the people in my office. Having planted my first garden around then I was much taken with the imagery of that endeavor: analogies flourished about the child being a little seed planted in the sun, watered and looked after. And I was equally taken with the significance of my perceived role as a gardener in this intra-psychic landscape. The images may be a bit threadbare but truth resides in them nevertheless. Both the little seeds and little children who are cared for start out with a better footing and enjoy a developmental advantage over the ones who are left alone or thrown away.

Back in the early seventies it was my experience with those who had been thrown away years before which left me astonished they had made it through life at all. Now, bearing down on the mid-1990s, I am still in awe. What I find most astounding at this time, though, is that there is a life force so powerful it propels people toward wholeness, toward their potential, in spite of the ways events and conditions may seemingly have joined to squelch their growth. Let life just *try* and prevent someone from growing.

Many years ago while I was still working with JoAnn, I remember climbing a mountain near my hometown in Kentucky. When I came upon a strikingly robust tree growing out of the solid rock face of a cliff, I was struck with how the scene reflected my image of her. At the risk of overcultivating the gardening metaphor, it was clear somehow a seed had landed in a crack in the rock where there was enough dirt for it to sink a tiny root. It had clung to life in what looked like a totally unyielding environment, and had grown into a strong and unforgettably impressive tree. Given half a chance to take hold, living things will defy all odds to convert their circumstances into sustenance. Having set their roots, once-tiny seeds *will* prevail. That's the fact of it. And the miracle of it as well.

As interesting as JoAnn's story turned out to be, so was the way she got to it, the "how" of its unfolding. Initially it seemed all I did as her therapist was express my interest in knowing what had made up the background so hidden from her present. Being determined to move ahead with her life she became committed to reclaiming her past. Impatient with my plodding ways and tedious questions, unsatisfied with the limitations of our one or two hours of therapy each week, she found a way to do the necessary work which uniquely suited her.

How does a forgotten life get resurrected when one is long on curiosity and short on trust? Familiar with self-sufficiency and unused to feeling things emotionally? JoAnn sought out her memories when and where she felt safest: alone, in the privacy of her home. She began writing there, and gave herself over to it completely. Hours a day, every free moment, she wrote. She brought in everything she wrote for me to read so we could use it in her therapy (the material was well over 4,500 pages when she typed it years later); all that she shared I read and found riveting.

Somehow JoAnn discovered a free-associative way to suspend her rational, thinking mind. Doing so allowed long-forgotten voices and scenes to reemerge from a vast warehouse of consciousness where it is thought a trail remains of everything that has ever happened to us. She recalled things from such an early period in her life many people will surely challenge the idea of the brain's ability to remember anything at that stage of development. I was certainly skeptical at first of recollections from her infancy, partly because I can't remember anything from *my* very earliest years. But then I never thought it was crucial for me to fill in those blank pages. Most of us, I suspect, feel that way.

JoAnn's writing was unquestioned, uncensored. She simply allowed it to come, and gave it a voice. Later she reflected that if she had thought about what she was writing she probably would not have done it; she'd have been stopped dead in her tracks with disbelief.

But write she did, with disbelief on hold, so she could know and then be free of her past. She did it entirely for herself, during an uncharacteristic period of self-centeredness. Yet the writings she shared struck me as a most generous gift. They taught me more than I ever learned in a classroom and seemed to dislodge me from a cozy pew near the altar of science. My usual tools of understanding failed in explaining not only how this woman survived the abuse and cruelty she was shown as a child but how she managed to arrive at her present state of peace and wholeness. I consider this gift a price-less one. It has helped return me to the terrain of wonder—a place I loved being as a child—where there was much I didn't understand but little that escaped my enthusiasm and appreciation for the mysteries of life.

CHILDHOOD'S
THIEF

1

FROM THE
THERAPIST'S CHAIR

Everybody has a story to tell.

Long ago our ancestors used to sit around their fires in caves or on the plains and recount the dangers they'd faced during the last hunt. Since they had to rely on each other for survival their connectedness was crucial; they must have spent hours telling the younger ones where *their* ancestors had come from and how they made the journey. In the great rush of our lives today little time is set aside to talk with each other, to recount how we survived childhood and how we got to where we are. We don't even know it's important.

Today's firepit is often that space in the psychotherapist's office around which an elemental ritual takes place as the helper and the one seeking help come together. The patient, or client, is hoping for a change: perhaps to feel less depressed or more confident, to be more assertive, less anxious, to stop crying, to be able to cry, to function better. The therapist, trained to listen, is there to facilitate that change. The change happens in their interaction, through the telling of a story and through the listening to it. I've begun to see that in their coming together both people are transformed.

I'm a therapist and I've also been a client. Most of us who seek help don't know we have a story worthy of telling; we simply want to feel better. In my own case, I went for help when I had lost a sense of perspective about myself after a loss I never imagined happening. My life had not been a particularly difficult one to live, especially compared to the lives I heard about in my own office when I sat in the therapist's chair. Still, I'm convinced nobody has an easy life. Not that we should, either, but some people have to deal with much more hardship than others. So even though I didn't consider my own problems to be traumatic, as I talked to my therapist across the safety and light of the fire she tended, my life assumed proportions I hadn't previously granted it.

The process of giving voice to our own narrative is an honoring of our experience. Talking about the forces and events that shaped us is the means by which we inform ourselves of what we've survived. We begin to hear our own story through the telling of it to someone else. *Their* listening helps *us* listen; if they pay close enough attention we listen carefully enough to hear our own pain, to validate our struggle and recognize our strength. I think it was Gregory Bateson who said, "It takes two to know one." We do indeed need each other if we are to know ourselves.

While talking to Celia throughout my own therapy it was as if I borrowed her ears in order to experience myself anew. During that process the feelings I'd minimized and the senses I'd dulled assumed something closer to their original intensity. As I became aware of how clearly she was allied with me and how much attention she paid to my throwaway lines, I started to treat myself with a measure of the same interest and kindness. How could I do any less?

Gradually I began to draw myself in more vivid colors, and with a bold range of subtle shading. Not only did I come to feel more three-dimensional but eventually I found my place on a canvas stretched to include my parents, grandparents, and the many nameless ancestors who formed a grand processional ahead of me.

Living, when you think about it, calls for a heroic effort on our part. Enormous faith is required for us to believe we can navigate clear of the shoals, and to try to do so with battered, hand-me-down compasses. Every single one of us starts out with a secondhand compass, passed on to us by our parents. Some of these "heirlooms" hardly work at all. When we dare look at our lives it's clear how little control we have over what happens to us. And yet were we truly conscious—in the way Thich Nhat Hanh, the Vietnamese Buddhist monk, means when he urges us to be aware even of having a non-toothache—we'd also see how countless miracles fill each day we make it to another sunset. I may not have been able to articulate it at the time, but part of my discovery in therapy had to do with learning and appreciating how I fit into this epic journey that dwarfs all of us.

That I discovered many surprising things during the course of working with Celia came as no shock to me. I expected to change in some way as a consequence of the experience; it's what I was there for. Most of us who undertake the "talking cure" when we're feeling some degree of desperation probably fail to regard the enterprise as an adventure. But that's what it is nevertheless. As with many situations, it isn't until we've gotten past something that its meaning can be recognized or understood.

When I'm the therapist, and have the emotional distance necessary to be of help, the adventure lying ahead for my clients is obvious to me. Even if they don't see it that way, I regard the opportunities awaiting them as exciting, and view them as offering a challenge for myself as the helper. Yet in the role of therapist I haven't always considered the exchange to hold the same potential of adventure for me, the listener, too. But that *is* what often happens nowadays as my clients and I sit beside a fire whose light seeps into the surrounding shadows and creates an area safe enough for them to begin trusting me with their stories.

These days I'm finding that in hearing their stories I discover previously unfamiliar aspects of my own expanding narrative. This change, for me, has been a gift from JoAnn and the work we did together during her therapy. She has been as important a teacher for me as I was for her years ago.

If I'd been an artist when I met JoAnn in 1980 and she had hired me as a portrait painter instead of her psychotherapist, my painting of her back then would surely have been titled "A Study in Black and White." It would've suited perfectly. Her short, thick hair was distinctly and decidedly salt-and-pepper. She dressed immaculately, quite stylishly, almost always in striking black and white patterns. She tended to view the world in that color scheme, too. Things were either right or wrong to JoAnn. Her clear and strong opinions seemed to divide the good and bad without hesitation. Uncomfortable with ambiguity, she did not live easily in the gray areas of life's uncertainties.

It all fit, of course, with her efforts to bring a measure of control to a life bred in chaos. But I hadn't known that when we met.

As is always the case in psychotherapy, neither client nor therapist knows what's in store when they set out to work together. With JoAnn that lesson was particularly vivid. The degree to which the past was hidden from her consciousness is not so very rare among our clients. What was unusual about her was the commitment and determination she brought to the search for the repressed events of her childhood. Where others may be content to unearth just enough of their past to see the foundation on which their lives are built, JoAnn had to get to the bedrock. Her black-and-white, all-or-nothing approach led to another characteristic dichotomy: the search moved her from almost nothing remembered to practically nothing forgotten.

It's doubtful I'll ever fully know why she allowed those memories to surface when she did. Still, since I'm always curious about what's underfoot at the point in one's life when a sea change takes place, I've wondered why it happened then. Usually when we decide to take a step that shifts our life's course it's a confluence of many factors. JoAnn had been in therapy a number of times before, in a variety of settings. The crisis which brought her in for our first appointment—telling her visiting mother to leave the house—didn't appear any more destabilizing than previous junctures when she had sought and received help. Yet the material for transformation was gathering.

Unhappiness seems sometimes to reach a critical mass. When misery becomes this dense the addition of even a "small" hurt or disappointment can tilt the emotional scales dramatically and the reaction often appears out of proportion to the triggering event. I think it's possible the visit by JoAnn's mother carried with it enough psychic weight to alter for her what had been a manageable amount of emotional material, and so she became determined then to get at the core of her unhappiness.

Many of us, approaching fifty, are less tolerant of outer conventions and our own reflexive behaviors that we realize are wasteful of energy and time. As both energy and time grow more precious we may begin to question the reasons for doing as we've always done. Perhaps at that point, in the early 1980s, JoAnn's courage to delve deeper was partially a factor of age and the growing sense of wasting her life.

Even though repressed feelings or memories, because they're unavailable to the conscious mind, may seem to cause no problems, *something* is required to keep them that way. It's reasonable to assume that some measure of human effort is necessary to not "know" what one knows. There isn't any question but that constant vigilance takes a crippling toll on both body and soul; such watchfulness eventually wears down physiological processes as well as psychological coping mechanisms. So maybe by age forty-seven JoAnn had grown too tired and no longer had the strength required to maintain her customary level of control.

All these factors may have played a part in what happened. Other things perhaps did too.

Naturally I've wondered about my own role in the unfolding process of JoAnn's therapy. There are a few things about me, and that period in my life, which I think influenced how we responded to each other. First of all, since being in control is not a major issue with me, I tend not to get into power struggles with clients who especially need to feel they're in the driver's seat, even as they acknowledge lives which have gotten off course. I was comfortable with letting her set the pace, although I wasn't always comfortable with the pace she set.

And part of my interest in understanding JoAnn, I think, had something to do with a previous case, one which had left me quite distressed. About a year or two earlier I'd briefly seen an anxious young woman who came to therapy extremely concerned about leaving her daughter at home when she went shopping or had errands to run on the weekend. She'd nearly panic until she got back and found the little girl was okay and that her husband had taken care of her. There was nothing she could identify as causing any reason for her to worry, and she couldn't recall anything from her own life that might have seeded such a concern. But as we continued to approach the area of her fear, which she always dismissed as

irrational, she quietly told me about having had two dreams—at
least that's what she thought they were—in which men she didn't
know scared her awake on several occasions after she was sent to
bed. Similar to JoAnn, she hardly remembered anything about her
childhood. Her mother had died many years ago of liver problems.
She guessed her mother might have been an alcoholic; she'd been
married four or five times and there had always been a boyfriend or
husband around during those early years.

I'd thought our work was proving fruitful and my client was
becoming more comfortable with this talking scene when she suddenly dropped out of treatment, without ever saying a word. I
wasn't able to locate her either. When I thought about her I ended
up feeling perplexed: What had happened? Why had she fled? Was
it something I either did or failed to do? I suppose all therapists have
cases that stir up memories of uneasy endings, of unsettled out-
comes. So, when JoAnn appeared and made a few comments which
reminded me of the young mother who'd left a hundred questions
in her wake, it occurred to me this might be a chance for a different
resolution this time, albeit with a different patient. I don't know
whether or not JoAnn sensed my interest in knowing what had
taken place in her life, but the interest was there and had probably
been simmering on a rear burner for a few years until she came
along and stirred it up again.

All of this is just a kind of guessing on my part that springs from
wondering why JoAnn made a quantum leap in therapy this time
around. It happens often, of course, and not just in psychotherapy:
the observable signs and circumstances appear the same, but one
day a person does something notably different with the situation she
or he is in. JoAnn herself never expressed any interest in the point.
In fact she once told me—as we were dealing with the ending part
of therapy—that she would have done the work some day, some
way, whether or not she'd met me. I believed her, too, when she
said that.

Those of us who set out to be helpers are dependent for a great part
of our learning on the patients and clients who come to us. After
years of schooling and training are over, our heads filled with infor-

mation and theories, we still require direct case experience to become truly competent. Blessedly for those who seek us out at that stage, our untrammeled enthusiasm and interest tend to compensate for a lack of experience. There is something to be said for the energy and optimism of the novice in any field or profession, quite a lot to recommend the initiate's sense of *possibilities* over the knowledge of *probabilities* weighed by the veteran. And because a sense of hope is essential for healing there can be an advantage in the newly trained care-giver not knowing what she or he is up against, or what the odds against success actually are.

I believe JoAnn and I were just about equally unprepared for what lay ahead when we agreed to work together. I've also come to believe our respective ignorance was not a terrible hindrance. JoAnn could acknowledge the fact her childhood was a blank, and she wasn't apologetic about not understanding what had happened to her later in life as a result of those missing early years. Throughout the course of therapy she had the clear head not to blame herself for what she hadn't known. I think because of her diligence in every undertaking she was able to accept her efforts as having been the best she knew how to do at the time.

Unlike JoAnn, though, I was not as accepting of my own ignorance. At times I felt defensive about what I didn't know, apologetic about my obvious limitations. I accepted that I was supposed to know how to help troubled people in troubling situations; it was my job. I wasn't without experience or expertise, either, but in the area JoAnn's memories began to lead us my experience was sadly lacking.

In fact both of us, at our first encounter, were the bewildered beneficiaries of systems that had failed to meet our separate needs. Obviously JoAnn's family, as well as the school system in which she'd been enrolled for ten years and the community to which she belonged for fifteen, had all let her down. The system that failed me, I see in retrospect, was the educational process of my own professional training. Though excellent by all standards, it certainly hadn't adequately prepared me for the cases I faced in increasing numbers. The larger truth is that during the 1960s our society as a whole was not disposed to deal with the issue of how women and children were being treated, especially how they were being treated in their own homes. Because schools simply reflect their time and culture it's no wonder I hadn't been better prepared by my professors. Their heads were as deep in the sand of status quo as were the rest of ours. In the mental health field our patients, once again, were the ones who instructed us.

2

A CLEVER LOCKSMITH

JoAnn hadn't impressed me as a particularly likely instructor when we met. She was seriously depressed, barely able to function in the routine of her daily life. It was all she could do to maintain her appearance, which looked to be the careful focus of her efforts to communicate stability and normalcy. Clearly she was well read but her speech conveyed that little attention had been given to many of the basics of an education. She seemed to be a hungry and solitary reader who apparently neither discussed, nor heard discussed, the ideas she roamed among. A large vocabulary, along with pronunciation that often missed the mark, suggested she knew how to track down the meanings of words she read but had never been taught the rules of phonetics or been exposed to people with similar vocabularies and interests. My impression was of a keenly curious person, an isolated student, used to absorbing ideas on her own from the pages of books instead of in dialogue or from interaction with others. All this indicated someone for whom self-reliance was a cornerstone of life.

As she began to describe the concerns which had brought her to our clinic, JoAnn's self-appraisal was to the point and painfully honest. I found her earnestness most compelling. It also unsettled me. In spite of showing no emotion she managed to convey how seriously she regarded our initial appointment. Without pleasantries or small talk she cut to the core of why she was in my office: friends and co-workers believed her to be happy but she thought death would be preferable to the hollowness of her existence. Regardless of how I may have later recoiled from the reality JoAnn eventually pieced together, from the first time we met I believed her.

It was stark, her approach to therapy. She operated without fuss or flourish, often without even the normal civilities of social convention. (She agreed with that observation when I shared it with her years later, saying there had been times early on when she resented my using part of her session to say "Hello.") She had no tolerance for wasting time. And perhaps her lack of affect, an absence of feelings associated with the words she spoke, enabled her to pare away all the nonessentials. There was no fat in the way she related, no padding. Since she was neither defensive nor judging, she offered neither apology nor blame. With this as an opening, JoAnn set the tone for her participation in our therapeutic work together.

During some of those early sessions I wondered if I could match her intensity. The bare-bones, full-throttle pace of JoAnn's style was not exactly *my* style. I thought at least my efforts stood a fair chance of being accepted because JoAnn already had a positive transference toward therapy. She'd viewed her previous experiences as helpful and was favorably disposed toward any situation where she saw there was a chance to learn something.

A year earlier she'd been seen for a short while by our clinic's staff psychiatrist, given antidepressant medication and discharged after a dozen or so sessions when she reported feeling better. The greatest benefit of those appointments, she mentioned on several occasions, was hearing Dr. Cunningham say, "You don't have to do anything you don't want to do." It seemed to have been the first time she'd heard such an idea and she clung to it like a talisman.

When she phoned the clinic again in 1980, after ordering her mother out of the house, Dr. Cunningham realized JoAnn didn't need medication; she needed to talk. In making the referral, she suggested that JoAnn, at a loss to remember her past, probably had weathered a horrible childhood.

The first several months of therapy were straightforward as we tackled the crisis at hand. In the process JoAnn was quick to see the response to her mother's visit exceeded the proportions of the event itself. Because she didn't attach blame or guilt to what she realized was an overreaction on her part she could allow room for her curiosity to spread out unimpeded. It was to be a common pattern: being undefensive about her behavior meant she didn't need to justify her actions. Not having to justify her actions allowed for understanding them instead, thereby providing a chance to find out more about herself. I think JoAnn's desire to learn and to understand became the most powerful motivating force in her therapy.

As I became caught up in the excavation she undertook, a similar fascination began to play a central role for me, too. Perhaps it was another factor that accounted for the connecting link between us despite the differences separating us. In our work together I was frequently uncomfortable with my limited knowledge about sexual abuse. It was sometimes a humbling thing for me to admit, but there was no point in doing otherwise. I obviously wasn't sure of what to look for in JoAnn's unfolding story, what questions to ask, what to follow up on. However, I suppose that what must have come through as I sat with JoAnn, overshadowing the distress and inadequacy I felt, was my wanting to understand and be helpful, and my rapidly growing appreciation of her indomitable spirit.

It's an exaggeration to say JoAnn didn't remember anything about her childhood. When she started to feel some slight relief and indicated a desire to go beyond understanding her presenting crisis, I began to ask more about her family and what she recalled about growing up. Her childhood wasn't a total blank. She had two memories from those fifteen years before she left home. One was of washing dishes as a small girl and throwing the pan of dishwater at someone, then getting in trouble for having done so. The other recollection was of sitting out by the mailbox in front of her house, waiting for her mother. *That* was her past; the images weren't quite like the pivotal few fossils a paleontologist might use to construct the entire skeleton of an animal extinct for millions of years.

I was curious about who she had grown up with during those early years, where and how the family had managed to live in that period at the end of the Depression, when she was born. Often she seemed surprised that I asked questions about her relatives, saying she never gave them any thought at all. But regardless of how quizzically she regarded me, or with what forbearance she tolerated my inquiries, right away she would call or write her mother to ask the questions I'd asked of her.

Soon after JoAnn had gotten the name of the man she was told was her father, I'd wanted to know exactly who were the people in her family back then. A week or two later she came in with a long list and a shaky idea of birthdates, or at least a notion of birth order. We constructed a makeshift genogram, a kind of family tree, roughly covering three generations. If I traced backward to find the small, nearly unnoticed-at-the-time gesture which signaled the initial step in what was to become a life-altering event, I believe it was here, at the moment in her therapy when JoAnn first put pen to paper. She created a short, piercing description of several people in her family, some of whom she hadn't even remembered until giving her nonthinking mind permission to go grazing in her memory's field.

She then started collecting information, and just as quickly grew skeptical of everything she was told. After hearing her mother's version of an event, she might call one or more of her aunts and get their reading of the same situation. This exercise yielded memorable lessons for JoAnn about the power of an individual to create her own reality.

There wasn't much agreement about anything among the people she questioned. For the most part she was met with either disinterest or what she described as a "what's-in-it-for-me" attitude. She felt sure she'd have gotten more cooperation if she'd thought of how to tell people they stood to gain something by talking with her. At other times she faced downright hostility: Why did she want to know? Who cared about stuff that was over and done with years ago? What the hell difference did it make anyhow?

So even though she went about gathering information, nothing she heard seemed to be effective in dislodging the stone blocking the crypt into which her past had been placed. Yet I'm certain the work she did was necessary because a background slowly assumed shape.

The human mind is a wondrous creation. And the part of it we call the Unconscious is as full of marvel and mystery as any aspect of it. If a person is forced to endure something she or he experiences as unbearable, an escape hatch is mercifully provided. In effect, the horror of an assault that is unacceptable to someone's physical or emotional integrity gets shunted aside to a well-protected chamber where the body's wounds and the psyche's pains are sealed away. Unknown and powerful forces stand guard there for as long as the world is perceived as an unsafe place, thus allowing the person who has been nearly destroyed to continue living.

Another amazing thing about the mind is that it seems to have the ability to do this, at least when repeated childhood traumas occur, without demanding an effort on the part of the person who is in such danger. I think of this gift from the mind as the psyche's equivalent of the body going into a shock reaction, assuring that vital processes immediately slow down in response to crushing injuries or life-threatening physical trauma.

Though no effort may be initially required to survive in this way does not mean it's done without cost over the years that follow. If the abuse continues, especially to children, the cost is great indeed because eventually they learn to shut down when detecting even the *possibility* of danger approaching; "not feeling" might then become a more conscious choice. Occasionally, later on, some people sense they are paying too high a price for living hobbled lives. Sometimes they choose to broach this inner fortress and discover what's been stored there, to understand how it affects them. This is a monumentally courageous act. Frequently it seems to me the thicker the walls of the fortification, the more fragile is that which has been secured in the keep.

If the Unconscious could perform only one feat, that of being able to sequester still-intolerable pain from a too-vulnerable being, well, that alone would be enough to capture our respect. But it possesses still another source of wonder in its willingness to release—ever so carefully, in the majority of cases—that same material when the self is strong enough to deal with it.

Our Unconscious mind knows us better than we know ourselves. I can see now how evident this is when I look back over the evolution of JoAnn's therapy. The key to unlocking her past was not provided by the questioning of relatives about family matters. Apparently they still posed too great a threat and JoAnn didn't feel trusting enough of them, though she probably didn't understand that at the time.

I think my belief in her, and my interest in knowing what she so fiercely wanted to know, was gradually wearing away at the caution and distrust that had forged the prow of her contact with life. An embryo of trust was developing as we set out to learn together. And if my presence and interest provided adequate light to glimpse the outline of her secret vault with its shadowy lock, the key itself was custom made for her particular situation, by her mind's own clever locksmith. As is so often the case, the key came from an unexpected source during a chance encounter.

JoAnn worked as a secretary for a large, suburban construction company. Already at the job for ten years when I met her, she was well known and highly regarded by the hundreds of staff and clients who would have reason to contact her desk. One of the many people who stopped by to conduct some business, or chat a few minutes on his way through, was a middle-aged, soft-spoken black man. Regardless of how hectic the day or how much pressure everyone was under, she felt he bestowed a sense of calm, like a benediction, every time they spoke. It was after a week when he'd been in several days in a row about building permits that JoAnn's first memories shook loose.

The first piece of childhood to be released for her consideration was the gentle and calm presence of an elderly black man stopping his horse to offer a ride on his wagon. What she remembered was how he talked, the tone of his voice. She realized the man hadn't wanted her to get hurt, so she had to make sure the horse was perfectly still before he let her climb up on the wagon.

Later on, when we looked back in one of our puzzle-solving exchanges, I could see how several bridges had emerged to connect the present with her past. JoAnn was beginning to feel a little more safe in my office; because our times together offered the only tranquil outpost in her life, I think she had a framework within which to freshly resonate with the calmness of the subcontractor at her desk. That he had such a gentle manner, was friendly, courteous, and, above all, radiated a sense of calmness opened her further to the past. His being black was surely the essential factor allowing her to recall a man who had functioned as the first sip of water for the parched child she was in 1940.

·   ·   ·

JoAnn talked a lot about those early encounters with the man and the horse, trying to describe her response to the experience. (In spite of never knowing his name, she soon learned his wife always referred to him as ". . . that Man." Likewise, when she heard him speak to or about his wife, he called her "Honey." So those were the only names she ever knew for the two of them.) Since she was so detached from her feelings, she didn't know how to label the sensations she was remembering. After several weeks of working at this she brought in a page or two of something she wanted to read me. She'd written of an incident involving the Man which she thought perhaps illustrated a point we'd been talking about, and wanted to know if it was what I meant by a "feeling."

Unlike JoAnn, who was beginning to remember in detail, I don't recall the exact incident she described or the particulars of the occasion. But what I *do* remember, again in contrast to JoAnn, was exactly what I *felt* at the time—because that moment perfectly revealed the essence of the woman sitting across from me. In her understated and low-keyed style, seemingly offhanded (except she obviously had come prepared) and in a voice which was expressionless but for communicating a passion about wanting to understand, she read not more than a few paragraphs.

If one of those cameras aimed to film bank customers had been focused on me that morning, I'm certain it would've caught me staring, slack-jawed and speechless, at someone who—without benefit of a sound track—could have been reading a recipe for Yorkshire pudding. I was astonished, simply astonished. And I'm sure I probably stumbled around trying to collect some elusive words to connect me with what was going on. I felt as if JoAnn had let me look through a pair of binoculars trained to see, amid a swirling fog, an etching-clear picture of a scared and ragged child riding high on the seat of a horse-drawn wagon beside a tall and smiling black man.

The scene she presented, the image I snagged, seemed worth weeks of therapy sessions to me. I believe I told her nothing else had helped me understand as much about what she experienced in that long-ago place. I *hope* I told her that. I must've conveyed something of the kind because she then started bringing in Garfield and

Snoopy spiral notebooks, such as fourth-graders carry in their book bags, crammed with writing which was ever so much more expressive than her voice. Many years later she told me she'd already been writing for a month or more before that session, but until I had spoken of its value, she'd been throwing the pages away as soon as the ink dried and she'd reaped the harvest of memories recovered.

I always perceived JoAnn as having written just for herself. My impression about that hasn't changed, though now I see a loop in the process I never noticed ten years ago. JoAnn *did* write in order to help herself, but when I explained how useful it was to me, too, I think it may have amplified her purpose and she wrote, in part, to help me so I could better help her.

Over the months and years to follow, her longhand-filled pages would tell a story in themselves. Even if you couldn't understand the words because you didn't know the language, the lines on the paper would tell you something about the writer as she worked. This wasn't quite so evident at the beginning because the material and her moods were not especially highly charged. Later, however, when she would plumb deeper into the more painful areas of her childhood, the *way* she wrote added an extra dimension to *what* she wrote.

If you flipped through any one of JoAnn's notebooks, or riffled through a stack of wastepaper she sometimes wrote on the back of (out-dated memos, for example, rescued from the incinerator), you'd see extraordinary variety in how the pages simply *looked*. Sometimes the writing would be fluid and expansive, sometimes scrunched and hard-edged. Occasionally lines would be loaded with capital letters; you might find a whole page that held only seven or eight sprawling, explosive words nailed by several six-inch-high exclamation marks. Often, when describing Honey's kindness or caring, she would draw a tiny lop-sided heart on either flank of Honey's name. At other times she sketched little teardrops falling from words like "sad" and "hurt." You might've wondered if this was the work of a precocious five-year-old comfortable with an energetic cursive script. With only a little training you could've "read" her inner process beneath the words, as an EKG reveals the vagaries of a heart. There was a primitive and unself-conscious artistry in the very act of committing her language to paper.

When JoAnn decided to hand over this material to me many years later she was determined to do us both a favor. First of all she wanted to get the avalanche of paper out of her house. Then she thought it would reduce the volume considerably and make it easier for me if she typed a copy of everything from her sometimes diffi-cult-to-read penmanship. This was a major undertaking, done only with a great expending of time and energy over a two-year period. Unfortunately, from *my* perspective anyway, JoAnn's efficiency re-sulted in as big a loss of one sort as was gained in another. I didn't know until later that she'd been throwing away her notebooks and papers as soon as they were transcribed to type. Typically, she had no comprehension of the unique way in which she originally gave form to her remembrances. Gone forever are the spontaneous and priceless, exquisitely personal, handcrafted touches to the rushing written stream of her consciousness. I mourn their loss.

The stacks of typed pages she gave me remain, though, and serve as the central thread around which our two stories are woven. Starting with the gentleness of her first few memories, here is how the past revealed itself to JoAnn, a most courageous traveler through a deeply shadowed landscape. The words are mostly her own. The editing I've done, however, has been extensive and, I hope, judi-cious. Where I've added content or structure it has been born of knowledge gained from our years of talking, with the intention of clarifying or explaining her writings.

JoAnn's memories surfaced with their own unconscious logic, not in linear, chronological order. I've tried to reconstruct the gen-eral way in which they appeared in her writings and during our sessions in my office. Thus a chapter might contain a sequence of memories that shifted from the writer as a five-year-old, to her ado-lescence and back to a memorable event in a fourth-grade class-room. Sometimes clusters of recollections sprang up around certain themes or ideas related to what was going on in therapy or in some aspect of her current life. In this way a picture assumes shape as the reader becomes part of the process of weaving an unexpected life.

3

CANTALOUPES AND OVERRIPE BANANAS

One of the first places I remember living was on a country road. I was about seven then and it's the place I can picture most clearly. Down from us was a black man and woman. I don't remember much about the woman, but I remember the man had a horse and a wagon which he drove to restaurants in town to collect garbage. The horse would plod down the road, tired and slow, coming home at the end of the day. So tired he was, just barely able to put one foot in front of the other. He had blinders on so he could only look straight ahead.

I can still see it in my eye's memory. We'd be home after school. As usual I had to watch Little Bobby, so we'd walk down to the road to play and wait for the horse and wagon and the man.

The man would say, "Well, well, are you children waiting for us? Ol' Horsey, looks like these little children are waiting for us." He'd take his hat off and wipe a sleeve across his forehead. They'd slow down even slower until they came to a stop and he'd say, "Climb on up, you children. Climb up and you can ride this last little ways home with me."

The man would stop the horse and help us on the wagon for a ride. One of us sat on each side of him. "Come on, Horsey, we's almost home now. Lordy, what you two been up to today?"

We would sit up there high above the wagon on a wood seat

that was just a board. I felt as happy as I could be riding that last "little ways." The house was on the right side of the road. He'd turn in very slowly, and his wife would be on the porch to wave to him. We'd all wave back. The old man would say, "I found these children along the road and brought them for a ride."

When he'd get Ol' Horsey unhitched and put away, we'd help him push the garbage off the wagon. He would go, hot and tired, to the porch to get water for his horse. His wife would sometimes hand him a dipper of water for himself.

There is a sense I have of peace and affection between them. They were an old couple, worn down poor, but they had a soft and warm feeling around them that I never before had come across.

We would go through the garbage and look for treats when he went inside with his wife to eat supper. They had a kerosene lamp on the table. The table was covered with an ancient oil cloth that was nearly rubbed colorless from her wiping it clean. Everything was cleaner than I'd ever seen.

I can remember one time I was so happy to find a rotting banana on the wagon. I was so hungry, and here was a whole banana he said I could have. We never got bananas at home; I'd never even eaten one. To this very day, some forty years later, I do not eat bananas unless they are way overripe.

Well well, today I can say why overripe bananas comfort me so. I never knew why they did until right now.

Now I can remember that *then* I thought we went there for the half-rotten fruit. I can still feel being content and waiting peacefully for the first sight of the wagon, and I know I went there for the peace and comfort of being near him and the horse. It was because of his being "glad to see you children. Hop up and get a little ride."

Nobody had ever been glad to see me before.

Little Bobby wants to ride on the wagon but he don't want to wait out by the road and look for it. So he sits me down at the end of the yard and says, "Wait here, JoAnn. When you see it a coming, you yell for me. Do you hear me? . . . No, you can't come too. Just stay right here and lemme know when you see him up the road a ways."

All Bobby wants to do is go for a ride. Francie's been told to watch for the old nigger. Grannie told her to go watch for the damn nigger to see what he would give us off his wagon. They don't want to wait and miss getting to play. Both of them tell me how they can't sit here all day and wait for the nigger and his wagon to come along. But I better keep a eye on the road and call them the minute he comes unless I wanta get beat up.

Francie grabs my shoulders, turns me around and shakes me hard. "Do you hear me, dummy? Do you? I'll teach you a lesson if you let him get by here without calling me!" and she runs off with Little Bobby.

I'm glad they're gone.

I need to pee, but I can't leave or take my eyes off the road. I just stand right there and pee. Don't even move or think about it. Just pee in my pants right there in the sandy dirt. I see how it turns dark where I'm standing, and then I move over from the wet place to where it's dry. I don't know where the pee went to, but I slide over and watch how the dark sand turns back to dry in the sun. After a while I take a stick and make pictures in the dirt; play with the stick and look for the nigger's wagon. The pants dry right on me.

Cantaloupes. That's what did it: cantaloupes.

One day the man had drove by coming back from town where he sold things from his garden. Bobby and somebody else had seen him and yelled out was there anything in the wagon they could have. The old man gave them some cantaloupes. I watched his easy kind of way with the shouty kids.

Grannie just couldn't get over it when they took them melons inside.

"What the hell you so excited about?" she asked them. "These things is almost rotten. Lookit them soft spots! You'd think the least that dumb nigger could do is give us something halfway decent."

She grabbed one of the cantaloupes and cut it open, started scraping out the seeds. "It ain't no skin offa his nose. Don't cost him a damn cent, does it? Why, he's got more stuff on that wagon than he knows what to do with."

Grannie said there wasn't enough for us kids to eat some now and have any for supper, so we'd just have to wait. She stood right there and stuffed herself with a whole cantaloupe, except for giving Little Bobby a few bites. And she whined about how "you kids eat up everything in sight, so there ain't none for anybody else. By the time you get all these goddam seeds out and cut out the soft spots there ain't nothing left. That nigger's got plenty, I tell you, and it wouldn't cost him a red cent to give us what he don't need."

Grannie was eating one piece after the other of that cantaloupe. She didn't give me any. Said, "Here's you a bite, Bobby," in a coo coo sort of tone.

I didn't care. I didn't smell it, didn't even want it. I watched her cut another one up and put it in a bowl, shoo some flies off the table, then cover the bowl with a plate. She didn't think the kids needed any anyway, seeing's how there wasn't enough to go around. She gave Bobby one last bite.

Grannie always gave to Bobby, petted him, did for him. I saw her give him some of that cantaloupe but I didn't even feel a thing about it. I knew not to. I knew it wouldn't do any good.

"I'm not in the habit of tellin' anybody what they had better do, little boy, and I ain't about to start with you. But I can tell you this for sure: I don't have to put up with this foolishness outta you on my own Place! Now you can just make up your mind to that, boy."

The Man didn't usually raise his voice but this time he did. "Why, I don't think you want to learn a thing. Don't know what's gonna become of you iff'n you keep this up, little fella. Best thing for you be to get yourself on off to where you belong! I don't like to start tellin' nobody what to do, but you better get offa my Place now. I think you just better beat it on home."

Bobby had got mad and called the Man a goddam old nigger. "Who the hell do you think you are, a tellin' me what to do?!" he had shouted at the Man.

I'd been watching the Man, a lot more than Bobby was. Little Bobby was not used to paying attention to how people acted around him 'cause he was so used to getting his way. I'd had to be on watch for how people were doing around me for so long that I'd seen the Man cut his eyes at us. At the time I didn't know it was "cut his eyes," but I knew it was an odd way he looked at us when we didn't listen and mind him real good.

'Specially I remember about waiting for the horse to stop, and jumping in the wagon. The Man said he didn't like Bobby jumping around in the wagon. And he told us we were to STAND BACK until he stopped the wagon dead still 'fore we came out and got on. Our family didn't know the meaning of the word STOP. We didn't know anything at all about stop or about listen.

"Now you wait till the wagon stops still. I don't want you all gettin' hurt none. This here horse and wagon ain't no plaything, boy." But me and Bobby didn't wait. Didn't know how to wait.

The Man had told us. Then he told us he had done already told us. "I don't mind tellin' you oncet, and I don't even mind tellin' you twicet, but when I have to say the very same thing again then that is too much! Now I'm gonna have to draw the line with you, boy. I can't hardly drive this wagon with you jumpin' 'round ever which a way. So I ain't gonna have you ride with me no more less'n you learn how to do right!"

That's when Little Bobby started to cuss and carry on. He screamed at the Man, asking him just who the hell did he think wanted to ride on his old nigger wagon anyhow?

"You ain't nothing but a goddam old shit in your pants nigger!" Bobby yelled. He was like Grandpa in one of his temper fits.

So the Man put him off his Place right then and there.

"It seem like to me he just want to show hisself, Honey. Most all the time. I don't know what's wrong with the boy. Looks like he's all right, but seem like there's sumthin' wrong with him that you just can't see." The Man's voice was like he was trying to puzzle out the answer of why that boy wouldn't listen to him, why he wouldn't try to do better than he'd been doing. I heard him sit down at the table for supper. I was hid under the house.

After he put Ol' Horsey up for the night, he washed his hands at the pump on the side of the porch. He dried his hands and tole me he is going in to supper now. Tole me to get along on home. I sat on the steps while he dried his hands on the rag they hang there to dry your hands on.

"They be waitin' your supper for you down there, chile. Time to get on home," he said to me.

That's dumb. I knew they wouldn't be waiting my supper down there, but I didn't talk. I never talk. When he went inside I crawled under the house.

"I don't think I ever seen no child so hardheaded as that boy, Honey," he says. "He just got to do it all his own way. So hard-headed he ain't 'bout to listen to a thing I tell him. I hate to say it, but that boy is MEAN, Honey. Got a mean streak in him 'bout a mile or two wide. I just don't know how he could a got so mean in so short a time! How old you reckon he is anyways?"

I hear the woman moving around the table. I can't make out the words she's saying, but I can hear the Man. "I done give that boy plenty a rope, Honey, and he went right ahead and hung hisself! Why you shoulda seen the fit that little fella throwed. Whooweee!"

Oh, Little Bobby had really showed himself. Jumping all around and cussing and spitting to beat anything the Man had ever seen. He had looked just like the little man on a string that jiggled and danced when you moved it. Like the cheap toy somebody brought home once with a crazy dancing man that threw himself all over the place when somebody pulled the string he was hanging on.

The Man had walked Little Bobby out to the road and pointed down toward our house. He told the boy to get off the Place since he didn't try to act right. Little Bobby stood on that spot like a cabbage, crying and yelling and cussing at the Man's back as he turned around toward the porch. Yeah, he stomped and hollered something terrible, but he didn't come an inch toward the house. I never figured on seeing anybody make Bobby do something he didn't want to do.

※

I remember a house in the middle of trees, in the middle of fields. It was the first house I can remember us living in. There was a long dirt road leading up to it with a dirt yard all around. No grass, just worn bare dirt everywhere. We played there in the dust and dirt. Even in rain the yard wouldn't have fat, happy mud. It was so hard-packed and trampled down that it wouldn't hold water; the rain ran off. I suppose the people were so packed down that they wouldn't hold life's water either. Any care or love just ran off of them.

Our family was dirt poor. Worse than dirt poor. They were sharecroppers for a while. The whole family worked in the fields. Grannie worked and the children played between the rows until they could pull weeds or pick cotton. Babies were slung in a holder in a shade tree or put down for the nonworking children to watch.

Marie Deborah Foley was the oldest of eight children. She gave birth to one child, me, when she was seventeen years old. Unwed, evidently she believed Grover Clay would marry her. She always said they were going to get married, but while she was waiting he married someone else. He didn't even tell her. In Mama's explanation, *his* mother was cast as the villain of the piece.

It was Depression time. There was my mother, a young woman, attractive, unskilled, poor, and desperately unhappy. There was a house full of hungry brothers and sisters, and she had one hungry girl of her own. All this in an Army town, full of young men with Army pay just laying in their pockets waiting to be spent. My sense is that she might have been a streetwalker in some form.

When I called Louise yesterday to ask about the past, she was quick to remember those long-ago days. She was an old friend of my mother's, and easily recalled how she—along with my mother and Aunt Susan—would go out and get some money. They would buy food, bring it home, Grannie would cook it, and they'd have a feast. Grannie was such a good cook, she said. They would enjoy the food and laugh and gossip, with the little children all around the floor. No man was in the picture she described. There wasn't any mention of the father. Louise said she didn't really remember me, just a floor full of kids.

There was the Grannie and the women and the kids. My feeling on the phone was this was a party time, full of good memories for

Louise. That wasn't my assessment of the situation. How poor must have been her life for this to have been such an obviously warm, happy memory.

My mother worked as a seamstress during the war, out on the Army base. We lived at home until I was in junior high or thereabouts. For some reason we had to leave in a hurry so we moved to a room with a hot plate, and shared the bath. Mama expressed the feeling that we were finally on our own, away from the family. She said this as if to appease me. I was glad when we moved, though I soon knew we weren't away from them. We were still tied to them. Mama seemed to hold on to them holding on to her. We lived across from the high school and I went there. I remember it now.

Some while later we lived on Branch Road, in a one-room, two-story shack. The bottom was a storage area and above it was the room where we lived for a short time. There was another place where we moved, a terrible place. It was a large, lovely home but every inch had been made into rooms-to-let. At least five families, if not more, lived in these chopped-up rooms. Some shared baths and kitchens; we had a bedroom and a kitchen with an outside entrance, and shared a bath. The place was owned by a fat and quarrelsome, nosy woman who fed off the tenants' miseries.

Why in the world did we move so often? It seems we were always slipping away from one place and having to hurry and find another.

My young, pretty mother went with Mr. Shepherd for years. She said she couldn't marry him because of me. All through the years she was trailed by "female problems" because of when I was born, and not having a doctor or proper care. I used to think, *Well, that wasn't my fault you didn't have medical care; how come you blame me? I wasn't even there, and yet you blame me.*

I never put it together before but she was almost always ill, and it wasn't explained to me. I don't believe she ever really understood anything beyond being sick and in pain, going to the doctor and taking the medicine. I don't believe she had any understanding of her body.

I left school after the tenth grade, when I was fifteen, to get married. My mother married Mr. Shepherd one month later. She was unhappy from the first day. Years of delaying because of me were suddenly over for her. She had moved past postponing any further unhappiness.

She worked hard, my mother, trying to win a place in the family, but she failed. I see now that she was in terrible competition with the other seven children for the love of her parents, especially her mother. Like a two-year-old she was desperate for my grandmother's good will and approval, or even a smile. She never got it. There was some wall she couldn't scale that existed between them.

This was the world into which I was born . . .

❋

"Tell you, Man, I is worried 'bout that chile. She's the strangest little tyke I believe I ever come across."

"Aw, she ain't so strange, Honey, I don't think. A little scared, maybe. Kinda quiet."

"Kinda? Too quiet to suit me!"

I can hear 'em talk. He tole me it was time to go on home, but I sneak back and crawl under the house and listen to their voices.

"That chile's a pretty good worker. Why, you should see her help me empty that wagon load. Seems happy to work right alongside a me. I ain't so sure 'bout that boy though. Seem like to me he wants a FREE RIDE, Honey. Reckon I try and wait a bit to make up my mind 'bout him, but it do appear to me like sumthin' is WRONG with him! Still, you're right when you say that little girl is quiet. She don't hardly say a word to me either."

"Well, I just knows sumthin' is bad wrong with that chile."

"You don't think it might be 'cause that chile not take on to you, do you, Honey?"

"No, no, that ain't it, Man. I just think sumthin' is bad wrong when a chile act too quiet. There's sumthin' not right when a chile act like that. Why, that chile not do a thing, not say a word. Don't even say hello! And you know what else? I ain't ever seen that chile smile! Did you notice that thing yet, Man? Now sumthin' is baaad wrong with no chile what don't smile at me!"

"Lord help, woman, the way you do fuss! That chile is just

quiet, that's all. Let her be for a while and she'll come 'round. You'll see."

"Well, I hope sumthin' can bring her 'round. She sit over there near the trees and just watch. Watch me come and go, do my chores. Never say a word, just watch. Seem like she's a waitin' for you to come home. Why, today I'se find her in the garden eatin' carrots. Eatin' 'em RAW, Man. Dirt and all! Chewin' up alla carrots she can get her hands on. Chile is HUNGRY, I tell you! Makes me uneasy, that chile do. Mighty uneasy."

The Man says something about Honey's just the right one to put some meat on that little chile's bones and make sure she get enough to eat. And make her smile, too. He says if there's anybody got the gift of love, why he's pretty sure that somebody is Honey. He figure she can make that chile come 'round if anybody in this whole world can.

Now he ain't a "gamblin' man." He know it don't do to go around bettin'. But one thing he *will* do, he'll bet a nickel, a whole nickel, on me bein' able to do that. Yes, a whole nickel; he takes out his change and we look at it. Just three or four coins. Two is pennies, one nickel and one quarter. He says I can take them two pennies for myself. Did I ever have a penny all my own, he asks me? Fool he is. I never even seen money up close. For sure no one ever give me any.

Well, he thinks I need to have a little money, a little change on hand. He says, "You can take them two pennies for yourself."

. . . No, no, he ain't a giving 'em to me. No, he says I worked for 'em. He says, "You is a pretty fair hand when you wants to be, chile. I tell you the truth, this is yours and you earned it. You been a big help to me, chile." (I don't believe it really. I'm so no account and worthless, ain't good for nothing 'cause I can't do nothing right piece a shit.)

The Man says he can keep the pennies in his pocket. I move a step or two away. I should've known he'd take 'em back. ". . . 'cause you ain't got no pockets, chile, and I don't want you to lose 'em."

I wouldn't have let go of them two pennies if the world had

ended right there. A bomb could have fell outta the sky on us and I wouldn't have lost them pennies!

And I wouldn't have lost what he said: I was a right fair worker when I took a notion. "Man couldn't ask for no better helper'n you, chile," he had told me.

The Man is near and dear and inside my heart, he is. His were the first words of praise I ever heard. I'm sure of it. He was afraid I'd drop the pennies and we'd never find them. No way. No way in this world I'd ever have dropped them pennies. I held them so tight, one in each fist. I don't believe Hercules could have prized my fingers loose from them pennies. If I'd died right then, they'd a had to bury me with two fists, a penny in each.

It's a wonder I didn't wear them out a looking at them, but I knew looking wouldn't "wear out" pennies. I'd sit with one in each hand and I'd look and look at them. First thing I did when I got to their house was look at them pennies.

But I did have to learn to stop and speak to her and that cat before I got them pennies out. Wouldn't do to run right in and not even have a "Howdy do" for Honey and the cat.

"Well, how you think she feels you come in without a howdy do, and her a layin' up here waitin' for you half the day?" Honey asked me.

That old mammy cat was so lazy she told Honey to wake her up when that chile come on to the Place. That's what Honey said.

"That cat was ascairt she'd sleep past time for you to come, chile. Why, she act like I don't have one other thing in the world to do 'cept wake her up!"

We was kinda friends, but not too friends yet. That cat was my friend more'n her. But I was "taking on" to her a little bit. I heard her tell the Man that one night when she called the old cat to come in the house.

Man said he just don't see why she couldn't let him have one little chile. He tole her she was a jealous woman. He just be darned if he ever would of thought such a thing, and after all this time!

She didn't know what he was talking about, if he's wanting to know the truth of it.

Old as they was and here she was a getting her back up over a younger woman!! Now if that don't beat all he's ever seen. He can't pay a little bit of attention to no other woman but what she comes along and gets jealous!

She was "put out." Honey was put out that I didn't take on to her. She said, "Sumthin's the matter with that chile!"

"Isn't neither," he said. "Seems like to me that chile is right nice. Funny how that chile taked on to me, ain't it, Honey?"

It was time, she thought. 'Bout time somebody taked on to him.

What did she mean by that? he wanted to know.

She mean just what she said, that's what. What did he mean by "what did she mean"? Can't he hear?

�֎

We had a long table in the kitchen, and all the Foleys crowded around it to eat. There was no room, no quiet, no ease. Sitting there was like being surrounded by a pack of wild animals at feeding time.

It scared me, getting hemmed in by so many people hurrying to eat before the food was gone. I thought they ate like our half-starved dogs who fought over the few miserable scraps Grandpa would throw out in the dirt yard. I was actually afraid of being eaten up in the rush and confusion at the table.

There was so much bad feeling when we'd gather in the kitchen that usually I'd want not to be there. But if I didn't show up, oh that was awful!

"You missed your supper, dammit!" Grannie would shout. "If you can't get your ass in here when food's on the table, you can just do without! There may be a biscuit left, but you can't expect me to save anything for you if you don't get in here on time. It ain't my fault if you starve!"

Honey didn't eat like that. Honey ate nice, and talked nice to me.

She'd say why don't we have a "nice little visit" while her and me eat the jelly biscuits.

I don't like her too much yet; mostly I wait for the Man to come along home. She says, "May as well have a bite a sumthin' while you wait, huh maybe?"

I gobble up the biscuit! She says not to do that! Tells me there's

no call to hurry 'cause the biscuit ain't gonna run away. "You end up
with a stomachache iff'n you eat like that, chile. I not like to see that
happen. I shore not. Be best iff'n you take little bites, and chew
chew real good."

※

The Man says iff'n you need to know something he thinks you
oughta ask everybody what's got good sense in their head. It appears
to him like it's the best way to get some pretty good answers.

"Talkin' to them what's got good sense, why you learn a right
much thata way. Listen and learn, chile. Listen and learn. When you
is listen and learn a lot, then you think and think about it"—he
points his finger at my chest—"then *you* decide what *you* a gonna
do. You has to remember to decide for yourself, chile. Won't do to
let other folks decide for you. Just won't do. The best thing is to
make you own mistakes in this life. Then if you make a mess, well,
it be your mess, huh, chile?"

He do think I'm gonna find this thing out for myself 'fore I get
too far along the road. He think it is the best thing, pay more in the
long run, if I do like him and listen a right much and talk a right
less. He believes it has helped him get along this far on the road.

"I found it out a long time ago, chile. Been a watchin' folks from
offa that wagon seat for a right good while, and I has found out a
long time ago that listen more and talk less is the very best
way. . . . Listen to them? Sure I do. Well, chile, can you tell me
how I'm ever gonna find out what they know if I spend all my time
tellin' them everthing I know and I not listen at what *they* got to say?
People do like to talk. You know that, don't you?" He smiles at me
like we know that thing, sure enough.

"You be a lot better off just to keep quiet and open up your ears.
Course that ain't gonna be no trouble hardly atall for you," he says
in a soft and sweet good-little-me tone, "since you is got such good
sharp ears, chile. Be no trouble atall for you to teach yourself to
listen at everthing! Then you be smarter when that fella goes on
down the road 'cause you know all you know and all he knows too!"

The Man taps his ear with his finger and say if I just learn to
listen and learn then I be a heap sight further ahead than most folks.

"Now the best way to get a fella talkin' to beat the band is to listen to him real good. And the other thing is this, JoAnn—now listen good to me—you make the other fella think you is just a dumb ol' nigger what don't know nothin'. There ain't nothin', chile, not one thing, what makes a man start talkin' more than to be 'round somebody who he thinks is dumb. Now I don't know just what makes it that way, but you get a man to thinkin' he knows a whole heap more'n you and the first thing you know, chile, that ol' fella done told you everthing he knows and what's in his pockets, too!"

He don't want me to take his word for it. No, he wants me to go out and try this thing for my own self 'cause that's the only way I'm gonna be sure.

"Here we go to Ko Ko Mo. Kokomo." I sang and sang about Kokomo and thought what a good song it was.

"Up-see-daisy, up-see-do to you, little lady. Up-see-do to you!" It was the Kokomo soldier and he was walking me around on the tops of his combat boots.

Mama sulked. She said I was messing up the shine on his boots, and told me to get off, to leave him alone.

"Get off" were about all the words she used, but what I heard was the threatening tone. The tone said, "You'll get yours later!"

He walked around with me on his boots, singing along with me. I thought he was nice.

It was some time later when I heard him telling Mama that in spite of everything he'd thought she was somebody special. The "in spite" meant in spite of the family. But now he'd found out everything was just a bunch of lies. Every word she ever said to him, he told her, was a damn lie. He'd learned she was lying about everything!

"You'd believe anybody before you'd believe me, wouldn't you?" Mama yelled at him. And here he was supposed to LOVE her!

It hurt my ears, like a bee stung me in the ear, and I didn't want to hear it. They were yelling at each other. She whined that someone had told lies on her.

But he had heard it from too many places, from too many people. It wouldn't do any good to fuss over it now. He said everybody knew the story but him. He asked her why she couldn't have told him the truth. Didn't she think about how he felt? Being the joke of all of them who knew?

It seemed like she didn't care about his feelings, not even a little bit. She didn't even hear him.

She said she reckoned it was all just BIG TALK, all his big talk about loving her! She should have known better. They were all alike, all of them! Then she grabbed his arm, hung onto his sleeve, and said it wasn't true. She pleaded for him to listen to her instead of believing them!

The Kokomo soldier said he had tried to. He had tried real hard, had shut his eyes to a hell of a lot that was staring him right in the face, but he just couldn't get around THIS. He was TOO DUMB TO SEE IT, he cried. He'd been a fool to ever listen to her, to her and her kind.

He knew the family was trash; he wasn't so dumb that he didn't know trash when he saw it, for God's sake! But he had listened to her lies and he'd believed she meant what she said, more fool him! She had been just as much trash as the rest of them. Lying in her teeth, every word a lie trying to fool him.

He tried to treat her like a lady, tried to get her away from HERE—he said "here" as if there was a bad taste in his mouth—and then to find out that all the time she was just a two-bit whore. Well, he shouted, damn her to hell and back!

The soldier from Kokomo said he couldn't trust her for nothing! There was no way he could live with a lying woman, even though he'd thought he loved her. Yes, he sure thought he had.

He didn't say he loved me. He didn't include me at all, and I was hurt. He guessed he probably still loved her, but a pretty face wasn't enough. So he'd just be damned if he wouldn't have to get over it. Hard as that might be, it couldn't possibly be any worse than THIS was!

About then Mama lost the thin coat of niceness. "Go! Go, goddam you and see if I care. Do you think you're the only man in the world? Well, you're not, damn it. You sure ain't the only man around here who's AFTER MEEE!"

He said he knew that. He sounded sad when he said, "I know it, Marie. That's the trouble."

She screamed at him to go, to get out before her Papa got his shotgun and came after him. Her Papa could shoot him for what he'd done to her, and the law wouldn't lift a finger against her Pa for doing it! He wasn't worth shit, and she would be glad to be shed of him! She was sick of him, sick of his AIRS! Sick to death, she was, of HAVING TO PUT ON AIRS FOR HIM!

"Get out!" she shrieked. "GET OUT! AND DON'T EVER COME BACK!" She got rid of him while she was in a fit, a Foley tantrum that was as familiar to me as the daily setting of the sun.

"Here we go to Ko Ko Mo," I sang. But we didn't go to Kokomo with the soldier. No, we didn't go anywhere with him.

I asked Mama where he was and how come we didn't go to Kokomo with him. She yelled at me not to ask about him. She said that he was GONE! And he could just go to hell for all she cared.

Gone? Gone to hell? What was she talking about? I didn't understand. I felt unhappy about him being gone. I had liked him. I thought he was nice.

"Well, chile, I reckon I is right content with my lot. Reckon so."

Me and the Man walk around the Place before it's time to go in for the night. We have a little "look see" to make sure everthing is all right. He tells me about being content. He explains it's like when he says, "I'm sure pleased with you, chile." Only this time he's pleased with his own life.

"Tell you the truth, chile, a whole heap a peoples is got it a lot worse'n I ever *thought* a havin' it! I been to war, and I tell you right now the best thing 'bout it for this ol' fella was to GET HOME! Now I ain't talkin' 'bout nobody else or nothin', but I reckon when a man is born and raised on a place, well then it just appears like a little bit a him is tied down tight to that place!"

He talks slow and easy to me. I know he's thinking about what he's saying, and means it real good when he says it.

"Don't mean to talk 'bout nobody, chile, but seems like lots a them folks ain't livin' all that good 'out there'! Me? I be right glad to get back home, myself."

He talks about "down on the farm" days to me. Says you can have them big times, chile, and them big towns, 'cause seem like to him he was a missin' the heart outta his own body while he was away in the war.

"And that's the truth of it. Reckon I just not take too kindly to it. . . . But still, tried to do my best, like I 'spec I got to do. Tell you the Lord's truth though, chile, I was mighty glad to set this pair a feet back on the road to HOME.

"I sure was glad to come 'long and see things lookin' 'bout like I left 'em. Guess I was a mite afraid things be changed when I come on down that road from town. Yep, I seen the tops a them trees from waaay back there," and he points down the road with his long skinny finger, "and I said to myself, 'Well, that's the Place, sure enuff!' "

"Whatcha think done happen to this Place, Man?"

"Don't know, chile. Don't know what I figure might be changed. All I'se sayin' is I be awful glad to see it look 'bout the same!"

Man says his Daddy come to get him. Brought him home in the wagon. Oh, he was mighty glad to see his Daddy. . . . 'Cause his Daddy meant a whole lot to him, is how come.

"My Daddy didn't fare too well 'long 'bout then, to tell you the truth, chile. That was one reason I hate to leave this Place then. Hate to leave it on my ol' Daddy like that. But have to do some things, chile, you just not wanta do. Seem there ain't no other way."

We stop back by ol' friend Horsey's house while he tells me about his Daddy. The Man keeps on a talking and I poke in the dirt with a little bitty stick, trying to make them letters right. He done show me how to make lotsa letters in the dirt, but now I forget it. He takes the stick to draw it for me.

When he hands me the stick back I do like he does, real slow and nice.

"See there how easy? Easy as pie, ain't it?"

"You ever see, Man, when you know how to do a thing, why, it looks real easy. Don'tcha think so, Man?"

"Why, that's the way it seem to me, too, chile. Now think a that;

a little mite of a girl like you notice that thing!" The tone of his voice says my my my how smart you is!

He keeps on smiling at me and says, "Lord, I can 'member my Daddy showin' me how to do a thing when I was a little tadpole like you is now. Seem like some things was hard to catch on to. I be goin' along tryin' to do like my Daddy tole me, and you know what happen, chile? Well, one day I look around and see I be doin' that thing without even thinkin' 'bout it! Didn't even hardly have to think 'bout it no more after that. Now that's the truth of it, chile! There I was one day a doin' just like my ol' Daddy did."

He tells me it might seem right hard till I catch on to it, but he thinks first thing I gonna know is them letters be REAL EASY 'cause I done learned 'em just fine! Says I have to work on it, though. Things don't come without you work on 'em, he says.

I practice in the sand with a nice little pointy stick. I can do 'em over and over and just smooth right over the wrong places with my hand.

The Man says, "Yep, I do believe you gonna 'gree with me when you get a bit older 'cause I can tell from lookin' that you is a right smart little girl. I reckon you gonna learn this thing for yourself when you get on out in the world. Many a time I notice how you can't 'spec to learn a thing without you work on it and tryyy hard till you know it. I be pretty sure you gonna take notice a that thing, too, Little Girl Who's Learnin' Them Letters!"

4

SCARED TO DEATH

For a short while we seemed to glide along fairly smoothly in our sessions. The few memories of JoAnn's which had shaken free were quite pleasant and touching. I was fascinated with how she could circle the same scene, turning it over and over again in her mind until yet another telling particle would surface. She was like a connoisseur of the arts, long blind, whose hands moved exploringly over the piece of sculpture before her; hungry for discovery, her fingers would grow ever more sensitive to line and shape, even to the variations of texture most people would overlook in a marble surface. The same incident might come up time and again in our conversation and in her writing, each time revealing fresh detail or another facet reflecting light from another angle. She would not be content unless she'd wrung out of every memory its complete text.

I don't recall how long we camped by this oasis at the distant side of JoAnn's childhood, but something was in place which permitted her enough time there to take on needed strength. Having gained entry to her past by riding up high on the wagon seat beside the Man, she wasn't about to shut the gates again until she knew what was there. She'd been talking and writing extensively about how quiet the air around him was. Though not able to define her *feelings* about people and events, she was becoming adept at describing the *sensations* she recalled experiencing. The attention she paid to the "calm" which bracketed her encounters with the Man became all the more significant as she was next buffeted by the howling storms within her family's orbit.

Yet even those darker images that spilled out of JoAnn's unconscious were emerging at more of a crawl than a blast. Once again, looking back with the knowledge of what followed, those early recollections landed toward the milder end of the spectrum of family pathology. "Mild" is a peculiar description to use when the spectrum ranged from horrendous to atrocious, but I think she was still somehow being protected, or was protecting herself, by easing into material which held the potential to overwhelm.

She remembered lots of yelling and agitation, people fighting; the glint in her grandfather's eye as he tossed a single bone out in the yard for the pack of half-starved dogs to fight over; her hair being set afire; getting hit and kicked, taunted by the other children in the house; Grannie, in the kitchen, threatening with a stick of firewood by backing her up against the cookstove until she burned herself.

In addition to having more recollections about the Man, his horse, and the woman who was happy to see him come home, when JoAnn started remembering the part of her life on Wade Street that related to her family it was as if two streams had merged. Suddenly a fast-moving river was born, hardly recognizable from a walk along the banks of either one of its tributaries. The volume and intensity of her memories and her writing increased so rapidly I struggled to find my footing and catch my breath.

I think it was around this time JoAnn brought a tape recorder to one of our sessions. The idea to do so was prompted by her frustration. She was tired of taking up part of our fifty minutes together to question or clarify something which had been troubling her since the last time we met. It shouldn't have surprised me, but it did, that she was leaving my office and reviewing our therapy sessions in her mind with as much attention to detail as she was conferring on the scenes her memory was then restoring.

Certain she was missing a lot during our appointments, she asked whether I'd mind her turning the recorder on while we talked. Such a simple question; it instantly brought up every trace of those feelings of inadequacy and ineffectiveness I still had. I'm sure today's technology can't deliver figures to a computer screen any faster than I was struck with that dreadful response. But, catching myself after a few seconds, I thought if she was interested enough in what we talked about to listen to the whole thing over again I'd just have to get past my self-consciousness.

Even if I'd been more knowledgeable about childhood sexual abuse I might still have had a moment's pause when she asked that question. Like lots of people, at times I'm gripped with a fear of exposure: now, finally, everyone is going to witness just how . . . fill in the blank with a relevant negative trait . . . I really am. When I catch myself in this sort of worrying, the paradox usually doesn't escape me. A hefty ego is required to believe so many people are actually going to notice how, for instance, unremarkable I am. I try to remind myself that if I and others like me are truly as inadequate as we sometimes feel, the chances are nobody's even going to be paying attention.

So she *did* start recording our sessions—the only client I've ever had do that—and I *did* get over my initial self-consciousness. JoAnn helped immensely, of course, because she was completely focused on her own self-discovery. Several lessons made their way to me in this process, all part of what I was beginning to learn from her.

Although she had lots of opinions, strong ones, about the world outside herself, JoAnn was spectacularly nonjudgmental around the business of seeking to understand herself. She may not have liked what someone said, or been comfortable in an interaction, but she always kept a mind open enough to ensure that something of value happened to her. During this period I can't recall hearing her say anything she did, related to her therapy, was a waste of time; it was simply that she proved willing to turn her consideration even to the smallest and most fleeting things. (For example, she might talk for fifteen minutes as she explored the effect on her of someone's smile when she sensed it didn't match up with words the person was saying.) Nothing was too inconsequential to be judged as unworthy of her attention. While I may have questioned or doubted my contribution to her therapy at times, I was also learning that if anybody could find treasure among dross, JoAnn would.

As a result of having a verbatim account of our exchanges, she now brought to our sessions comments like, "Remember when you said I needed to be aware that people paid attention to things I say? Was that what happened in the group when Gloria was upset about . . . ?" Or "When I told you last week that . . . such and such . . . I think it wasn't just right. What I meant was . . ." She would listen to each session's tape before we met again, and closely enough to notice when one of her comments or descriptions hung even slightly askew on the wall of her intention.

I smile now as I think of how concerned I first was about what those tapes might reveal to JoAnn regarding my competence when all she wanted was to figure out what was going on with *her*. This incident of the tape recorder served up another portion in an ongoing lesson I've long strained to digest fully: the Judge who lives "out there" (or the Bully, or Victim, etc.), to whom I have such a strong reaction, is not the one I need worry about. Far more formidable to deal with is the Judge who still resides within me, beating out all others who would pass sentence on me or my conduct.

As she worked harder than ever at this time in her therapy, the dam across the reservoir of JoAnn's memories seemed to give way, suddenly powerless to hold anything back. I realized much later, however, that I just hadn't been familiar with how, when given the go-ahead, the Unconscious mind functions during the process of retrieval. What appeared to me then to be a torrential outpouring of a force too-long held in check was nothing compared to the flood released later when JoAnn, although exhausted, was stronger and had more of a support system in place. Back then, as it was happening, I couldn't imagine this wasn't already a flood.

One thing had become obvious to me during these months: I simply wasn't a big enough container for JoAnn anymore. She was relentless in her efforts to remember and communicate those events of her childhood, and she was driven to understand how they had exerted an unknown control over her life for the last forty years. I was the only person with whom she was talking about any of this, and I was at the clinic only two days a week. Throughout this period we met once a week; at the most, when possible, I managed to see her twice a week. In addition to thinking she could benefit from other resources our staff provided, I knew that I could benefit from some backing up. At times I even needed shoring up. Aside from the effort she was putting into remembering, writing, and talking about her past, she also had a present that required tending, and I couldn't focus on all those areas with her.

Among the various kinds of groups I ran then, for several years I'd been co-leading a weekly women's therapy group. After discussing these concerns with Bev, my colleague and co-leader, I decided to refer JoAnn to our group.

I don't think she was enthralled with the idea of opening her life up to a circle of strangers who were there because they, too, were having problems. Most clients who've been working individually with a therapist are not initially delighted about the prospect of joining a group. But she was respectful of the reasoning behind my recommendation—and certainly she was aware also of needing more time than we could muster individually—and was willing to give the group a try.

At the first session she attended JoAnn told the other members her purpose for being there was to learn what feelings are. Being there was not easy for her. For that matter, no part of therapy was easy for her; she may have put in long hours and been creative in her approach, but nothing came easily.

She used the opportunity afforded by the group to speak about the difficulties she was then having with her ex-husband and with their youngest child, an adolescent son who was the only one still at home with her. In talking about these matters, and in responding to other members, JoAnn began to get an understanding of why she often felt troubled in her relationships. Basically she operated from the belief there was nothing unique about herself, that others shared the same values and wanted the same things out of life. But she was continually confused by the discrepancy between this premise and how she observed people actually acting. Despite what might be obvious to many, she started to realize other people weren't like her. She found this to be a shocking awareness, but it helped explain why she had such trouble understanding others and why so many interactions left her puzzled.

JoAnn had no patience for anybody she thought wasn't, in her words, "trying to do better." In the group—as elsewhere, I'm sure— her style was to slice into all the explanations and excuses people made for their predicaments, and fillet the rhetoric being served up. She was humorless, brutally direct, unrelenting, without tact or subtlety. She was also guileless, a scrupulous listener, and so unconcerned about anyone's opinion of her as to be not intimidated by anything. She was a powerful force in the group, an accepted leader; someone not necessarily comfortable to be around yet someone who garnered the respect of other members. Everyone knew where they stood with JoAnn. It was invaluable for me, as her therapist, to experience her around other people. I also found it supportive to have the perceptions of a colleague to compare with my own, and was relieved to know another therapist was involved in her care.

Somewhere around this time JoAnn also saw a notice on the bulletin board in the patients' waiting room announcing the start of a Systematic Training for Effective Parenting Group. The twelve- or fourteen-week course was a structured series of meetings designed to give parents some guidance as they scrabbled across the talus on the slope of child rearing. Naturally that prospect caught JoAnn's eye since she was starting to realize the lack of adequate training she'd been given for the task of parenting. Bev and I both agreed that if JoAnn thought she could manage another therapeutic resource—this one aimed at helping her cope with an unhappy son— it would let us focus with her more appropriately on her interactions in the group.

So, in spite of being by far the oldest parent in the S.T.E.P. group, she threw herself into the meetings with characteristic intensity. I believe she recognized the group as helpful although, typically, she struggled to be tolerant of people who said they wanted help but who, she perceived, spent most of their energies casting themselves in the best possible light. Why, she would wonder time and again, do people who know they need help work the hardest at trying to convince others they're doing the best job possible?

JoAnn was continuing to write and remember more about her life during that critical year on Wade Street when she was seven and her family lived down the road from the Man and Honey. She continued recording and listening again to our sessions, attending the weekly group and a parenting class, plus working twenty-five to thirty hours a week at her job while raising a teenager from whom she felt increasingly alienated. I sometimes worried her circuits would become overloaded because she seemed unable to slow down or rest.

The following paragraphs were among the pages she left on my desk one week around this time:

I am at a point in my growth where I can no longer afford to shut out memories of my childhood. A few years ago I learned from Dr. Cunningham that it was O.K. not to remember my past if I chose not to, and so I have been unconcerned about my lack of memories. Some months back I was told by RME that at this point such an attitude was only going to hinder my progress.

It is important to note that therapy for me is a most highly prized process, not a case of being sick, crazy, or any other such carelessly used label. Instead, it is the most urgent and important thing in my entire life, ranking only after food and shelter. RME has wondered about my inability to pinpoint fear in my therapy; she says fear is a normal factor in change. As I sit here I realize that I am scared. Scared to death. I am afraid NOT TO CHANGE.

I feel so dead and wasteful of my inborn intelligence and capabilities that I sense I am truly not alive. I'm just existing and taking up space, dead from the neck up. Dead and just waiting for God to take the breath of life from me. I must change myself because I have a destiny of more than mere existence or why else was I born?

I do not want to stand on Judgment Day and see myself and my life as a Nothing; to have God shake his head and say, "Ahh, you have missed the very spirit of life as I intended it for my created children." There is a joy and aliveness in this life which I have missed and was not even aware of. Now I am scared, just like RME and the books say.

But my constant and real fear is not of changing. I am rather stone cold scared in my soul that I have been too slow to learn; the long delay in starting to change frightens me to death. My living and breathing fear is of this terrible ignorance, because *that* must give way for me to be the best me possible.

I feel absolutely smothered by fear and ignorance. The fear inside is so strong that I MUST drag all the past up out of the pits and examine it to learn what things back then have contributed to me being as I am.

Originally, in the beginning of our work together, I'd thought of JoAnn as having ardently thrown her energies into the role of Student, with herself as the subject of study. It had seemed to me a duck never took to its favorite pond more enthusiastically than JoAnn had taken to therapy. But she herself didn't regard her participation in therapy as a matter of choice. (We often argued about the aspect of "choice" in one's life.) What I had first thought was a decision she'd made to invest in therapy, what I took for her enthusiasm, I finally began to see as an act of desperation.

Maybe I heard her at last. Finding this one-page statement among the papers so matter-of-factly left behind in my office helped me put the undertaking in *her* framework instead of shaping it to fit *mine*. In this age of inflation, where even words are oversold and one risks losing credibility by stating something too strongly, I nevertheless believe JoAnn was, like many others in the healing process, fighting for her life. She knew it, too, long before I did. Truly her greatest fear was she might die having missed the whole point of living. It was that fear which contributed to the urgency of her mission to look under even the faintest recollection, into the most ghostly of recurring images and around whatever intense response she had.

5

THROUGH A
WINDOW NEWLY
WASHED

I was just an hours' old baby when she pushed me away. Mama could not have even known what kind of baby I was yet. But the anger and hatred had started before that, before I was born.

People would know she was pregnant, they would be able to see. They would "know our business, be butting in and nosing in our business!"

There was such fear and anger misplaced onto an unborn child. And in spite of all she could do I wouldn't miscarry and go away. Some people, she would cry, could get rid of them so easy! She was not able to dump me, but she tried. They tried.

I spoiled everything. I grew in her, which made her fat. I grew and she got ugly like an old woman. She'd never be able to be a pretty young girl again. Her breasts were all swollen and stretched; they'd be horrible, like an old woman's breasts, and no man would look at her.

Thinking of no longer being pretty made her cry—not despair and sorrow, but mad tears because her pretty clothes would never fit her again. All because of this goddam baby that she never asked for!!

My mother had become ugly and fat and sick. Sick as hell. Sicker than anybody else ever. Oh how she wished I had never been. I was ruining everything! She deserved a little fun, and now she was so ugly and fat nobody would even give her a second glance. She wanted to break the piece of a mirror because she couldn't stand to see how awful she looked.

The mirror was a cheap one with wavy lines through it. The cheap silver backing stuff had peeled off here and there so that in some places it wasn't a mirror at all. There just wasn't any more backing to make the reflection. There were places where her image didn't exist, only holes where you could see through her.

"Who in the hell needs a goddam squalling baby?" she wailed. She turned away from the mirror and flung herself across the bed, crying and sobbing. Grabbing handfuls of the bed covers in her fingers, Mama herself wailed like a baby.

"It's all BECAUSE OF YOU!" she shouted. "Damn you to hell. You ain't got no business being, spoiling everything for everybody. I wish you was gone! I DIDN'T ASK FOR YOU, GODDAMMIT!!"

It was a soft, slack bed with springs that were no good. It bounced when she threw herself on it. Oh, she was sooo broken-hearted from the loss. To think she had been the prettiest one, so young, and now she was losing her beauty. She hadn't even got a husband yet. She was crushed, just crushed. She was dying. She'd rather die than be so fat and ugly, so old-woman looking.

She hated me always; it was not new when I was born. Already it was old in her, that hatred.

"Look at you!" she screamed. "You ain't even pretty. All this, and you ain't even pretty."

After all the hell I'd put her through during the pregnancy and then the birthing, I was just so unworth the trouble I'd caused. "Look at YOUUU!" she shouted as she threw me across the bed.

Soon after birth I was thrown aside like an old rag. It was a simple action, without thought, but it perfectly forecast my place in the family for the next fifteen years. Abandoned before and after birth.

It is fascinating to wonder how they reasoned it. The two adults were not to be held responsible. No blame was attached to them.

The seedling child was the one at fault. I had been thoughtless enough to come uncalled for—unwanted and unbidden—and ruin a beautiful young figure and a chance for happiness.

As I think about it now, I believe it wasn't that my mother hated me. She hated what I cost her. I always cost her trouble of some sort. And she could never get past herself to me. Nor did she ever try. Never, not once that I can remember, did she consider my feelings first. I simply would not be as she wanted me to be, as she wanted her girl to be for HER!

I see it now, finally. I can see the back side, as clear as a window newly washed. I can see right through her, like when she sat in front of the cheap mirror with some of the backing gone. Now I realize how she—and all of them—blamed me for everything that cost them anything, starting with my being conceived and born.

What I don't know is why I was the one to get all that blame.

Little Bobby was Mama's younger brother, and Grannie's very favorite child. Actually Grannie had an even younger child, a boy named Crane, but I don't remember much about him except that I was between him and Bobby in age.

I had to play with Little Bobby and keep him out of trouble. I was his "whipping boy," just like in the Old South in the slave days. None of the Foleys like me—I think I served as the family dumping ground—but mostly I was Bobby's whipping boy. We played together and went to school together. Somehow we were just always together, from the crib up.

Since we were never apart, when it was time for him to go to school he wouldn't go unless I went with him. Little Bobby was about seven or eight months older, so he had to start school before me. Grannie sent me with him to school on the first day, just to shut his mouth because he kept carrying on about how he wouldn't go unless JoAnn went, too.

Grannie told him he had to go to school. Bobby didn't care. He was scared and he wasn't going to no damn school! He was not used to being made to do anything he didn't want to do, and he thought he would get out of school.

"I ain't going. I ain't going by myself, not to school I ain't," Little Bobby shouted.

While Grannie tried to talk to him, to get him to go with the other children, he just stood there yelling and screaming, without one real tear. All her sweet talking didn't change anything, and neither did her pleas: "You have to go to school or Mama will get in trouble with them. All you kids is got to go, or they'll be out here after me again."

"Do I have to go?"

"Yes, you got to."

"Well, send JoAnn with me, too!"

"No, I can't do that."

"Well, I ain't a going without JoAnn." Little Bobby said he'd go only if I came and stayed with him when his older sisters, Francie and Warnie, my youngest aunts, went to their classes.

"Okay, okay," Grannie agreed. "Go tell her to get ready then."

They let him take me along as if I was a favorite teddy bear or blanket. I went along to keep him company on his first day. When we got there they registered me, too, because Warner or Francie lied about my age. So I started school a year early.

The nice lady was taking me to the new room with the nice teacher. She thought I was a baby and she had to show me to the room 'cause I couldn't find it by myself. I wasn't no baby. But I liked it, the feeling from her. It was so important to her for me to be all right, and I could tell it. She was concerned, that's what I felt.

But where was Bobby? Oh Lord, where was Little Bobby? I didn't dare leave him! I had to take care of him, and I couldn't understand what was happening. I walked a few more steps with her. She was talking easy to me.

"No, no. He will be fine where he is. . . . No, he can't come with you. He has a teacher of his own, and we're going to take you to a nice teacher for yourself. Won't that be nice?"

I knew it wouldn't be nice for me, leaving Little Bobby behind. She was telling me that I would like this teacher just fine, and that "your brother is all right and you'll see him after school so you can all walk home together." I was having trouble hearing her.

"But now you have to come with me," she said.

She was tensing up. I stopped. I tried to think; I couldn't think.
I was so afraid. What could I do? I would not cry. I'd be a big girl.
But Bobby . . . Grannie would kill me!

I was "supposed to take care of that boy! Do you hear me,
JoAnn? IF ONE THING HAPPENS TO LITTLE BOBBY, I'LL SKIN
YOU ALIVE! You stay with him and you take care of him. Do you
HEAR me, you dummy?"

Grannie was mad with THEM for telling her what to do with
her own kids. She took it out on me. All this fuss and crying from
Bobby was driving her crazy! She had to get him to school or they'd
be ". . . RIGHT BACK OUT HERE TELLIN' ME WHAT I OUGHTA
DO FOR MY KIDS . . ." and that she had to get rid of the flies and
fix the screen and cover the water bucket and everything.

Grannie hated all of the world, I think. Back then I thought she
just hated me, but now I believe she hated everything in her world.

Right there in the school hall I stopped in my footsteps. I
couldn't leave Bobby or Grannie would kill me. Did I dare tell the
lady? Could I even put it into words?

I went with her to the classroom. All I could do was wonder
what was going to happen.

Grannie would never have sent her Little Bobby to school if
they hadn't made her do it. She was as bad as him; they both went
crazy at the idea of being separated. And somehow they both expected me, who they couldn't stand, to make the separation bear-
able for them.

They didn't pay the Preacher's Wife for the eggs she sent to Miss
Foley's. Grannie wouldn't go to get the eggs herself, partly because
she was lazy and partly because she owed the woman money. She
sent me for the eggs instead. I went sometimes just to see her flowers, and she was pleasant then. But the Preacher's Wife felt different
to me when she knew I had come to get eggs. When she heard that
Miss Foley wanted eggs, something changed in her even though she
was still nice to me. She was mad about them not paying her.

·   ·   ·   ·

I walk through the hedge and she is in the front yard. She has on a big floppy hat to shade her head.

"Hello, child. What's bringing you over here today?" She feels fine, she smiles at me.

"You come to see me today, did you? . . . Yes, yes, I'm really proud of my flowers this year. Well, of course pride is a sin, but STILL, I do work hard on my flower garden, child." She has a garden and she has a flower garden. "See the size of my zinnias, and all the colors? . . . Yes, just like a rainbow."

"Grannie wants a dozen of your best eggs. . . . Yessum, she sent me. She said to 'go tell the preacher's wife to specially pick out a dozen of her best eggs for me. Some of them eggs last time were very, very small, and not worth what she charged me for. Tell her not to let it happen this time or I will have to buy my eggs some- wheres else.' I am not supposed to fall and break them eggs either if I know what's good for me." I am telling her just exactly what Grannie had told me to do.

She asks me if my grandmother had sent a bag for the eggs with me. I tell her, "No, ma'am. I could carry them in my skirt tail. . . . Well yes, I may crack them that away." Now I am troubled. ". . . Yes. Yes, she'll be mad if I crack them. Please would you give me a bag to carry them in. I'll run home and get one if you want to save yours. . . . Yessum, I do know bags don't grow on trees. . . . No, I'm not crying, ma'am. I'm too big to cry. It's only I DON'T WANT TO GET A WHUPPING."

"Poor, poor child. Poor little child, it ain't your fault," the Preacher's Wife tells me. "They's just trash. You deserve better, child, you sure do." She almost hugs my shoulders, but not much. She knows I don't like it too much, to be hugged. She don't know it is that I don't like to be touched.

Her arm is kind of on my shoulder as we go around the right side of the house to the back door to get the eggs. She says, "You are an angel, that's what you are, child. The Lord knows His own ba- bies. Yes, He knows His own. Now you get a nice drink of water at the pump here and hush up your crying. We'll fix you right up. Wash your face now while I pump you some water."

I hold my hands under the spout and then splash a little of the cold water on my face. The Preacher's Wife keeps on talking.

"Won't do to let her know you was crying, I don't expect. I'll send the old woman some eggs. I'll fix them up so she won't have no excuse to beat you over them. Lord knows, it don't take much for her to whup you, does it? Seems like you're the one, child. There's nearly always one that gets it all the time. Looks to me like you is it. Don't cry. Now don't cry, child. You're upsetting the Preacher's Wife. She feels sorry for you."

She dries my face on her apron and takes me through the back door into the kitchen.

"You don't have to feel sorry for me," I tell her. "I'm a big girl and I can take care of myself. . . . Yes, yes, I can. You should see how fast I can run now. I can run fast and hide before they can get me. I never go in if I can help it. Not even to eat . . ."

I stop 'cause I hear myself rattling on. She's watching me, and she sees my look fall on a plate in the middle of the table that's got two or three biscuits on it.

". . . Well, no, I'm little and I don't need too much to eat," I say. ". . . Well, if you ain't gonna eat it, and you don't mind."

I look at her. I don't like the feeling, so I tell her, "I ain't really hungry. Maybe you want to feed it to the chickens to make eggs?"

She says no, she thinks the chickens have had plenty to eat already. And she believes they've started on laying eggs by this time; she's pretty sure they start early in the day with making eggs.

I take one of the cold biscuits off the plate she holds out to me. ". . . Thank you very much, ma'am." I eat it slow and tell her I sure do appreciate it. It's right tasty. Not that I'm hungry. She gives me one more biscuit. Two whole biscuits.

Somewhere there had been trouble over me telling someone that I was hungry. There'd been a terrible fuss and beatings for telling LIES! For spreading LIES that they didn't feed me. That is why I had to be so careful not to tell that I didn't eat at the Foleys'. They had beat it into me real good over that trouble.

The Preacher's Wife knows I'm hungry, and I don't like her to know that. I can see it in her eyes, and I don't like it. I don't like her feeling sorry for me. I don't like it at all.

She has another biscuit in the stove, up in the saver place.

"Well, I'm not really hungry now. See, I'm eating so slow. I still have half of this one left. . . . No. Well, I could just hide it here in this pocket, just in case I might get hungry later on."

She watches me take little bites and starts talking kind of easy-like and asking me things as she gets the eggs together. ". . . Yes, I do like it here. It's so quiet and pretty with all of your flowers. Grandpa says you can't eat flowers so they ain't worth having. . . . Yes, I think so, too, but not my Grandpa. They're so pretty, but they'd just get tromped down at our house."

"Lord, child, they's natural born destroyers in this world. Hand-maidens of Satan is what they are, and you've ended up with a passel of them. Here now, here's your eggs. Get on along home now. Take care with them eggs. They're my best ones. I picked them out especially for you, child, to satisfy your grannie and keep you out of trouble."

Back at the house all I get is yelled at by Grannie. "Good God! She wants twenty cents for these puny little eggs? I swear people will always try to beat a poor woman out of her money. . . . No, they ain't her best ones either. Look at that, Miss Know It All. I just oughta not pay her for these things. That old nigger preacher's wife, she probably sent us the worst eggs on the place. Them dumb niggers is so jealous of us they don't want us to have nothing!"

"Why're they jealous of us, Grannie? Their house is better'n ours."

"There you go again," she screams at me. "Always got something to say to bother a person to death. You're enough to drive me to drink." She is stealing a drink from Grandpa's jar of white lightning.

She says it is my fault she needs this, so I sure as hell better not tell Hank on her. She puts a little water in the jar so he won't notice some is gone out of HIS whiskey.

She will hunt for his jar when she knows he has one, and she'll say she deserves a little nip since she has to "put up with YOU, Goddam you!" I am so bad, or else she wouldn't be drove to drink on account of me. It just wears her out having to "put up with YOU AND YOUR CRAZINESS ALL THE TIME!" Grannie wears herself out trying to beat some sense into my hard head.

※

"Lord, Lord, chile, this is a ol' made up story. It ain't no way real. Lord, whatsa matter now, chile? There ain't no such thing in this world as that. That be a made up story what I tole you. . . . No there ain't such a thing. Why I wouldn't scare you for the world and all its riches, chile. I cut off my hand first, I would." She hugs me, rocks me back and forth. Honey is upset 'bout me being so upset. "Oh lord, chile, ain't no ways real."

It was a made-up story she told me. To this day I do not like made-up stories. I really don't. I just don't read them. And I don't like a lot of television stories because they appear so unreal to me.

The Man hears about what happened when he comes to home. He says they don't hardly tell them kinda stories no more. Hmm-uhmm. They tell stories 'bout the animals in the woods and 'round the farm.

"No more a them stories at all atall. Hhmmumhmm, no siree Bob. Well Lord, Honey, whatcha tell them bad stories to this chile for? I can't leave this Place without you go scare this chile? Why, next thing we know this ol' woman be scarin' them chickens so they can't lay no eggs. They swell up fit to bust if she go and do that thing. Get so heavy with them unlaid eggs, they waddle 'round this Place like sumthin' you never seen. Come on along with me, chile."

"Where we going, Man?"

Is he mad at me for something? For telling him I'm scared. Is he gonna throw me off from this Place? Oh, I am ascairt. I cry inside and hang back 'cause I don't want to get throwed off this Place yet. I don't wanta go! It ain't turned dark yet. He aims to GET RID OF ME 'cause I told on Honey.

"Well, I 'spect us need to check on them hens, chile. See is they able to lay us any eggs today, what with that ol' woman a scarin' everbody in creation to death. They liable to be puffed up and rolled away."

Oohhh, I can breathe again now. They don't have a fit on account a me.

"Let's us go, Man. Wait for me. I'm gonna hold your hand down these steps, and go 'round to check on them ol' hens with you, okay? I think they didn't hear that bad ol' story 'bout them children and the witch and the oven. . . . No, 'cause, well, you see, Man, we was just a resting for a spell under the tree. An them ol' hens they was pecking for their dinner, and we was a pretty far piece away from 'em. I don't think they got scared outta their wits at all, atall. I just don't think they did. I think they is just fine. Be layin' eggs okay, I think."

Oooh, I stop. Mr. Man is looking at me. He's gonna say WHO YOU THINK YOU IS TO BE THINKING YOU CAN THINK! JUST SHUT YOUR MOUTH, YOU DAMN HARDHEADED DUMMY. YOU AIN'T GOT NOTHING IN YOUR HEAD TO THINK WITH ANYWAYS! I hold my breath.

Man says, "My, my, I hope you right 'bout that, chile. I do like a egg of a morning for my breakfast. Nice fresh hen egg do set you up of a morning to go 'bout your day's work. I fairly hope you is right 'bout them hens, chile."

We walk on, looking over things. He says, "Honey won't tell no more made up stories like that. . . . Lord, I hate to see them ol' hens be scared outta layin' them eggs for us. I shorely would hate to see that. I 'spect Honey have to be careful 'bout them hens hear them stories. Them ol hens ain't smart like you and me, chile. We can think 'bout a thing and learn 'bout it. Them hens, they can't think it out like we can. No, they believe everbody that comes along and tells 'em a thing or two. Can't think a thing out like we can, chile. We know better than believe everthing we hear. Ummm-hummhh, we do, don'tcha think? We ain't chickens, are we?"

We walk along, look that Place over. I hold his hand and have to take big, big steps to keep up with that Man.

Grandpa was stomping around, mad as an itch.

Babies weren't a thing except another mouth to feed. It was all Elsie's fault, having all them kids. How'd anybody expect a man to get ahead with a wife that kept having more mouths for him to feed! Damn no good kids. Damn no good Elsie.

He sure as hell didn't need nothing else to feed. She oughta DO SOMETHING about them babies! Why, he's not sure how many of 'em are HIS anyways! Damn half-breed bitch!

He kicked me out of his way, Grandpa did, so he could keep

stomping without losing stride. I was little, a toddler I'd guess. It didn't take much to shove me aside.

Grannie had just had a baby. Crane they named him, and Grandpa didn't even want to see him. He'd seen too damn many babies before, for Christ's sake, to waste his time looking at another one!

"Now, Mr. Foley, you don't mean that," the neighbor lady said. "You're just worried and upset, that's all. You got a fine boy baby, and everthing's all right."

Grandpa had been up HALF THE DAMN NIGHT listening to all that noise! He was mad 'cause Grannie kept him awake, and him with his work to go to. She could drag ass in the damn bed, but he had to be out there the same time as usual!

Besides, he wanted to know, who was gonna take care of HIM while she was laying around in bed with everybody making over her?! You'd think dropping them babies was the biggest thing in the world, the way they were all carrying on. Now he had to go to work and try to make enough to FEED 'EM ALL! He had to do it all himself, and now he couldn't even get a little sleep.

He was watching Mama.

The woman was telling Mama to get some rest. They were all tired, she said. It had been a long night but everything was all right now, so she should get to bed. They all needed some sleep. She would let herself out the front door.

The woman did not know the Foleys, but she did not like it here in our house. She had only come to help out a neighbor, and was glad it was finally over. She thought Grannie should have had a doctor. Too old to be birthing a baby, is what she said. She didn't like our not having a doctor for a woman that old.

I could feel that the woman didn't like us. She was just answering a call from a neighbor. Now she was relieved to be done and going home. No need for her to come back, she told Grandpa. His wife would be all right. She couldn't refuse a cry for help, no matter who it was. It wouldn't do to turn your back on somebody in their time of need. As the lady left she told Mama again to get some rest because she'd have to take care of things for her mother tomorrow.

Grandpa was still thinking about who was gonna take care of him while Grannie was laid up. I watched him watch Mama. As I see it again now, with the freshness of an undisturbed memory, I know what was in that look. He was going to take her to bed with him that night.

※

"Them garden peas is talkin' to us," Honey says as we walk along the row.

"What they say, Honey? Huh?"

"What they say to us two ol' womans? They say 'Come here and get us. Come here and get us right now. We's ready, ready! Now's the time. We's ready to be picked.' Why, can'tcha hear 'em callin' out, chile? They be sayin' 'Where at is that little girl what's been waitin' and a watchin' with that ol' Man. Ever time she drag him out here when he gets back to home they be a lookin' at us, checkin' on us. Well now, where is they at when we ready to be PICKED?!' That's what they is all a sayin', chile."

Honey says we gotta pick 'em now, then we fix 'em and eat 'em right uppity up! She gonna can some, too, for them to have this winter. I start to worry about them little peas.

". . . Naw," she says, "it don't hurt 'em a bit, chile. They can't feel a thing at all, atall. Naw, 'cause that's their place in this world. They has been put right here to be eat up. That's what God made 'em for. To be food for us, His chillens. That's what they's growed for, chile. It don't hurt 'em, not nary a bit."

I think how it hurts me to be eat up. It hurts me in the dark, but I don't tell her that.

"Everthing God makes do have its own place, chile. Its own place and its own time. Just you wait and see, chile. You have your time for glory, too. Sure as God make you, He got a job in mind for you. Now He don't bother makin' you less'n He does. He don't make nooo waste, chile, He shore don't. He just don't believe in wastin' His time, so we got to make the best use of everthing He sends us, chile. God don't like no wastefulness like some people do with theirselves!"

I know who she's talkin' about: Grannie and Grandpa and Mama and all them others who don't do good. Honey don't want me to be like them "don't do" people.

"No, no, no! No siree, God plain don't like to see that! 'Deed He don't. Makes Him purely sad. Makes Him cry like a chile."

I look at her like she's gone crazy.

". . . Well, a course God cries, too. Ain't nothin' wrong with cryin', chile! Lord, everbody what's got any sense knows that! Them tears wash away your hurt sometimes. They do."

Honey gets quiet a little bit. She says, "A chile like you shouldn't be havin' no such worries on her like you got. Now that's the truth, chile. . . . Yeah, I be sure. Ain't I a ol' lady what knows? I know. I sure to God do know, chile. I see the rain. I say 'Oh my. God done cry His eyes out over the bad troubles in this ol' world of His.' He got a plan for you, JoAnn chile, but for right now sometimes He just needs to cry. 'Deed He do."

I heard such confusing messages about school from my family. We had to go because Grannie complained, "They'll be out here after us if these goddam kids ain't in school!" It got us out of her hair. Like a baby-sitter, it was a way to "get them goddam kids outta here before they drive me CRAZY!"

School was never seen as a place for learning. Some of the time it was viewed as an interference or intrusion. If somebody wanted you for something, then the officials at school were "a pain in the ass for telling us what to do with our own damn kids!" When we didn't want to go, or were needed around the house, we wrote our own notes to get out of going. And the teachers knew it was all lies, but they couldn't do anything about it.

They went to Recess and left me. I was not part of them. They were the class, the good and clean little children. Not like us. We were dirty and bad. The teacher had had the Foley children before. Every year there was another one, like dogs with their litters. She did not like the Foley children. They didn't know things, didn't know how to act, how to line up. They did not do what they were told to do.

"Since you can't do right like the rest of the class, JoAnn, you can just stay in here and do your work. You be quiet and get your work done while we go out for Recess."

She didn't like me, this teacher, and she didn't want me in with "her" class. I was glad to stay behind. She thought I wanted to go out for Recess but I didn't like all the noise and running around out there. I liked being in the classroom by myself. I knew not to let her know I liked it, so I'd do things to make her make me stay in at Recess. I'd sit there while they filed out and left me all alone.

Alone and sullen; a sullen child huddled up in the desk chair with the pencil in the right hand.

The teacher had shouted at me to ". . . use THIS hand, the RIGHT ONE! You can't even use the RIIIIGHTTT HAND to hold your pencil! Take it in THIS hand, JoAnn, your RIGHT one."

What was she saying? It felt wrong to me to be in this hand! How could I do it right if I used the WRONG hand? I couldn't explain it so she would hear.

"If you can't do anything else right, at least you can hold it in the RIGHT HAND, can't you?!"

I felt the anger in her. It was held in check, held down by the use of enormous energy. She was a mean and hostile woman. I think she would have been like the Foleys except she was held in check by the "they" of the school system. The feeling that came off her, though, was just like the Foleys. She wanted to hit me and she had to hold it in. Maybe she didn't know it, but I sure as hell knew it. I knew the principal was the Mama she didn't want anybody to tell on her to.

The Ruler. The teacher's Ruler was her escape, her safety valve. She could use the teacher's Ruler, and nobody would make anything of it. Smack!

Smack! SMACK! across the wrong hand.

Smack! I was free. I was free 'cause the class was gone. The teacher was gone and the door was closed. She meant for me to "be quiet and do this work." I was glad they were gone. I hoped they'd all go to hell!

I liked the schoolroom without the teacher and the class there. Once in a while I would even sleep. It was so quiet I would just sit and rest myself. The teacher thought it was such a bad punishment for me to have to miss Recess. All I missed was being teased and called names by other children on the playground.

MyMotherSays was one of the worst ones.

"Uggh, you got a snotty nose!" she sneered. "Just look at the snot running outta your nose. My mother says you're DIRTY and I might catch something from you! Miss Adams, tell JoAnn to blow her nose."

She was a small child, afraid she might get something dirty and bad off of me. Her mother said it.

Her mother told the teacher she didn't think decent children should have to go to school with Trash like me.

The teacher said the woman's daughter would just have to anyway. "We can't put her out of school. . . . Because, Mrs. Hunt, she has not done anything to be put out of school *for*."

The woman thought I should be sent somewhere else, somewhere away from her precious blue-eyed daughter.

"My mother says you are TRASH, nothing but White Trash. White Trash is worse than Niggers. My mother says Niggers is Niggers and can't help it. But White Trash is a DISGRACE!!"

Buzzz, buzzz in my ears. They were all out of the room at last. That little girl is a pain in the ass. My mother says this. My mother says that. My MOTHER is all she can talk about. Well, I wish her and her mother would drop dead and go to hell!

❋

Bobby says he's going to the store, ha ha!

"Whatcha going for, Bobby?" I ask him.

"Nothing. I just got a nickel to spend."

A nickel! Oh, Little Bobby has got a whole nickel to spend! It surprises me to hear it. I don't think I ever have a whole nickel. I have pennies sometimes. One or two mostly. You can buy penny candy with 'em.

He's going to the store to spend his money, so I tag along 'cause I'm always suppose to keep an eye on Little Bobby.

The woman who works there is not ever in a hurry. She lets you take a long time to decide which penny candy you want.

"Well, just let me know when you make up your mind," she tells him. "It's hard to decide, I know. Take your time. You can decide without me helping you, can't you? Just call me when you're ready. I'll hear you."

Six jars. Different candy in each one. There's six kinds of candy, but you can only get one kind with a penny. Peppermint. I don't think I like that. Burns a little bit in my mouth. It's awful pretty, though. Pretty colors: red and white. I like red, yes I do! Bright red is pretty. They're made of red and white stripes. I'm not suppose to open the jars and touch 'em, but I can touch the jar. I put my finger on the jar, move it on the red stripe here, the white stripe there. Peppermints are pretty but I remember they burn my tongue and I don't like 'em very much.

Little Bobby wants a Tar Baby. They're black, shape like babies. They don't get wrapped up by themselves like peppermints. Tar Babies is what he wants. Little Bobby says he can tell they ain't boys 'cause they ain't got no THING. He asks for a boy one with a thing so he can have that much more candy.

The lady in the store don't like that. I can tell she don't like Bobby. I can tell.

"Hurry up now, boy. You got your candy, so go on home now!" she says to him.

She thinks he is dirty. I hear her when she's not talking to us. I hear her say to another lady there that he's a DIRTY LITTLE BOY. On account of that smart mouth talk about the Tar Babies.

I know she only says "dirty little boy," but inside myself I hear her talking about "THEM DIRTY LITTLE CHILDREN." Since I'm always suppose to be with Little Bobby that's what I hear her say.

※

School was terrible because they made you mind and you couldn't do what you wanted.

"JoAnn, you can't bust in line like that!"

"JoAnn, you have to stand up now."

"Don't be late, JoAnn. You have to leave with the class."

"JoAnn, you can't just do what you want. This is the time to get our books out."

We had to ALL get our paper. We had to ALL get our pencils out. We had to ALL get in line. Meant we had to do it together. The teacher said we had to "do it together."

Do it.

"Do it" meant sex to me, and it scared me when the teacher said it. Doing it. They're doing it. Somebody at home was always telling me, "Don't go in there, JoAnn. They're doing it."

How old was I then? What grade was it? Early in elementary school, I'm sure. It couldn't have been kindergarten because we didn't go. Some of the other children in the class had been to kindergarten, but we started in at the first grade. The teacher complained we Foleys weren't ready for school, we didn't know anything. She had to spend her time teaching us to listen and mind her, which the others already understood.

I thought the other children said they'd been to a "kinda garden," a nice place with flowers.

MyMotherSays was one of the privileged ones who had been to kindergarten. She knew lots of things: how to mind, how to behave. She knew everythinggg! At least she thought she knew everything.

I knew about sex stuff. I knew, but I didn't know the words to identify it or say it. I had lived with sex and sexual behavior all my life. I saw them doing it lots of times, the people in my family. I did.

The teacher was forever saying we had to all get our paper out, all stay in our seats; we had to "do it" together. The poor woman would have fainted if she'd known what I thought she meant.

6

THE SISSINGHURST APPROACH

JoAnn's memories slid gradually from verbal assaults and physical cruelty into the area of sexual abuse. When she *talked* about what happened to her she could've been telling me about a trip to the hardware store, for all the life she put into her words. But when I read what she *wrote* of those times, her stark descriptions frequently left me in tears, or tossed between the Scylla of enormous sadness and the Charybdis of a pacing kind of fury. The emotional sea is a rather tricky one for a therapist to navigate.

Essentially we're trained not to respond emotionally to our patients, at least not outwardly. The picture of a bearded doctor, silent and expressionless, writing in a notebook poised on an elegantly crossed leg has probably printed itself forever into our collective image of psychiatry. I think there are a few elements in that well-entrenched approach with some merit, too. The purpose of psychotherapy, in the first place, is for patients to focus on understanding their feelings, thoughts, and behaviors, not to provide a format for the care-givers to be absorbed with their own. It's crucial that both parties in the therapeutic relationship be as clear as possible about whose feelings are whose, but because of the inherent difference in their reasons for being there it's necessary for therapists to be more aware than patients of personal attitudes, values, and feelings which underlie their emotional responses. Also, if therapists are *too* emotional, patients may either worry about having upset them or look to strike a middle ground, and thus respond with less emotion in their exchanges. Still, there are a lot of reactions to hearing disturbing material which fall between that impassive note-taker and a helper given over to a completely emotional response.

When JoAnn and I began to examine her memories she had no idea there was anything unusual about the way she grew up. Perhaps intellectually, if for no other reason than she was an inveterate reader, she recognized that others had different experiences from her own. But she really had no concept of there being anything out of the ordinary in the way her family lived and treated each other. Time and again, as I questioned her or struggled to piece together what she was saying, she'd look at me as if I were slow-witted. Occasionally frustrated and impatient with me, she could be as incredulous about my not understanding her world as I was unbelieving that she had no sense of normal.

"Aren't you listening to me?" she asked more than a few times, her voice rising with exasperation. I was trying to understand how a seven-year-old could stay away from home all day, time and again, and not be missed. "If you paid attention you should hear what I keep telling you. Nobody cared if I was at Honey's all day. Nobody noticed. People in my family only noticed when you were underfoot and bothering them. I told you that."

(It's true I had trouble taking this in; no doubt she could only gather that either I was stupid or not listening. She had no way of knowing what my experiences had been. I ran away from home once when I was about seven, on an afternoon when I was helping my father rake leaves. I had worked hard to get all the leaves together in little mountains; as soon as I did my younger brother, Carl, jumped into the middle of them, obliterating my effort. Worse yet, he did it a couple of times. Still worse, my father didn't make him stop. So I shouted that I was leaving, that I wouldn't be back, and I pedaled my bike wildly to Carol's house, one street over. At the time I didn't think about it but I'm sure they knew where I was going and I'm pretty sure my mother called while I was over there. Carol and I played together the rest of the day, and they asked if I wanted to stay for supper. Soon after we'd eaten, while there was still a little time until sundown, her mother suggested I'd better get back home. When I walked into the house my brother was coming down the stairs and said I was just in time for the story. It seemed as if everybody expected to see me. Even though my family didn't talk much about this sort of thing, without fanfare they had made room for my afternoon of rebellious independence. So we went about our usual evening routine: Carl got up on one arm of the big, over-stuffed easy chair, I sat on the other, and our father started reading the story where we'd left off at bedtime the night before. I remember the book was a story about the adventures of a little goat. I think it was called *Billy Whiskers, Stowaway*.)

When patients are unaware of their feelings, as JoAnn was, and haven't been exposed to how other people live because of their own isolation, the therapist's emotions are a way of revealing that, in-deed, another reality exists. So I told her when I was incensed about something that was said or done to her, that I was appalled by how cruelty was so commonplace within her family. I wept frequently while reading the notebooks I took home over the weekend; often-times I'd tell her about how they had affected me. I was determined not to respond to those brutal scenes from her youth with the equa-nimity she showed while sharing them. Gradually she began to stop regarding me as an alien with no knowledge at all of her homeland or language. Gradually I began to realize that her world was ex-panding.

Over the years JoAnn returned many times to this issue. She found it painful that so many people are never exposed to life be-yond the circle in which they stand. Finally she found a quote that spoke to her experience in this area. Typically she had to paraphrase the statement since she paid more attention to its meaning for her than tangential things such as who wrote it, where she read it, or the exact words used. The quote, she said, went something like, "It would be impossible for a fish in the ocean to discover water."

The topic fascinated her. Others, of course, coming up with variations on the subject have crafted similar statements: "If one grows up in an insane asylum then it's the world outside that looks crazy." It summed up one of the haunting themes in her life: how different things would have been for her had she never met Honey and Mr. Man. Most assuredly, she believed, she never would have found her way to psychotherapy. Instead she'd have been just another page in her family's history, a carbon copy of everyone else in that tragic volume.

The women's group was an important adjunct to JoAnn's individual therapy. Despite having little trust for the other members, she revealed things about herself in that setting which continually surprised me. Once she realized something about herself she didn't hold any of the material back out of shame, embarrassment, or fear, as happens with many people. It became apparent from her interactions there that she understood things intellectually long before she experienced them on a feeling level. Knowing and Understanding seemed to be the twin beacons on JoAnn's horizon by which she set her course.

In the group I was able to witness the repercussions for her of not having a ready avenue to her feelings. JoAnn's observations were keen, her insights quite profound, and almost always her comments were to the point. It wasn't so much what she said but the way she said it that caused difficulties for some of the other women in their dealings with her. When she believed she understood the underlying dynamic of somebody's painful interaction, like when she got a bead on her own, she tended to pound the point home until satisfied she'd been heard. After a lifetime of feelings not heard, she apparently believed the pounding was necessary if she was to have any effect. So, as she'd give feedback to someone, or state an opinion, there was a detached and rather severe quality to her comments that often left the recipient feeling pummeled. It was a problem of style, not substance. Gentleness was not in her repertoire, nor was tact. Since she preferred people being straightforward with her, the more direct the better, I think she assumed everyone preferred being treated that way. And because her feelings were never hurt (maybe protected by something akin to emotional callouses), she was always genuinely surprised to learn she'd had that effect on another person.

It was never easy for JoAnn to let anyone know when she needed help. Usually she worked things out on her own and then informed me, or the group, of how she'd handled a given situation. But during several consecutive group sessions there was no getting around the fact she was obviously angry with her ex-husband and heading for a showdown.

He kept dropping in at her house, she said, any time he took a notion. They'd been divorced eight or nine years by then and he'd been remarried for most of that time. If he was unhappy about something, perhaps having to do with their son, he would show up on her doorstep without phoning, or just let himself in when she was out, in order to complain or tell her what to do. Although she didn't quite know why, it was starting to get to her.

"Why is it bothering you now?" people wondered. "You said he's been doing this for years." All JoAnn knew is that it was intolerable for her now and she was unsure of how to confront him with her changed feelings about this familiar behavior.

Willing to see if some role-playing might be helpful, she "set the scene," selected someone to play Wesley, and tried to put into words what she wanted to say. I think what came out of that session turned out to be one of the most valuable contributions the group made to JoAnn's therapy.

If clients are able to give themselves over to a simulated encounter like this, the chances are good the experience they'll have won't be an intellectual one. And that's what JoAnn discovered. Her composure seemed to vanish as she spoke; there was a not-heard-before insecurity in her voice, and the bargaining, placating tone which seeped into her talk with Wesley took us all by surprise. None of us were more surprised than JoAnn herself at hearing the sounds and words which emerged from this make-believe confrontation.

I'm quite sure what then came up for JoAnn in the following weeks, both in the group and in her individual therapy, was a result of the emotions touched off during this session. Realizing how hard it was for her in the exercise to set limits with her ex-husband, to draw her rightful boundaries, she had a different understanding— this time more of a *feeling* awareness—of an ancient sense of powerlessness that permeated dealings with her family. What affected her, in turn affected others in the group.

She started to talk there about some of the memories of abuse then beginning to tumble out into her writings and our individual sessions. It wasn't long before almost every woman in this group of young wives, single college students, and middle-aged divorced mothers was remembering and recounting incidents of beatings, incest, and rape. Bev and I were stunned. One or the other of us had known and worked with each of these women individually before they joined the group; none of them had spoken of these traumas before.

This scene would presage similar revelations in several different groups I led over the next few years. Gradually in those groups, as trust grew among the women who were there for a variety of problems, as repression and denial fell away, we would discover together an unanticipated commonality among a majority of the members was their history of having suffered various forms of sexual violence. Having landed in a setting where they were finally not alone with a secret burden or their inexplicable confusion, they could begin to acknowledge what they knew to be true even if they didn't want to know it. After a while I ceased being surprised at the revelations, though I wasn't any less troubled by realizing those traumas had such long-lasting effects and were the cause of such a staggering range of symptoms among our clinic's patients.

A year and several months after JoAnn's initial appointment with me, she'd settled into a familiar routine with therapy and was writing extensively. While the routine, or structure, provided by our sessions might well have become familiar to her, what happened within that structure was anything but predictable.

I made my first trip to the world-famous gardens at Sissinghurst Castle in Kent, a bit southeast of London, while I was still seeing JoAnn. Despite having grown up with well-tended lawns and flower beds, I was not much of a garden fancier then. Yet something about that piece of the Kentish countryside caught me in its sublime grip. Later, as seems so often the case with me, I realized why. At a depth of which I wasn't fully aware at the time I felt the work JoAnn and I were doing together in her therapy resonated in some way with the collaboration I saw there between Harold Nicolson and Vita Sackville-West on those exquisite gardens. It had seemed to me one of my roles in our therapeutic relationship was to supply the trustworthy setting and regular schedule—rather like Nicolson's orderly design of the grounds—so there would be a safe environment in which JoAnn's memories and writings could thrive in all their spontaneous and profuse abundance—as did the passionate plantings of Sackville-West flourish with exuberance in those carefully laid out gardens.

Our own collaborative effort proceeded; different in form, yes, but perhaps not appreciably in effect. Each week JoAnn was bringing more written material to our sessions and leaving the pile on my desk, usually without comment. Perhaps the total wasn't really that much greater, as I think back on it now, but the incidents she was recalling were far more intense. It may have just seemed like I was taking more pages home to read.

One of the reasons I believe the "fit" worked as well as it did between us then was because I had plenty of time available during that period. It was a matter of no small significance. Had my schedule been like that of colleagues I can't imagine carving out the hours necessary to read all the material she handed me, to sift through it and work the crucial areas into her therapy. But as fate would have it, time was my friend in 1980. A year earlier I'd made the decision, since there were other things which interested me, to cut back from a full-time position to working half-time instead. Fortunately, when JoAnn's captivating writings later came along, I had the luxury of enough time to read and study them. I'm convinced that having a gentle schedule in my life during that period made a viable balance possible between her degree of dedication to therapy and my own willingness to invest in the work.

She had to have been aware back then that there was a great deal I didn't understand about what she was describing, but still each week she handed me those raw images that frequently left me feeling sickened, as they sometimes left her stunned. Throughout the tumultuous early years of our collaboration I think she clung as desperately to a shaving of trust in me as I clung to an instinctive belief in her.

The truth is I always believed her. And from the beginning it was that way, from our first appointment when the woman with the salt-and-pepper hair, wearing the black-and-white dress, sat down in my office and began talking. In fact, I think the most important thing I did during our work together was to believe her.

Believing her was sometimes a struggle for me, however, though it had little to do with JoAnn. There was nothing in her behavior, nothing I picked up from her—either factually or intuitively—that struck me as deceptive. Any of the problems I had with belief had to do with me, not her.

My own background and life were idyllic in comparison to the childhood she was remembering. My small hometown of Berea, Kentucky, dared to spring up, before the Civil War, around the first southern college to offer an interracial education to the young people of the southern Appalachian mountains. JoAnn's Georgia hometown prospered in the early days around a slave market, and then later received a great financial boost from servicing the needs of a nearby military base. The pronounced differences in our backgrounds extended back through time to vastly different historical settings and community purposes, perhaps even having influenced our respective families generations earlier.

At a more personal level, my family existed somewhere near the other end of the spectrum from JoAnn's. They were positive and supportive where her relatives were negativistic and tyrannical, educated and service-oriented while her people scorned all schooling and exploited those on the ragged edge of society. My parents had deep roots in the town; the house I grew up in was where my mother had been born, the house her parents built on land the college sold them in 1908. JoAnn's family, forever in hot water, led an almost fugitive life. I can't recall seeing my parents at a loss to find some shining aspect in the bleakest of situations. Having grown up without even hearing them argue, there were times, especially as an adolescent, when I wished they would cuss or drink beer like other kids' parents did. Such were *my* complaints!

Indeed my early experiences could hardly have provided a less likely background for understanding JoAnn's early life. I knew such people and attitudes existed, naturally, though it was only an intellectual kind of knowing. I had been a hungry reader in school, particularly of literature about the poignant nature of the human condition, about the drama of human suffering. Clearly I was looking for color and texture, for the complex and mysterious about people I went so far as to think more fortunate than I because their struggles and tragedies spoke of primal passions. I found in books what I could barely imagine happening in life, at least mine or anybody's I knew of. In fact, the worst scandal I recall hearing during high school had to do with an affair our mailman was rumored to be having. And then there was the sorry news of a family on the other side of town who threw their sixteen-year-old daughter out of the house when they learned she was pregnant. This last incident made such an impression on me, I think, because of my mother's response to the story I told her I'd heard at school. I was fifteen at the time and well into an adolescence bent on establishing myself as less admirable than my parents. We were getting supper ready; she was making gravy as I set the table. She stopped stirring the bubbling, thickening juices for a moment and looked at me levelly. "If that ever happened to you," she said, in a tone surprising for its seriousness, "we would never throw you out of the house." It's all she said on the subject but I've hugged those words to me countless times.

So, almost twenty years later when I was well into the business of helping people sort through their own stories, when JoAnn sat in my office and began to follow the trail back into her past, I was a most eager listener. But the dramas in my family and hometown hadn't prepared me for giving the same credence to her real life history as I'd granted the literature to which I'd always been drawn.

No, there wasn't anything about JoAnn that caused me to doubt the truth of what she began to recall. I believed *her,* the teller, but sometimes stumbled in believing the tale. It was relieving to me that she, too, occasionally had trouble with this. Once when she remembered and wrote about having gone as a small child to her mother for protection from groping hands in the night, only to be shoved away so her mother could get some sleep, she interrupted the writing to address her balking, rational mind. "Brain Self," she warned, breaking off her own memory mid-sentence, "don't you even *think* it might not be real. It is and you know it is! It is real or you would not of thought of it. It's time you stopped this stupid unbelieving attitude . . ."

Much later, pondering her look back over stacks of notebooks filled with recollections, JoAnn wrote: "Sometimes I think about myself and wonder how I was ever able to believe my own senses and my own memories when the memories came. The facts seemed not possible, so at variance with what the family fairy tales have been and continue to be. How hard it was to think such things

actually happened to anyone—much less to me. When repressed
memories are so monstrous and in such direct opposition to the
family's myths it is indeed a major job to make yourself believe your
own memories."

When I had trouble accepting what she said and wrote about, I
thought it was due to my having come out of such a relatively placid
childhood. I figured it was because I'd been trained by kindly, trusting parents who seemed unable to think ill of anyone. If JoAnn, who
lived those events, fought her own disbelief, it puts my struggle
during that eye-opening decade in a more sympathetic perspective.

7

SEE SPOT RUN

She wanted it and she asked for it, he was telling Grannie. The girl was such a pretty little thing, and waving it in his face all the time! She asked for it, the prissy little bitch. All the time prissing around in front of him, driving him crazy. She wanted it and she got it, and loved it, too!

"I'd do it again, too, 'cause she loved it, I tell you!" Grandpa was disgusted with all the ruckus. Jesus, such a fuss over a goddam little kid.

"Shut up now, Elsie. YOU'D JUST BETTER SHUT THE HELL UP IF YOU KNOW WHAT'S GOOD FOR YOU!" He smacked Grannie hard across the face. He didn't think she'd be so high and mighty if she didn't have him bringing in the MONEY!

It was not me.

When I first remembered this I thought it was me—but it happened before to someone outside the family. And the Foleys had run. They had been told about it by the family of the child, and they packed up and ran away as fast as they could. Grandpa got in big trouble then.

The brothers of the girl had come with their father to find out about it. They had had no trouble believing it of our family. We worked as sharecroppers for them in those days. It was the first place I remember us living, the scene of my earliest memories.

The girl's brothers saved Hank Foley from being killed by their father. The man had an old timey buggy whip, and he said he would beat the fear of God into Hank Foley for what he had done to his little girl. He beat Grandpa with that buggy whip until the sons pulled the hysterical man off him. They were afraid their father would kill Grandpa and then he would go to jail for murder.

The father was crying and yelling at Hank. "She's not no more than a BABY, for God's sake, man! How could you do that to her?!!" He beat him with the buggy whip. The man was in terrible shape, crying and swinging that whip at Grandpa.

The father and his sons had to go to town to get the law and bring them out to the country so they could put Hank Foley in jail. It was hard to get to town, and there were no phones near.

The Foleys grabbed what they could of their junk; they had to help Grandpa get around because he'd been beaten so bad. They packed up and ran before the man came back with the law.

Grandpa went to be a carpenter then so they couldn't find him so easy. He had been furious with Grannie for yelling at him for making them have to move. He kept saying that little girl was growing up, running after him all over the place, and she sure as hell had asked for it! Besides, he had done so much for the farmer, and the man had never appreciated all he'd done around the place.

I guess he thought all he'd done made it all right to attack the man's little girl. I never remember hearing another word about this event after we moved. Not one. It was another of the Foleys' many secrets, known but not mentioned. I suppose the family was relieved it turned out as well as it did. After all, if Grandpa had gotten taken in by the law what would have happened to the rest of them?

So another secret was added to the family's history.

"Go get the shovel, chile," Honey tells me. "Gotta get this mess up. No, we just can't have this here. . . . There ain't a thing wrong with whatcha did, chile. Tell you right now you be in trouble iff'n you *not* do that." I run get the shovel and give it to Honey. I know she's some upset with me but I ain't sure if she's gonna be mad and yell.

"No, it ain't bad to go to the toilet, but you have to learn to do it in the TOILET, chile. It hurt you baaad if you don't go. Just you do it in the toilet, not no place else. Okay, baby?"

I had gone and shit in the yard. Mr. Man and Honey's yard. And she ain't never heard tell of no such a thing. She says I'm too big for this now. But she don't scream and hit me. Says I'm too smart for any such a mess like this here. I don't tell her, but I do it at home all the time.

Honey lifts that mess up on the shovel. "Let's take it right along to the toilet where it belongs to be. Gonna get rid of this now, chile. You have to do it in the TOILET, that's all. . . . Okay, okay, we won't talk about it no more, but just remember this: you has to go, else you be sick and your stomach hurt you bad. But it won't do to go poo poo in the yard; you just come along here and do it where it's supposed to go."

Honey tells me to hold the door open for her, and she'll put it in the toilet hole.

". . . Now don't say shithouse. It's a TOILET, that's what it is. Not do to say SHITHOUSE!"

"But that's what everbody calls it."

"Well, YOU ain't gotta call it that, chile. . . . Why? 'Cause I say so."

I go to hold the door open for her but get scared she's gonna push me in.

". . . No, no, baby. You can't fall in the hole. Oh no, I not let you fall down there! Lord a mercy, chile, long's this toilet been here we ain't never lost no little chile down the hole." Little Bobby and the others always laugh about pushing me in the hole. I hate to go in there.

"We'll get rid a this now. You has to go pee pee? You run out here to this toilet. Has to do your business? This where you come to. Ain't a thing in the world gonna hurt you in here, chile. And don't you say shithouse, neither. . . . 'Cause I not like to hear it, that's why."

Honey holds the door open and says, "See there. It ain't a

stinkin' mess at all. It's all nice and clean. We got to have a toilet on the Place, chile. See, you is too big to fit in this here hole. You not ever have to worry yourself 'bout such foolishness, chile, 'cause I tell you we ain't never losted no little girl in this good ol' toilet."

Honey says them not want that mess all over the place, so the Man made this here toilet for 'em. She don't want me to go any old place I take a notion to anymore. 'Cause them not take kindly to stepping in that mess and tracking it all around.

"Why, it get tracked all over the place before you know it maybe, and we got a heap better things to do than clean up what somebody done STEP IN!! Don't you think so, Little Missy?"

Me and the Man is riding in the wagon the last little way to home. He says he got sumthin' today, a surprise for us two womens. I don't have Lu Lu Belle yet; two is just me and Honey. He tells me he went in a store in town and bought it for me and Honey. I can take it in to her iff'n I want to.

"Sure you can, chile. Reach right in there in that pocket and get 'em." He has a jacket on that fits kinda loose, that just hangs on his long tall self.

I don't like surprises. Don't like this at all. I'm scared to go in his pocket. He wants something and I'm not gonna reach in there. I won't do it! Surprises, to me, mean "Gotcha!"

I'm hid under the house and I hear 'em talk. The Man talks more'n he usually does.

"Well, that chile cloudy up, and I don't know what in the world happen. I thought she'd be plum happy to bring 'em to you, Honey."

"She was. Come on in here with you, didn't she? Act all right to me."

Man say yes, yes he knew that. In the wagon, though, he could tell things wasn't just right. He tole the chile 'bout that surprise in his pocket what he brought from town. He put it there in his right hand pocket so that chile be sittin' on that side, up on the wagon seat, and she could reach right in without no trouble. Yep, there might just be a little surprise for her to carry in to that ol' woman. He said it seem just fine till he tole her to reach right in there and get them seeds out. Said she could see for herself what that surprise was if she just get it outta his pocket.

Oh, he tell Honey how everthing change, how that chile cloudy up of a sudden.

"Don't rightly know why. Just don't know what happened. . . . No, can't think of a thing I done wrong. We was ridin' home and that chile was chatterin' away like a little ol' squirrel. You know how she does, Honey."

"Well, what d'ya say to her, then?"

"Didn't say ANYTHING to her! You think I go 'round scarin' little children? D'ya think all I has to do is GO 'ROUND SCARIN' SWEET LITTLE CHILDREN?"

Honey say Whoa! Say for him to hold on a minute. Iff'n he didn't say sumthin' to that little girl, then what's the chile's TROUBLE? What'd he do when she cloudy up like that?

Man say he pull that pack a seeds out, and that was all there was to it. Pulled 'em out and hand 'em over to her. Tole her all 'bout them seeds, and what a nice surprise they be for you two womens. Chile brighten right up! She play with them seeds all the rest a the way home. Happy as you could ever hope to see. She changed back just like you turned a switch on her.

"I just dunno know what happen, Honey, to bring a smile back to that little girl's face. Why, you'd think she never seen a pack a seeds, the way she carry on! Ask so many questions it make my head swim! I tole her she have to ask that woman 'bout them flowers. Yep, I done tole her I ain't too much on how to *raise* them flowers but I reckon I know how to *look* at 'em pretty good. I said most a the flowers 'round this Place been raised up by you."

"Well, that ain't quite the truth, but iff'n I was to have my way, it would be. Course, these good ol' seeds gonna help out right much," Honey tells him.

She was pleased with that Man about them seeds. I could tell. He just seen 'em in town and thought about us two womens. Bet some of them is marigolds, he said. Mary Golds, I think, is sure a pretty name. Reckon they make a nice little flower some day.

✳

Mother and Father and Dick and Jane and Spotty dog. See Spot run.

I know the book is not right. See Spot run. The book is not right. There's too much smiling on the faces.

I know it's a lie, but the teacher tries to explain the story to me. I tell her it doesn't make sense to me. She says it is hard to explain.

"Parents care for their children," she tells me. "Dick and Jane can have lots of brothers and sisters and come from a big family like you do, but this story is about one Dick and one Jane. One Mother, one Father, one Spotty dog." The teacher talks to me in a soft tone.

"You don't need to know. Why do you keep asking me about THAT? You don't need to knowww, dammit!"

Mama is in a bad, bad black mood. She says, "It's bad enough without you reminding me all the time."

I don't know what she is so mad about. I had asked her about the story that the teacher told us, about the family that has a father, mother, and children.

"Of course I'mmmm your Motherrr," she says in a don't-bother-me tone. She is in a hurry to get ready to go out. "I'm just too busy for you now. I gotta get out of here. Jesus Christ, who do you think puts up with you? Of course I'mmm your Mother! Here, hand me that purse off the bed."

She looks for her makeup in the little pocket purse. She don't want me to bother her is the feeling I get.

". . . the teacher said? The teacher said WHAT? What in the hell business is it of HERS, I'd like to know! Just tell me that. Just tell me what business it is of that BITCH'S? Who the hell does she think she is filling your head full of SHIT LIKE THAT?!"

Mama throws the brush down on the dresser and tells me I'd just better learn which side my bread is buttered on around here if I know what's good for me.

Pigtails. Mama grabs my pigtails and PULLS. "Do you hear me, you little bitch?" She YANKS and YANKS on my two pigtails. "Your father? YOUR father? You never hadddd no father! Do you hear me? You never did. He left before you were everrrr born. He never wanted you, stupid. I was the one stuck with you, and NOT HIM!

And you had better learn who to listen to, do you hear me?" She yanks me around by my two pigtails.

Mama says, "You better learn who to listen to, and it ain't that stupid teacher, either! DON'T YOU DARE EVER OPEN YOUR MOUTH and tell that filthy lie again!" She slaps me and shouts DO slap YOU slap HEAR slap MEEE slap slap??!!!

Mama is scared. She is scared because I tole the teacher that Hank Foley is Papa.

The teacher said, "Papa is another word for father, JoAnn. It just means the parents, that's all. The parents take care of the children.

"Marie is your mama," the teacher said. ". . . Yes, that's another word for mother. It's the same thing, only a different word. Yes, yes I know it's hard to understand, dear."

The teacher called me "dear," and tried to explain it all. But I had tole family filth to the teacher. Mama beat me, tole me not to do it again, not to tell anybody THATTT!!

"It's none of their goddam business!" she cries. "Papa is MY Papa, not YOURS! He's your Grandpa, dummy, not your Papa!"

Oh, she is mad. Mama says when she wants me to talk I shut up, and then I go and spill my guts to some bitch at school when they tole me to keep my ugly mouth shut.

She is scared, too. She is afraid of Grandpa "finding out" what I said, and he would blame her for getting him in trouble. Ohhh, Jesus, she thinks Grandpa will blame her and she didn't DOOOO anything!! So she let me know not to tell filth about the family by slapping me and yanking me around by my pigtails.

". . . No, Grandpa," I say nicely, "I don't want to go to the store. . . . No, I just don't want to go."

I could count on Grannie not letting him take me if I was helping her, so I used her to avoid him by doing chores for her when he was around. She didn't care about me, she just wouldn't let her help go.

"No, I don't care to go, Grandpa. . . . No, there's not anything wrong, Mama. I'm not sick. . . . No, I just guess I don't like Pepsi anymore. Thank you for buying me Pepsi, Grandpa, but I don't want them anymore."

He is angry and he can't say too much. I will stay around Mama. I will stay around people. Grandpa is looking at me. I have to stay with people, any people. I am safer with some people around. He is glaring at me with his soulless blue eyes. I don't think he'll say too much in front of the others. I remember he has told me NOT TO TELL! I can't tell.

He is mad but he doesn't want them to know what he's mad about. Stay with people and he won't make too much of a fuss. Remember we can't tell, so I know he can't raise hell without telling, and he said, No Telling! It is like a cold and quiet war between us. And I know I will win. I just watch out all the time and either hide or stay with people.

There's nobody here.

Where is everybody gone to? THERE'S NOBODY HERE!!

I was hidden and I did not see them leave. They did not ever all go off at the same time, ever. The children never went anywhere except to school; the grown-ups were never all gone at once. Until now. I came in from hiding, walked up the front steps and into the hall. I didn't notice anything wrong or different. I was nearly into the dining room door when I felt that something was not right. It was the quiet for one thing. And something else in the air, in the living room especially. It felt wrong; the very air felt wrong. I turned. I was scared. I was scared to look. NO PEOPLE! Where was everybody?

He was hidden behind the door, kind of hidden by the half-open bedroom door. There was Grandpa, hidden on the daybed in the front room. I froze. He saw me. Don't run. Think! Get out! Think, think! What to do?

"Look what I have for you, JoAnn. Look what I have for Grandpa's good little girl. Come and get it." He lowered his voice, trying to sweet-talk me. "Come over here and get it now, JoAnn."

"No, no, Grandpa, I'm not your good little girl."

"YOU COME HERE, JOANN."

"Where is everybody gone to, Grandpa?"

"Don't you worry about them, they'll be back later. You come on now, JoAnn girl. You haven't been fair to your old Grandpa, now have you." His voice switched from oily smooth to harder and colder. "Don't act so stupid and hard to get. I seen you looking after me. They won't be here for a little while, so you come on over here by your Grandpa. You know I like you the best, don't you, JoAnn? Don't you want this candy bar; it's your favorite kind. I been saving it just for you, JoAnn. Oh yes, old Grandpa knows what YOU LIKE," and there was a nasty, slimy tone on the words "you like."

He was unbuttoning his pants! "I have THIS BIG OLD THING FOR YOU! You come on to your old Grandpa now and I'll GIVE YOU SOMETHING GOOD!"

Leave. Leave, run. Leave him. Leave the candy bar and run. Run legs, run. Don't stand here or he will get you. Run fast. THE BACK DOOR IS HOOKED! I CAN SEE FROM HERE IT'S LOCKED. Get it open and get out of here, get it open! Hurry, he is coming. Out, get outside. Run legs, RUN! Not into the woods. Oh no, not into the woods. The road! The road where people may be at.

The closest place to us was the little colored settlement. I ran like wild dogs were at my heels, up the road toward the colored people's houses. Someone will be there and they will be out in the yard. Oh run, run to where there are people. Remember this has to be OUR LITTLE SECRET NOW, JOANN. He did not want me to tell.

Old Aunt Reanie was out in her yard, as usual. She lived in her yard from sunup to sundown in the summer, just working on her flowers. She seemed very old to me, moving slow and easy to get around her place. I went into her yard and told her I just come to see her plants. She was always happy to tell me about her plants, how each one was doing. She would show me this one and that one. Finally she said maybe I better start on down the road. It was almost getting dark.

I told her I could stay longer, that there wasn't nobody at home but Grandpa. I think she knew something was wrong the way I said his name. "I guess I just better sit here on your porch and wait until the other kids get home."

Her porch was lower than the road, and the yard had bushes across the front so that her porch was kind of hidden from the road. She asked me where did they go to and leave me by myself?

"I don't know. I just don't know where they went, Aunt Reanie. I was left on account of I was playing in the woods. I guess they forgot me. I am easy to forget, I know. . . . No, I don't mind if you go to bed. . . . Your rheumatism's bad, huh? Well, I won't make any noise." I promised if I could stay I wouldn't bother her any.

"I can't go home yet, so I'll just sit right here on your porch and be quiet, and you won't even know I'm here. Okay, Aunt Reanie? . . . Well, I can't go home because, you see, I bother Grandpa. He says I bother him because of I am so bad. . . . No, I don't know what he means by that."

I thought hard and I told her that I purely don't think anyone ever told me what it is I do that's so bad. But I have heard tell of it a heap of times, I have. I told her I wasn't sleepy a bit. I was wide awake.

Ooops, my head jerked up. . . . "Oh, I was only closing my eyes for a spell. . . . No, I won't fall over. . . . Yes, I could lean over here and lay down. That's better, yes."

"They treat that child like a stepchild. Come on now and let her lay. She's done fell asleep, Aunt Reanie. Come on." It was a younger woman in Aunt Reanie's family. She was helping Aunt Reanie up off the chair. She told the younger woman just which one of her quilts to cover me up with. The younger woman came back after she helped the old woman into the house. She put me in Aunt Reanie's chair and tucked the quilt in around me as I fell asleep.

I wait. I take my time. I tell her not to hurry me, not to hurry me 'cause I have to get this thing just right now so I won't mess it up. I talk to her like does she think I'm a silly goose that don't know nothing?

"Well, I ain't got time to stand out here all day, chile, a turnin' this here rope and you not even jumpin' it! Do you think alls I got to dooo is mess witcha the live long day? Chile, ain't you never gonna GO?"

I can tell Honey is starting to get aggravated with me. "Well, I know you has to take your time but, Lord, chile, I is gettin' plum tired a turnin' this rope for nuthin'."

But she's not mad. I know Honey don't really mean it, 'cause the words still sound soft.

She knows it don't pay to Jump Off Too Fast. No, no, no. She is sure I'm gonna go just as soon as I make up my mind, but maybe she set down a little minute. Or move over and lean against the tree, "on account of I don't think you, Little Missy, is in no hurry to make up your mind, is you?"

But I watch that rope go up and over and down to hit the ground, over and over it goes, and down and down it goes. And each time it goes down it hits the dirt with a slappy sound and kicks up the sand. I watch it close. I decide to GO . . .

I get a big breath and take a little running start to get right in there where the rope hits, and JUMP, JUMP, JUMP!

Honey is real sure I can do that thing when I get ready, and I do it, too! I'm so surprised I can jump rope as good as I do. Why, I can hardly believe it's me a jumping!

Now, of course, I realize she was turning the rope easy to help me be able to do it. Sometimes she would just rock the rope back and forth, and I would hop over it. For a long time she just did that. But I finally could jump the rope by myself when I tried real hard. I don't think I ever got very good at it, though. I had to leave too soon, before I got real good at anything but remembering.

Honey covers me up. She holds me gently and rocks us both.

After what happened in the chicken pen she's ascairt of the fit I throwed. There ain't no phone and nobody around. She rocks me in that chair until the Man comes to home. He don't see her where she oughta be, where she usually waves or calls or something. They was old, and he was full of worry. No telling what it meant to him, but he didn't panic or run.

He calls out for her first, then stops the wagon and looks around for her. It don't feel right to him; it's too still. She ain't on the porch, not in the yard. He don't hear her voice call back, no singing or humming.

He takes the steps two at a time, we can hear him. I know she "don't like you a jumpin' up them steps! Could hurtcha self." He's quiet as he hurries in, just in case.

"Whatsa matter? Whatsa matter, Honey? What happened?" His voice is quiet, like he's ascairt. "God, Honey, what's wrong? What's happened here?" He thinks maybe she done got hurt.

Honey ain't hurt but she's wore out. It's before noon when we was in the chicken pen and I scared her so bad. We done sit there all day long in the rockin' chair. Nothing done all day 'cause she just rocks me the whole day long.

Honey covers us both with the quilt. I mumble and push her hands away. I don't like to feel I can't move around. I'm just laying over her.

"I is ascairt to death, Man," she whispers when he squats down beside us. "Oh, Lord, I'm so glad you're home. I done been a sittin' here for hours 'cause I don't wanna wake this here chile. I'm tryin' not to move. She stirs iff'n I do."

Honey starts to cry a little bit now that he's home. She don't let go till he gets back, and now she's so glad he's here. I feel it. "Oh, Lord," she says, "I think you never come."

Seems like it's old, an old feeling in them.

"I'm here, I'm home. It's okay now, Honey." He pats her shoulder and loves her up without hugging her while we keep rocking.

I go with Honey in the henhouse to help her find the eggs. While she's looking for eggs, I go looking for the little chickies. She tells me to leave them chickies alone 'cause their mommy don't like me messing with 'em. But the baby chickies is so cute I don't wanta leave 'em alone. When Honey ain't looking I try to catch 'em and play with 'em. The mommy hen gets mad and comes after me. It scares me and I scream and run 'round the chicken pen and yell for Honey.

"Stop it now, you hear me! You just hush up, chile!" Honey says she is plum tired a this, and she ain't gonna put up with me!

"No!" she shouts. "Now you listen at me, little girl. You done scare the feathers offa these chickens, and I ain't a gonna have it!"

Honey swings 'round and raises her hand up to stop me.

The onlyest thing I see when she turns 'round is that arm go up in the air. I can't hear her 'cause I'm lost. I just see all them Foleys, and that's all I hear.

Hank Foley rose up from sitting at the table and he was a GIANT towering over everyone and everything in sight. He was bloated and swollen with anger, mad as hell 'cause he didn't get what he wanted SOON ENOUGH!!

"Goddammit, Elsie, do you think I don't mean what I say?! Huh, you bitch?!!"

Grandpa yelled at Grannie that he hadn't "been drinking"! Well, maybe he'd had a drink or two, SO WHAT?! He sure as hell deserved a little something for himself. He don't get nothing at home for all his hard work, and he wasn't about to put up with no woman telling him what he should do, by damn!

As he shouted at her he came up out of his seat, bumping the table and knocking his chair over backward against the wall. He swelled up, his face got red, and he grabbed the edge of the table and flipped it over on all of us sitting there. He pitched a fit, is what he did.

And such a fit is what I throw there in the chicken pen the next morning after Grandpa ruined everybody's supper.

I scream at Honey. I cuss like Grandpa, spit a flyin', two fists in little balls and my face getting all swole up. I shout all the filth at her that I hear at home.

Honey looks at me without moving; she can't even talk. She don't move a inch while I cuss her out. She don't do nothing until I fall down on the ground 'cause I done wore myself out.

"Lord, Man, if you'd a heard what come outta that chile's mouth!" she told him later when he got home. She'd stopped crying and she could finally talk. "Well, you'd a not believed your ears."

Oh, she was so glad to see him!

Someone said I thought I was a princess living in an ivory tower. What in the hell did I think I had that was so special?

"You can't tell 'em apart in the dark, can you, Papa? Pussy is all the same." One of the boys was talking to Grandpa.

"Get. Get away," I said. "Don't you come near me."

The boys were laughing and said to look at me, a little kitten who thinks she is a great big cat! "You ain't got no claws, kitten. Ha ha. One day, just you wait . . ." and they leered at me like they couldn't wait for that one day to come. I knew they were picking on me, trying to scare me. I got away and hid and watched them. I watched them all, all of them. All the time.

They were like dogs, the ones that hung around and rode on the mother dog when she was in heat. She couldn't get away. They wouldn't put her in a place away from the male dogs; it never crossed their minds to do so. It was entertainment for them. They fed off of it in some way. They would get out and watch the male dogs snarl over the mother dog and then talk about how they were getting her good. They said to look at how he was doing it to her now. All those dogs would chase her. Dogs I had never seen would chase her, waiting for a turn at her. The boys and the girls and the grown-ups, too, would watch. It was like a show.

"What are they doing?" I asked Grannie.

"It's just dogs having fun. They're riding the dog."

"She looks hurt!"

"She ain't hurt, Dummy, she likes it. She's in heat and she loves it. Why don't you watch? You might learn something."

"In heat? It isn't hot. What's it mean In Heat?"

"You're making me mad with all them questions, JoAnn. Shut up or go on," Grannie yelled at me.

I was in the kitchen, and I asked where did all of those dogs come from all of a sudden. There were dogs in the yard I had never seen. Mama was complaining that the damn bitch had pups before and she will again. That damn dog don't do nothing but eat and have pups for her to mess with.

Grannie said, "No, you can't run them off from her, Dummy. . . . No! Water in a bucket won't run them off. Leave them alone to have their fun. Once a man or a dog gets the scent, they won't leave until they get screwed. They're all the same, men and dogs. A pack of males just waiting and watching for some pussy to priss along. Yeah. Yeah, your Mama knows."

I did not ever like it when Grannie said "Marie" or "your Mama." The tone in her voice sounded like something was very wrong. I couldn't quite name it.

". . . a baby-faced bitch," Grannie screamed at Mama. "No, dammit, butter wouldn't melt in your mouth but you'd lead your own father on, wouldn't you? Huh?" SLAP, SLAP, SLAP.

Grannie hit Mama back and forth across her face. She wasn't through with her yet, though. "You! You been sneaking in bed with your own father, ain't you? Well, there's your reward, right there," and she pointed her finger at me. "A goddam dummy! A crazy dummy kid that nobody'd have! I should have drowned her, the little dummy, and saved us a lot of trouble! I should have drowned you when YOU were born. I knew you'd be nothing but trouble!"

I just remembered there was a song called, "I'm My Own Grandpa." It always made me terribly uneasy to hear it but I never knew why. Well, the unconscious thread was there all along. That's why patterns are repeated endlessly. We bury the root cause, the feelings we don't even identify, and repeat the patterns in ignorance. I have lived most of my life that way. Only if the feelings are pulled out and investigated do the patterns emerge for anyone to see who wishes to look. Otherwise they lie buried, but alive and rotten, seeping through from the unremembered past and contaminating the present. Unknown but strong and deadly, on and on into tomorrow and all eternity. Unless we remember and change the patterns.

❈

"Lord God, it ain't no ways right. No ways right." The tears come up in her. I feel it in her. "Well, we's just here a short minute on this earth, and it ain't for us to question why. We got to keep on. Keep on a haulin' this load, chile.

"Got to trust in the Lord and do our best. Lord knows it ain't easy. No, it shore ain't easy. You got a right heavy load on you but seems like that's the best thing to do, chile. When times is rough you just keep on a pluggin' along, doin' your best. Can't lay around on our backside and 'spect Him to DO IT ALL! Man's got to help hisself, too, you know!"

"And us, too, Honey?"

"What?"

"Us, too? Us womans, too, Honey? We got to help ourselves, too?"

Honey laughs. She laughs and says, "Lord yes, chile. We's alla same to the Lord. Mans and womans, too."

"Girls, too, huh, Honey?"

"You too much, chile. Yeah, girls, too."

"Birds, too?"

"Birds, too."

"Cows, too?"

"Cows, too."

"Horses, too?"

"Yes, good ol' Horsey, too."

"Chickens?"

"Yep, chickens, too."

"Roosters, too?"

"Yep."

"I'm ascairt of roosters. Did you know that, Honey?"

"Course you is, but he ain't agonna hurt you. Nope, he just a lotta noise, a lotta fuss and feathers, chile."

Later we go to get eggs. Honey sees me hang close to the gate.

"He ain't agonna hurt you, chile, humm mummm. You hear this woman, ol' Mr. Rooster? You come 'round here a messin' with this sweet chile, oooh ooohh! Why, you find yourself a sittin' up in my stew pot! . . . Now don't you go a lookin' at me like that, you ol' rooster. You may be king in this here chicken pen, these ol' hens may be bowin' down to you, but this ol' henhouse won't be a missin' you iff'n you go and scare this here chile!!

"You do that and we be a measurin' you up to fit in my big stew pot. Ain't nothin' so good as a rooster stewed up inna pot, mumm mummm. 'Specially a rooster that thinks HE is the boss! Iff'n you go ascairin' this here chile, we gonna see how that Man like to have some good ol' chicken stew one night. Just keep up your ways, ol' feller, and we gonna see!"

Honey looks over to where I'm waiting. She says, "He heared me. He just gotta do his fuss and feathers in front a his hen friends here. But you can BELIEVE he knows 'bout ascairin' you. He heared me a talkin' to him. Yes you did, didn't you ol' feller?"

She's looking at that big rooster. Yep, looking right at him. He's a walking off! He ain't gonna come 'round to bother us no more. Honey tole him. She is done tole ol' Mr. Rooster to leave her sweet chile alone! We's snug as bugs, me and her, a feeding them hens, and ol' Mr. Rooster not a bothering us one bit. Oh no, no.

One time that ol' rooster had jump up at me. Honey done tole me to stay away from ol' Mr. Rooster but I think he's pretty and I want to see him close. Oh, it surprised me bad. I think he's gonna kill me, and I fight to keep him off me.

Honey tells the Man, "I was ascairt that chile gonna kill herself, a rollin' and a jumpin' round all over the place. Yellin' and cussin'! Don't believe I ever heared no such a hissy fit in all my born days. Liked to scared me to death, Man. I wait for the first chance I get and grab that chile quick! Hold onto her tight, Man. Hold on for dear life, I tell you. Ohhhh, that baby do carry on but I hold her tight."

I had scared Honey bad. She done thinked the devil hisself is took aholt a me! She shush, shush me, and falls over onto the swing place. Holds me tight and says, "Shush, shush baby. You is my little baby girl. You is all right, chile. You is all right now, baby. I is gotcha now, baby."

Honey tells me not to be ascairt. She not let NOBODY or NOTHIN' hurt her sweet chile. She coos and talks soft to me. "Don'tcha worry youself one bit, baby. I be here and I take care of you. Iff'n that ol' badness come back on you, well I get him good! I chase that ol' badness away, awaaay!"

I know she do that thing, too. Even while I'm wore out, I know she do it. I hear her say she take care of me, save me from that badness. She just take her BROOM and come a running!! I know it. I be in her arms, hear her talking soft, and I let go. She don't even know I can hear her; I just let go.

"You think I let that ol' badness mess 'round with my little Missy Girl? Well, I won't. Now I just tell you the trooth, chile, I not

put up with none a that messin' 'round on this here Place, and that's
all there is to it!"

Oh, she be so happy to chase that ol' bad Meanness away from
meeee iff'n he ever comes around. She gonna walk right up to HIM
(I think she means Grandpa) and she say, "Whatcha doin' ON THIS
PLACE, you ol' Badness Man?!" She gonna get her broom and chase
him clean off from this Place. And she's gonna tell the MAN on you,
Ol' MR. MEAN BADNESS What Don't Care 'Bout Nothing and Nobody!!

"And do you know what, baby?"

I'm dozing off. I don't answer her.

Honey says her and the Man is gonna chase that Old Meanness
Man plum clear outta the county iff'n he puts his foot on to this
Place. Now, that's the trooth she is a tellin' me. Think she let that ol'
badness take aholt a her BABY?? When he comes 'round here he's
just gonna FIND OUT. He's gonna find out for sure!

Ohhh, she gonna fix him, she will! And iff'n he don't listen to
HER, well he's gonna be some kinda sorry when that MAN gets to
home!!

For Honey, who heard me babble on about my family and saw me
act out the ways I learned at home, Grannie and Grandpa and Mama
and Little Bobby and the others came to personify all the bad and
wrong things in this world. Poor old woman. She sure took on a
load of extra trouble and woe when I came along the pike.

8

A CRISIS OF FAITH

JoAnn's employer was impressively supportive about allowing flexible scheduling in her work hours to accommodate the various therapy appointments she had. I imagine she must've been seen as the sort of valued employee who isn't easily come by.

As previously locked-away recollections crept into her sensory range, JoAnn became more seriously depressed. She couldn't stop the memories from their attempts to surface. Actually I'm not sure she tried. It appeared she was writing practically nonstop. Perhaps she figured that, as one might bundle up to sweat out a fever, she'd give way to whatever was burning in her to reach daylight. Intensify the experience rather than dilute it.

I grew worried about her. She looked awful, was hardly sleeping, gave no thought at all to personal care, could find no respite from her pain. No, she didn't want to talk with one of the staff psychiatrists about medication. She didn't want her senses dulled. Drugs scared her; she'd taken plenty of medication over the years, agreeably prescribed by a host of doctors. No, she assured me, she wasn't suicidal. I was concerned she was plunging into exhaustion and wondered if she should be hospitalized.

At first she didn't want to go to the hospital, felt it wasn't necessary. I spoke with her about needing to rest, wondered about the benefits for her in not having the pressure of keeping a household going and answering the demands of a job. She found the idea appealing, all right, until I phoned our liaison there to ask whether they had any beds available and get an update on the details of their psychiatric inpatient program.

As soon as I told her the unit had a structured and well-designed program of various therapies and activities, she was not at all interested. What she wanted instead was to be in a place where she'd be left alone, to be free of worrying about anyone or anything other than that which her mind, like a somber butterfly, alighted upon. She wanted to be left alone, not locked up and ordered around.

I consulted with others on our staff, discussed her situation in our case review meetings, spoke with Bev about her view of JoAnn in the group. There was no clear consensus. Opinions were about evenly split as to whether she might need hospitalization; it probably reflected the ambivalence embedded in my concerns each time I talked about her.

This point in JoAnn's therapy was a test for me, a crisis of faith, I suppose. My trust in her, ever so firm until this period, was wobbling. Was she so obsessed with turning herself inside out that her usual perceptions were pitifully skewed? Had she now become manic, responding to a pressurized inner rhythm that contained its own lonely reality? I wasn't sure. The trust I had in myself, not always as solid as the trust I had in JoAnn, was under siege.

Feeling much uncertainty and little solace in the position of figuring out what would be most helpful to someone whose life was in crisis, I realized it finally came down to whether I was going to trust that JoAnn knew herself better than the rest of us did. She had, over the last year and a half, followed the conviction of her instincts and the imperative of her own pace; it had seemed always to result in what she felt necessary to reclaim her life. Either I believed her or I didn't. Maybe the harder task, after all, was to trust myself. I had to trust that I knew her well enough to believe her capable of making a reasoned judgment about what she needed and could manage.

We talked about my concerns and what I saw as some options. She continued to decry mention of medication or any hospitalization where she'd have to heed someone else's directives. What she wanted was a chance to know and then rid herself of everything festering in that great tyrannical void of her past. She'd recently remembered how Honey once lanced a boil which her family had let go too long unattended on her thin child's back. That act left a dramatic impression: the way to get over a blinding hurt was to look it straight in the eye. So she longed for enough time out, free of distractions, to do the required work. In her bones she believed the only way to overcome her pain was to head right through it.

We devised a strategy. I strongly felt that JoAnn had to take off a block of time from her job and, if nothing else, at least keep all her therapy appointments; we would have as many during this marathon as we could possibly schedule. She was granted leave from work, about three weeks' worth, and showed up for a heavy dose of sessions throughout. Our staff witnessed an enormous change in her. She was still depressed but now let herself be regressed as well.

This once stylishly dressed matron took to wearing a muumuu on her trips to the clinic. Sometimes she showed up in bedroom slippers, carrying a well-worn rag doll. I think the doll was one of the few things that gave her comfort then, a bit of grounding provided by a loving symbol from her days of being mothered by Honey. In light of what she was going through, when any comfort was precious, I thought having the doll at her side was a fine idea.

Many years later I also learned about another consolation she found at that time. Instead of simply listening, before we met again, to the tape she made of each session, I discovered that for many months she had been listening to each of the tapes more than a dozen times altogether (sometimes even while washing dishes or driving to work). And during that particular period she would often put one of those tapes in the recorder on her nightstand and, in the absence of someone to read the dawning little girl a bedtime story, would play back our familiar voices while she drifted into coveted sleep.

One day she sat crouched on the floor in a corner of my office, her eyes swollen with fright, for a whole session. She talked of her terrors, though, and I simply pulled my chair a tiny bit closer as we spoke. Maybe she looked like hell and was acting crazy, as some said, but what she talked about and the writings she brought in made perfect sense. I tried not to worry.

Some important things happened as a by-product of this admittedly risky undertaking. JoAnn acknowledged that, even though she wanted to be alone, she hoped her friends would occasionally check up on her; she had some fear of "going out too far and not coming back." That in itself was different, admitting her fear. Therefore she asked a neighbor who was also a friend to please come by and look in on her a couple of times each day. Anna, terribly frightened for JoAnn, did just that—with loving intent if no sure understanding of what was happening.

She also asked other friends to come by, people from whom she'd never asked anything. Some went shopping for her, some brought food by. A co-worker from her office stopped in, she told the group one morning, and gave her an envelope. They'd taken up a collection for JoAnn at work; the envelope held a check for seven hundred dollars. Seven Hundred Dollars! She didn't know how to relate to such a gift. For all I knew it may well have been the most money she'd ever had at one time, but the thing that truly unsettled her was why so many people would go to such lengths on her behalf. It's impossible to be gracious in accepting a gift when you're used to looking for the strings you've always found attached.

Emerging in our sessions from this period were sharper pictures of JoAnn's relationship with her mother. The sepia tint of earlier images was fading away, with the forms now in clearer focus. She could summon forth innumerable instances of feeling powerless, like when her mother said through clenched teeth as she dressed for a night out, "Now stop that crying, dammit. I've gotta get outta here, so you better behave yourself! Just do what Papa says, JoAnn, and he won't get mad." As she began to process those pictures differently the anger grew in her, and it was consuming.

To offer a channel for that anger, instead of seeing it splatter in every direction, I urged her to write a letter to her mother—not necessarily with any thought of mailing it, but simply to express her feelings within some framework. True to form she wrote the letter right away, even before our next appointment. And, just as characteristically, she sent it off without editing or second-guessing herself. I think she figured her own puny words couldn't express her age-old anger any better—especially to a mother who had yet to hear her—than the effort she'd just made.

Perhaps it was my imagination working overtime but I thought

I could hear echoes of Honey's thundering tones in that letter, getting wound up enough to "preach your funeral . . ."

Dear Marie,
Well, I shall try to explain what I have been doing in therapy for over a year now. I do not offer this information with any hope that you will even attempt to understand. Nevertheless I will speak my mind: I feel nothing but a passionate anger toward you and the sick family that raised me. I am outraged about the inhumanity shown to me when I was a mere child. You were simply the biological mother of me, not a real mother. Never were you. A real mother would never have allowed such a terrible childhood for her only child.

The horrors released from my unconscious now are so painful and so alive in me that, even after all these years, I scream in agony as each new outrage surfaces. I lie here in pain like you've never felt and know it is all from the life you subjected me to. Nature pushed me out, a tiny infant who came naked and defenseless, and you had not the courage to defend or provide for me. I was put aside to be a good, quiet baby. And I was. It is the way I survived.

Marie, I WANT YOU TO HEAR ME: IT IS UNIMAGINABLE TO ME HOW ANY HUMAN BEING WOULD CLOSE HER EYES AND EARS AND ALLOW SUCH ABUSE AS I HAD TO ENDURE. Physical abuse, emotional abuse, sexual abuse, abandonment. I was abandoned on day One.

You have lied to me always. Even now you are lying in answer to the questions I've asked, and you are angry I dared ask any help from you. Trying to get information about things that happened years ago is too much to ask of you. And it doesn't matter to you that this is so very important to me. No, once again you can not be bothered!

It's useless. I've tried and tried but you simply do not love me today and you never have. You can not offer me any goddam thing of true value and you will not even answer a few questions that would mean so much to me. But you could leave me to the untender care of your black hearted witch of a Mother, who was such a cruel woman that I would be eternally sorry if I thought for a moment she had escaped burning in hell until the end of all time.

And of course you could also leave me with my loving Grandpa. An abusive, drunken, perverted fool, too cowardly to approach adults with his temper and violence, his sexual perversions and demands. He fed off his own children like a shark. You chose to leave me there.

There is no excuse. There is no reason.

I am grateful to my Father in heaven that I have not the responsibility for making judgments. I truly am, for I would be less than perfect. I would be far less than perfect. Gladly would I condemn your soul to hell for eternity were it up to me!

You made your choices for forty-six out of my forty-eight years. Now I will advise you of a choice which I have made, and this choice is not open to revision—not now, not ever: I CHOOSE NOT TO BE YOUR DAUGHTER. I FREELY CHOOSE THIS.

I have buried years of memories until I grew strong enough to say this. You abandoned me always. The reason is that YOU DID NOT CARE ABOUT ME.

Beware to approach me. Be fairly warned. I am no longer your daughter. You cut yourself away from me before the cord was ever severed. That thoughtless act inflicted awesome, terrible damage and waste upon my life space. So now I cut myself away from you. Stay away from me all the days of your life. If you do not I shall skin you alive and hang your guts out for the crows. This rage which rises in me is the anger that leads to murder. Even if I did strip your skin away as you gasped for breath, your pain would not come near to what I feel now because of what you allowed to be done to the child of your own body, the only child God bestowed upon you.

Believe me I could stand and watch you die, just as you stood and watched me die by inches, just as you took part in the killing of my child self. AND I WOULD NOT SAVE

YOU. I leave you to God. You are in good hands with Him. He will judge you for Himself. I only know that I have anger towards you all, anger which surpasses any which you ever saw in that filthy bastard of a father of yours and mine.

I WANT YOU TO HEAARRR ME! My anger towards you is monstrous. I want you to envision Hank Foley at the peak, the very peak, of his most terrible drunken rage. Remember it? Then I urge you to feel your fear, let it come up and cover you. Just let go and re-live it right now. There. Feel that fear?

Know you this: IT IS NOTHING. NOTHING! WEAK! It is as weak as cow piss compared to the anger I have for you.

I would give up to you the truth as I see it: you need to fear me mightily. If you possess any degree of intelligence or instinct for self-preservation you will open your ears and your mind to me. At least for this one time you will hear me speak.

I despise you for your heartless lack of attention to my needs. So now I choose not to attend to your needs. You have not a child as of this moment. I am lost to you as if I were dead. You are the loser, but doubtless too self-centered to appreciate your loss.

I care not to see nor hear you ever again. I leave you to God for He may show you more mercy than you will ever again have from me. Do believe me, Marie, because you know I do not lie.

JoAnn sent the letter, apparently, unsigned.

9

RIBBONS

I hold the bag with the ribbons in it and run to her house. I don't really know it is her house but I know she is in there. Like Grannie is always in our house.

I was not too warmed up to Honey yet. Mostly I went there to wait for the Man. I was beginning to understand that he wasn't there on the Place all the time. It was hard to understand because I didn't know what "time" was, just that he wasn't always there. I didn't like it. I was learning that I could stay around with her and then he would finally come along.

Sometimes she would see me coming and say, "Well, here you is come again, ain'tcha? Oh, I know you ain't come to see me, chile, but you mays well sit here while you're a waitin' on that Man! Look like you could have a little bite to eat while you're a waitin', don'tcha think?"

But this day I'm happy that I'm gonna see her. This day I'm so pleased with myself that I can't hardly wait to show her all these pretty ribbons I got. They're so bright and the colors are so pretty. I want Honey to see how shiny and new they are and how they're all mine. But I know to walk nice up the steps and knock on the door. Won't do to go barging in and scare her plum to death. Oh no.

I stand nice and tall and knock on the door. Honey tells me to come on in. She talks nice to me 'bout how it looks to her like it's a really pretty day today, don't I think so? She is doing her works but tells me she done saved me a biscuit. She wipes her hands on her big ol' apron and reaches up in the saver place on the stove to get the biscuit.

"Well, I save this here biscuit just for you, chile," Honey smiles. It's a soft tone when she says "for you, chile." She's not mad she has to save it for me. Then she puts some jelly in where she cuts it open, and says for me to sit up to the table so I can eat it. I'm not used to having anybody do anything for me. She turns back around to her works and I eat the jelly biscuit. I want to show her my ribbons but I remember she has tole me I have to learn to wait till she's done with her work. When she's done with her works is when she can pay attention to me. I know not to keep on asking her things till she is finish her works.

I eat slow and nice, just like I know you're supposed to do, and I finish the biscuit. I got my elbow on the table, leaning my head on one hand while I'm picking up crumbs with my other hand. If I lick my fingers then the crumbs are easy to pick up. Then I lick the crumbs off my fingers. Honey wipes the table clean and takes the plate to wash. I tell her thank you for saving me a biscuit. They been teaching me how you get a lot further with sugar than vinegar. They been saying how "thank you" is a lot like sugar.

I wait while Honey finishes her works. I lay the ribbons on the table and put my finger on the end of one piece. I drag it around the table like a choo-choo train. It drags out long behind my finger and I can see all the pretty colors in it. So bright and so new and crisp. I had seen ribbons in the hair of the girls at school. Sometimes the ribbons were in bows. Tied in their hair or pinned on their dresses. I knew what they were and had seen them lots but I never did have no ribbons of my very own before.

". . . for your very own."

That was one of the things the man said to me. His voice was kind of pleading when he said wouldn't I like to have this for my very own? I knew he wanted something from me. It was a tone I'd heard in my family. It was the same tone as in the Foleys' voices when they tried to get you to do what they really wanted you to do. It was a familiar tone, but one that wasn't usually used on me, or to me. There was not the element of "if you don't do what I want then you'll be sorry you made me make you do it!"

No, the man's tone was more like pleading, without the threat of "I can make you do it." The voice belonged to someone who could not get back at me so openly. Someone not a Foley. This man who said ". . . for your very own" was someone outside the family. As much as I hated his tone, I think there was also something in it I liked. He was trying to bribe me, to buy me. To get me to do what he wanted by paying me. Maybe it was a feeling of having some power that I liked. I certainly wasn't used to it. But here someone was pleading and bargaining with me instead of forcing me to do what he said. He would give me something if I was quiet and did like he said for me to do.

I was gone away inside, hidden from all the drinking and cussing going on in the house. I knew it would end up with the men drunk and getting in a fight. It always did. Men would come by to see Grandpa and drink and play cards until they all were madder than hell at each other. So I had gone to the corner of the porch, hoping nobody would need me for anything. I just wanted to be left alone. What I did was hide inside myself from everybody's sight.

It seems like the man had bent over or squatted down to see me. I hadn't seen or heard him until he had been talking awhile. When he couldn't tell if I was listening to him he reached out to touch my arm. I came up out of myself at the touch and jerked my arm away.

He talked quiet and easy, in a tone like he wouldn't hurt a fly. But the words he said didn't match the feeling of him. Not a bit. He was feeling much different from his words, and I knew the feeling he had. He wanted me to do something to him. Or for him, or with him. I could feel the intense wanting in him, and some part of me just knew I had to do it. Just do it and get it done with so he would leave me alone. It was old in me already. I didn't even think that he would not do to me whatever he wanted. It never crossed my mind. He wanted something from me and he would get it.

But then he was whining and wheedling. I hadn't heard him at first, but he didn't know that. He had got up to the point of not being sure he could get me to do what he wanted. And then I heard him, whiny like, saying he would give me some ribbons.

"Look at these ribbons," he said. "Wouldn't you like to have these pretty ribbons for yourself? Don't you want them? I'll give them to you. All for you. You can keep them for your very own." He waited. His voice had a begging sound to it as he kind of whispered, "You'd like that, wouldn't you?"

I knew he wouldn't try to "make me"! I knew he wasn't going to try and force me. Maybe it was power I felt; he wanted something that he could not make me do. I wasn't used to this feeling.

I had gotten the ribbons first. First before I did whatever it was for him. I'd seen enough from everybody in my family to know that's how you did it. Even at that young age I figured out I had to get the ribbons from him first or he wouldn't have to give them to me after I had done it.

So I am dragging the ribbons around and around the table. Honey stops to see what I have. She's so pleased to see my pretties.

"Oh my, chile," she says, "they be so pretty in your hair." Says she'll fix me right up. "Did your Mama give them to you?"

She's stupid. I don't say anything but I think she is dumb to think my Mama give these to me! She's listening for my answer.

"Man. A man that come to the house. . . . No, not our Mr. Man. Just a man and he gave 'em to me," I tell her.

"He did? Well, he must be a right nice man to think a bringin' you such pretty things. Sounds like he must like you, chile. That's a right nice thing for him to do, ain't it? Is he a friend of your Mama's?"

Honey sounds like she don't know who this man is. Like she don't know how things are at my house. I tell her I don't know who he is. He's a man and he give me these ribbons.

I watch the pretty ribbons as I move 'em all around the table. Pretty colors. Somehow I just start to tell her how it is I come to have these pretty ribbons. I tell her I got them from a man who stopped off to have a drink and play cards with Grandpa.

I decide to tell her all about it, just like I have learnt to tell the Man "everything that happened today" while he was gone off to town with ol' friend Horsey. He was so pleased with me when I could tell a story about what me and Honey did all day while he was away. He thought he never did hear nobody tell it any better. Say he feel like he knows just how it was, like he had been right here hisself. "Oh, chile," he'd smile at me, "you do have mighty sharp little eyes and ears to tell me all that business what went on 'round here today!"

So I know how to tell her about it, like I 'splain to the Man how we did the wash and picked the beans while he was gone. So it makes sense. I tell Honey how I went on the porch to get outta the way. How the man had come out there and talked to me. But I hadn't listened to him at first. Wasn't till he reached out to touch me that I jerked back and heard him talking. I tell her he said I could have these ribbons. They'd look pretty in my hair and I could keep them for myself. Don't tell, he said. He wanted me to just touch him and not tell, and he would give me the ribbons. But I tole him no. No, he had to give them to me first. I knew 'bout how people say you can have something if you do so-and-so, and then after you do they tell you no, they never said you could have it to keep.

I tell her all 'bout how I got my hands on the ribbons first 'cause he might not give 'em to me later. I think I am right smart to do that thing. I tell her he wanted me to touch him and not make any noise. I did like he said for me to. I knew about doing that for men. I did just like that for Grandpa.

I'm chattering on, just so proud of myself for telling a good story so it makes sense. Like I tell the Man about things on the Place while he's off to town. I have to try to get it all right and in order so's it makes sense. When I'm telling her what happened I hear her make a sound in her throat but I keep talking 'cause I'm so busy telling the story just like it happened. How I got the ribbons for sucking the man and touching him in his pants. I hid the ribbons and now I bring 'em here to show her how pretty the colors are. Don't she think they're pretty?

At first I don't feel it. I'm so busy telling the story it's hard for me to let it in. But then there's too much feeling coming offa her. Honey sucks in her breath and sits down heavy in the chair. I know not to jump in the chair like she falls into the seat. I know to sit down nice, nice. But Honey kind of falls into the chair, like the bones in her ol' legs is just give out.

I feel scared. I know it's not like her, and I'm scared. She looks funny. Different. I stop moving the ribbons around. I stop talking. I don't know what's the matter but I know something is wrong.

Maybe I did something wrong. I'm learning not to be scared on the Place but now I'm plenty scared. Maybe 'cause I count on things being the same on the Place. Now it's not the same. There's a scream in my head: "What's the matter? WHAT'S THE MATTER?" I am sooo scared . . .

"What's the matter, Honey," I ask her. I don't want her to tell me, and at the same time I do want her to say. She's so different and it makes me think she is sick. She looks at me like she don't see anything. I go around the table to her. Touch her arm and say, "Is you all right, Honey? D'you want a drink of water?"

I am about to cry, that's how scared I feel. I don't know nothing anymore 'cause she is just so different. Things on the Place are supposed to be the same!! She finally looks at me. Looks and sees me.

"There, there, chile," Honey says. She is come to herself now and sees the fear in me. ". . . No. No, there ain't nothin' the matter, chile. No."

She moves slow, reaches around my shoulder with her arm. She don't grab me and make me. No, just lays her arm around my shoulder and says, "No, you didn't do anything wrong. Not you, chile. You is the best thing in this world. Honey just sit down a little too fast. That's all. That's all, chile. Don't you worry none 'bout me."

Honey takes a deep breath and hugs me good. I can feel she's tired. Like she is sometimes late in the day after we done work hard all day long. It ain't the end a the day, though, and here she is sitting down so heavy. I don't know what it is. She is about to faint.

"I was just 'bout to faint," Honey tells the Man later on. I hear 'em from under the house when I'm supposed to be gone home. It ain't too dark out yet so I don't really go home. When the Man goes inside I swing back and crawl up under the house. I hear Honey say she was 'bout to faint when she "heard them things come out of that sweet chile's mouth. It was awful, Man. Terrible. Just terrible!"

Honey tells him, "Everything started out all right. That chile come into the kitchen with a little brown bag she's a carryin'. You know the kind a bag I mean. The kind you get penny candy in, or like you brought home them seeds in. I wasn't thinkin' nothin' about it. Give her a biscuit, while I'm doin' my works, and tell her to eat up. I wasn't really payin' her much mind. She said she wanted to show me sumthin' pretty. Chile pulled some ribbons outta that little bag and said she knew the names of all the colors. Asked me did I wanta hear her name 'em all? She just talked on a mile a minute— you know how she do, Man—and I just listened to her talk. Got my hands in the dishwater and not really payin' her no mind. I tole her how pretty them ribbons was, all right, and how we could fix 'em up in her nice dark hair. Soon as I finish with my work. I figure it was a good chance to get her head all washed clean, and then fix her hair up pretty with them ribbons. I tell her I think that ol' Man be so surprised when he come 'long the road and see her a standin' there all nice and clean. Bright and shiny as a new penny, and with all them pretty ribbons in her hair. She think you gonna take one look at her and say, 'Whooo is you, little Missy?' She don't think you even gonna know who she is with them pretties in her hair. Oh, she was just so happy, talkin' 'bout that Man sayin' to her, 'Now whooo is you, little Missy? Don't believe I seen you 'round here before.' "

I hear Honey get up outta her chair and walk back and forth. Heavy and slow. On the floor up over my head I hear how wound down and heavy she's moving in the kitchen.

"The chile was talkin' lickety split. You know how she do," Honey kept on. "Got them ribbons spread out all over the table, pointin' to the different colors. Say, 'Here is little Miss Red. Here is little Mr. Green.' Names all them colors so good. I ask who give her the ribbons. Was it her Mama? Chile say no, and go on talkin' 'bout this here little feller, Mr. Yeller. So proud a herself for gettin' the names a the colors right. Then she just go prattlin' on 'bout some man that give these ribbons to her. I was just half listenin'. At first I didn't think I heard what I heard. Thought maybe my ol' ears is give out. She was tellin' me 'bout touchin' some man's thing. I wasn't payin' her much mind so I thought I missed sumthin'. You know how it is, Man, when you ain't payin' attention? Didn't make any sense to me, so I ask her what'd she say about playin' with a thing. I figured maybe he done brought her a play toy or sumthin'. I asked her did he bring her a play pretty besides the ribbons?

"Well, the chile answered me nice enuff. She said, 'No, ma'am. No, he didn't give me nothin' but the ribbons.' But I could tell she was put out that I wasn't listenin' real good."

From where I'm sitting I hear the Man's voice but not what he says back to her. Everything Honey says comes right through the floorboards, though.

Honey tells the Man it was awful, just awful. "Made me sick, I tell you, to hear how that chile got them ribbons. I just don't know how anybody could do thataway to a CHILE! Any man who'd do like that"—her voice gets louder—"why, God in heaven oughta strike him down!" She sounds like she's callin' down a curse on top of his head. Says she hopes the Lord will strike him dead for what he done to that sweet chile.

Honey's winding herself up, she is. Sounding like a preacher now 'cause her tones is deeper and you can tell she means every word she says. Get him. She wants the Lord to just reach down and get him! Get him and skin him alive for what he did to her baby! Oh, she is like to skin him her own self. Skin him alive over hot coals!!

"I tell you, Man, I never thought I could hurt no living creature of the Lord's till I heard that chile tell her story!" Honey shouts out how she'd like to kill him. Kill him and anybody else who'd do such awful things to one a the Lord's own children.

Then it sounds kinda like her voice cracks. I feel a little bit of a surprise to hear Honey saying them things 'cause she don't like to even hurt a fly. I think maybe she's surprised, too, at hearing what comes outta her mouth. She starts to cry. I don't really feel bad that she wants to kill them Baddies, but maybe she don't like to be saying them words.

Honey just breaks down and cries like her heart is broke. Cries and cries like her world is fall apart. The Man talks soft to her, coo and pats her. I'm not in there but I know how they do me: listen to me and pat me but not grab me, just sort of coo in a soft tone; say they feel mighty bad to see me feelin' so bad.

Oh, Honey do cry and wail. She has tole me, "It's okay to cry your tears out, chile." I know she just has to cry herself out. She done tole me that a heap of times. "There ain't nothin' for us to do," she has tole me, "but just sit here and cry it out, chile." She don't touch me, don't do nothing but let me cry it out. I hear her talking to the Man now in the kitchen up over my head and I feel mighty bad. I know there ain't a thing in the world to do but just let her cry all her tears out.

In between her sobs and wailing, she tells him she can't stand to think a them trashy folks gettin' their hands on her baby, and that chile not even knowin' what she was doin'!

I stay scrunched up under there trying to figure out what happened and why Honey's crying so hard. She's right about me being put out she wasn't paying attention to what I was saying. I was tellin' her real plain about the man on the porch, in a way like they both use to 'splain things to me. I tole her all 'bout it. Like I tell Mr. Man how things was going along on the Place today while he was gone off to town!

"No, Honey," I had tole her. "He didn't give me a play thing. I played with his THING. You know, his thing in his pants, Honey."

I tole her what I did to get the ribbons. But first how I get 'em from the man in my hands before I do anything he says. So he can't snatch 'em back and not let me have 'em. I think I'm a "smart feller" for knowing to get the ribbons first!

Oh, I did think I was smart. When the man poked me to get my attention, I heard his whiny, begging tone and knew he wouldn't be doing like that if he could "make me." I figured he didn't want anybody to know what he was up to there on the porch with me.

He'd just come by to see Grandpa. I could feel him looking at me while he was there. I think he must have seen me before; after all, he'd come prepared with the little bag of ribbons in his pocket, hidden from the Foleys. He pretended he had just come out on the porch, not really looking for me. But I could soon tell he was trying to talk me into something he hoped I'd do.

I don't think I'd ever heard anyone bargaining with me before. No one needed to because they could always make me do whatever they wanted. The man with the ribbons didn't have them backing him up to enforce his getting what he wanted from me. There wasn't anybody waiting behind him to threaten me: "You better do like you're told, if you know what's good for you, dammit!"

"Dammit to hell!" Grandpa had shouted. "Wait a goddam minute and I'll talk to her," he'd yelled. He didn't shout it to the man with the ribbons, though. No, Grandpa had said it to some other man. Someone else at another time, earlier. Someone else had paid.

"Goddammit, Hank, I paid my good money. I paid my money

and she didn't do like I told her to!" There had been a bad-smelling, fat man who was crying big tear-words. He was a lot like Grandpa; so full of "Poor Me." I couldn't stand him so I just closed down. I just didn't do anything.

But I heard the man, this earlier man, whining to Grandpa. About how he'd paid his money to be taken care of and then I wouldn't do anything for him.

He was just whining because he was too weak to demand his money back. There was not a single thought about what he'd paid for, what the deal was about. Two full-grown men stood there discussing a business complaint about services paid for. The bad-smelling, fat man had bought a service and didn't think he had gotten his money's worth. He'd paid to have a small girl touch him and make him feel good. They were talking like it was not much to buy. Like it was nothing at all to sell.

"A man's got to make a living, you know," Grandpa told the man. "Sure as hell ain't nobody ever give *me* nothing! Why should you get something for nothing? You had your fun now. Are you telling me you didn't?" Grandpa had a sly and sneery tone, like trying to jolly up to the man.

The man didn't take to the jolly talk. "Oh, yeah, she did it, Hank. Now you know I ain't one to fuss, but she didn't do it like I told her to," he whined. "That's all I'm saying, Hank. Hell, if I wanted to have a hard time getting it, I could have just stayed at home." Ha ha, what a laugh. Oh, us good buddies know how it is with them damn women.

The man didn't really make a big fuss though. He liked little girls too much to get Grandpa mad at him. I remember that he wanted a little girl. He'd paid because he liked it easy. He liked to just lay back and tell someone what to do to make him feel good. And to "make this thing jump out at you." Oh, he thought that was so funny. I was little because he told me it was magic.

I hadn't seen him at first, the bad-smelling, fat man. He was so much like everybody else that he just blended in with all the others around me. He wasn't even noticeable in the mix. I didn't hear him until he said something about the magic. He could do magic, and asked me if I wanted to go with him and see how he could make things grow. It was so slick and funny to the people sitting around. I didn't know why they were laughing. Fooling a child made it so much fun. And made him feel smart, like a hot shot.

He had taken my hand, had led me off to another room so I could watch him make the magic thing grow and jump out at me. He thought it was so funny, and I wanted to see the magic. I had taken the bait like a fish. But when we got in the room and he undid his pants, I knew he had lied. There wasn't any magic. I had seen lots of pants unzipped before and knew the feelings men had about their "things." He was a liar. I was sad with myself for listening and thinking he would show me magic. So I closed right back down, became like a little robot. The man had not been pleased with that.

"It just ain't right," he told Grandpa in a whiny voice. "I've been fair with you, Hank. I paid good money and she didn't do me like I told her to. Now you know that ain't fair."

But he wouldn't stand up to Hank Foley and demand his money back. The discussion was all about whether or not he'd been cheated. Why should he have to pay for services not satisfactorily rendered by a young child? It never occurred to anyone the child had been cheated. A young girl being cheated out of her birthright was nothing to get upset about.

I hadn't remembered the fat man who wanted to show me his "magic" when I told Honey about the man with the ribbons, but I think the lesson from then had stayed with me. I wanted Honey to know how smart I'd been to get the ribbons before the man could cheat me out of them. And I wanted her to know she should pay attention when I was trying to explain something to her.

I'm dragging the ribbons 'round the table and looking at all the pretty colors and just talking away. I tell her how I do it. How I play with his thing and suck on it. But not too hard. No, not too hard or he'll be mad. I know what happens if I hurt Grandpa when I play with *his* thing. It had happened before, and he'd taught me never to do that again. He'd taught me with his fist.

Grandpa had jumped and yelled and hit me in the ear with his fist when I hurt him. Said he'd teach me to hurt him! He was absolutely furious at the idea of me sucking too hard and hurting him when he was feeling so good. He balled up his fist and hit me in the side of the head as hard as he could. Grandpa screamed that I'd

better not ever hurt him or his thing again if I knew what was good
for me. I knew I'd be sorry if I hurt men's things. It was a lesson I
learned at an early age.

So I told Honey how I had not hurt the man who gave me the
ribbons. I was proud I'd been able to do it right. I think it was
offered up to her as something I knew how to do right. It never
crossed my mind she wouldn't like me to know how to do that. She
always liked for me to "know a thing or two." And for me it was just
something I knew how to do. I knew the men did not like it when
you sucked too hard and hurt their things. I think it was important
that I felt like I had done something right. That's what I was bab-
bling on about to Honey. I told her like I tell her anything I had
learned to do right. I would run in and tell her when I learned to do
things like tie my own shoelaces. Or how to whistle. And she would
say, "My, my, my! You don't say so, chile?" She would be so pleased
to think I could do that all by myself.

I tell her how I get the ribbons and hide the little bag behind
the outhouse so he can't snatch them back and not let me have
them.

He had given me the ribbons and I told him he had to wait.
Told him I had to go pee first. Be right back after I go to the toilet, I
told him. I hid the little bag behind the outhouse. When I got back
to the house he whispered for me "to come on over here and do it
like I told you to." I was well trained. That's how I got the ribbons.

I had heard them joke about starting them early and training
them how to do what you want. Oh, they laughed and laughed at
the big joke: get 'em young and train 'em right! Really there was no
such thing as too young to start training them.

While Honey finishes up her work I rattle on about the fat man
and getting the ribbons. I'm so busy talking and telling the story so
it makes sense that I don't take no notice of her. Then she all of a
sudden sucks in her breath and kind of falls down heavy in the
chair. Not suppose to sit down in the chair any ol' which a ways.
She has tole me lotsa times you have to sit down nice. That's what
gets my attention, how she sits down. Her eyes is open but she
looks strange; she don't even see me. I get down offa my chair and
go to where she's at to see what's a matter with her. I'm not used to
seeing her be so still. She's so still even her eyes don't move.

I touch her on the arm. Real easy-like I touch her big, fat, black arm that's lying on the table so still. She raises her arm up and puts it around my shoulder. It seems hard for her to do, like she's just too tired to move. She gives me a little hug and it seems like she wakes up. When she comes to herself is when she tightens her arm around me. Then her feelings start to wake up, too.

Great waves of feeling start to roll off Honey, one wave after another. She is throwing off heat and feelings like sweat pops out of the Man's skin when he uses an ax in the sun. Oh, she is so upset. She's scared, just plain scared to death. Honey says she never did think she'd hear such a story come out of nobody's mouth! She don't know what to do, what to say. She asks the Lord, "Tell me how to talk to this chile." She is kinda praying as she talks to me. Tells me she don't like how them people is trying to drag me with 'em down to the devil.

Honey is not mad at me, though. No, she talks quiet and steady. Tells me to listen real good and remember what she says. She reaches out and touches the ribbons with her fingers. She don't pick 'em up. No, she touches 'em like they're snakes. Like they might bite her. I can tell she don't want them on her table or even in her house.

"Some things we don't need," she says. Her tone is dead serious. "There's some things that you is better off not to have, chile. Not if you is got to pay too dear for them. You have to think about this for yourself, now. Have to make up your own mind 'bout these here ribbons. I ain't a gonna tell you what to do with them, chile. But I tell you that I is not touch them things iff'n they was give to you for that man to mess with you!"

I can feel the heat coming offa her. Honey's feelings are boiling over and out of her. She is scared that man is gonna drag me down into the fires of hell with him. Oh, this is terrible; I feel all turned around. I don't know what to do 'cause I'm thinking how much I like these pretty colored ribbons, but now Honey don't want to touch 'em no more. Not even to fix 'em up in my hair so Mr. Man can come along and say "Whooo is yoooou, little Missy?" when he sees me standing there. Much as I want the ribbons all for my very own, I don't want Honey ascairt them people is gonna drag me into the fiery furnace after them. I reach out and push all the ribbons far away to the other side of the table. Far away as I can push 'em.

I tell Honey I guess I don't want them ribbons after all. It's hard for me to say it. Mostly what I don't want is for her to fall down so hard in the chair. I don't want all these bad feelings pouring offa her. I don't want her scared for me. So I push the little pile of ribbons away from me. When she asks me if I'm sure I don't want 'em no more I nod my head Yessum.

Honey says, "They ain't worth it, chile. No. You don't need no ribbons iff'n you got to get 'em thataways! Won't be worth it, chile, 'cause one day you have to pay. I tell you them folks that do like that is marked by the devil. They gonna burn up in the fiery furnace, chile, for all them trashy ways. No, no, we not have no truck with folks like that."

Honey gets outta her chair and goes over to the stove. She takes the lifter-up-the-lid thing and lifts up the lid to the stove. Then she picks up each one a them ribbons by the end, like she'd pick a dead fly outa the sugar bowl, and takes 'em all to the stove. Holds 'em out away from her as far as she can. "We gonna burn these right up, baby. Not have nothin' more to do with this ol' badness."

She holds the ribbons over the opened-up place in the stove. The pretty little ends start to curl up from the heat and fire in there. Honey drops 'em in the hole like as if they was burning her fingers. There's just a little smoke that comes out, and then she puts the lid back on. I think the ribbons burn up in the fires of hell like she says them bad people do.

Later on, when the Man gets back from town, I tell him all about it. "You shoulda seen how Honey burned 'em up, Mr. Man," I say after he unhooks the wagon. I'm watching him take the strap things offa the Horsey. He hangs 'em on the nail where they go so he always knows where they are when he wants 'em.

"My, my. That ol' woman did that, did she, chile?" The Man looks at me and shakes his head.

"Yep, she sure did that thing, Man. She said, 'We don't want no such trash as this, do we, baby?' Honey tole me that pretty is as pretty does, Man. Said she's as sure 'bout that as she is of anything in this world! You shoulda seen how she scrunch up her face and say, 'Ohhhh, ohhh, ohhhh. We not can keep these now, chile. Can't have no truck with the Wages of Sin!' "

I show the Man how Honey scrunch up her face and hold the

ribbons with the tippy tips a her fingers and "put 'em right straight in the fires of hell." Honey tole it in a kinda sad tone that them Baddies is going to hell. I talk like her but I ain't one bit sorry. I hope Grandpa and all of 'em go ahead and burn up along with the ribbons.

"Honey put 'em in the stove, Man. Soon's they burnt up she said, 'Let's go on the porch and get us some fresh air, chile.' She talked like she didn't wanta be in the kitchen where the ribbons was. I tole her I wasn't never gonna do thataways again. I promise I not do any more a them trashy ways with them no account people."

I walk over to where the Man is rubbing his ol' friend Horsey on the neck, and I do like he showed me. I pat the horse's neck real easy like and I tell the Man, "Honey said I didn't need those ribbons 'cause she was gonna give me something better. She done comb my hair and tied it up with pieces off the scraps from the scrap box. Pretty clean scraps a ribbons that she ironed all nice and neat. Honey said they was just the thing to set off my pretty little head."

"Well, I reckon she was right about that, chile," the Man smiles at me. "Don't think I ever seen anybody that's got any nicer bows in her hair."

We go out the door of the horse's shed and head for the house. I see he's got a grin on his face. "Sure was a good thing Ol' Horsey recognized you when me and him come along, don'tcha think? Why, if he hadn't a slowed down I reckon I'd a drove right on by you, chile. Yep, and when I got to home I'd be a wonderin' who was that little lady back there with such nice bows in her hair."

I think to myself I ain't touching that baby and get my head knocked off. Clean off my shoulders, for sure!

Honey's watching me. She says, "Well, Lordy, what's a matter? Don'tcha like her? I know she ain't like the picture, chile. Maybe she ain't Shirley Temple but she's a nice baby, don'tcha think?"

I ain't too sure what's goin' on. Don't know if somebody's playing a trick on me or what I'm suppose to do.

I tell Honey she looks pretty nice, I guess.

"Well then, why don'tcha pick her up, chile?"

"Is she really *mine,* Honey? Is she really and truly for me? My own baby doll that I can keep?"

The Man holds up his hand. "I declare I think she's YOURS, chile. Seems to me I done seen Honey a sewin' on that baby for a month a Sundays now. Just for you, chile. I just don't see nobody else 'round here but you what needs a baby doll. Do you, Honey?"

Oh, Honey does think every little girl needs a real baby doll. Even ME! Oh my. Ohhh my. She's so pretty and so clean, I'm ascairt I mess her up. I walk over to where she's sitting. I look at her. "Ohhh my, what I do with her, Honey?"

"Well, chile, I believe that baby needs to be took outta that blanket. It seems right hot today for that much coverin' up."

"You sure, Honey? You sure she not be catching a cold without her blanket?"

"Lord no, chile, not in this nice warm kitchen. No, I do believe she needs a little air. Course, you is THE MOTHER, ain'tcha? You do whatever you think be the best thing for that baby."

They get busy then. Get the Good Book out and open it up. I never hear one word of the story that night.

With that raggity doll I'm in another world. Me and Baby. I don't name her yet; she is just "Baby." I take all her things off and look to see if she has all her arms and legs where they suppose to be at.

"Chile, I swear to goodness I don't know where you get it, but you is 'bout to set me plum crazy." Honey fuss and fumes at me, and says for me to go ahead and get her box.

Oh goody, she's gonna do it. I go open the drawer and get out her sewing box and look at all the buttons! While I look at the pretty buttons, Honey wets her finger and then threads the needle.

"Well, come on now. You hurry me up to do this thing for you, I done set mysef down to do it, and now what's a matter witcha, chile?"

"I gotta decide, Honey."

I done already decide a big thing: call my baby Lu Lu Belle. I think it's a pretty name.

"Here I think you was in such a hurry to get that raggity baby all fixed up, and now I just gotta wait till you two make up your

minds. Lord, Lord, what am I gonna do with the two a yous? Such a
mess you'uns is!" But she don't yell and be mad and hit me.

"She don't know what in the world to do with us, Lu Lu Belle,"
I tell my baby, "and she don't know what in the world to do without
us." And we just laugh and laugh 'cause we know *she* is a mess, too!

Honey says she just go on 'bout her business now, and when I
decide what I want then I can tell her 'cause she is plum tired a this
messin' 'round. Says she can't tell which one a us is the worstest.
Can't tell who is the raggity baby and who is the CHILE!

"Well, you do know, Honey, it just don't pay to go jumpin' off
without thinkin' 'bout where you gonna land. Don'tcha know that,
Honey?" I talk in a tone just like her. "There's a lotta buttons in this
box, Honey, and you know I wanna get the very rightest one for Lu
Lu Belle."

She reckons I make a whole lotta sense. If she's gonna sew one a
them on Lu Lu Belle's tummy, well then seems like it oughta be the
prettiest belly button we can find.

10

SANCTUARY

Marie called as soon as she got JoAnn's letter. I was curious about her response.

"The only thing she said," JoAnn stated, "was 'Why did you write those things to me?' She didn't deny anything and didn't confirm anything. All she wanted to know was why I said those things *to her*. If you'd heard the tone when she said 'those things TO ME,' well, you'd know she hadn't paid any attention to what I actually said. She was upset only because I'd said it to her! Like *that* was the outrage here, not the things I'd written about. I told her I didn't want to talk with her—I was very calm and polite—and I hung up."

Her mother called twice more within the next few weeks. Each time, before hanging up the phone, JoAnn simply said, "I have no interest in talking to you."

She shook with anger, though, when telling me about those brief exchanges. She was surprised that Marie could disregard the written injunction she'd packed with probably as much emotion as she'd ever risked on her mother. I was shocked, too; I found it hard to conceive of getting a letter like that and ignoring the warning. However, after thinking about it a moment, I wasn't surprised at all.

"You've always said she never listened to anything you told her," I offered. "Looks like this is just business as usual." I seem to have a knack for knowing when to prevent the obvious from going unsaid.

Maybe it wasn't unusual for Marie but this time for JoAnn it was different. Never in her life had she felt any power in regard to her mother. It simply hadn't occurred to her she was entitled to have a say in their relationship, that she deserved equal consideration.

Almost two years before this, when we began working together, it was after JoAnn had ordered her mother to leave the house, insisting the six-month visit was over. She hadn't felt empowered by that action back then, however. If anything, aside from feeling confused, she'd been frightened of her anger and perplexed about why it had suddenly erupted to overtake her usual measured reactions.

Despite our role-playing session in the group some months earlier, I think at the time she wrote that angry letter I didn't understand the full extent to which JoAnn felt powerless to keep people in her family from intruding into and controlling her life. She'd always appeared so self-assured to me, confident of being able to manage whatever challenged her. It's not that this assessment was so far from the mark, either, at least in my experience with her. But old training, especially from one's first teachers, is the hardest to change.

When children have been systematically indoctrinated into believing the needs of their caretakers are what matters most, the process of learning to assert their own claims is similar to mastering a basic life skill. And if a child is cursed and knocked over every time she pulls herself upright to take a step in response to her body's natural desire to walk, the desire to walk will most likely be short-lived. Unless someone intervenes, or the youngster is blessed with a fiery will, the chance of discovering how to travel under her own steam is slim indeed.

In the past we've tended to think that brainwashing flourishes only in distant, war-pocked countries or far below the smooth and humorless smiles of beleaguered cult members. It's just recently we've been comprehending that, in truth, it happens within even the most normal-looking families in neighborhoods across the land. So the task for JoAnn of learning how to set limits with her mother was an undertaking I didn't completely fathom in the early 1980s—until I began to see the consequences of her efforts there. The moratorium she had declared on their communication rolled into months and then stretched into more than a year.

During the early part of that long period JoAnn was hit with a bruising awareness of how vulnerable she'd been as a child. I think for the first time in her life she permitted herself to feel the age-old impossibility of keeping out of her own space anyone who chose to invade it. That personal space included everything from surrounding airwaves, time enough to pursue an interest, freedom to craft an opinion, to the right of privacy, her bed, and her own body.

As I sat with JoAnn in my office talking about these things it occurred to me I'd never *not* felt safe. The realization was shocking, especially since I had an adventurous streak and sometimes took risks on the far edge of prudence. Maybe I'd just always shown a trait I regarded as my family's belief we could handle ourselves while harm roamed elsewhere. It wasn't until later I began to wonder if we merely denied that danger was sometimes present in our lives. Either way, whichever it might've been, the result was uncomplicated: I did what I wanted to do without much thought as to my safety.

On looking back, I suppose the most frightened and vulnerable I'd ever felt was in the mid-1960s when a friend and I drove to Prague while our husbands were on Army field maneuvers in the German countryside. We had to surrender our passports at the hotel where we stayed, something I'd never been required to do. When we anxiously walked around the city, under a watchful and pervasive military presence, it was without those seemingly all-protective documents; and I wasn't sure if anybody knew exactly where we were. The fear I carried on that trip made even more sense to me some while later when the newspapers printed stories about the Soviet government, shod in heavy uniform boots, suddenly trampling on the Czech citizens in Prague.

I came to see that in the few, relatively brief instances where I might've been in danger, it was always with my having chosen to be in the situation. And *that* difference made all the difference. In JoAnn's life the element of choice had always been appropriated by someone older or bigger. Aware that I'd grown up knowing I could decide what seemed right for me, always trusting that my decisions would be respected, now left me acutely grateful for a blessing I'd offhandedly assumed to be an entitlement.

I wondered what it would take for JoAnn to believe that very same blessing was a condition to which she actually was entitled. I started talking about setting limits, about defining her boundaries, establishing a sense of safety in her life. It seemed essential to me that she consciously work to create a physical space where she'd feel protected enough to keep exploring, if she chose, the emotional aspects of long-ago dangers which still numbed her.

"Where's the place you feel safest?" I asked.

It took no thought. "In my bedroom," she replied instantly.

I'm not sure JoAnn had ever given any consideration to the notion of safety before, or even defined the term. But she knew right away what this was all about. A single word, serving as a nucleus around which she wrapped an idea, was all it took for her to understand the concept. In effect she then gave herself permission to draw a protective border circling her bedroom; in there she could risk gradually exposing her vulnerabilities further still.

Her mother stopped calling. JoAnn nestled into the room that was becoming her sanctuary, a place she could find refuge enough to continue her quest. She brought together in one spot all the tools of her new trade: notebooks, paper, pens, books, her tape recorder, tapes. She no longer feared they might come into someone else's hands, as had occurred with anything else she'd cared about. In that place she also gathered up things which gave her comfort, like the rocking chair where she must've found a familiar motion to help ease out her pain. She gave way to a natural rhythm and flow that seemed to seep from some recessed wisdom or guidance instead of responding to a standard of behavior mediated by her overfunctioning mind.

And she slowly grew stronger. It was the first time in her life she began to feel safe, the first time she realized that throughout forty-nine years she had maintained a state of constant vigilance. Later on I learned that during this period JoAnn undertook yet another method of purging herself of the past, something I don't believe she'd have been able to do without feeling safer in her newly created environment.

There were times she simply didn't have the strength to write or didn't feel like confining herself to the two dimensions of a sheet of paper. So after banishing her mother (who surely must've also represented the whole family), and gaining access to more emotions since carving out her sanctuary, sometimes she would speak into a tape recorder of the feelings she couldn't express any other way. At those times any other way would have meant imposing some degree of control when she was fighting so hard to relinquish control.

I'm not sure how long JoAnn had been using this outlet before she brought in a few audio cassette tapes she'd recorded. Unsurprisingly, she put them with a batch of papers on my desk before leaving and would've left without comment if I hadn't noticed and asked about them. It was practically as she walked out the door I learned that she'd discovered another way of moving her therapy along. Again she taught me what was helpful to her.

Eventually JoAnn probably turned over twenty or thirty tapes to me (only part of those she recorded), along with the usual supply of papers. Thankfully—from my standpoint, at least—she didn't tape record her process as much as she continued to write about it. I found it nearly unbearable to listen to the tapes she brought in, and yet I understood why she chose to record those particular things. A piece of paper could not possibly have contained their messages.

I heard several of those early tapes left behind at the end of our sessions. They often started out with her speaking in a soft voice, dreamy-like, sometimes with a rhythmic cadence (the way you might talk to a baby who doesn't quite want to sink into the crib where sleep will overtake him). For want of any other framework, I pictured this opening as a sort of self-induced trance. It probably is a fair description, too, because that technique seemed to lull her away from a head too stuffed with thoughts and ideas, a mind whose job was to make sense of her world. Thus when she recorded those tapes—as when she wrote—she gave up on the idea of making sense out of things and, instead, spoke of whatever wanted to come forth from her interior world.

I tried to listen to the tapes, I really did. Partly because I felt I owed it to her since I had contracted—at least in my own mind—to be with her on the scaffolding as she reconstructed a childhood that had collapsed on itself. But I couldn't do it. Or I could only do it occasionally, for limited periods of time. It was just too hurtful. I suppose it came down to practicing what I was preaching: I needed to be able to set some boundaries, too.

When the voice on the tape was talking, just talking about whatever incident was freshly floating into consciousness, I could manage it. But when JoAnn would connect her never expressed, nor even experienced, *feelings* with oncoming memories, she'd often start crying or crack apart into agonized sobbing. Either that or she'd scream with raw fury at the absent person who never had and never would hear her. When this sort of thing happened in my office, even if I felt uncertain about what to say, at least I could just be there with her, sit it out with her. But when, through the marvel of technology, I listened to those sounds of anguish come off the tape so excruciatingly real and yet disembodied, it was more than I could handle. I couldn't stand to feel so helpless.

That sense of being powerless was something JoAnn had begun to identify as a constant factor during her early years. I knew she didn't have any choice about what had been handed her, but I also knew that I did. Just as she'd found a way that best suited *her* to create a portrait of her life, I'd also found a way that best suited *me* to let that effort enter into mine.

For me it was a balancing act. I needed to have time enough away from work to renew my energy to do the work. And since the part of my work that involved JoAnn was so dark and shadowed, I managed to deal with it best in a setting with as much light and calm as could be gathered anywhere.

Sometime during part of the four-day weekends I had every week, I took JoAnn's material with me out on the deck to read in the quiet of a piece of the West Virginia countryside enveloped in woods thick with oak and hickory trees. In the winter, when I couldn't sit outside, I claimed a spot between the woodstove and a series of long windows looking out toward the garden. Apart from our sessions in my office these were the only places from which I could tolerate entering her world. I couldn't do it when I stayed in the city; the noise and the pace and the clutter of people and their things kept me too revved up to spend time with stories that frequently left me churning of their own accord.

A friend from Texas understood this and once put it another way. After visiting a few days, he said, "I can see why you love this place. It's like a big generator you come here and plug into. Then you go back to the city and your patients plug into you." I felt this was particularly true in my work with JoAnn; being able to plug into that generator was part of what helped keep me going.

To put down a small notebook of her disturbing recollections and then look up to see seven or eight deer move cautiously from the trees into a clearing by the creek was just the kind of balance I required. If I stayed very still, sometimes they came to within fifty feet of the house, eating weeds and grass and leaves off low branches as they slowly munched their way along. Eating everything in range, actually, with the sort of panda gusto Ling Ling showed while she feasted on bamboo at the National Zoo.

But even these simple pleasures could strike me with their dark side as I sifted through JoAnn's material. A doe, for instance, might come to the edge of the clearing first and stand perfectly still a few moments before looking around. There'd be such alertness in her huge eyes I wouldn't even know I'd been holding my breath until I ran out of air. Sometimes her wobbly-legged, spotted fawn would stop a little way back among the trees, not moving a muscle, waiting for the mother's signal that it was safe to come ahead. They'd both graze, but the mother deer would look up while chewing every mouthful, always watching for any sign of movement that might signal a threat. Then of course when I glanced down at the papers in my lap, I'd be saddened to concede that not all mothers looked after their young with such watchful care.

Lots of days I had the queasy feeling that comes of changing directions too fast, like being in an elevator that stops suddenly. After I'd read on one page of Honey soothing JoAnn's skinned elbow and would then watch her mother deliver an end-of-her-rope slap to this same child on the next page, the contrast could leave me terribly unsteady. I suppose there isn't any paradise without its own kind of poignancy.

One thing I knew: deer wouldn't walk by and hummingbirds certainly would stop zipping in to tank up on the sugar water in their garish feeders if I assaulted the quiet knolls with taped sounds of sobs and screams.

JoAnn found the tape recorder liberating when she had powerful emotions to dispel. I was glad she used it and found help there. It was not liberating for me on the other end of the loop, though. As I steeped myself in her childhood I craved stillness and light and the earth's natural turn instead of technology that could fracture the air with cries of human pain.

11

HENRY'S GIRLS

She is patting her hair, making the little curls lie just the way she wants. Putting on lipstick now. She loves the mirror and what she sees in there. She is just about ready now to go out and have some fun.

I had told Mama I wanted to talk to her. She said to come on in the bedroom with her and we could talk while she got ready to go out.

I tell her not to go out tonight, but I can't tell her how bad it is for me when she's away. It's getting nearly too much for me to stand anymore; I don't know what might happen. She says she's gotta get out of here. Mama can't stand it if she can't get out of this place for a few hours. She tells me, like she always does, to be a good girl and don't cause any trouble for Grannie or Papa while she's gone.

"Well," I think to myself, "you can't stand to stay here with these people one minute more than you have to, but you don't hesitate a second to leave *me* in this stink hole by myself!" That's what I THINK, but I don't say it. What I want to say to her is much more important.

It was immensely important to me, and I had thought it out very carefully. I wanted her to realize that we had to move out of there. It was an unheard of idea in my family, so I started explaining and telling her what we could do and where we could go. I'd thought it all out, even where we could move and how we could manage. On some level I must have realized I was being devoured in little pieces there and had to get out or I'd die.

She is sitting on the little cheap vanity seat leaning toward the cheap wavy mirror, looking to see if her lipstick is on straight. I ask if she is listening. I have to ask three times before she says, "Yes, dammit, I am listening to youuu, JoAnn!"

But I know she's not. It is suddenly so clear to me that she is not listening. I start to repeat words and phrases, pure junk. Only in a talking kind of voice. I know it doesn't make one bit of sense. She doesn't catch on. She doesn't even know I am talking gibberish. I keep it up, keep it up in a kind of conversational tone, like I am speaking sentences. She never notices. I do it until I get sick and tired of it.

She never hears anything wrong because she had never listened to me all my life. Naturally she doesn't hear that I am just sing-songing trash at her! She lets me go on. She lets herself think we are HAVING A TALK, and all the time her full attention is on the cheap dirty mirror in the front bedroom of the house on Pine Ridge Road.

In spite of my thinking so hard about telling her we had to move away, the whole effort was just a waste. When I realized she didn't care, when I KNEW she wasn't hearing me, never had and never would hear me, ahh what a feeling came over the child I was. How old was I then? Not much. A girl, a still undeveloped girl. But starting to develop. And it scared me that people were starting to notice. Ten comes to mind, but I do not know for sure.

That was when I started the gibberish talk, just to test her on it. Even though I KNEW she wasn't listening, I guess I didn't really want to believe it. So I had to check it out again.

Like we were learning to "test out" the arithmetic problems in math class . . .

A girl, another student in the class, had told me how to "test out" your answer. "And if you do this, JoAnn, you can tell if you've got it right!"

She was trying to help me. Step by step she went over how to do it. She said, "To test it out you just put a little line here, like this, and then you add this and your answer and if you get this number right here, then you did it right! See there. It's easy once you know how to do it, isn't it?"

We were at Recess. She said she would try to help me "get it." She said her mother always says it is sooo hard when you're learning a thing, but you'll be surprised how easy it'll be when you know how to do it!

It was her tone of voice that I remember so well. I was sitting, doing nothing. That girl had felt terrible about the teacher talking to me so mean. Her mother said there wasn't any reason to "talk bad" to anybody.

She sat down. She had been talking to me, standing there, and I wasn't paying her any mind. I knew someone was there. I could feel it and see her shadow in the dirt. I could feel her first, coming up and standing there. I closed up more. Drew up inside, preparing for the bad thing to happen when somebody would come up on me.

I was not listening, but her tone got my attention. I was keyed up and waiting for the hits and yells to happen, but instead she was talking soft. There was sadness in her voice. She had told her mother she did not like the way "that teacher did you, JoAnn." Her mother did not like it either.

She told her mother when she got home from school. Her mother would want to know "what happened in school today?" So she told her about the teacher and about me. She liked her mother, I could tell. When she said "Mother" it was with a cooing tone. Her mother said anybody can learn, but you had to be shown how to do things.

The girl said she could help me, she could show me. Her mother and father had showed her how. The teacher didn't show her. She didn't like the teacher. That was another thing which drew me up from the darkness. I felt that she and her mother (coo coo) did not like the teacher either.

She sat down and fixed her dress over her legs. "Would you like for me to show you how to do it, JoAnn? I can. I couldn't do it either at first. Then I told my father, and he said he would explain it to me. It didn't even take FIVE MINUTES!"

No, it didn't take long to learn because her father knew how to talk to her and how to make it easy for her. Now she could do all the adding and subtracting problems, she could. Just as easy as pie.

"Would you like for me to show you?" She waited.

She did not rush in and sit down and shove and push all over me with her feelings. She waited, and I never talked. I kind of pushed over a little bit. She sat down with her back to the big tree. I was sitting there with my back flat up against the big tree. I was protecting myself by being against the tree.

She sat down and got out her paper. She drew the letters and numbers real carefully. She made a neat paper because her father always told her "the reason for writing something is so someone else can read it," and if you scribble scrabble—well, how could a person read THAT?

So she wrote slowly, and talked so easy and calmly while making up the "problems." She was so calm that I got a little bit calm, too. I listened to her. I watched the paper, saw her draw the lines and the numbers. She showed me how to work the problem and then test it out to make sure the answer was right.

Mama is finished primping now. She yanks off her old blouse and throws it on the floor. She has a new one to wear tonight when she goes out.

"Well, I deserve to go have a little fun once in a while, don't I? Goddammit, JoAnn, I'm not an OLD WOMAN!" Mama sees in the mirror that she is still the prettiest one of the Foley girls. She stands up in her new blouse and tucks it in so it will show off her beautiful waist!

She does not know that I live and breathe. As I sit there on that creaky old cheap bed I think to myself she WOULDN'T EVEN NOTICE if snakes were growing out of my head! I am as sure of it as I am of the dirt clay road that runs by the whorehouse we live in. I don't even know why I bothered to test her on it.

"You is STUPID, Lu Lu Belle! I break your damn arm and it serve you right!"

I try to put Lu Lu Belle's arm in that sleeve, and she don't help a bit. I'm gonna break her arm on account of she don't help when I'm working so hard. "Stupid goddam girl! You don't do a thing RIGHT!"

"Chile, WHAT ARE YOU DOIN'?" Honey cries out to me. "That ain't Lu Lu Belle's fault. You do like that, the first thing you know you yank that baby's arm clean off! . . . Well, she can't help it. She's a raggity baby what can't help herself one little bit. You gonna hurt her like that. You have to take your time and do right. How many times I tell you that, chile? Now I just not like to see no poor little rag baby get treated like that."

"She won't put her arm back in here, Honey. It won't go."

"Well, you oughta thinked about that before you taked it off her! I know Lu Lu Belle not ask you to take her dress off her, did she? Now you think 'bout that thing before you answer me. Think before you open your mouth, chile."

Honey picks up that rag doll from where I pitched her. "Poor baby, you come on here with me. I love you, lil' baby. Way that girl treats you, makes me unhappy to see. I do hate to see her be sooo bad to you, Lu Lu Belle."

She's a goddam pain inna ass, that raggity doll is. And Honey loves her! Oh, I cry inside. I don't like to see her love that baby. Makes me wanta hit her. Beat her up. Smack her and shake her head and teach her a lesson! Teach her to mind me when I tell her something!

I'm so sad. I get closer to them but I don't hit Lu Lu Belle. I don't say them words like I want to.

Honey says, "Mummmhuhhhh, chile. I just don't like to see it when a mama don't treat her baby right. No, it purely do upset me."

❈

"This is sad times for that man. Yeah, sad times come to us all, chile."

Honey tells me 'bout the stranger man what come onto the Place. He done sleep out there with Ol' Friend Horsey in the horse's house. The man chop wood for her. He cut up all that wood for the stove.

"Good work," she tells me. "He do good work. Pile up alla that stove wood just as neat as a woman do. Times is hard, chile. Times is hard for him 'cause he's down and out. . . . Well, it don't hurt to help somebody out once in a while. Don't hurt a bit. . . . Why? 'Cause we never can tell, that's why. You just can't never tell." And her voice has a sad tone when she says how you just can't never tell when you might need a helping hand yourself someday.

"Things go up and things go down in this ol' world, chile. Lord, yes they do. Lucky. Oooh, we is lucky to have this Place. Always have a place to lay our heads. That ain't the way it is with him, though. Poor man. Poor man."

Honey talks to me while I eat. She fixes up a little something for the tramp man to take along with him. He eat already; done had his breakfast today. He's out cleanin' up after hisself from sleeping in the Horse's house. She tells me he's gonna catch a train. Going off to catch the first train what comes along.

She thinks we got enough. "Taste mighty good to him, don'tcha think, chile? We mebbe not know where he's goin' to but at least we know he have a little bite to eat!"

Honey packs up a little something for the tramp man to eat. Well, she knows we don't have to do it but she figures "we have a plenty, and you just never can tell where that man be at tonight when he gets hungry. Might turn out that he be glad for a few cold biscuits, a little piece a cheese, and a jug a cool water out the well."

I don't want to give him any cheese. I wanta keep it for myself. I do. I know she don't like to hear THAT. But I know not to lie to her, too.

She says, "Ain't a thing the matter with you a wantin' to eat that cheese. I like cheese myself, too, but we is got so much, chile. So much that we can spare a little bitty bite for him too, don'tcha think?"

I wanta make her pleased with me. I say, "Yessum. Yessum, we is mighty blessed." And I tell her I know it be the best thing to share with that poor ol' man what is got his troubles.

"Lordy, I think so, too, chile. I sure do. Can't tell where he's likely to be tonight, and be a comfort to us just knowin' he's got a bite to eat no matter where he's at, don'tcha think so, chile?"

She cuts me a little bite off that cheese, and she takes a bite then cuts a piece for the tramp man.

"Oh, it do taste mighty good, don't it?" she says, and rolls her eyes around. "Taste mighty good to him, too!"

I'm almost pretty sure we have enough, but I ain't really glad to give him any cheese. Honey says we have plenty, though, and we eat a bite and get all warmy. We have to help him 'long his way, Honey says, 'cause it be a terrible thing not to have a mouthful a food come nightfall.

"Yeah, chile, I know how I feel iff'n my man be out a wanderin'. Well, well, hope that man find his way home. Have a family a waitin' for him somewheres mebbe. Mebbe so. Mebbe so . . ."

※

School was such a mystery to me. The teachers talked, and I hardly understood anything they said. I was not used to being talked to when I went to first grade; yelled at, yes, but not talked to. I was totally afraid there, frightened of the halls, the rooms, the other children. There was too much confusion in the air, and it scared me.

At home they had all complained about how awful school was, how the teachers there would finally "teach me a thing or two!" Of course "teach me" meant hitting and beatings and cussing me out, so I thought school would be just like it was at home.

But it was more terrifying at school, really. When the teachers talked it might as well have been in Latin. I was so used to not knowing anything that I just went on along being upset and not understanding a thing. I just went along as best as I could, learning a little bit each time. It was truly hard for me.

I remember learning where the toilet was, then finding out I didn't know WHAT a toilet was. I only knew an Outhouse as the place you went to pee. I don't believe I had ever been in an indoor toilet until I went to school. The water scared me, running in the faucet and flushing in the commode—the force and sound of it seemed somehow violent.

A sign by the door said GRADE 3. I knew the number 3. When I got there the teacher, in a soft voice, said, "This is the third grade."

I must have mumbled that I was in the wrong place because she started questioning me.

"You don't belong? Are you supposed to be here in the third grade?"

I did not know that the "third grade" was the same as "Grade 3." It seems preposterous to me now that a child would not know how to read by the third grade, but I'm sure my placing of the time is right. I remember overhearing someone say in a kind of pitying voice that "she's so slow." It wasn't said in a harsh, angry tone that blamed me for not moving fast enough to suit them; I knew it was a different kind of "slow" they meant.

I don't think I did much of anything in school except move when shoved or pulled, like a dumb animal who has been battered into submission and neither can, nor will, move an inch on its own for fear of it being The Wrong Goddam Way! I may as well have been a piece of wood, just doing like I was used to doing at home. I had never been taught; I didn't know ANYTHING!

So in school I simply blundered along, watching everything in my deep confusion, trying to figure it out with all those small people milling about in the room. Outside was even worse because there were many more children running around and playing. Only it was not play to me. It petrified me!

I hung back in the room, not wanting to go out. One of the teachers said, "Of course you want to go out." I knew the words "go out," but that was most all I understood of what she said. I realized it was time to go out, except I was far more frightened of being outside than staying in the classroom.

She told me I had to go out and play with the other children. "Of course you want to go with all the others, JoAnn. It's Recess," she said simply. The teacher had to think for a minute until she knew which little girl I was, but she said my name.

She had seen me sitting in the little chair-desk thing, doing nothing. Sometime earlier I had been told to stay at my desk because "you can't just get up and wander around all over the place!" And now here was this big woman leaning over and asking me what was wrong. That was it. That's how it started. She had walked by and seen me in the chair . . .

·   ·   ·

"She was just sitting, not doing anything. Not doing a THING, I tell you!" Her voice was starting to lose some control, and with it there was a low level tone of "don't blame me" as they talked.

The woman had not even been my teacher in that room. It was Recess and she had walked by and seen me sitting in the room. The thing was that she knew no child should be in the room at that time, so she first thought I was being kept in.

"But when I asked her, she WOULDN'T ANSWER ME! She didn't say a WORD!" The feeling that poured off of her was like it was all my fault for not answering her question. If only I had answered her the way I should've then none of this would have happened.

She had just asked the child what she was doing in the room. That was all. "And I told her she should be outside playing in the yard because it was Recess time. Good lord, don't all of them like to go out and play every chance they get?" All she had done was what she was supposed to do, and the first thing she knew that child had come at her like a CAT!

The young teacher was hurt and frightened by what had happened, but startled more than hurt. She did not like being questioned about what she had done to "make JoAnn do that."

They were saying that it wasn't like her, was it? She was always so quiet, so slow. They did not think the child was quite right. It happens sometimes "in cases like this." They meant in families like the Foleys, white trash families with stair step children where nobody even knew who was mother and father to who.

"God, what a mess," some woman said with a sigh. She felt bad about "what is going to happen." All they could do was to do what they could and hope for the best, but she just couldn't see anything good happening to them. Such a terrible waste, she thought.

She was the principal of the school, the woman who sounded saddened by her experiences with people. Miss Stayer was her name, at least that's what I thought it was. Miss Stayer. It was hard for me to get her name, but I remembered it by thinking "stay," you have to Stay Here.

Miss Stayer was finishing with the teacher, figuring the young

woman was all right now. It was not an easy thing, she acknowledged. Not an easy thing for the "new ones" who had so much to
learn besides what was in the books. No, it certainly wasn't easy for
them, coming in without knowing so many things.

The young woman said something and the principal laughed.
She said no, she didn't mean that. Far as she knew the teacher's
preparation was good, she'd finished school and gotten good grades.
She didn't mean anything like that, she told her.

They were fixing themselves some coffee. The principal stirred
her cup slowly, thoughtfully, like she was weighed down by old
feelings and worries.

It had been a mess to straighten out, but they had to get it
straight. That's all she was trying to do, get it sorted out so she
would know what had happened.

I didn't know what had happened. I hadn't even been in my
body; it was just another instance of being hidden deep inside,
completely unaware of life around me. There was something in the
principal's urgent voice, though, that made me come back and pay
attention.

She was trying to keep everyone calm so she could get the story
straight. She had to know what happened before she got there to the
room. Reports had to be made, questions answered, and she had to
know. It didn't feel like filing a report was the most important thing
to her. No, it was more a matter of her being puzzled and wanting
to know what had occurred before the incident, before she got
there.

No one seemed to know. They just heard it out in the hall and
came in to see what all the noise was about. No one knew, so it all
came back on the teacher. The young woman did not like it either.
She felt they were accusing her, and she hadn't done anything!

All she did was ask the child what she was up to in the classroom when she should have been at Recess. That was her job and
she did it. A child should not be in the classroom during Recess!

"I don't KNOW why she was sitting there," the young teacher
tried to explain. "She wouldn't say anything! She just sat there like a
statue, that's all. I DIDN'T MEAN ANYTHING!"

She had been telling the principal as much as she could piece together, and I suddenly remembered. I think it was because Miss Stayer was trying to calm everybody and understand. It was her concern that grasped my attention and drew me back to the room.

I remembered how the teacher had TOUCHED ME. She had put her hand on my arm, probably just to find out if I could hear her since I hadn't responded, and I went crazy when she TOUCHED ME! Never, never had I liked being TOUCHED!!

I came up at her like a living flame that had been drenched with gasoline. Unable to keep me off her, she was filled with terror of the child who went crazy for no reason at all.

I guess I can understand, recalling this some forty years later, how frightening it would be to have a quiet dummy of a child all of a sudden turn on you like a wildcat. It shook her up severely, my secret fight that none of us comprehended.

Yes, school was certainly confusing and a mystery to me. I stayed away as much as I could, which was considerable because nobody noticed or cared either way.

I was a dullard. I just sat.

I didn't "do" anything except come and go, fetch and carry, do as I was told to do by the Foleys. I might as well have had no brain of my own. Unable to bear my life, I simply left it; my body was all that was there. How long I was like that I can't tell, but I still recall the feeling and that sense of being empty. I had fled from inside. Just the husk of me remained.

As shut down as I was, I didn't like going with Henry's Girls. I had to go to The Joint with them, and I hated it. Even more than being at home with the Foleys I hated going to The Joint with Henry and his Girls. We were nothing—my mother, her three sisters, and me—just collectively "Henry's Girls." I was about eleven years old when they started making me go with them.

At times I would try different things to get out of going. For a while I'd be good about going, getting dressed when they told me, and not arguing with the Girls. They were not very happy about having to "make me go," but they were afraid of Henry, who was always telling them to watch me and get me ready. No matter what happened, or what I did, they were afraid to tell him I wasn't ready or that I wouldn't go.

If I caused any trouble Henry would go crazy. As the oldest son, he had taken over the little kingdom Grandpa once ruled. And now everybody was afraid of *him*. He would scream and blame them for not being able to do a goddam thing like he asked them to do. He asked them for sooo liiittle, and still they couldn't even handle a goddam dummy, for Christ's sake!

When he pulled up out front, we would be herded out in a bunch to Henry's car. One dusky night while they were getting in the car, I broke away and ran like hell into the woods across from the house. Before they even realized it, I was long gone. Long gone at least for the one night. I knew they would be eager to get going, and not expecting any trouble from me at that point. They were so easy to read. Stupid is what they were. One thing I hated most was how stupid they all were. They never learned a thing.

Marie, especially, never learned. She wanted me to promise to "be good," and she wanted me to remember to keep my promise not to call her "Mother." She simply was too young to be such a "big girl's mother." It wasn't right to her. It wasn't right for them to know she had a big girl like me for a daughter.

Ohhh, how she hated the thought that she was old enough to have "a big girl like JoAnn!" Everyone agreed with her, and she would touch her hair and smile because everyone agreed JoAnn COULDN'T POSSIBLY BE HERS!! Be HER girl? NO!!! Marie's daughter???

All of a sudden I was watching her as she talked to me for the Millionth Time. I was drawing with my finger in a wet place on the table. I saw her, and saw it was getting near the end of the game, the little pattern we played out almost every day when she came home. Soon we had to get dressed to go to The Joint, and she went through the ritual to straighten me out.

I knew she was going to touch her hair, finish the last of her coffee, and I knew she would tell me how I'd just better do like she said, how I'd better MIND HER tonight! I sat still as she got up from the dirty old stinking table to go primp. She told me to take her dishes off the table.

I smiled at her. I hardly ever smiled, almost never. She looked at me funny, kind of puzzled, and STUPID. She was so damn stupid!

I slid over and picked up the dishes. Staring at her like a copperhead, I threw them on the floor and jumped on them. My heel shattered the plate but not the cup because it was that thick white mug stuff. She looked at me like she was choking.

Very quietly I said, "No."

We stared at each other. Marie said she would "teach me a thing or two!!!" God, I'd heard that all of my life.

I said, "No, I think not. I think not."

"What do you mean, JoAnn? What do you MEAN?"

"What did I say, Marie? Are you so old, Mother, that you can't HEAR me? Are you so old you can't hear your 'little girl'? ARE you?"

I swung out and hit her HARD, as hard as I could. With every bit of strength in me I hit out. I wanted to knock her damn head off her shoulders. I wanted to kill her!

Ahh, I was a Foley. It was just that simple. I was a Foley in miniature. I kicked her and hit her. I punched her like a man would do, like I had seen them do since the day I was born. Like dear Papa did, like all of them did, from the littlest one to the oldest ones.

Marie's nose was bleeding. I hit her breast, I think maybe because she was sooo proud of her beautiful breasts and her waist, this "prettiest one of the Foley girls." She was always looking at herself in that goddam vanity mirror while I was dying dead in that hell hole.

I beat on her until I heard the screen door open in the hall. Only then did I stand away, to see who it was. It was Grandpa coming to see "what in the hell is going on in here?!"

Out the back door I ran, like a scared rabbit runs. I hid in the woods all night long. I heard them call me and tell me to come on in before they locked me out. Ha! As if I cared. As if it was even possible to lock that old shack up.

The energy flowed when I was angry, and it was wonderful to turn on them, to see them afraid, to feel the balance of power sway, and have some force of my own. The Foleys' world was ruled by force. Force was the first means, and the second was "slick." You had to have power or else be smart.

Without strength you were lost unless you could be slick enough to outsmart the forceful one into doing what you wanted, while making him think he wanted it. Or to make him think it was his idea to start with.

Sometimes, when I couldn't find a way to keep from going with them to The Joint, I'd try to start trouble there. I thought if I was a big enough pain in the ass maybe they'd leave me home. It didn't work, though. Too many of the men liked having "that young one there" for Henry to leave me home.

I'd slick up to two men at The Joint, and it would end with their being so mad at each other over me that they would get into a fight, or else leave and forget about me. I'd just sit there like Henry told me to, like I didn't even know what was going on. I'd smile and be quiet and so innocent! I liked it. I really did. The only fun I had was in beating the Foleys, one way or the other. Either with my fists or my head.

Beat 'em with my fisties or my head full a senses.

"One or the other, baby. One way or the other, you is gonna win. You is a gonna LEAVEEE THAT PLACE AND THEM FOLKS, chile. I know it!"

I didn't remember Honey's words at the time, but underneath everything they still tugged on me.

What a good apron Honey has that she wears alla time. Wish I had one just like it. I ask if I can wear hers a little bit. She takes it off and hands it to me. Oh, she do laugh and laugh. Honey laughs till she cries.

It surprises me, them tears after all that laughing. "What's a matter with you, Honey?" I ask.

"Ohhh, I be laughin' so hard, chile, I can't even talk to you. . . . What a sight you is in this here apron a mine!" Tells me she gotta sit down and get aholt a herself.

Then she fix it. Ties her apron on me real good and says to let her see this sight a me in her apron. Laughs to beat the band!

"You oughta see yourself, chile. You is a sight! A SIGHT!"

I parade around, walking in her apron, stepping high so I don't step on the apron tails. Ohhh ha ha ha. Honey says I is better'n a picture show, and we just fall all over ourselves a laughing.

"Lord, chile, it's too big for you!! Lordy, we can wrap this ol' apron 'round you twice over. Tell you the truth, you sure is a pitiful sight without no apron a your own! Ain't you now?"

I remember how Honey says a woman wasn't worth her salt less'n she has a apron to keep her nice dress clean while she's a working. "I just can't be a thinking how that never come into my head before this, Honey. Well, you know it ain't fitting for me not to have MY OWN APRON, don't you, huh?"

I look at her. I be thinking how I never ask for anything before. I don't out and out say "I want" to her. If I do that at home, all it gets me is a slap in the head. I just say to her it don't hardly seem fitting for me not to have a apron of my very own.

She laughs and says, "Well, chile, I 'specs you is right 'bout that! No, it don't hardly seem fittin', what with all the work you do to help me 'round this Place. Lord, the size a you, it not hardly take much to put together a little apron just your size, now would it? Sure be a help to keep your dress nice and clean, huh?"

When's I gonna get my apron, I wonder . . .

". . . Now don't go a rushin' me, chile, 'bout this here apron business. I know how you is! You take a notion 'bout sumthin' and you wanta do it right now, lickety split! Well, some things just ain't that a way. Ain't thataway at all, atall. . . . Don't go and cloudy up on me now, chile. All I'm sayin' is you gotta gimme TIME. Aprons ain't made in a day, you know. . . . No, not even little bitty aprons, the ones your size for little girls. They all takes TIME. Now that you know that thing, well then you just gotta wait!"

"Wait don't do nothing, Honey. You said so yourself. 'Wait done broke the wagon down!' That's all WAIT do, you said it lotsa times, Honey," and I put my little hands on my hippies and look at her! "Now didn't you tell that to me, Honey?"

"Well, do tell! Dooo tell! I never seen the like. Whatcha mean a blessin' me OUTTT, chile, right here in my own KITCHEN? Lord, a little bit of a thing like you is!" She stops. Puts her hands on her hippies. "Now, chile, the notion come on me one a these days, and you find yourself with a apron all your own. Till that day come, you just gotta make do with whatcha got!"

I talk with Mr. Man about this apron business.

"Oh, chile, she full a fuss and feathers, she is. Just like a ol' setty hen. She gonna sew her eyes out makin' you a apron one a these days when she gets a chance," he tells me. "You wait and see!"

I'm so excited she's gonna make me a apron just like hers. But it'll be little, lots more little than hers. I tell the Man how her apron is tooo big for me, so I need a littler one. I think about how I wear my apron that's like Honey's, and we go 'long to hoe our row in aprons just alike. Why, we be just like two peas in a pod. I think the Man won't be able to tell us two womens apart!!

Honey stops and turns. She looks at me and says, "Chile, chile, I just give up on you, I declare I do. You best better help me finish with these dishes now, then I don't care iff'n you spend all afternoon in there with that apron on your mind.

". . . Look at them scraps all you want to, chile. . . . Yes, I 'spec any one you be a wantin' is all right. 'Cept there's one I got saved up 'cause it's three or four a the same kind. Can use 'em for a dress or sumthin' for myself. I hate to cut 'em up for the little bit we need to piece together a apron your size. . . . Course, iff'n you like it best of all, I reckon you could have it."

"No, Honey. You keep it 'cause they's all the same kind. I'm pretty sure I find lotsa pieces I purely do love for my apron." I coo coo when I say "my apron."

"Well, I do want you to have one you like, chile. Ain't no sense in makin' one you don't like." She tells me one piece in there got pretty little roses on it. Another piece is blue. Nearly almost as pretty as blue sky.

She done said her piece now, I can tell. I best better leave her alone.

I talk with the Man when we sit on the porch.

"She do it soons she can," he says. "You know how she is, chile. . . . Hmmm, I reckon I need to be puttin' up a peg for you to have for your very own apron, don'tcha think? Can hang it on that pantry door. Course it have to be down low so's you can reach it yourself. . . . Lord, chile, I do seem to recollect there might be a peg there already. Whatcha say let's go have a look?" Him and me go in the house to look.

The Man opens up the door to the pantry and his face lights up like a plate of hot biscuits. "Well, sure enuff! That was my girl's peg when she was a little bitty mite of a thing like you are now! Why, I just 'bout plum forgot it, I did. Reckon it's near on to perfect for you, chile. Yep, I figure it's just whatcha need when you get that pretty little apron!"

Me and him goes back to sit on the steps out front. He starts to whittle. We sit quiet awhile. But I'm still wondering about how long? and when? and what I'm gonna do till then?

". . . No, to tell you the truth, chile, I never made no apron MYSELF. . . . Well, I 'spec lots a people make aprons ever day. . . . Could I? Why, I don't rightly think so, chile. Leastwise not too good! . . . Ol' Mr. God? Sure He could make a apron. Sure He could. I think He could make a wondrous fine apron iff'n He set His mind to it. . . . Yessir, think you is right. Wouldn't be nothin' to no God what made this ol' world in a few days to make a apron in a minute! Trouble is, chile, the trouble is I don't rightly know how to get the Lord's attention on no such a thing as this apron.

"Course now Honey can make a real nice apron, but I reckon it take her a little while. . . . She ain't no ways gonna forget you, chile. Now you do know that, don't you? 'Spec the best thing be to kinda back off a little from that apron awhile. Honey tole you she's gonna make one for you, just like her own, and that woman sure is good for her word, chile. She knows it'd be a TERRIBLE thing iff'n you don't got a APRON A YOUR OWN! So just grab on for now, chile. Okay? She ain't ever gonna forget about YOU!"

12

OLD DIRT

During that period of near exhaustion when JoAnn took leave from her job and set aside everything except for working toward the mending of old wounds, some of my colleagues may have been right when they wondered if she was having a breakdown. Certainly her psyche's way of previously handling things *had* broken down. And the fact is it needed to; the regression she allowed proved to be a self-correcting adjustment on the path she'd chosen to take.

When forest fires race out of control over great expanses of wilderness, fire fighters are sometimes able to stop their devastating spread by planning and setting a series of controlled fires. Whether she realized it or not, I think JoAnn orchestrated something similar to this on her own behalf in the area of her emotional health. Following her intuitive lead, together we set some structure in place around her sense of purpose. That form, once again, acted as a container which held the feelings she let rage in whatever direction the winds of her energy blew.

In our widely scattered, anonymous society few people today are offered the family or community support needed to go through the kind of upheaval it sometimes takes to break free of one's own emotional constraints. JoAnn, after writing her mother, seemed gradually to regain both her strength and perspective. Her leave came to an end and she returned to work.

I remember one session as she was coming out from those dark memories and angry feelings when she told me she had "lost it" the evening before. That day she'd gotten a letter from her mother, along with a check and instructions to buy herself a present. No mention was made of any previous communication.

"I was furious," JoAnn said. "I started throwing stuff around and broke everything in sight."

I wondered what she meant by "everything in sight." She told me that several years ago her mother had given her a set of dishes; after the letter with the check came, she broke each one of the ninety pieces in the service, every single place setting. Then she tore up the check and sent it back to her mother, without comment.

This is what I remember JoAnn having told me about the incident at the time it happened. And it would've been like her to boil the meat off the whole story and get down to a few bony sentences before moving on to something else she wanted to discuss. Many years later we talked about this episode again.

Nothing else was pressing on her mind then so she filled in for me a whole stew of details she hadn't served up earlier: her mother had made her usual big deal out of giving such a generous gift; the dishes were part of a sales promotion where shoppers buy various plates or cups at rock bottom prices along with their purchase of groceries; JoAnn neither wanted nor ever liked the dishes; throwing them all to the ground left the floor space in her small kitchen covered with about an inch of broken pottery, which she walked around on and ground underfoot into even smaller pieces until she swept up the whole mess the next day.

My own slant on the incident was that JoAnn finally dealt with the tyranny of the gift. It isn't unusual for people to deny part of themselves on occasion because of a present they've been given. Few folks find it easy to refuse a gift or to acknowledge they don't like what someone's given them. Some kinds of "generosity" are nothing if not intimidating. More than one tired sitcom has been built around the dilemma of whether to bring out of hiding a detested vase or lamp bestowed by an imminently arriving relative. Many presents are simply bribes in gifts' clothing and are used as a not-always-subtle way of controlling the recipient. In fact the whole subject is emotionally loaded for people because precious little giving is done cleanly and purely just for the other's benefit. JoAnn's explosion ended another way in which her mother maintained an unwelcome presence in her life—even if only as a reminder that valuable shelf space had been usurped by unwanted dishware.

As for the coda to this story, there'd been a lot more to it than the angry tearing up of a check. Since money had always been the most powerful tool for manipulation in her family, JoAnn figured that her mother would be more insulted by a rejected check than hearing her dishes had been smashed. To make her point she took a pair of scissors to the check instead of just ripping it up. She described spending the next several hours methodically cutting the check into the thinnest strips of paper one could possibly imagine. Three or maybe four hours it took to transfigure that check. Confetti, by comparison, would be coarse and bulky. With the remnants of the check gathered onto a sheet of typing paper she funneled the hundreds of slivers of paper into the envelope she mailed. I imagine, in reality, Marie may not even have known the pile of paper shavings in her hands had once been a blank check in her purse. But JoAnn never seemed to need other people's reactions in order to explore the fullness of her own, and she was pleased with the effort she concentrated on obliterating her mother's bribe.

This was the kind of freedom she gave herself during those months of finally relinquishing some control over emotions which had been kept just beyond her reach for so many years.

Off and on there were stretches of fairly smooth going in therapy, interspersed with times when an issue from JoAnn's past might erupt to capture her attention. And just as I was doing with regard to how much of her material I could read, and under what conditions, JoAnn also struggled throughout this period with her own version of finding the right balance in her life. One of the hardest aspects of that involved the pulls between her therapy and her children, especially the youngest son still living at home.

Reentering from the recent awareness of how unprotected she'd been as a child, her focus slowly spread to the world beyond herself. It seemed as though she was birthing a spiral of concern, with its seed planted deep in her interior. She became intensely attuned to how vulnerable all children are in their dependency on others to take care of them.

It hurt her, she said on many occasions, to hear the way parents talked to their children on the street and in the supermarket. She kept noticing youngsters whose eyes were polished by fear, whose faces held no joy. After having located vulnerability in herself, JoAnn felt raw when she was around people. She had a sense of somehow being exposed, without an invitation, to their unhappiness. Over a number of sessions she described having recently found herself knowing things about people—even strangers—she had no way of knowing; things people might not even have realized or been able to articulate about themselves. Yet she knew these things. Even if it made no logical sense to her, she couldn't deny that knowledge. And she was deeply troubled with being able to do this—or, more accurately, with it happening to her, because she certainly wasn't consciously *doing anything*. Unable to keep the world out now, she was losing the protective detachment which had cloaked her childhood in its only shabby source of safety.

What was once helpful to her long ago had become a liability in the present; that capacity to split away from a child's pain had left her out of step with herself as an adult. But the changes she was now undergoing and the progress being made also exacted a price. I found the following half page among her writings one day:

Ah, me, I can sit here and feel her, the little child inside. Yes, I can feel her: a little, skinny, dirty child who is bone weary tired most of the time. It is a tiredness beyond tired. Like dirt. In my mind the difference is so clear. There is dirt, and there is Old Dirt.

Old Dirt is ground in, ages old, stale and an unquestioned part of the life of the child. It is what you see in a child who is neglected and uncared for. It's a part of the child who can get up and go to bed and never wash up; a child who starts the new day by crawling, still tired, out of bed.

I can feel the child with yesterday's filth on her, getting into yesterday's clothes at the start of each new day. What

new day? There was never a "new day" in that child's
world! There was just the never ending, never changing dirt
of childhood years. Old Dirt is not like fresh, clean, just-
got-on-yourself dirt. It is ages old and ground in.

All too often I see that Old Dirt in the sad little children
around me, and it is painful every time.

JoAnn grew especially concerned about how life had been for her
own children during *their* childhood. We talked about this many
times, and its impact was always double-edged.

I'd be hard-pressed to imagine any wife and mother of the
1950s and 1960s who studied more diligently than JoAnn how to *be*
a wife and mother. Although memories of Honey and the Man had
been repressed along with everything else from her early years there
must have been a remaining awareness that it was possible to live
differently from the way she'd experienced with her family. She set
about discovering a better way. Books were her vehicle. She taught
herself to cook by reading cookbooks; learned to sew by the study
of sewing manuals; found out what was expected of young house-
wives in those days by reading magazines. In order to do what was
customary in her suburban neighborhood she went to PTA meetings
when her children reached school age, volunteered in the school
library, even held several offices in the PTA. Those were the things
she saw other mothers around her doing; she wanted to be a good
mother so that's what she did.

Above all, she wanted to be a good mother. Perhaps one of the
things about which JoAnn has continued to feel best is that she
didn't hit her children. Over the years, as she dug out her history
and then began to study the problems of physical and sexual abuse
in families, she's probably taken the most comfort from that fact. At
least, she reasoned, she didn't contribute to perpetuating that particular insidious cycle.

But while she could be grateful that she hadn't hit her children,
as her perspective broadened it was upsetting to realize that neither
had she hugged them. She had fashioned herself from the printed
page. Books, after she'd gotten away from home for the first time as
a fifteen-year-old bride, became her parents. They were certainly

more trustworthy than the people she'd known. Yet despite their power to instruct, no book can teach a person how to feel. Therefore she parented from her head, processing the works of respected authors on the subject of parenting through the sieve of her intellect.

Here's another piece I came across which JoAnn had included in a notebook she passed on to me during that time when her feelings and her thoughts were becoming acquainted:

> I carry with me such a sadness about what I was not able to give and share with my children. There is indeed a great sorrow within me for their loss. I would like to have had their lives enriched and expanded by those intangibles I couldn't provide. Still, I will be glad that they suffered only those deprivations, and not a repeat of my own childhood. That alone is a notable advance in life.
>
> Perhaps they will find nurturing from others which will help them toward maturity. I shall have to shelter that thought in my mind as some consolation for myself. Their father and I did way, way better with them than ever anyone could have predicted if they'd had any knowledge of our backgrounds. So in my viewing of what they lacked getting from me, I need to hold that realization against the sorrow in my heart. How much worse, how terribly much worse, it could've been. But, even so, it fills me with tears and drenches my soul in enormous sadness.
>
> The child in me can feel their fears, can sense the lack of emotional support they've had. I know they never received adequate recognition of their feelings, their own being. In some ways I think this awareness may be harder for me than remembering the rest of my own childhood. Back then I was DONE TO, but in the lives of my children I will be partly the DOER, one of those responsible for the lack of warmth and sufficient caring in their lives. I believe I have enough knowledge from my own experience to see the damage I myself have inflicted on them.
>
> It is painful to realize and acknowledge how another generation has suffered. I can only hope that my children

will learn other ways and not repeat the mistakes of their parents. Otherwise how do we make progress?

As we talked about these things during many sessions, JoAnn readily acknowledged that rather than risk either imposing her will or being intrusive in her children's lives, as *her* family had done, she may have gone to the other extreme and not provided input or guidance when it might've been helpful. And since touch and touching had forever in her life meant hurt and force, she believed she was offering her children a personally unknown freedom and respect by keeping her hands out of their physical space. If she didn't know the difference between appropriate cuddling or comforting and inappropriate touching or using then she'd refrain from anything that might reach over the line.

Her youngest child, Danny, was in the throes of a most difficult adolescence when JoAnn was coming to this awareness about her limitations as a parent and the effect it had had on her children. All she could hope to do with this youngest was better than had been done with the others; before this she'd been so shut down she hadn't seen the signals of trouble in their lives. Now she couldn't miss the signals Danny was sending out in all directions.

She'd recently ended her therapy with the group after nearly two years, feeling she'd gotten as much as she likely would in that setting. Within several months she and Danny came in to see a child psychologist on our staff as she tried to understand what was bothering her son and to improve their communication. He was missing a lot of school, complained about feeling sick even though the family doctor could find no physical basis to the complaints, seemed angry most of the time, was resentful of her discipline and guidelines for coexistence in the house, scornful of his father who, JoAnn sensed, he was able to manipulate at will. Together they began family therapy. Before many months passed she was feeling a little more hopeful about their living together as a result of the work they were doing with Dr. Stephens.

In one of our sessions I asked whether Danny had been around when she broke all those dishes. She said he was upstairs in his room when it happened. And his reaction? Primarily, she recalled, he'd seemed startled. He'd also been concerned about her. She'd never lost her temper like that before, so it was no doubt alarming to him. Perhaps he was used to outbursts from his father, but not from her.

I found it hard to believe he'd taken it as calmly as she indicated. JoAnn minimized the effect of this on Danny by saying her family tended to view her as strange anyway, so she didn't think any of them would get thrown off stride by whatever she might do.

This didn't put my doubt to rest. She was uncannily sensitive to other people's moods and feelings, but such sensitivity usually didn't hold up when she herself played a leading part in a given interaction. After having discussed dozens of examples of this at length I was not surprised anymore about how blind she could be when it came to assessing her own impact on someone else. I suppose all those early years of feeling unheard and unseen had left her with a greatly damaged ability to realize how she was experienced by others, even as an adult.

Some of my probing about Danny's reaction to her sudden burst of anger was surely in part because such a reaction from *my* mother would've been upsetting to *me*. As therapists we tend to use our own experience, the way everyone else does, as the most basic reference point from which we try to understand other people. Yet that's not to say our own lives are the norm, the standard by which we should measure what is healthy in the population. Hopefully we realize this.

I knew that my coming from a family which never got angry—or at least didn't express it directly—was something of an extreme, just as the people in JoAnn's volatile family were toward the other end of the continuum. So I was conscious of trying not to project my feelings onto Danny. Still, even if he'd grown up around anger and violence to the extent it was "normal" for him, yet hadn't seen any of it coming from his mother, I thought her breaking all those dishes must've been unsettling to him. For many years, practically through all her therapy, I believe JoAnn's ability to judge people's reactions to her was possibly her most poorly developed and least effective sense.

•   •   •

For several years it was a rocky trail the two of them traveled while JoAnn was going ahead with her own therapy. Like many parents of adolescents, she found this passage to be over uncertain terrain and without familiar signposts. At times they seemed to get along fine; at other points she felt completely frustrated, puzzled by indefinable concerns.

During one of their confrontations, Danny said he would rather live with his father than conform to what he regarded as her unreasonable rules. She took his declaration seriously and evaluated it within the framework of what she considered essential in being a parent and necessary for a person newly coming alive. They talked about these matters at length with Dr. Stephens, who helped them through this time of transition. Still, it didn't make it any easier for JoAnn to see her son make that move.

13

A PHANTOM MIRROR

—

"You ain't hurt one bit, dammit!" Mama yells at me. "Not a goddam thing wrong with you, and you better not go acting like that anymore. Go ahead, lie to them. It ain't gonna get you nowhere. They won't believe you, you little liar. It ain't gonna get you sent home from school no more, so don't be acting like a fool and making them call me to come and get you again! Now do you hear me?"

HIT—!—HIT—!—SLAP—!—HIT!

Mama was furious. She beat me to show me a thing or two. What had happened? What was that all about I wonder . . .

. . . something about the school calling . . .

The school had called her to come and get me because I was sick. She had told them to just keep me there and send me home with the other children, with Bobby and Francie or Warner. They said no, it was important that she come to school and get her daughter. The lady at school told her I was really quite sick and would need to be looked after.

So she did get to school. At least that one time she managed to get there.

Mama always said, "Yes, yes, I'll be there." She always planned to go, promised to get to the school for whatever it was they wanted the parents to be there for. Her promises were like some horrible birthday present: you'd be so eager to unwrap it, and when you'd lift up the lid to the box beneath the bright paper and ribbon all you'd find inside was however much air the box could hold. But that one time, when they called her from school to come get me because I was sick, she actually did get there.

For our sixth-grade graduation I was all dressed up in a white dress she had made for me. She was so proud of that dress, it was sooo pretty! And I hated her for it. Down deep I hated her for loving the wrong thing.

(Pretty is as pretty does, chile. It ain't enough to just BE pretty! You gotta DO pretty in this ol' world!)

"You go on ahead, now. Take the bus and go on to school with Bobby," she told me. "I'll be coming soon, coming soon's I get a ride. . . . Yes, I'll BE there, dammit!"

I knew she wouldn't be there.

We were upstairs in the old elementary school. The girls were all hanging around the windows and watching the parents come in up the front steps. "There's MY MOTHER!" "There's MY FATHER!" they would shout. "Here comes MY BROTHER!" "There's MY FAMILY!"

I didn't go over there to look. I stood on the side and looked for a while at the people coming in. I knew she was not coming. She had better things to do. Somebody probably came along and took her out to have fun.

Later, back at home, I was just getting out of my clothes when Mama came in. She said, "I meant to come, JoAnn. I really did mean to, so don't call me a liar. Something else came up, that's all. I knew you were all right. Besides, didn't I make you that dress so you'd be the prettiest girl there? It took a lot of work to make that, you know?"

Without taking my eyes from her, and hearing those questions hang in the air between us, I began to tear up the dress. Even though I was stone calm on the outside, the little child inside me was in a screaming frenzy of despair and fury as I slowly ripped into the beautiful long, white skirt she had worked so hard to make for me.

. . .

"Well I do declare you maybe don't know everthing in this world, Honey. I just think you don't. My Mama, her heart won't bother her A BIT!"

"Why, I can't hardly believe that, chile."

"No, no, I tell you it won't. She go right out and do that thing. She would!"

Honey looks at me funny. Says she thinks that hurt my Mama right much to do that thing.

Won't neither, I tell her. I know it won't!

"That man gonna do it, Honey! Just wait and see. . . . You sure he don't? You sure about that?"

Me and her is sitting at the table with the Good Book. She tells me about the picture of that man with a knife over top of his son. God done spoke to him and tole him to kill that boy.

"He's gonna DO IT sure enough, Honey."

She says, "Well, sure was hard on Ol' Abraham, chile. He got to do like God say, but he don't wanta do it. Hard on that man to do it either way, chile. He is catched between a rock and a hard place, 'deed he is."

I ask her, "How come he catched between a rock and a hard place?"

" 'Cause on account of God tole him to 'kill your boy,' " and she talks in a deep voice like her is God talking. "He best better do that thing when the Lord tells him, chile."

"We know he best better do what the Lord wants him to, don't we, Honey? Old Lord God don't like no lazy shiftless folks what 'won't do!' "

"Well, you is right, chile. Still, some a the time it ain't so easy to do like the Lord say do!"

"He's got a sharp knife, Honey. 'Cause God tole him to kill that boy? He suppose to listen to what God tells him, huh, Honey?" I'm watching her now. She feels a little bit different to me.

"Ah well, it ain't easy. No, it ain't. We all gotta try to do the best thing, chile. . . . Don't matter. Don't matter if ol' Abraham didn't do it. Main thing is he try. He try to do his best. He don't wanta do it, but he loves the Lord, and Lord God tole him to do it. Not wanta do it 'cause he loves his son. Very hard for him to do, chile."

I think on this a little while. Then I say, "Honey, she do it in a minute."

"What? Who you talkin' 'bout, chile?"

"My Mama could kill me and it not hurt her a bit." I tell her that my Mama be plum glad to get RID a me! "I think she don't love me at all, Honey, 'cause I ain't nothing but a pain in her ass."

I sit and talk to her nice and easy, just talking away. All at once something feels different and I look to see what she's doing. Honey's closing up the Good Book. Says she don't want to look no more. Don't feel like looking right now.

"How come, Honey?" I ask her. "We ain't finish with the picture part yet. How come you don't wanta look no more? . . . Whatsa matter, Honey? Why you crying? Did you hurt yourself, Honey?"

I turn from the book and touch her hand. I feel so bad about her feeling bad hurt somehow. She pleats her apron between her fingers, looking upset and full of worry.

I put my arm around her neck and say, "Whatsa matter, Honey? Are you hurting inside like Abraham? Are you, Honey?" Oh, I hurt inside 'cause she's hurt, with her eyes full of big shiny tears.

"No, chile, no. I'se all right. Just sad, chile. I'se sad to see bad-ness winnin' out in this ol' world. Ain't right, you know. Just ain't right, chile. The truth is them folks is purely bad. But YOU, chile, you's a pretty little angel! A Brown-Eyed Angel of God!"

Honey puts her arm around my little waist while she's sitting in the chair and I'm standing beside her.

"Don't matter, Honey," I tell her, "it don't rightly matter. We just gotta do the best we can, like you alla time tell me. And Ol' Mr. God gonna say 'Don't you two worry yourselves now. You go on along your row and leave the rest up to me!' Now, don'tcha know that's the truth, Honey? . . . 'Deed you do 'cause you done tole that to me lotsa times!"

I hear Honey talk to that Man while I'm hid under the house. She tells him it was bad.

"Was bad, Man! That chile sit there and say the worstest things to me in that little sweet voice. Oh, I tell you, Man, it like to tore my heart out! Then when she see them tears come in my eyes, she tell me we just got to trust in the Lord. And she say, 'Honey, that Man done said a whole heap a times we got to believe that God knows what's best for us! He say God loves us just like we love EACH OTHER!' That chile say 'each other' means God loves the three of us, us two womens and that Man, and the house and chickens and ol' Horsey and the cow and pig and EVERYBODY! Oh, that little angel done pat my hand and tell me how the Lord God not ever gonna take His eyes off us! Now, don't that just beat all you ever heard, Man? Hummmhh?"

"Well, JoAnn, you can just go over there and think on it. Over there in the corner." The teacher tried to keep her voice level.

I knew. I knew the answer but I was afraid to talk. It was safer to BE-QUIET-DAMMIT. I was never sure what were the right things to say, so it was better to not speak at all.

The teacher never thought I knew the answers. Seemed like she just asked me things so she could send me over there. In front of everyone.

"Over there, little girl," she ordered me. Her voice was getting higher. "Right now! Right in the corner. Maybe you can think on it and get the answer. You just need to try harder. Can you really be that dumb?"

Would a teacher say that to a child? Call her "dumb"? Am I remembering this right? I know someone said "think on it and get the answer." It had to be a teacher who said that . . .

"Now, class, don't look at her. We will just forget JoAnn Foley for now. Yes, JoAnn, you can think on it until you get the answer. . . . No, you only need to stand there until you think up the answer. You should be able to do it if you read your homework like you said you did."

Her tone said she didn't believe me. It was a "see, class, JoAnn lied" tone. I had told her I did my homework. (I DID, TOO!) It didn't matter if she believed me or not. She had had Foleys before. All the Foleys were nothing but TROUBLE.

She felt just like Grannie to me. Only instead of hitting me she sent me to stand in the corner.

"Face the wall now, JoAnn, and don't bother us. . . . No, turn on around. Now, class, we will just go on without JoAnn Foley."

It wasn't simply me. It was the other Foleys, too. She was so sick of all those Foleys. She'd had them before. It wasn't right for her to have them in HER CLASS. Her nice class. She was sick of those Foleys. How many little brats have they got anyhow? And all of them causing trouble; it made her sick. They didn't know anything. White Trash is all they were. Lord knows what went on out there with people like that. White Trash shouldn't be allowed to come around decent folks.

I felt her fear. Of me? Was she afraid of us Foleys?

Too close. It was too close. Or rather I was too close, too threatening to her. She had worked and scrambled to get above her raisings, and here she was getting rewarded by being stuck with someone else's White Trash brats. Like her sisters and brothers. She had been stuck with her sisters and brothers when she was little, I will bet you. I could feel it in her though I couldn't name it at the time. It was just all the feelings I picked up from her. To her this was worse than being the oldest one at home. She hated what we represented to her. Yes, she was scared of all the Foley children who had ever sat in her classroom. The teacher was panicked over the unacknowledged memories for which we blindly stood as phantom mirrors.

How would I know this? I'm sure I never heard her talk about her childhood. Sometimes it frightens me how I know things I can not know. But I do know it. I know!! I'm sure that woman hated us for reminding her of a life she had scratched her way out of. She was so hard-won decent. Well, I hope she found a world without Foleys. I can't even imagine who has suffered more, me or her . . .

"Honey says I'm right good com-pa-KNEE! Did you know that, Man?"

"Why, yes, I know that. Reckon that woman tell it to me a lotsa times, chile."

Me and him walk around the Place, take our time looking

things over. He stops and breaks off two branches. One is for him and one is for me. He takes the biggest one 'cause he's the biggest one. He needs a branch a little bit bigger than mine.

"Here's a right nice one just 'bout the size for you, don'tcha think, chile?" he asks me.

I look at it and think a minute. When I know I ain't jumping onto a answer without thinking first, I tell him it seems like to me it's just the right thing.

We're gonna whittle! But he tells me we have a lot to do yet before we start to whittle. Have to get ready, have to pull all them leaves off and get that good ol' stick ready first. When he does all that, he reaches in his pocket and gets HIS knife and MY knife!

Oh, that knife is just my size and the Man got it just for me. It's the color a blue that's the color a sky like in the pretty apron Honey done made for me, the apron I just love all to pieces.

Honey says I can have that knife but only if I use it when the Man can watch me. I tell him Honey says she just "not 'bout to have you cut yourself when that Man has gone a traipsin' off!"

He hands me my pretty little blue knife. He allows as how "we know she ain't mad. She is just a fussin', chile."

"Yes, she do fuss sometimes, Man. I done notice that thing."

"Now, ain't that sumthin'. A little tadpole like you has done take notice a that yourself!" He is so SIR-prised that I is done notice that without nobody having to say a thing about it!

He thinks she just has to have somebody around to fuss at. "Now I know that sounds kinda funny, but I be right willin' to bet on it, I would! Yep, I sure would."

We think about that. He looks at me real straight-faced.

Man says, "I just 'bout be willin' to bet that them hens is layin' a lot better now since you be 'round here, chile." He don't look at me, just keeps a whittlin' on his stick. I KNOW he's gonna tell some-thing! I do 'cause he got his Straight Face on so he won't "let on" to nothing! I try and cut a little bark offa the stick with my knife, like I see him do alla time. That way I don't have to look at him.

"It's the truth, chile. Before that woman had you to fuss at, she used to be after them chickens every day. She did! Like to keep them poor ol' hens in a UPROAR alla time! Done keep 'em worked up so bad they couldn't hardly lay no EGGS!" And he stretch his face sooo lonnggg to think a them hens what can't lay but a few eggs on account a that ol' woman!

"Now that's the truth of it. Lord, I just don't know if ME or them HENS was the gladest to have you 'round this Place, chile!" He still don't look over at me. "Well, all I know is there's a heap more eggs 'round here now. Heap more'n there used to be 'fore you help me out by comin' on to this Place, chile!"

I bust out laughing and fall all over him a laughing. He says, "Well, what's this, chile? Don'tcha believe me?"

He says "don'tcha believe me" in that tone Honey says he takes on when butter won't melt in his mouth. She knows he's up to NO GOOD when he talks like that!

I tell Honey what all he says about them hens laying more eggs here lately. I tell her all about it when she's cleaning off the table after supper is over and the dishes done. Soon she be getting down the Good Book for us to read before I has to go home.

"That Man!" Honey says with a hand on one a her hippies. "You mark my words, chile, that Man is up to no good when he come 'round here a tellin' you such trash as that, in that ol' voice. I just don't know what's gonna happen to him. I do my best, work myself near to death a tryin' to get him fixed up and on the right road."

Honey cuts her eyes at him. "Now look atcha! Just look at how you act 'round that chile! Never thought I'd live to see the day, but here 'tis. Now, chile, don't you believe a word he says! Not a word 'cause he is a RASCAL. And I'se just 'bout to throw my hands up in the air and give up on him once and for all!"

Oh yes she is, but I think SHE is trying to keep a Straight Face a her own. Honey ain't done with him yet. "Now I know I said it before, but this time I really MEAN it, chile. I just can't put up with this now. No, I can't! Think I gonna wrap him up in some paper, stick a ADdress on his backside, and let the postman take him away!"

I look at her to make sure she ain't serious. Seems like there's a laugh around behind them words.

"Trouble is," she says, "I think he be too big to fit in that mailbox!!"

All of us break out laughing. All three of us can't hold it in a minute more.

The Man says he be right glad to see us two women laugh. Lord, he thinked his bag was 'bout to be packed for sure this time! Whooeee, he sure did. Lord, he be a sweatin'! But now he guess mebbe he have time to drink a cup a coffee 'fore he gets put out on the street. Oh, he's right glad of that . . .

✳

I can't hardly wait for the Man to get in from putting Ol' Horsey in his house for the night 'cause I got lots to tell him.

"Some man come around here acting so big and smart. Oh, you oughtta seen him, Man!"

I'm so excited to tell Mr. Man what happened on this Place here today that I almost trip over the story; I got too many words to say and not enough mouth.

". . . Honey just listen at him talk, Man. Listen real good and hold her piece. She did, Man. He be a smiling and a talking at us two womens, talking on a blue streak. Ain't that right, Honey? But we hold our piece, don't we, Honey? Tell him what you tole that city fella, Honey."

I'm so happy we fool that man from town what don't think we know a THING. He thinks us two ol' womens just been hatched outta our shells this morning! That's what Honey tole me. Yep, we hold our piece, me and Honey. Find out all he knows and what he wants. And now me and her tell our Mr. Man what that City Slicker was here on this Place for: we done figure out that city man was wanting to have this ol' Place for hisself!

"I sure am glad I got you two ol' womens around here," the Man tells us. "Makes my load a heap lighter just to know you is here when me and friend Horsey come on down that road. Sure do, chile. You two womens is a blessin' on this ol' man's head!"

He looks at his Honey. They don't laugh but something is going on with 'em. He's right pleased with us for fooling that City Slicker into thinking we is just hatched out. That city fella done show off in front of us dumb ol' niggers and end up telling us all he knows!

"How you 'splain this chile to him?" he asks Honey.

"Tole him the Lord's truth. Tole him that chile, her Mama be off a workin'. Good heavens, Man, you know I ain't gonna tell no lie.

Even to that man who knows it all. Or least-wise he's a thinkin' he knows more'n this poor ol' woman." She hangs her head down and says "poor" like "poooorrrre," then looks at him and laughs. "Lord, Man, was a sight to see. I wish you'd a been here to see it. Make you laugh fit to beat all!"

I jump around, waiting for Honey to stop so I can say some more. There's a lot I need to tell him.

". . . Well, Lord, chile, how'm I gonna tell that Man anything with you squawkin' like a magpie? Now you sit yourself down here beside me and help me out with these ol' boot laces."

Honey's helping him get his boots off. He looks at me and says, "Now lets us be quiet and listen Honey out."

I start to cloudy up. I'm afraid he's gonna read me the Acts if I don't HUSH UP now.

"No, you not do nothin' bad, chile. Just let her have her turn now, that's all."

He's not mad. I don't like him to be mad. I hate it when he takes it into his head to read me that Riot Act. No, HhuhhUuhh! I already heard it enough times.

Well, Honey and Mr. Man out-slick the City Slickers. I hear more about that business, I do. They tell me all about it one day when I get there.

Them men what think they're so smart come out from town a few days later and talk to the Man and Honey. Say they give 'em money. Lotsa money for this ol' Place. Outta the goodness of their hearts! Wasn't worth much, they say. Wasn't worth nothing, to tell the truth.

"You're getting on in years, you know," them men say. "It's too much for a old man and woman to handle a Place like this at your age. Naw, at your time of life you oughtta be setting back on the porch without a worry in your head.

"Now I tell you what we're going to do. You take this money and go off and find yourself a nice little Place you can keep up, handle for yourself. Don't like to see an old fella work himself to death on a no good patch of dirt like this. This Place ain't worth a damn, to tell you the truth, but we're going to do you a favor and take it off your hands. Getting to be too much for you. I tell you I'm going to come out the loser on this deal. But what the hell!? If a man can't help out another man once in a while, what good is he, huh?

"You just put your mark down here and I'll give you all this money for your old Place here. . . . Think about it. Lord, you'd be better off somewhere else. You think about this, but don't take too long now. We just might pick up another little farm around here and then we wouldn't be able to help you out any."

Quiet like, the Man tells him, "Well, I do reckon we'll just have to take that chance. Don't do to leap before you look. No, don't wanta do that. Just have to think on this awhile. Don't pay to jump off like a frog till you look 'round to see where you gonna land. Got to watch where you land in this world."

That ol' City Slicker looks at the Man. The Man's telling him how he has learnt it's better to think a thing out before you do something you gonna be sorry 'bout the next day. I think the Man's maybe telling him to go jump in the lake, too, like a frog. The City Slicker thinks the Man's saying he wants to find another Place to land on for a home. He is about to out-slick hisself.

"Well, well, now I can just see you're right about that, old man," the fella from town says. "I guess you're gonna need to find a nice little piece of land before you'll be wanting to spend this money, won't you? Can't fault you there. I think probably we could be on the lookout for a nice little Place you and your wife can settle in to. Why, I guess we could even throw that in the bargain, too. Now, think it over and let us know if this sounds all right to you folks. But don't take too long getting back to us, you hear . . . ?"

Oh, we do get a good laugh offa them men what got all that money falling outta their pockets! The Man says his daddy give him this good ol' Place, and that's 'bout all him and Honey needs for to be happy the rest a their days.

For some reason we had to leave Grannie's house in a big, mad rush when I was in junior high. Mama and I moved in for a little while with her younger sister, Warner, who lived in the Longstreet Army

Housing Project while Jay was overseas in Germany fighting in the Second World War.

I pretty much served as the unpaid baby-sitter for Warner's three children. I knew Jay would be glad I was looking after their boy, Jakey, and the two little ones while he had to be away. Warner and Francie, Mama's youngest sister, went out a lot to "have a little fun before the good times are gone."

"After all," Warner would say, "you don't expect me to sit here all the time with them damn kids, do you? Hell, I'm still young, you know! It wouldn't do any good to sit at home anyway. It wouldn't help Jay for me to stay here with these kids and rot!"

Francie agreed with her, saying she needed to live it up a little, too. Besides, it wasn't *their* doings. *They* didn't start the war, so why should they have to sit home with a bunch of kids all the time when it wouldn't do anybody any good?

Warner and Francie would get all dressed up and take off to have some fun. "Just watch the kids, JoAnn. When they go to sleep you go on to bed. Don't wait up for us."

Warner hated that place. She'd whine and cry that the damn Army quarters weren't worth shit. I remember a utility room next to the kitchen, a small room that was always filthy. All the trash from the rest of the place would be swept in there and left on the floor. The living room looked better when anyone came in because she'd close the kitchen door and not let them see the mess in that little room. It was hidden behind closed doors, just like they hid the truth of their lives from sight.

For a short while another family lived next to her. They lived right next door, yet it was another world. I baby-sat for them once or twice before they were transferred. The woman didn't leave her baby much, but once she had to go out with her husband so I went to sit with the baby. The minute I walked into the house, the very first minute I set foot there, I knew they were a different kind of people.

The living room was identical to Warner's living room, only facing the other direction because it was on the opposite end of the building. It was as if I'd walked into another world on the opposite side of the earth. It was a world I knew nothing about, but I could tell it was real. There was no fake face to show to outsiders.

They had asked if I'd baby-sit for that one night. The father said to sit right here and listen, to take good care of the baby. He did not say "kid" or "damn kid." He told me to just sit and listen, and the baby would probably sleep till they got home. Not "back to this damn place!" No, they said "home," like they hated to leave it and would be glad to come back.

Sit and listen for the baby, I heard him say. I had a lot of practice doing guard duty, and he was leaving me to keep watch like a sentry over his baby. Not just to "stay there." This was different. He was leaving me to sit and watch, so I sat and watched. I listened for the BABY.

I sat in their house in a wingback chair. I didn't move. That's why I can't picture anything else about the place; I never left that chair. I just soaked it in until they came home. She went right in to check on the baby as soon as she got there.

". . . No," I told them, "the baby never cried. I sat right here and listened. And I watched real good, too. You didn't need to worry about the baby. I can come again. I can come back whenever you need someone to baby-sit."

He said the packers were coming the next day and they would be leaving. "Thank you for coming, JoAnn. Thank you very much for watching after the baby."

It was kind of like keeping watch over little Jakey and the babies for Jay. I knew Jay would be glad I was there and the children would be safe while he was fighting in Germany.

But unlike Warner, the lady next door would not have run the streets while her husband was away. She would have watched the map of Europe and her poor heart would have stopped in between his letters home.

The mail had come, and Warner was frantic for her allotment check. I remember thinking my allotment check could've burned in hell if it would have brought Jay home one minute sooner.

"Well, yes, there's a V-letter in there somewhere, but I haven't had time to open it," she said impatiently. "My God, you don't know what it's like here all day with these damn kids, JoAnn. God dammit, ain't I got enough to do without you telling me I oughta read his letter first thing?"

"Can I see it then?"

"Yeah, take the damn thing. Take it outside and take them kids with you." She needed a minute's rest from her hard work of watching them kids because they were driving her crazy.

She did not care to read the letters from Jay. She always said they were "the same old thing," and you couldn't half read that damn stuff anyway. They weren't written on regular paper, those V-letters. It was on special thin, thin paper folded up to be an envelope. The war letters had tiny writing, but not so small that you couldn't read it if you wanted to bad enough.

"Take it! Take it and get to hell out of here, JoAnn. Jesus, you drive a body nuts with your questions! You can have it; it's just the same old junk. Take it outside to read, and take these damn kids out there with you."

She was mad. She wanted to go. If damn Francie would get there they'd leave me and the kids and go downtown to have some fun. I had to take care of the kids. I had to do it for Jay. He couldn't help it if he was overseas. Warner didn't care that he was gone; she didn't care if he was gone forever. He had gone to fight and maybe die, and she sat there whining and fussing.

"He acts like I don't have a thing to do," she whined, "but sit and write letters. My God, what does he expect? Aren't things bad enough without him bugging me about a damn letter? I got more to do than write to him all the damn time. And besides there's nothing to say 'cause I don't get to do anything but sit here and watch them kids. He just doesn't think about how bad it is for me here!"

So she quit reading his letters at all; what mattered was that the allotment check came every month. The important thing to Warner was that the Eagle flew over and shit his money for her. She didn't even open his letters, and she certainly didn't write to him. She was so dumb she didn't know Jay could get people to check on her if he did not hear from her.

Someone came to the house once, from the Red Cross or the Army, because of her not answering his letters.

". . . No, I'm not here to check up on you, Mrs. Hawke. Now nobody's accusing you of anything." Something was odd about her tone, though it started out all right.

Warner went to pieces and started in about how her husband

didn't know how hard it was for her. She sat and twisted her hands and got more and more nervous, thinking somebody had lied about her and said she was running around behind Jay's back.

I knew as soon as the person came in the house and saw and heard Warner's crying words that she did not think much of us or the house or the way Warner acted. She was not happy about a thing to do with us, so she lied and soft-soaped Warner for all she was worth. She was upset that the poor husband worried why he hadn't heard from anyone when he tried to find out why his wife had not written. He was afraid something had happened to his family. She was biting her tongue and trying to get Warner to write to her husband.

"I know how hard it is for us 'war wives.' Everybody knows just how hard it is for you, Mrs. Hawke, especially with three small children to care for."

Very patiently she told Warner that the mail meant so much to our men overseas who are so far away from all they loved, and it just was not fair to make them worry needlessly, was it? Yes, she knew Warner would be sooo glad to have them all come back home. But in the meantime all the wives must do whatever they could to keep their husbands' spirits up.

The Red Cross lady was losing, in fact she'd lost, with this approach because Warner didn't care. She saw it, too. It was then she said, "I would sooo like to make a good report on this case for you, dear. You know how much trouble the Army officers can make for us if they want to. Yes, if you could try to keep in touch with your husband, Mrs. Hawke, I just don't think the Army would bother you."

That woman told Warner off very politely. She would hate to see Warner troubled with all the red tape the Army could put her through. She could see that things were hard enough without the officers at the Post bothering her on top of all she had to take care of. She was masterful in her job. She knew what we were, and knew what to do to make Warner "behave" towards Jay. She despised us. She truly felt sorry for a man gone to war whose wife didn't even write to him and then cried about how hard her life was.

No, she was not happy with us for letting Jay worry about his family when he had it so bad overseas in the war. Being very calm, she let Warner know to behave if she wanted her allotment check. It was not said, but even I got the message—and I didn't hear all of it because Warner sent me out with the children.

The woman from the Red Cross scared Warner, and she finally wrote to Jay after that. I don't know how much, but she wrote.

I knew the woman from the Red Cross would never need to talk to the lady next door like she talked to Warner. The lady with the baby would be writing her husband all the time, telling him things like how the baby was trying to speak and how things were going for them at her parents' house.

14

BETWEEN
BLACK AND WHITE

Sometimes I thought JoAnn was held hostage by an obsessive nature and implacable will. She readily admitted the work on herself wasn't always an endeavor she welcomed.

The awakening which started as a pale perception of what a defenseless child she'd once been now spilled richer colors over that same nearly invisible little girl with so much still unspoken. Because she'd always operated out of a survival orientation and from a realistic base she wasn't used to voicing "nonproductive" thoughts or feelings. Consequently, any talk of "if only . . ." or mention of what-might-have-been was routinely decried as useless. But just as she'd recently permitted uncensored words to appear in her notebooks and on the tapes she made, she also began speaking in a way which made room for conflicting sentiments.

There were many times, especially during the second and third years of therapy, when she'd arrive for an appointment saying, "I almost didn't come today." Or, while in the throes of a wrenching kind of resistance, she would be on time for her session even as she walked in announcing, "Believe me, I really don't want to be here!"

Among the papers JoAnn left regularly with me, occasionally I'd find part of a notebook recounting her ambivalence about therapy. The inner, angry struggle was always between, in her definition, the Brain Self and the Child Self. She found a way of describing the mind-body split that professionals speak of in their work with survivors of sexual abuse.

Here is how she reported one such skirmish from the front line in the battle of the Therapy Wars:

> *I do not want this pain anymore. I would leave it laid away in a beautiful box, each hurt carefully wrapped in tissue paper. But I can no longer bear the pain of storage. There's a song about how you can't go over it, can't go around it, and you can't get under it. All you can do is go through it. Each of us must pass through the pain. I am sure I shall make it through if I live long enough. And be better for it, too.*

Better for it? Better for it? Then how come you look so sick?

Because my stomach doesn't believe my intellect yet.

You BETTER believe your STOMACH, Old Lofty Head! You think it's so safe in that ivory tower up there in the clouds. Well, I'm down here in your guts, in the blood and guts of the trenches, with all these warring emotions. It's not safe here! For YOU it's so easy and safe. You make the dumb decisions and then expect ME to do whatever you say.

Now, now, Little One . . .

Now, now, nothing! You think it's easy for me. Well, it's not. It's hard. It's lonely and cold here. There's trouble all around, and you don't even consult with me. MY FEELINGS DON'T COUNT FOR SHIT! Do this. Do that. You think it up and I have to DO it all. "Respond but don't feel" is what you want. Well, I DO feel. I feel it in my stomach, in my bowels, and in a back that aches with memories of being kicked and hit. I HATE YOU! I hate the sound of your stupid brain tick tick ticking away. I don't even think you're human. You're just a computer going tick tick tick. I'm tired of being trapped by you and your stupid brain! You oughta been born an idiot for all the good it's done you! Things weren't so bad for me till you had to go tell her.

I can't stand her, that Rose Mary. What a stupid name.

I bet she's a Stupid, too. There's lots of Stupids a roaming
the streets, and maybe she's one of 'em. Leave it to you to
fall over one! I told you not to tell her. I told you to keep it
buried. You listened to me for a long time; everything was
fine then. So, who asked you to dig it up now? I don't have
a choice about it, but YOU DO! Christ, the dumb therapist
herself said you do have a choice! I don't know what in the
hell going through all this is gonna get you. What happened is over and done with, and I don't want to go back
there anymore! Maybe, just maybe, one of these days I'll
figure out a way to make you listen to MEEEE!

When JoAnn voiced her emerging ambivalence about therapy, it was
the first time I had heard her acknowledge negative feelings. It made
for one of those moments in the therapeutic process where the views
of client and therapist are dramatically different. Frequently this is a
point when many patients decide to leave treatment.

I saw the conflict JoAnn was talking about as an encouraging
sign of her progress. She saw it as hell, maybe the birth of a self she
never wanted to be. Intellectually I'm sure she could understand the
clinical implications of the work she was doing and why I was
excited for her. But on an emotional level I think she was simply
feeling as bad as she ever had, perhaps worse than ever, if only
because she was so much more conscious now. Although it was
hard to imagine her dropping out of treatment here, I admitted to
myself she might.

Troubled pilgrims commonly stumble over a watershed along
their travels through the psyche when they grapple with whether to
continue stunted but familiar lives or risk the unknown of change
by going further into the void. JoAnn survived almost fifty years like
she remembered the Man's old horse doing: plodding down the
road wearing blinders to keep out all peripheral distractions. She
had made it through life by not wasting time or energy on matters
that fell outside the focus of her simple goals to do right and do the
best she could. Concentration like that was the binding compound
which held together the various elements in her compartmentalized,
all-or-nothing approach to life, and why it worked for her as well as
it had.

So, not surprisingly, this sudden amalgam of newly identified "warring emotions" caused JoAnn some distress; she'd never really let herself feel anything which might cloud her vision. Now she was expressing whatever insisted its way up through her usual control. Even though she sometimes railed against my presence in her life— as well as criticizing herself for remaining in the situation—in truth she was not seriously deflected from the direction toward which her spirit's compass had somehow long ago been set. Like those of us who've been raised to be gentle and nice but come to accept our negative emotions as also part of who we are, once she'd voiced her darker feelings they lost their power to overshadow. She could, after all, exist in a current of eddies swirling in various directions. And more important, she could temporarily land on one shore without having to renounce her citizenship on the other. Maybe the greatest fear which had stalked her accumulating years was that she would become like other members of her family. The Child Self she'd recently named, a being who wanted what she wanted and didn't worry about the consequences, was so frightening at first to JoAnn because she reeked of the Foleys' legacy of total self-absorption.

Although ambivalence and resistance are a predictable part of treatment I marveled at the disclosing of this process in my office, largely because JoAnn chronicled it so thoroughly. As we explored the shifts taking place I felt another area of commonality begin to materialize.

Admittedly, one of the least exciting or colorful things about me is that I've always been far more used to living amid shades of gray than in settling down on either the black or white. Ambiguity and ambivalence have been as much a feature of my daily landscape as clarity and definitiveness were in JoAnn's world. Generally I tend to see, instantly and effortlessly, at least two sides to nearly everything.

Most of the time I find this to be helpful, yet there are occasions when it's either blocked me from making a quick decision or left me feeling immobilized for a while. I've never been sure whether this tendency was a blessing or a curse, though I suppose it's been a bit of both. (Of course this *would* be how I'd see it!) Nevertheless, I've admired people who know in a flash how they feel or think about any issue. JoAnn had always been that way until this point in therapy, and a part of me was sorry to see a loosening of her grip on the kind of certainty for which I sometimes longed. However, when I realized she was feeling some of the vulnerability, so well known to me, implicit in trying to stare down contradictory feelings, I saw it as one of the mixed blessings of her less rigid face-off with life.

Contributing to JoAnn's stretch of ambivalence about therapy at this juncture were two kinds of pain she was experiencing more intensely. It didn't surprise me she felt increasingly attuned to the plight of the little girl locked away inside her forty-nine-year-old self, or that she was also more sensitive to the misery her antenna detected in those around her. She wasn't as able any more to seal off her emotions from her awareness. But what *did* astound me, what I hadn't expected, was her inability to seal off her body from the past.

Physically, she was hurting. The type of physical pain assailing her was notable for a couple of reasons. It needs to be understood, first of all, that JoAnn never complained. Even when she should have complained, in my opinion, she didn't. Complaining was the same thing to her as whining, and it had consistently been the most basic way her family disavowed any personal responsibility in their lives. It was another one of their behaviors for which she had no tolerance. So she seemed determined, even if not verbalizing it then, to distance herself from those cries of "poor me" already starting to litter her memories about the Foleys. This resulted in her almost never talking about her physical being; the rare exceptions were when her body betrayed her by interfering in some serious way with her mental and emotional functioning. The denial of her corporal self seemed just another manifestation of the technique discovered long ago when she detached her feelings from the mistreatment her body had to endure.

What I noticed as she came for our appointments during this period was that her posture, her bearing, the way she moved, was changing. She walked slower, more carefully; sitting down looked like an effort at times, getting up seemed a chore. Her face, initially so unlined as to be remarkable for a woman of almost fifty, now revealed shallow furrows between tensed eyebrows. As I thought about it, the only times I'd seen such smoothness in the faces of mature adults was with people who were devoid of animation in their interaction with others. Now, however, JoAnn's face was growing more expressive because she was feeling more; and what she'd come to feel was a sharper awareness of how much her body hurt.

One afternoon as she gingerly lowered herself into our standard issue clinic chair, never characterized by anybody as particularly comfortable, I asked if she was in pain.

This time, instead of dismissing me with her usual, "No, I'm all right," JoAnn said, "I just had some trouble sleeping last night."

"Why couldn't you sleep?" I asked. "And why do you look so uncomfortable, the way you're sitting?"

"My back was hurting yesterday; it still is. I think that's why I didn't sleep much." She leaned forward just enough to re-arrange herself in the chair.

"Did you do something to your back?"

"No, I didn't do anything to it," she answered in her sometimes not-very-forthcoming manner. She could be stingy with her words in our sessions, as if irritated at being robbed of precious time while answering something she didn't think important.

"Well, what happened? Do you know?"

She looked at me and said quietly, "I know what happened. I don't know if anybody will believe it, though."

JoAnn was right about one thing: she knew what happened. In this instance she knew precisely what had taken place in her life, despite the fact it occurred forty years ago. She didn't need to wonder about being believed, as far as I was concerned, because the power of her conviction always carried with it enough force to make a compelling case for whatever she said about her life. And whatever she told me about her past was never said cavalierly. This was consistently true in my experience with her, even when she spoke of things I had never before heard or imagined.

In this particular case she remembered going to the store one day with her grandfather when she was about nine years old. He beat her savagely as they were walking home along the path through the woods; then he kicked her in the back, for good measure, while she lay there in the sandy dirt.

She reached around with her right hand to the mid-section of her back. "This is where he kicked me. I'd been feeling sore here for about a week, but it really started getting worse the last few days. Yesterday I was writing something about his always wanting me to go to the store with him, and then I remembered the whole thing. This is where the bastard kicked me, after beating me into the ground."

With this incident, JoAnn was pushed to deal with an entirely different kind of memory. During the next two years she would suffer wretched soreness and a variety of pains and aches that appeared to come out of nowhere, for no discernable physical reason. Time after time, within days or weeks of living with increasing discomfort, she'd manage to uncover a connection from the past which put her probing mind to rest. Her pain, as we pieced it together, functioned to create a focal point around which her memories gathered. Using the now-familiar technique of permitting undirected images to appear on the screen of her awareness, she was able to inform herself of what her body knew but her unconscious mind had repressed. The memories had remained in her muscles, bones, and tissue, however, and in organs like her kidneys, which ached anew from ancient blows.

Often JoAnn wouldn't talk about how terrible she felt until she'd discovered the specific inscription on her psyche's half-buried Rosetta Stone with the pertinent translation of her body's hurts. She was convinced that if, as a child, her mind had let her feel all those beatings from her family she surely would've died.

Still she hadn't gotten off without paying a price; in the early 1980s their brutal treatment from decades earlier was catching up with her. Now, in the present, she experienced the agony of having had her arm almost torn from its socket as she was yanked up off the porch floor by an enraged Hank Foley; her head ached from the power of Henry's full-grown fists trying to teach the stubborn child-woman a lesson about submission; her coccyx seared with the pain of having been a favorite target of the nearest impatient boot.

I'd never witnessed anything like this. It was one thing to hear JoAnn remember what happened to her long ago in childhood; it was altogether another to see her re-experience, in the present, physical responses to those events. I'm not even sure if "re-experience" is the right word since I think it's likely she had never actually "experienced" those events in the first place—at least not in the sense of *feeling* them.

Yet again my life provided little knowledge of the things about which she talked. I've never had a broken bone or even needed a stitch, and only was in the hospital for a tonsillectomy at age seven. By the time I was well into my thirties—when just about everyone I knew seemed to be adjusting to a bad back—I got older feeling fine, with a great deal of gratitude for my good fortune and, I think, a whiff of self-righteousness about taking such good care of myself. In my thirty-sixth year, though, that smugness ran out of fuel with the first real discomfort to hit me. By the time JoAnn and I sat in my office, I'd become another numbing cipher in the statistics on Americans with back problems. Like her, I knew what happened to me. But neither the cause of the problem nor my awareness of its effect was ever far from my ken.

Competitiveness had gotten me in trouble, on a spring day that was sunny and newly warming. Carl, who had long since outgrown the stage of destroying piles of just-raked leaves, was visiting for the weekend. Since he was only a few years younger we had spent our childhood playing together and fighting with each other. I suppose tennis was the perfect outlet for those impulses because we both learned quickly when our father taught us the game; at the time we got our first rackets I was a gangly thirteen years to his towheaded, less-complex ten.

When we initially faced each other across the net I definitely had the advantage, if only by virtue of being bigger. Then for a while we tested each other about equally, both of us challenged to hustle faster, hit harder, think smarter, and play longer. After a short period, though, he'd out-paced me by an insurmountable margin; we competed in tournaments against others in our respective age brackets, or else we teamed up on the same side as partners.

We hadn't played together for quite some time when we took to the court on that sparkling April afternoon. Things began okay as we practiced but I gradually grew frustrated and impatient with myself for not being able to hit the ball with the grace and strength he had. As a measure of my desperation, I asked Carl to show me how to hit a two-handed backhand, thinking maybe it would give me an edge the younger players of the day seemed to be enjoying. While neither of us had ever used the stroke, he understood the technique better than I and provided some coaching. Just when I was starting to get the hang of it, and just as I decided to really hit out at the ball, I twisted or pulled up or I don't know what but my back went into spasm—and I've never been quite the same since.

Even though my backaches have been mild compared to what others endure, they are reminders to me, when I pause to think about it, of some traits I don't prize in myself. When I'm in a kindly frame of mind, I try to use the soreness and stiffness as a prompt to work on those troubling things that were embedded in our tennis game, like the competitiveness I mentioned, or a sometimes frightfully high standard to which I hold myself and therefore am all too often found wanting in my own eyes, and a susceptibility to value the product more than the process, the outcome instead of the doing. A connection to my back's pain and what it represents to me has been a daily presence in my life from the moment I did myself that way on the tennis court.

JoAnn's experience, so very different, was completely alien to me. Information was only beginning to emerge at that time about Post-Traumatic Stress Disorder; we still knew almost nothing about the ways in which people had managed to survive an array of inhumane traumas. I listened in wonderment as this woman who had come to me for help kept leading me through new concepts and into psychological states I hadn't previously fathomed.

Her efforts to connect with injuries nearly half a century old, in many cases, required a sizable segment of our sessions for well over a year. Unable to get away from her body anymore and finally feeling what she hadn't felt as a child, she could sometimes barely keep going. Occasionally she stated—with only a smidgen of hyperbole, I think—a desire to just outright die instead of trying to outlast the pain. An examination of those memories held captive in her body left JoAnn certain that years of consulting medical specialists for countless health problems, including several instances of surgery, were necessitated by the physical and sexual abuse her body and mind had disowned.

So, I surely wasn't surprised at her ambivalence about therapy at this stage. And although neither of us may have understood what was to be gained from that part of the work she was then doing, we both knew there wasn't any turning back. I had to believe that JoAnn's opening up to, and reclaiming, her physical as well as emotional pain was an act of releasing its furtive hold on her.

One day, much later, as we were talking about the sequence and significance of various aspects of our work together, I asked what she recalled about that period of ambivalence when she was in such pain.

JoAnn threw her head back and laughed. Without missing a beat she said, "You know what I remember? I remember reaching a point in therapy where I was hurting so bad I practically screamed at you, 'All right, Evans, you sure as hell better be telling me the truth about things improving! 'Cause if it turns out you're lying to me . . .' "

Neither one of us could recall how she'd finished that sentence back then, but at least *this* time we could laugh about it.

15

"BUT, GRANDPA, MR. LINCOLN FREED THE SLAVES."

Mama never knew how to cope with me. I was always a burden, and she let me know it from the outset.

"I didn't even want you, goddammit," I remember her yelling at me. "I didn't ask you to be born, and I don't need no goddam baby to tie me down! I never asked for no shitty baby to take care of."

The problem was I took up too much. I took up space, I took up room in the bed. All I did was TAKE UP. I took up her money, 'cause she had to buy things for me. Mostly I took up her time. She didn't have no time for me. She was so pretty and so young and she had to take care of herself. There was no time for a baby. She needed time to primp and get herself ready. It was awful the food that I took up, the water I took up.

The water was a big thing because we didn't have plumbing or running water then. It had to be pumped and toted for washing my shitty diapers when I was a baby. So they didn't change my diapers very often, and that way they didn't have to wash them all the time.

As a toddler I think I must have learned that making a mess in my diapers was a terrible thing. It felt awful, since I only got changed when somebody couldn't stand the smell any longer. I learned that soiled diapers made people mad at me. And it was all my fault. I think I tried to control my bowels before I even physically could. I suppose it's no wonder that later I sometimes got constipated.

"Chile, chile, you is plum tore up!"

I was. It was the castor oil. Or Castoria, some patent medicine for constipation. I'm gone to Honey's house and I'm terrible sick. Sick as a dog. Shit running down my legs and I can't stop it.

"TOO MUCH!" Honey says. She can smell the medicine in all that shit. She's mad at them folks that give "a whole bottle to that chile. You is have too much of that mess, chile."

I'm shitty all over, and throwing up, too. I throw up all over myself and shit all over the place. She's upset, but not with me. Sick as I am I know Honey's not upset with me. I get to her house and know I'll be all righty right. I'm covered in vomit and shit. She don't know what to do to make me feel better.

"Poor chile, poor little chile. They is give you a whole bottle of that mess, and you be runnin' off from both ends!" Honey worries about what to do to fix me up. She don't do like the Foleys and cuss me out for making a mess.

She don't know what to do first. Then she figures out to throw me in the tub, pour nice warm rainwater from outta the barrel over me. "We is got to clean you up and get them rags offa you, chile."

She takes them messy rags offa that chile and pours nice warm rainwater on that baby. Clean her right up. Rinse that baby off, dry that baby all up. Dry her good and keep her nice and warm. She sits that chile up in the big ol' rocker chair. That baby is snug as a spot on a bug in a rug.

Honey is mad with them Trash what make her baby sick. She thinks God oughta not do like that to a poor little chile, not oughta dump her with them Baddies.

She washes up them rags and puts them in the nice clean sunshine to dry. She tells me No I can't put her britches on. She laughs and says she ain't never heard tell of no such a thing.

"Why, them britches a mine cover you up from head to toe, chile." She laughs and laughs. Then she puts the Man's undershirt on me to keep me warm while my clothes get dry. It's like a tent, but I sit up in the rocker chair with it on just like I'm a real some-body.

Honey don't ever get mad if she has to clean me up. At least at *me* she don't.

It's a little bit of a rain falling. I'm laying on a quilt by Honey's chair.

"How you doin' down there, chile?"

"I is snug as a bug, Honey."

She asks if I'm about ready to rest awhile now. She pulls a cover up to keep the flies from bothering me.

"Be a little bit cool down there iff'n you just happen to noddy off."

But I'm thinking I ain't gonna rest. I ain't even tired. Mebbe I might miss something.

"Is you ascairt you gonna MISS OUT ON SUMTHIN', Miss Big Eyes?" Honey asks me. "Well, you can close them big ol' brown eyes a little bit, chile, 'cause you not gonna miss a thing in this world. I sit right here and I keep a eye out. If sumthin' happens, why I wake you right up to see it!

"Close your eyes for a little bit now. Rest yourself. We is got things to do later. I can keep a sharp eye out while you take a nice nap."

She covers me up real good now, right up to my neck. She gives me a hug and says, "I sit right here and tell you a story till you nod off. I might nod off a little wink or two myself, who knows? Just us two ol' womens, and we ain't got a thing to worry 'bout on this Place, now do we?"

I'm all tucked in, on a pallet, on the porch floor.

"It was a rain kinda like this one, chile. . . . Lord no. I wasn't even THINKED of in them days! Was a long time ago in the Bible days. . . . No, he wasn't born neither. Was a nice rain like this one, but the trouble was it rain for all a FORTY days and FORTY nights. . . . It says so in the Bible, chile, says so in the Bible. Good stories in that ol' book. Teach you a whole lot a things, sure will. Now you is done hear tell 'bout the BOAT, ain'tcha?"

Most every time it rains I get to hear about that Boat.

"They is go in two by two, chile."

Me and her is two. I know what is two. Me and her on my

fingers is two. Her and him is two. Me and her and him is three. Me and her and him is three and the horsey is gonna make four.

Honey is name all the animals what she can name that go in that big Boat. "And ol' Mr. Noah say, 'Is you two? One man and one womans? All right then, get on board now 'cause we ain't got no time to be wastin' round here. We is got our work to do! Gotta get alla you animals on board here!' You know this story, chile, now don'tcha?"

She reach down beside her chair and says, "You KNOWS, don'tcha, chile?" and she pokes my NOSE.

"But I forget it, Honey. Tell me again about that Boat what SAVE EVERYBODY." I giggle 'cause we NOSE I can tell that ol' story just as good as she can.

"Two cows?"

"Yes, he got two cows on there." She is right sure about that 'cause they need milk when they come offa the Boat.

"Two chickens?"

"Sure, he got two chickens."

I tell her that if only two chickens can go, that's gonna leave lotsa chickens in the chicken yard. I think mebbe they can get right up on top a that chicken house and be right high outa the water.

"Mebbe so, mebbe so," Honey says.

"Get on the very tippy, tippy top a that old chicken house and I think they be okay. Two horseys?"

"Yep, think so. Need good ol' horseys."

"Two worms?"

"Yep."

"Two fuzzy worms?" I only seen one a them kind a fuzzy worms in the flower bed. Not two.

"Well, that's okay, chile. When you is see one fuzzy worm like him is, then you know there's a whole heap more. Iff'n you is seen 'em or not. I'm right sure, come the time, they be two a them little fuzzy worms walk right up there into that Boat."

She goes on telling the story, but I just think about them little fuzzy worms. I think Ol' Man God must love them worms a whole bunch if He makes sure Mr. Noah gets 'em on the Boat.

I don't even hear her talk. I feel like one a them fuzzy worms. I noddy off, just like Honey reckon I do.

I'm walking back from the store with Grandpa, along the sandy path through the woods.

The woods were behind the house we lived in on Pine Ridge Road. We had to move there in a hurry, to a too-small house not far away from where we'd lived on Wade Street. Later I learned that somebody in the family, I think it was Mama's oldest brother, Henry, had pulled some strings to get us in that house. It had been closed down by the city, so it was vacant at the time. It was closed down and boarded up because people in the neighborhood had complained about it being a whorehouse. There'd been a big commotion about having to get us another house to stay in after we left Wade Street, so this was the place Henry found for us. I lived there in that one-time whorehouse for the next five years, until I was twelve and had to move away again in a big hurry. Seems like I lived enough to fill up a lifetime in those five years . . .

Grandpa slows down to a real slow walk.

"I don't wanta stop, Grandpa. . . . Yes, I wanta be your good little girl, but they'll think where are we if we don't get back home. If we don't want Grannie and them to know we stopped, we better go on."

He stops quick. ". . . No, no, Grandpa. I won't tell! NO, I DIDN'T SAY I'D TELL!!"

I duck my head to keep him from hitting it 'cause he is slapping and hitting on me. I tell him to stop it, he's hurting me. Stop it, please stop! I promise him I'll stop crying. I tell him I'll shut up, and ". . . yes, Grandpa, I'll touch your thing."

He says I like to do it, don't I!

But I don't want to do it. He won't ever listen to me. "I DON'T like to. . . . Do I have to, Grandpa?" I am about to cry again. He doesn't care what I want.

He just looks at me angrily with his blue fish eyes and tells me to SUCK IT. SUCK HIS THING. That's all he cares about, not if I want to do it. He is too busy thinking of his THING and how he wants to feel better.

"Suck it! Suck it hard, baby. Shut up your goddam crying! Do you want them to see you been crying? Jesus Christ!! You're just like your damn mother, making such a stink over nothing!" He punches my head with his fist and tells me to Shut Up!

Suddenly his tone changes. "There's a lot of other little girls who would be glad to have a nice Grandpa to buy them surprises. You'd just better count your blessings, JoAnn girl. Yeah, you know I have plans for you, don't you? Big plans for you and me. And I'll be different this time. Yes siree bob."

He says that 'cause he had learned his lesson with the other girls, especially Mama. Oh, he'd gotten in big trouble with Grannie over Mama! Grannie didn't like it that Mama was his favorite.

"You're going to be a knockout, yes sir. And you're MY little girl, you know. Yes sir, you sure belong to your ol' Grandpa. Ain't that right?"

He's excited, and I don't like it. Belong? Belong to Grandpa?

"But, Grandpa, Mr. Lincoln freed the slaves. There's no more 'belong' to anybody. There's no more slaves anymore, Grandpa. You're wrong. Some slaves stayed on the plantations, but they didn't have to. People don't belong to people anymore, Grandpa. You can't own people these days."

I am just so excited 'cause I know all about Lincoln and the slaves. "Lincoln said people can't belong to people anymore. He made a law and the slaves were free. You can't have slaves and you can't own people, either. It's the law now, Grandpa."

I'm all caught up in what I remember learning in school, talking and prattling along. "Don't you remember, Grandpa," I ask, "about Mr. Lincoln?"

I stop. I stop and feel it. I've done SOMETHING WRONG! I am so excited I FORGET TO BE QUIET! Oh, what have I done? What's wrong? What's going to happen?

"SHUT YOUR MOUTHHH!!!" He is screaming, and looking at me like he has never seen me before, as if I'm a snake across the path.

Oh God, I forgot. I talked, and I know better. I never talked like this to him before, and he is so MAAAD. His giant arm goes up and I fall down in the sand with the ants, and cover myself up to protect my head and ears. I know what is coming, but I don't know if it will just be a beating. I'm not sure if he will kill me or not. I don't even know what is "kill me," not really. But I have heard them say they'd kill me for as long as I can remember.

I lay in the warm sand with the ants, in a ball, and I try to be smaller and smaller.

"WHO IN THE HELL TOLD YOU THAT YOU COULD TALK TO ME LIKE THAT?!! I've had it with you, you goddam dummy!" he shouts at the little ball that is me.

He takes off his big wide work belt, standing over me, and hits me with it. Again and again he hits me with it. I don't know how long I lie there curled up as tight as I can get while he beats me with his belt.

Maybe he starts to get worried that we've been away too long because he puts the belt back through the loops in his pants. Then he kicks me in the back with all his force before walking away. His face is red from anger and the hard work of beating up a child.

Grandpa walks off, back toward the house. When he's way beyond sight I unroll myself and I feel like I have to learn how to stand up all over again; I can hardly straighten up. I wonder if my back is dead. Some while later I head in the same direction, but stay off the path so nobody will see me.

Up ahead I hear him answering someone who is at the cow pen. "I don't know where in the hell she is. The goddam little dummy wouldn't come on with me. Guess she ran off to play in the woods. You know how she is. Drives you crazy!"

He lies. Grandpa knows where I am, and he knows I'm hurt, too. He's lying 'cause he knows he beat the shit out of me and left me in a pile, in the sand with the ants. I'm nothing to him. He thinks he owns me, that I'm his pretty little girl. He doesn't own me! HE CAN'T OWN ME! People can't own people anymore.

That's the time I hide in the outhouse, when they leave the cow shed. I am hurt bad, and I go into the outhouse after they go to where everybody else is. I am almost crying, but I won't cry. I can't cry. It won't happen. No tears come. Someone might hear the noise, and it is all over if you let the Foleys see you in pain, or show weakness of any kind.

They're all in the filthy shack, at the table for supper. It is then I notice the inside of the outhouse pit. It makes me want to throw up. Their filthy shack is not much better than the outhouse pit, I think.

And I'll not live in either one. They'll not ever make me live there with them in that awful place.

I never remember going to the store with Grandpa again. I even avoided the stretch of the path where we had stopped. I'd go a different way around that piece of the woods' path. It was the longer way because that piece of the path was a branch off toward just our house, and it was less traveled because we were the only ones who used it. It was too dangerous there because less traveled meant less chance of being seen by someone, so I almost never went on that part of the path again.

✳

I can tell Honey ain't happy.

She looks at me and says, "Tell you the truth, I not be so pleased with you today. Now I just have to tell you like it is. I don't think you try very hard today, chile. That's all there is to it. I just don't think you try to do right today. Now did you? . . . Hummmpp, hummpp. . . . Well, I'se 'fraid so."

I be 'fraid so, too. Honey says the best thing to do is start all over with me today.

Oh, I do that thing. I jump right down and go start all over with her today. We done got off on a bad foot, and we need to start all over fresh before we get plum aggravated with each other.

Honey tells me to wait a minute. She walks over, picks up that raggity baby and says, "Don't forgets your baby. She needs to start all over, too! Even this baby done got off on the wronnngg foot 'round here today, she has. I declare it do seem like everbody 'round here is got off to a bad start!"

I take my baby that starts off on the wrong foot, and I feel so bad she is do like that. I tell her, "It's okay. It's okay, baby, we just go right out there and start all over again, and we forget this ol' badness now. Okay? We not talk 'bout this here no more," and I coo coo to her 'cause I ain't mad.

I know she ain't gonna throw us CLEAN TO HELL OFF THIS PLACE. I know we Do Try but we did get off to a bad start, so now we do the very best next thing: me and Lu Lu Belle go out and start off fresh.

Honey takes my things off the table, and I take my raggity baby

out the door. I wait a minute. I go knock on the door just as nice as
ever you please ('cause it don't do to just come in without being
nice).

Honey says, "It sound like that chile is knock on the door. Is
that you, chile?"

"Yessum." I say Yessum real nice to her.

"Well, chile, DO come on in here. I been waitin' on you, hopin'
to see you today!"

"Well, you're a fool for not wanting to go with us and have some
fun. That's all I got to say."

Mama is starting to get mad at me. But she's in a hurry to get
her makeup on and her hair to do just right, so she can't waste too
much attention yet on getting mad.

"What d'you think's gonna happen to you, for God's sake?" she
asks impatiently. "You'll be right there with all the rest of us, won't
you? God, you're so crazy! There's plenty of girls who would like to
be where you are. I don't even know why we bother with you."

She's tired of messing with me. It all falls on her. All the time it's
up to her to make me listen when Henry says I gotta go with them
to the beer Joint. "You can at least come with us and just sit there,
can't you?" she says, slamming the comb down on the dresser.

Mama is finished making the little curls hang around her face.
She spends hours combing the little ringlets around her face, and
she tells everybody about how her hair is so naturally curly; how it
just hangs in ringlets by itself. She doesn't have to do a thing to it,
nothing at all. Well, she would say, she wouldn't mess with making
them except they just fall that way when she washes her hair.

"You can at least come and sit in the booth! You can at least do
THAT MUCH, can't you? . . . No. No, dammit, you don't have to
leave the goddam booth ALL NIGHT if you don't want to. If you
shit your pants it's all right far as I'm concerned. YOU DON'T HAVE
TO LEAVE THE BOOTH! . . . Well, then don't drink much and
you won't have to pee! For Christ's sake, you're making a fuss over
nothing at all. It ain't gonna hurt you to be NICE! Now is it? A lot of

girls would sure like to have the chances you THROW AWAY, JoAnn!!"

She runs out the door. Time is getting late. Henry will be here soon and she won't have me ready. Mama is scared to death of Henry's anger when he would drive up to the house and find out I wasn't ready to leave. She goes out and yells for Grannie. "Mama, come tell JoAnn she has to go with us tonight. Mama, make her go!"

❋

No.

All I said was "No!" The steel-hard voice had told me to get in the house. He wanted me to "do it."

I was barely more than a little girl. I know because we'd only been living on Pine Ridge Road a few years then.

The hard voice, with its flat cold tone, was Grandpa's. I'm sure of it. He wanted me to get on in the bedroom.

It took me by surprise. Usually I stayed on guard so no one could sneak up behind me, so there'd be no "Gotcha!" But I was weary that night, tired out and worn down. When I'd finished whatever I'd been told to do, I went outside and sat near the edge of the porch, in the shadows, but not really hidden. It had grown dark and I had gone away inside where I could be quiet and barely breathe so as to be nearly invisible.

The voice, the command, startled me. I guess I'd allowed myself to drift off into exhaustion, and it was the being found, so unexpected, that did it. As I came out of the dead stillness, not yet alert, I heard Grandpa's order, and I said "NO!"

That was all. Just a word, nothing else. Just No.

I think perhaps that "No" surprised Grandpa as much as his voice had startled me.

"WHAT did you say??!" He seemed unable to believe what he'd heard.

So I said it again. "NO!"

"No WHAT?" he yelled. "What in the hell did you say, you goddam little bitch? D'you know who you're TALKING to?"

His mouth hung open and he stared at me, shocked at the nerve the stupid dummy had in saying no to the mighty Hank Foley. Then he reared back and kicked me, kicked me hard again and again. "You get the hell in this house when I tell you!"

So, as in other times when all else failed, he beat me up. He grabbed me by the arm and yanked me off the porch floor. I know I was not a little girl anymore because my feet never left the floor. When he used to grab me, before I was this big, I'd be yanked right up off the filthy floorboards. There's not a reason I can think of why my arm stayed attached to my body instead of ending up in his huge hands when he jerked me up like that. I almost passed out. Maybe I was bigger and taller now, but still he slapped and hit me like I was nothing more than a rag doll.

It didn't matter. It didn't matter at all, not at all. I would not DO IT. I wouldn't, and he knew that he couldn't make me. When I would "get like this," all he could do was beat the pure hell out of me. So that's what he did.

It didn't matter because I had learned. Even though I had no memory of Honey that night, her voice had stayed in some far-off crevice and I had learned the rule: NOBODY CAN MAKE YOU. "They can do things to you, chile, but they can't MAKE you! Do all they wants to, but can't make you be BAD. No, no, no!"

Grandpa dragged me into the kitchen. When he finally realized I was just dead weight that wasn't going to do as he wanted he threw me down and looked up at the people who were sitting around talking and drinking coffee.

A woman's voice said, "You can't do anything with JoAnn when she's like this! Might as well leave her alone when she takes it into her head not to listen."

It was Grannie, and she was glad that now they could all see what she had to put up with day in and day out. "Leave her alone," she said. "She'll get over it."

There in the filthy kitchen, with those words, the air took on an edge of tightness that seemed to suck the breath out of everybody. I could feel it. It was just unbelievable, as if spread across the sky in mile-high letters for all to read was the single word "WHO?"

They all felt it, too. Who will have to do the dirty work now that it won't be the little dummy?

Grandpa looked around and said, "Come on, Francie." He said it so simply, then turned and walked out of the dirty kitchen into the dark bedroom in the sure and certain knowledge that his command would be obeyed.

That was it. All there was to it. The King of the Cannibals had spoken. "Come on, Francie," he'd said. With all the assurance of a feudal lord in the Dark Ages, Hank Foley issued a command and left the room to be served, knowing he would be followed into the bedroom where it was dark except for a little bit of light from the kitchen. HE KNEW HE WOULD BE OBEYED!

I could hear the bed springs squeak and sag when he sat down on the pissy, rotten mattress. I'd gone away inside, still lying on the floor where he'd thrown me down, but the sound and smell of it was so filthy familiar.

The others were relieved Grandpa had taken Francie. The air was back in the kitchen, and everybody could breathe again. I could feel each one thinking: I'm glad he took Francie and not me!

No one had stirred. Not a finger was lifted, not a voice raised. There was just relief felt by all those who were not picked that night by Grandpa.

For me it was different. Honey had told me that nobody could make me do what I didn't want to do, and that night I felt the truth of it.

❋

I was worried about them greens. I heard the Man tell our Honey he sure thought it'd be nice to have some a them good ol' greens when he got back to home at the end of the day. I think we should go and finish picking 'em so she can cook 'em.

But Honey don't wanta do that now. "We ain't a gonna worry 'bout them ol' greens just now, chile," she tells me. "Lord no. You and me is gonna set a spell. Come on over here, JoAnn chile. Even GOD rests Hisself ever now and then, you know. . . . Sure He does, chile, sure He does. That Ol' Man ain't no fool. He knows He needs His rest."

She is thinking about some little girl chile who don't know when she needs to rest! Even the Lord knows to set a spell when He's tired, she tells me.

"Sure, He's the Lord, but He ain't no fool! Do youuu," and she rolls her eyes over to me, "do you think God's a fool, chile? Well, He ain't. He knows when it's time to cut them greens. And He knows when it's time to rest Hisself. He don't do like SOME FOLKS who don't know they need to take their rest."

Honey says them greens ain't a gonna run off like the little chickies do when I go to play with 'em. Nope, them greens is gonna be right there where them belongs at.

I ask her is she sure about that thing, and I start running around and looking like I is a green with legs. She is laughing at me.

"Is you plum sure about that, Honey? How you know them greens ain't got little legs? They might have little green legs tucked right up there under their green skirts." I'm just dancing all around all over the place. I reach down in the pan where we already picked some greens and hold up one of them leaves to show her how it is like a little skirt. "You best WATCH OUT now, Honey. They may run on off back into that field and we not ever get 'em."

Oh we laugh and laugh at the idea of them greens running back out to the field. She's about to fall over laughing and gives me a hug when I come running by her on my little green legs.

"They just wave their little arms, Honey, and say 'Don't eat me. Don't eat me.' Run, little greens, run!"

I don't like it. All of a sudden I am scared.

They're gonna eat me! Oh, they're gonna eat me. It's the Foleys! I'm ascairt they're gonna eat me all up. I start to cry. I am so ascairt of them bad Foleys.

Honey don't know what's the matter with me. I was so busy just a minute ago laughing and running around like a green with little legs. Now I stand here and cry like there's a well in me that somebody's pumping the water out of. She reaches out and pulls me to her. Honey is holding me and swaying with me. Under the big ol' tree.

It is ruinted. I'm so ascairt. I can't be a doing like them Baddies. I can't. I be ruinted if I do like they do!

Ah, there's a key.

No wonder I can't play. I don't ever just play make-believe for fun. I cannot relax and BE LIKE THEM! There is a message burnt in fire across my soul: I'll be ruined if I do like they do!

If I play I might remember what they did.
If I play I might forget and do like they do.

❊

Honey says she don't think too much a anybody that does like them Foleys. She sure be sorry to see me be like them folks.

She coos at me. I think I sure ain't gonna be like them. No, no, no. The onlyest thing she can tell me is she thinks them is the DEVIL'S HELPERS. I can tell from her tone that the devil's helpers is the very worst thing to be!

It makes her so sorry to see folks what do the devil's work for him. One thing for sure, she says, Ol' Devil will sure claim his own, and then it be too late.

I sit and play with Lu Lu Belle while she talks to us about this Ol' Devil business. I nod my head 'cause I agree with that woman. I listen and nod my head; I know to listen and learn what she's got to say.

"When Ol' Mean Devil Man come to get 'em," I tell my little Lu Lu Belle later on, "won't matter iff'n they say it ain't their fault. Oh no! Be too late. They have to pay for all them bad things they done! They can cry and wail all they want, and it won't change a thing. Be too late for all them what don't DO RIGHT!"

I think the devil looks just like Grandpa, I do.

I ask Honey if the Lord be mad at them Baddies? I ask her do the Lord beat shit outta them? I want the Lord to catch 'em all and kick the hell outta them. Beat the hell outta them like they beat me.

"Hush up. Hush up that talk, chile. The Lord be sorry, but it be tooo late for them folks. Be toooo late, chile."

I'm glad, but I don't tell Honey I'm glad. I hope the Ol' Devil get 'em and hit 'em and jump on 'em and smack 'em and kill 'em dead!

"Come time to settle their accounts and they be lost. Be too late by then, chile." She talks in a sad tone 'cause it be too late.

I ain't sad about it be too late for them Baddies.

❊

"Ah Lord, well, it's okay. It's okay NOW, chile."

I'm awful sick, in awful pain, and Honey's gonna "fix it right up."

She says to let her look see. ". . . No, no, indeed I not touch it. I 'member not to touch you, chile, less'n you say so. You know THAT, don'tcha?"

Honey gets all that pus stuff outta there, and burns that rag right up inna stove. She says, "That mean ol' Mr. Core! Don't know what he think he's a doin' to get in there and bother this here baby! Don't know how that Mama of yours can let a boil like this get so bad. I just don't know what this ol' world is coming to, do you, chile?"

She washes up, and is so glad to see that ol' Baddie Mr. Core is all gone now! She sits down in the rocker chair.

"Poor baby, poor baby. Don'tcha worry yourself none at all, chile. No, no, no. You gonna be all better pretty soon now. Now that Ol' Mr. Core is gone, you gonna feel all better real soon."

She tells me to rest. "Think maybe so you can get a little rest now? Don'tcha think so, huh?"

Honey covers me up so I can rest, and says she sure not gonna hit that sore place again. "So don'tcha worry yourself none 'bout that, okay, chile?"

I lay on a pallet, right by her chair. She rocks and talks, talks soft and low. I doze and doze but don't sleep tight.

She's not working on her string stuff; her hands is in her lap and she's a humming, talking and a singing soft soft soft. Making sweet, easy sounds . . .

I don't know how long before I let myself feel as bad as I do. I look at her, and I look at her. I listen at her humming and I crawl over there closer and I look at her. She ain't a paying me no never you mind. She just be soft soft, go rock and rock.

Honey's got her string stuff right in her lap, like always when she's in the rocker chair. But her hands is empty, just lying still.

I could fit right there myself, I think. Somehow I know I can. Reckon I done think of it before, when she's working on her string stuff. The little pile of stuff is there in her lap, and I think how it'd be to be there, but I don't do it ever.

I'm so close now to where she's rocking to and fro, and singing soft.

I do it . . .

I crawl right up in her lap with never a sound.

To us rock. Fro us rock. To us rock. She just keeps on, singing soft songs, and rocks me to sleep.

16

LIKE AN UNSHED TEAR

I've never met anyone who enjoyed leave-taking, who relished good-byes. Leaving, being left, endings: it's a lot of what therapy is about. Because it's a lot of what life is about.

Many times, over many years, I've thought you have to be a glutton for punishment to be in this psychotherapy business. Why would you want to work so hard at getting to know a man who's so little known to himself? Plenty of therapists, in fact, have patients they eventually get to know better than their own spouses, lovers, or friends. Why keep opening your heart to someone (even if it'll help her learn about opening *her* heart) when you know it eventually has to come down to your looking at each other one day and saying, "Well, it's time for us to say good-bye now"?

Parents do this all the time. It's what we therapists do, too. Over and over again it's what we have to do. Seems like a cruel joke often enough, like a masochistic job description we sign off on, agreeing to perform. Probably we do it for different reasons, but I imagine there are a lot of therapists out there like me who hope that learning more about this process will help us better handle the part of life which deals with letting go. Getting older is the best teacher of how much of life is involved with letting go.

Our patients don't have it easy, either; we're all in this "endings" thing together. The spacious floor of psychology is littered with theories about the jumble of problems stemming from separation.

Even with giving all those psychological theories—the classic as well as the exotic—their due, there's the inescapable *physical* truth that every one of us has suffered the most basic of separations: our birth. The fact that it's the sine qua non of our survival, that it's happened everywhere on the planet since cells began dividing, doesn't make it any less traumatic for the human species. And just because we can't remember the moment of being pushed or pulled from our symbiotic womb-home, literally severed from our mothers forever as the umbilical cord was cut, doesn't mean we haven't been affected by that life-altering event. In those few moments our first form of living was supplanted by an entirely different way of being alive. My guess is that each of us carries around unknown cellular and somatic effects of our birth that we haven't even begun to comprehend yet.

Then, as if that weren't enough, there are the emotional and psychological aspects of our difficulties with endings, an area of seemingly infinite scope. It isn't hard to compile a sorrowful list of traumatic separations for young people, including their being hospitalized in childhood, having parents divorce, being "given away" or "taken away," the illness or death of a parent; the list seems truly endless.

And thinking still of that earliest of separations, I remember having read—maybe, in fact, many have said it—that we never get enough mothering. The particular article was neither a piece of mother-bashing nor a diatribe from the "blame it on Mom" school. Actually the article was framed in a feminist perspective that considered our culture's role in the challenge of raising children. Since it's always been the job of women in our society to bring up children, and since women have traditionally had less power and prestige than men, the formidable task of raising healthy humans has fallen to those people who themselves have been undervalued. How, I recall the author wondering, can children develop self-esteem and gain a sense of having true worth if their mothers, their primary caretakers, were not granted that birthright? How can the next generation be taught to treasure themselves for who they are and not what they "do" if their teachers were not cherished in that way as *their* personalities were forming?

So, if we've never gotten enough mothering from mothers who never got enough mothering, it would seem that our hunger must be huge for an emotional connection to equal the physical intimacy we once experienced when we were truly part of our mothers, before being so shockingly separated from them.

I became especially interested in the issue of separation while I was working with JoAnn because the subject came up repeatedly as a topic in our sessions. At the beginning, however, I wasn't sure that's what we were dealing with; the first possible indication hardly seemed a clue at all.

JoAnn rarely missed any therapy appointments. Even if she had to move mountains of demands on her time to get to the clinic, she'd do it. She didn't treat the effort required as anything significant, either. Many clients, as any therapist will attest, go into excruciating detail about the traffic tie-ups which made them late, or an intractable work project that didn't allow enough time for them to call and cancel. I often didn't know of the lengths to which JoAnn had gone to make it for a particular session unless I stumbled on a question whose answer intimated the difficulties she'd overcome to be there in my office at that moment.

The second or third session I remember her missing was just after I'd gotten back from two weeks in Canada. A message left in my mailbox by the receptionist said JoAnn wasn't able to get off work that morning. I was curious about why on this particular day she'd had trouble rearranging her schedule when little had deterred her before. It was natural to wonder if there was any link between *my* going away and then *her* being away.

As we talked about it at our next meeting, though, her explanation seemed reasonable: having been back at work on her old schedule while we didn't meet had apparently lulled her supervisor into assuming she was available for more hours than she'd planned for or wanted. We spoke about this briefly before moving on to whatever insights had struck during the interim and left her brimming with energy to start exploring.

One of the things which kept creeping into our peripheral vision over the following months (maybe even a year), and certainly over the period of my taking several other vacations, coalesced around what JoAnn could only categorize as a sense of being unsettled. She was acutely puzzled over what it was that remained so ineffable, just beyond her verbal grasp. She spoke of feeling a tremor within, and made several attempts—particularly on paper—to discover its identity. The following lines reflect one of those efforts from that time:

> I feel so terribly like a huge trembling tear. An unshed tear. I'm frozen in mid-release, left to tremble forever on the very brink of being shed. I am alive with desire to be free, but am not able to let go yet. Why can I not release this huge quivering tear?

Gradually I started seeing an association between those pained feelings about which she wrote and a few happenings then squeezing time from our sessions.

The welfare of JoAnn's youngest child was the first such issue. Although in many ways it was easier to continue with the work on herself while Danny was living with his father, in other ways it was as if he still remained in her house. Her thoughts were never distant from what was going on with him, or at least with what she could see and hear for herself and as far as he was telling her. He had transferred to a junior high school he'd been keen on attending, was living in a much more upscale neighborhood, and had merely to tell his father he wanted something before he soon received it. But he was no longer near old friends from his old neighborhood and JoAnn worried that the material goods he kept acquiring could leave him feeling more empty than ever. He didn't like this school any better than the last one, hated several teachers, in fact, and even refused to go to his classes much of the time. Although he may have been living fifteen or twenty miles across town at that point, much like the moon's passage pulls at the tide his unhappiness always tugged at her.

I wondered then whether Danny's moodiness and hostility were causing her to question her decision to respect his wish about moving out. JoAnn appeared comfortable with her judgment about this, however, because all along she'd been steadily comfortable with her expectations of him. Nor was guilt a problem here, either, she said. Once again she'd taken stock of her behavior and feelings and said it wasn't a matter of feeling guilty about how things had turned out. Not that she was pleased with, or even liked, the present situation, but she accepted it.

She acknowledged, as I'd heard her do many times before, that she'd done the best she could, given the existing circumstances. She saw no reason to blame herself for not having known what she didn't know, or not doing what she hadn't realized at the time needed to be done. All she could deal with was the present situation and what she now understood. She was the voice of reason and practicality, discussing all this matter-of-factly with disarming candor and the same dispassionate quality which was becoming so familiar to me. Although she may have shown little affect in doing so, it shouldn't be construed there was disinterest or callousness on her part as we spoke about what was taking place with Danny or the edgy interactions between them. In fact she communicated, much as she'd done during our initial appointment, a deep concern and commitment both to understanding and improving the situation. She communicated all this with an intensity or passion I felt but couldn't *see* in the usual ways one senses strong emotions being expressed.

So, the situation with Danny kept reentering, at different points along the way and over a generous stretch of time, a circuit of subjects under our consideration. Another matter appearing frequently during this same period of disequilibrium involved one of JoAnn's friends.

Over the accumulating seasons of therapy as she talked about her current life and relationships, I had gotten the impression lots of people considered JoAnn a friend. In the majority of those cases she didn't use the same word to define those same relationships. However, while she hadn't spoken of Peg very much before this time, when she did talk about her the reference was always to her as "my friend." She'd known and worked with Peg for many years; they had been co-workers since JoAnn took her first job a few years after Danny was born. Some of their children were the same ages.

Closing one of her therapy sessions in this unsettled and unsettling time, JoAnn mentioned an encounter with Peg a few days before. She had caught up with her friend in the hall as they were going to the lunchroom. She put her hand on Peg's back, just behind the crest of her shoulder, in an affectionate gesture. It was a gesture, for her, not easily made. Through her fingertips she felt a shudder, as if Peg's entire body winced.

After that she learned her friend had been in quite a bit of pain for a while, even though she didn't believe it was anything of concern. Over the next several months JoAnn talked with Peg about her health and whether or not the pain was getting any better; along with their supervisor, she urged her to consult a doctor about what was becoming a persistently painful condition.

JoAnn's concern grew, even as Peg continued to minimize what was happening. In our sessions she talked more about this woman she once described as the "only person I know who is halfway normal." I think she was trying to figure out why she cared, why Peg mattered to her when the concern she felt for most people was in the abstract ("Well, I'd be upset if that happened to *anybody,* not just my neighbor.").

Whenever she felt a strong reaction to something, any kind of not usual response, JoAnn turned into a kind of undercover agent from the Unconscious Squad. She'd start tailing that reaction tirelessly, around the clock if necessary, certain that by retracing its movements and discovering its motives she could solve the mystery of why her attention had been nabbed in the first place.

So, she gradually amassed a file of information, and her accumulating observations took on the significance of clues. What seemed to impress her the most about both Peg and her husband was the genuine concern they had for others; their focus was never just on themselves. She was profoundly touched by the respectful way they treated one another. Even when they disagreed or argued, each one still listened to what the other had to say.

"I'm not used to seeing this in the people I know," was such a common refrain when she spoke of Peg and Gerald that it often sounded like the chorus from a familiar song. There didn't seem any doubt in her mind they had the best marriage of any couple she knew. Perhaps the greatest tribute JoAnn could lay at the doorstep of their friendship was to say their home was a place where she consistently felt comfortable.

Looking back over the ten or twelve years she'd known Peg, JoAnn recalled once behaving in a way quite out of character for herself. Although she never had been a particularly sociable person, she was always getting invited to a variety of functions and activities and many seemed to regard her as a trusted confidant. I imagine those same acquaintances would be surprised to have heard her acknowledge she really didn't like people very much. Despite that fact, JoAnn joined Peg and several other women from her office for a weekly game of cards.

She didn't like playing cards and didn't know anything about poker, but she participated anyway. In order to be sure a flush beat a straight, and three of a kind beat two pair, she even got used to checking the crib sheet they made for her and insisted she use. Remembering those evenings and how unlikely it was to find herself involved there, she realized she'd never have joined the group if they hadn't always met at Peg's house.

Talking as much as she did about her friend apparently served the function of informing herself, in a far more conscious way, about the importance to her of their relationship. And it was somewhere in these exchanges JoAnn understood that Peg and her family provided the only contemporary experiences reminiscent of the forty-year-old memories she was steadfastly harvesting from her days back on the Place with Mr. Man and Honey.

At last Peg saw a doctor. Even though she underwent batteries of tests, none of the findings could explain her discomfort. The problem, she continued to believe, was probably an infection of some sort. She missed more and more work . . .

Naturally enough JoAnn was uneasy about the situation and all its uncertainties. Finally she learned her friend was being treated at the area's best-known cancer center. Peg wouldn't talk about it; she withdrew from her friends and co-workers, becoming angry and bitter. JoAnn reread the ground-breaking work of Elisabeth Kübler-Ross on dealing with death and the stages of dying. She went to visit Peg after she'd resigned from her job, and for the first time ever felt not welcome.

As was typical, JoAnn's main concern seemed removed from her personal feelings. She worried how Gerald and the children would handle their loss when Peg died. She was distressed, during their infrequent meetings, to hear Peg so full of bitter complaints: hadn't she lived a decent life? More than a hell of a lot of people, she'd been thoughtful and kind to others and always tried to maintain a healthy lifestyle. Was this the payoff for her efforts? What kind of justice was there anyway?!

JoAnn had a tough time with Peg's withdrawing and with the rancor being vented. It seemed to me she focused a lot more around the effects of that anger on Peg and her family than on how it all affected *her*. She obviously cared about what was happening to her friend, spending hours of our sessions pairing up incidents with her reactions, but I don't remember hearing her speak about the impact of this possible loss on her own life.

Outwardly, JoAnn didn't appear to be drawing much of a connection between those two subjects: her life and Peg's fight with cancer. Intellectually, I think she may have, but not on a feeling plane. Her writings, however, were a completely different story because that's where she set her unconscious free to sound a deeper reality.

Gaining access to that place of essential knowing must have come from the interplay of several concurrent and overlapping happenings, exactly the way things occur in life. There's never just one thing going on at any single time in our lives.

The recollections then finding their shape in her notebooks were the product, in my mind, of JoAnn's making literary silk. The process reminded me of the transformation I'd seen in a drafty, noisy factory in the middle of Wuxi, a small city between Shanghai and Nanjing.

There, row after row of workers stood alongside vats of steaming water in which hundreds of small, white, oval-shaped cocoons floated. All those cocoons had once been temporary homes to caterpillars fattened on mulberry leaves by practitioners of an ancient craft I thought of as fabric farming. Mulberry leaves are the favorite diet of larvae eager to evolve into *Bombyx mori* butterflies inside the protective chrysalises they spin with a substance extracted from those leaves. The pupae in these cocoons never made it to that stage, though. Boiling water ended their lives; the cocoons they'd made now gave up their riches to the rows of watchful workers by the steaming vats. Hot water loosened each tightly spun chrysalis so a slender strand could be snagged and fed with seven other such strands to a machine winding them together onto a spool-like apparatus. Each cocoon contained two miles of filament that looked but a fraction as thick as a spider's web. And the filament from eight of those cocoons wound together made one thread, a single silken thread! How many threads had it taken to weave the ties and dressing gowns, the shirts and blouses upstairs in the sales room? I couldn't even imagine.

But I *could* imagine the memories JoAnn was weaving at this time as being pulled together from several strands of her life. One of those lines then running through her days had to do with Danny moving out of their house and in with his father. Even though she didn't know what she could do to help him feel better about himself, to help him be happier, she talked often of her concern about him. Another strand involved her friend Peg, a relationship to which she was just starting to attach words and feelings. I'm sure yet another element, though it never quite held up to much more discussion than a few minutes of mostly intellectual chatting, related to her still unclear bond with me. After my Canada vacation—which preceded JoAnn's missing a therapy appointment—I began noticing a connection between my schedule and some things going on with her.

The vacation I took in the midst of this period was not an easy time for JoAnn. She'd had a cold almost the entire two or three weeks I was gone; her work setting was undergoing massive changes and several people there had left or were planning to leave. As is true for many of us, change had never sailed in on a calm sea for her. Soon after I returned, she acknowledged having not wanted to come to therapy. It was made clear she didn't even want to write or bring in any of her notebooks! And then this usually unflappable and pragmatic fifty-year-old woman wondered if the little child inside her was angry with me for going away.

Quite a number of the pages she'd written during this and another vacation I took a few months later—all of which she *did* share with me despite her first impulse to the contrary—touched on themes of being left and feeling abandoned. One of those written

LIKE AN UNSHED TEAR

pieces, in fact, was delivered by her sense of that most elemental severance, the original separation from mother.

I was puzzled by several aspects in this material. First of all, I couldn't comprehend how she was able to remember those things. Second, I wasn't sure if what she wrote about were actual memories; maybe they were simply fantasies of how it had been. Maybe the scene was a creative rendering of her imagined entry into the hostile and unsafe world she soon came to know. Maybe it really didn't even matter if I couldn't figure it out and had to stay puzzled.

I read her description of her birth, ten or twelve lines scrawled urgently in the middle of something else she was writing about. . . . No, she'd never been told anything about when she was born. This is just what came out as her mind and pen interrupted their unguided wanderings through a stack of notebook paper:

> Resist   Resist   Resist   Resist
> "Push, dammit! Push, Marie. Dammit, Marie, PUSH! D'you hearrr me?"
> It is my legs. They are braced so I won't get out. I won't GO OUT THERE. It is a wrong place and I don't want to go. I DON'T WANT TO GO!
> *My back has been hurting so bad this past week. That's what the pain in my back is coming from: force against force. My force against her force. I know there's a connection to this pain in my back.*
> "Something's wrong. It's allll wrong, dammit. I never seen the likes! The goddamn baby is in ass backwards!!"
> "DOOOO SOMETHING! DO SOMETHING NOW! FOR GOD'S SAKE, MAMA, DOOO SOMETHING!!!" It is my Mama screaming to her Mama. "Do something, Mama. Help me!"
> My Mama is dying of pain from the damn baby who is ass backwards and won't come out so she can stop hurting.

My own birth had been well attended, an easy one, in the hospital just behind the playing field and college dorms across the street from our house. My mother was thirty, my father thirty-two, when I was born; my older brother had his eighth birthday ten weeks before. Early in my adolescence I remember asking why Bill was so much older than me. (I'm pretty sure that's how I put the question. When you're a teenager the entire world is in cosmic arrangement with you at the center of it all. I can't picture having asked about why I was years younger than my brother; that would've established *him* at the starting point.) When I questioned her, Mom and I were sitting on the side porch shucking a pail of lima beans Dad had brought up from the garden. She said they'd tried to have another baby but she'd had a miscarriage several years before I was born. And then I finally came along just two days before Thanksgiving. She said it seemed the right holiday; they were awfully thankful.

Oddly enough a couple of things have popped up in these last few years to get me thinking more about when I was born and what had been happening in my parents' lives around the time of my entry into their world. It probably isn't "oddly enough" at all, come to think of it. I was almost through rereading the whole of JoAnn's material. She'd recently converted it to neatly typed pages from the massive hodge-podge of papers and pages and notebooks which had been such allies in her effort to write herself. At that point I had just started to see if I could gather up some words of my own on paper about what we'd been through in therapy, so JoAnn and her life were very much on my mind then. As was my own life. It was already hard for me to think about one of those lives without also thinking about the other.

Driving home one day after therapy, my therapy, I was dreamily reviewing the session I'd just had with Celia. We'd been talking about my childhood, especially as it compared to a number of JoAnn's experiences I was trying to write about. For some reason there in the car—I really don't know why—I fixed on birthdays. I'd always liked the fact my mother and I were born on the same day of the month, different months but the same day. Don't ask me why I'd felt that was such a neat thing; seems a silly fact to have been attached to for so many years. But, as I maneuvered to get home through rush hour traffic, in response to a curiosity I didn't know I had, I counted up the months between my mother's birthday and my birthday. I've no idea what possessed me to do that. Nine

LIKE AN UNSHED TEAR

months. It came to nine months exactly. I was thrilled, as if I'd received a present.

I called my parents soon afterward, no doubt sounding like a kindergartner with a handmade valentine. Wanting to share my new discovery, I told Mom I'd figured out I was born nine months after she turned thirty years old.

"Did you know that?" I asked her, tickled with my cleverness. "Nine months TO THE DAY after your THIRTIETH BIRTHDAY!"

"No, I never realized it," she said. "Is that right?" Then she gave a little chuckle. "I guess we must have celebrated that night."

There had been two things, then, I unearthed while picking my way home through traffic that evening. The second one had to do with finally understanding why I'd been so intrigued with our birthdays for as long as I could remember. I think I must have always sensed there was more to it than both of them simply falling on the twenty-sixth of the month. On that particular day's drive home I gave myself a gift with the idea that *my* birth might've started with a gift on *her* birthday.

At the end of that year another surprise came my way, still relating to this issue of how one is introduced to the world. For Christmas my mother gave me a soft-covered volume of 8½ × 11-inch paper which had been printed and bound at the College Press. There were 165 pages between bright red, plasticized paper covers; most of the pages were handwritten, some were typed. A Christmas card clipped to the inside of the front cover read:

Dec. 1989

Dear Rose Mary,
When I cleaned the front room closet this Spring I spotted a box I hadn't noticed before. In it were all the letters I had written Mother in 1940, 1941 and 1942 when she was working in Kinston, N.C.

Since they were on all kinds of paper I decided to copy them. At first it was for you, but Bill was such a part of the letters I had a copy made for him, too.

Hope you will enjoy reading this and realize all the
happy moments you gave us. You were two precious children. I'm awfully glad Mother thought so and saved the
letters.

Lots and lots of love,
Mom

The effect of all this on me was at once bright and shadowy. My first
and overwhelming response was to feel deeply treasured. This collection of my mother's correspondence (part of it about me, the new
baby) to her mother, found after nearly fifty years of safekeeping in
a box at the back of a little-used closet, placed me in a kind of
generational receiving line. Through these letters I was given a retro-
active introduction to my young mother, hardly viewed back then as
a person in her own right by the infant me. Her gift invited me to
share in the connection she had with my grandmother, living nearly
six hundred miles away during my first three years. She was teaching weaving then at a reform school to young students who were
wards of the state and frequently referred to in those days as "way-
ward girls."

The compilation of letters began with:

Dearest Mother,
Your *first* granddaughter arrived Nov. 26, 1940! At 2:58
P.M. in the Berea College Hospital.

Dr. Dodd delivered her, and his first words were, "She's
a nice plump little girl." He also told me she was thoughtful
to come at such a wonderful time. "She didn't keep the
nurses up all night," he said.

Wilson is excited to be here with her. Billy is spreading
the news far and wide among his friends. Wilson will keep
you posted.

Lots and lots of love from 4 of us,
Ellen

Mom's epistolary account of my early life (including stories of a
whopping appetite, being wheeled up the street in my buggy to visit
neighbors, first steps, etc.) was just one aspect of her correspon-

dence about their busy lives. Equal to my feeling cherished by reading about my arrival into the family, was receiving her gift so many
years later recounting those events. Spread out before me was a
feast, dished up in my mother's narrative of our lives during the first
few years of the 1940s.

Yet somehow I wasn't able to relish being at this banquet as an
epicure would have. For at the same time during those winter
months that year I was pouring through the newly retyped pages of
all JoAnn's writings and finding stacks of torturous memories which
had come up during her therapy seven or eight years before. Some
of those memories were about her earliest experiences of being not
wanted, of being locked in closets, shut out of the house, of crying
to be left alone, and of being frightened at being alone.

Racing across the pages in my head then were JoAnn's haunting
words. Phrases, whole sentences, so many words had left tracings I
couldn't erase:

   . . . I was just an hours' old baby when she pushed
me away . . .

   . . . In spite of all she could do I wouldn't miscarry
and go away. She was not able to dump me, but she tried.
"Damn you to hell," she shouted. "You ain't got no business
being. I wish you was gone! I DIDN'T ASK FOR YOU,
GODDAMMIT!!" she yelled, throwing me across the
bed . . .

   . . . Mama grabs my pigtails and PULLS. "Your Father? You never haddd no Father! He left before you were
ever borned. He never wanted you, stupid. I was the one
stuck with you, and NOT HIM!" . . .

In my new, bright red volume of collected letters I read about the
light blue bathrobe Grandma had sent for my second Christmas,
and how delighted with her choice Mom was because "your granddaughter looks so adorable wearing it." I couldn't shake my head
clear of another image:

. . . Grannie hit Mama back and forth across her face.
"You been sneaking in bed with your own father, ain't you?
Well, there's your reward, right there," and she pointed her
finger at me. "A Goddam Dummy! A crazy dummy kid that
nobody'd have! I should have drowned her, the little
dummy, and saved us a lot of trouble!" . . .

What explains that natal toss of the dice? Why does one of us end
up over here and the other wind up over there, maybe with skin
another color, certainly with different dispositions and preferences?
The words written forty-nine years earlier and now shimmering
from my mother's book would have been exquisitely comforting if
they hadn't bumped up against JoAnn's words, ironically written
about *her* birth forty-nine years earlier:

. . . It is my legs. They are braced so I won't get out. I
won't GO OUT THERE. It is a wrong place, and I won't go.
I DON'T WANT TO GO! . . .

Quite a few of JoAnn's recollections at this time were opening onto
her experiences of being left, feeling not wanted, abandoned. It's no
wonder those memories of endings included echoes of her begin-
nings. Since the first separation for each of us begins with our birth
the two events are inextricably linked.

17

ALONE IN TIMBUKTU

I don't know where I'm at. I'm lost.

Lost and all alone. I'm all by myself, in the tall grass across the road.

Across the road. I'm not suppose to go ACROSS THAT ROAD! And I know it, too. Unless Honey is with me. I start crying 'cause I just about scare myself to death. Honey done tole me right many times to not cross that road by myself, but I see a rabbit go hop, hop, hop over the road into that strawgrass field.

I remember when the Man showed me the box he put out to catch rabbits in, and he tole me to stay away from it.

"Not do to get too close, chile," he said. "Ol' Mr. Rabbit got such a good nose on him he be able to tell you been around, and then he stay way far away! We never be able to catch him then."

The Man tole me all about staying away from them rabbits, but mostly I remember hearing about that box, and I think maybe it's in that field where the rabbit's gone hopping to. Maybe I can see Mr. Rabbit hop hisself into our box and get caught!

So I go over there. I go even though I know not to do it. I go over there and can't find no rabbit box. Instead I get all turned around, can't see over the high grass. I'm so lost! I cry and yell and scream for Honey. I don't know what else to do. Then I see her come high stepping across the road and run right into the tall grass after me.

Honey grabs me up in her big ol' arms and tells me everthing be
okay now. She looks me over to make sure I ain't hurt.

I start to get all calm down now since she is find me and baby
me till I can be quiet. I tell her what I come looking for over here as
we head back to the house. We're crossing the road when Honey
slows down her fussing enough to get her breath back. I ask how
come she don't come when I call her.

"How come? HOW COME!! Well, Little Girl, lemme tell you
this thing right now. Hows you think I could come and getcha?
Hows you expect me to FIND you? Don't you think I done look
EVERWHERE YOU WAS SUPPOSED TO BE AT?!!! First thing, be-
fore I knowed where you had got to?! Do you hear me, Little Missy
Who Was At The Laaast Place I'd Ever Look 'Cause It Was Where
You Didn't Have One Bit A Business Being At? Huhmm, d'you hear
me now?

"Didn't I run my legs off a lookin' for you and a callin' for you?
How I'm suppose to know you done went and cross THAT ROAD?
You stand here and wanta know how come, HOW COME I not fly
over here and getcha?! Well, I tell you, Little Girl: the next time you
cross this road, the VERY NEXT TIME YOU TAKE A NOTION TO
CROSS THIS HERE ROAD . . . !"

Well, it's so bad she can't even say it. She just looks at me. She
can't even get any more words out.

Nosy me. When I ask her later what she's gonna do iff'n there's
a next time, Honey says she's gonna leave me there, that's what
she do! But I know she won't do it. She won't leave me, ever
ever.

We go back across the road where we belongs to be at, and
where Honey says we better STAY. She just can't believe I go across
that road by myself! Honey says "across that road" like it was Tim-
buktu or the Moon.

"Well," Honey tells me, "all I gotta say 'bout this is once burned
is twice warned!" And she lets me know she ain't a gonna put up
with no such trash as THIS.

She is pulling me along by my arm and saying she just like to
paddle my backside.

"I mean it, chile. Never think I see the day I be wantin' to do
that, but I not know what else to do witcha!"

We get home and Honey falls onto the porch step, still a holding my hand. She puts her other hand over her heart and says, "Lord, chile, I thought they's done gotcha!" Then she busts out crying.

I don't know what's wrong with her or what she's talking about.

Honey says she don't know what she'd a done iff'n she got over there and find them snakessss a crawling all over me. Oh, Honey do cry! Cry and cry, sob and rock and hold her face in her apron! I think her crying scares me about as bad as being lost way across the road.

Honey's busy putting supper on the table. Tells the Man if she was a betting woman she bet he never guess where at she done found "this chile" today. She sets the biscuits on the table.

He says, "BET?" Oh, his eyes get big when he hears that word. "Well, my Lord, chile, if she be willin' to make a bet, I reckon this here must be sumthin' I'd never ever guess!"

He says Grace before we eat, and they pass the food around. He butters us a biscuit, one for me and one for him, and we set to eat this good food what the Lord is done bless us with. It cross my mind while they're thanking the Lord that I don't feel like Honey thinks she's blessed with me today. But I don't worry too much; I know she loves me.

The Man bites into his biscuit, looks at me, looks at Honey, says he don't believe that chile do a wrong thing when she knows better. He talks soft and slow. He says, "Honey, is you sure *this* chile was the chile that did it?"

"Far as I can tell this here's the same chile," Honey says. She looks at me, "You the onlyest chile on this Place, ain'tcha, little girl?"

"Yessum. Yessum, I do believe I is." I look at the Man's chin so I don't start to laugh.

Honey tells him all about what done happen today. I tell him, too, and about how ascairt I got when Honey was crying so hard after she drag me home.

He 'splain how she's afraid a them snakes what live in the strawgrass across the road. When she can't find me anywhere, and hears me crying from that strawgrass field, well, she just *knowed* them snakes done got me!

I tell him how she hauls me home, sets herself down on the porch steps, and lays me over her knee! "She do, Man. She lays me over her knee and says, 'I'm gonna warm your little BEEhind for you, chile.' She paddles me real hard, Man. She don't do it with a stick or a belt, just with her hand, but ohhwweee she sure does fan my backside. Says she hopes I learnt my lesson!"

I tell him, "I not ever, ever, ever, no more cross that road, Mr. Man. Not even to see if the rabbit hop in the box. I promise. Cross my heart. Cross my heart, Man, but not cross that road!"

"Well, chile, I'se sure glad to see you done learn that thing. Reckon it be a sight easier on Honey, don'tcha think?"

"Oh, yessir. She won't have to worry no more about them snakes getting me. Honey don't like it when she can't find me, Man. I don't like it, neither either, when she can't find me. Oh, I sure learnt a lot today."

"You did, did you?"

"Yes, sir," I say, and keep a straight face. Me and Honey done cook it up how to tell him. "Yes, sir. I learnt it's a lot a hops between MR. RABBIT and the POT!"

He laughs and looks at me. "It don't look like you is any worse for the wear, is you, chile?"

I think for a bit. "No, sir, that's what I figure, too."

"And you learnt sumthin', didn't you?"

"Yes, sir," and I rub, rub my little ol' BEEhind what she done warm up pretty good when she got me back to home. "Yes, sir, I sure learnt something!"

✺

Honey sometime gets that I-ain't-messin'-around-witcha-chile tone in her voice, and I know I "better not do like that 'round here now." I know 'cause she tells me that lotsa times.

". . . Why? 'Cause I'se the Mommy, that's why, and I say that's the way it gotta be. I ain't talking just to hear myself talk, now am I? No, I is the Mommy here. Iff'n you wanta decide not to try and do better then we just gonna have a partin' of the ways."

She goes in the house, and I decide not to mess no more with her now. I take my raggity baby doll what has on a pretty little dress, I hold her up careful and I say, "You is about to get yourself into big troubles!"

I set her down by the bottom step and tell her to stay right there 'cause I ain't gonna put up with no more a that foolishness. It's washday and I got my work to do. "Lots of work to do today," I tell her.

I turn around and look at her real good from the washtubs where I'm fixing myself up. I stop my work and say I don't know what to do 'bout her! I shake my "ol' gray head" and wonder 'bout "what in the world is gonna happen to you iff'n you is keep on like THAT, now Little Missy What Not Try To Do No Better'n This Here Monkey Business. Now does you hear me?"

I hold Lu Lu Belle up and look right at her. "I is just gonna leave you right here to THINK ABOUT THIS THING NOW, CHILE!"

Honey's walking by the door about then and sees me out in the yard by the wash pot. I done got all that stuff on my face and arms and I'm talking sooo serious to that little baby doll.

Honey throws her hands up, runs down the steps to where I am and says, "My, my, my. Lord love you, chile. Lord love you, sweet baby!" She drops down on her knees and hugs me up all to pieces.

"I don't know what in the world to do witcha, chile," Honey says, and she cries and cries. She holds onto me and cries, and she gets all dirty. I wanta make her better, wanta fix her up, but I don't know nothing to do about her crying and getting so dirty. All that stuff I done rub on me, now it's all over her and I don't know what to do! She just holds onto me and cries and don't even mind that her nice clean dress gets all black from that stuff.

I hear her tell the Man all about it after she says I have to go on home. But I don't wanta go home so I come back and crawl under the house. Can still see my hand.

"I never seen such a sight in all my borned days!" Honey says.

It's not too dark that I gotta go home. Honey alla time says I gotta get on home 'fore it "be so dark you can't see your hand in front a your nose!" I hold my hand up and I still can see it okay.

"I tell you, Man, I wish you could a seen that chile! Why, it look like she fell down the CHIMLEY! That chile was nothin' but one big mess. Now, you know how hard it is to get soot off, don'tcha? . . . Well, I wipe most of it off, and throw that rag awaaayyy! I think I ain't ever gonna get that lil' girl clean. Have to rub her hard, Man. Hardest thing, though, was to keep from laughin'! I not do it, but I sure had a hard time keepin' from it."

He wants to know what she do, how she clean up that chile. "What I do? Wasn't nothin' else TO do but throw that chile in the washtub and scrub her clean! . . . with LYE SOAP! I tell her, 'Hold your nose and close your eyes tight, chile. Ol' soap get in your eyes, they be stingin' like the very devil hisself.' I scrub that chile all over, from head to toe, right there in that washtub. Why, I tell you, Man, she done make herself black as you or me. Got that soot right off the bottom a that ol' washtub, she did. Make a mess like you never seen! Whooowee, she is sumthin', that one is!"

Hank Foley had me by the ankle. He knew his strength was greater than mine; he knew I couldn't get away. I felt him laughing at me. This was just a game of cat and mouse for him, and he was getting charged up by it. I could feel it in him.

I had fallen asleep under a tree a little way from the house. It was one of those times I was just too tired to keep my guard up any longer. Somehow Grandpa sniffed me out while I was sleeping there. Soon as I felt him grab me I knew I had to come awake fighting, but he had both my ankles before I could even get in a good kick. I grabbed at grass to try and pull away, then turned and twisted to get free of his sickening smile. With all my might I tried to kick free and smash his damn face in.

He had me, though, and nothing I did mattered in the least. I was kicking and swinging but it didn't matter. Even if it had been on the dining room table that he raped me it wouldn't have mattered. The people in my family would have stared and kept on eating. And enjoyed watching "you get yours." No one would have seen or heard anything upsetting.

He had me. I knew it and so I quit. I quit fighting and lay as still as a step. Inside I *felt* myself kicking and screaming and throwing punches but I did none of it. I felt it all but I held it inside because I knew Grandpa and the others loved to see you fight, to watch you plead and be scared. Oh, the next best thing to some good white lightning was watching someone cry and beg for mercy.

While he yanked my pants off and pushed my legs apart I never moved. I was a lump, stone still. I never did nothing.

". . . ain't doing a goddam thing! You may as well be a rock, goddammit. What the hell's the matter with you, JoAnn?"

I made him so mad, so damn mad, all he could do was hit me to make me "do something." It didn't matter. I was gone. I knew I couldn't get away from him so I hid as usual, way deep inside. I just left my body alone there with the son of a bitching bastard and went far away.

I never moved at all. Just lay there like ice on a pond, cheating him out of his fun. He went crazy because he had worked so hard to sneak up on me and then I went and cheated him! He beat the pure hell out of me, hitting me like a man hits another man with his fists. So mad! So CHEATED!

Grandpa got his little piece all right but he was furious that I cheated him of any fun in it. I beat him in a way, though, in the only way I could. He hated me for it, too. His eyes let me know it. Those dead, flat, pig eyes that never had any feelings for another living thing showed their only sign of life when they filled up with his hate for me.

I was hurt bad from the beating he gave me. I hurt for weeks and weeks. My body finally healed but he never got over it. I don't think his so called "pride" ever healed at all. Hank Foley never saw me after that but what he remembered was how bad I had cheated him. I could see it in his hate-filled eyes.

※

Honey ain't happy with me.

"If the Old-Fashioned Truth is starin' SOMEBODY [she means me] in the face, and that person don't pay attention, well I got no truck with such a PERSON [she still means me] as that!"

She walks on off. Waits. Says she done give me plenty a time.
She goes off a little bitty bit, then looks back at me. I look under my
eyes at her, and rub the sand with the flat part of my hands.

I'm sitting down. Mad 'cause she done walk away and leave me
there. She tells me the two of us is gonna go to war less'n I get aholt
a myself. First I rub one hand in the sand, then I rub the other one.
Both of 'em. She called it dirt! I tell her she's a dumb nigger on
account of she don't know a thing. Don't even know this is SAND!
The Man would say the same thing as me, I tell her. He knows it's
SAND.

Me and the Man's walking. I tell him, "Then she says to me, 'I go
'bout my work and not bother you while you make up your mind if
you wanta try and BEEhave.' And that old woman walk on off and
LEAVE me. She leave me right there! She do that thing, Man. Honey
knows I don't like her to do that! Makes me mad when she go off
and leave me."

"She did do that? Hmmmmuunnhhh," the Man say.

I hold his hand and I walk two steps, hop around in the sand
and tell him about the nerve a that Honey. She knows I don't like
her to do me that way.

"You think maybe she not like you to pitch such a fit as that,
humhh?" he say.

He don't think much a no such fit throwing as that, I can tell.

I'm mad at Honey 'cause she says I best better think about
what I wanta do while she goes off and leaves me alone. I say I tell
on her.

"I'm gonna tell that Man soon's he comes home. Sure as the
world I'm gonna tell him him on you, Honey. He gonna hit you for
that, Honey!"

He stops walking and looks at me. "Lord, is that what you tole
her? What'd she say to that?"

"She say, 'Chile, who do you think you be talkin' to? We gonna
settle this thing right now, once and for all 'cause I plum ain't gonna
put up with no such carryin' on. I not wanta bother with you while
you be thinkin' on this!'

"She reach down, pick up the bucket, and LEAVE me! She plum

leave me there. She's bad for doing that, ain't she, Man? Do me like that!"

"Honey do that? My, my. She do that, chile? Hhumm-muummm. That ain't like Honey. Not like her to be so mean to you, is it? You think maybe sumthin' you say to her done set her off? . . . Ohhh! Well, chile, you gotta 'spec her to get mad iff'n you cuss her out and call her names. She don't like no such fit as that. You don't think much a her leavin' you, and she don't think much a fits like that. Guess I better leave you two womens to settle this thing by yourselfs."

We walk along. We just be quiet. I'm thinking.

"Whatcha 'spec happen now, Man?"

"Lord, chile, I don't know what's gonna happen next. Time onlyest thing can tell what happens."

We walk along a ways more.

"Whatcha figure MIGHT could happen, Man?"

I hear that he don't know what's gonna happen, but I wanta know what he figures on being best to do about this thing.

"I 'spec she do the best thing when she tell you to think 'bout it. You think 'bout sumthin' and figure it out for yourself, chile. Only-est way."

Honey's mad at me and I don't like it. I don't want to leave this Place either. What am I gonna DO?

"Honey means what she says, Man. Alla time she's telling me to THINK ABOUT THIS THING. Well, how come I got to think about this thing alla time? Let HER think about this thing! Just let her go think about it her own self, Man! She don't ever tell HERSELF to go think about something!!"

"She don't, huh?"

"No she don't, Man! She alla time tells me:

'I THINK YOU JUST BETTER THINK 'BOUT THAT THING, CHILE!!'

'BEST THING BE FOR YOU TO THINK ON THAT NOW!'

'I RECKON YOU BETTER THINK THIS THING OVER, LITTLE GIRL!' She says that to me alla time, Man."

"She do? Lordy me, chile, you sure do sound like that woman. Yep, you sure got that down pat! . . . Well, you know, don'tcha, that you ain't the onlyest one she talks to like that? She talks to me like that, too, you know!"

"She do??? Whatcha say when she do that, Man?"

"Well, I go off and I think 'bout it. Most usually I just take her advice. She's right lotsa times, chile. Plum right. . . . I tell you she's one right smart woman, she is."

"Well, Man, I don't think she has to be right EVERY, EVERY time!! Do you?"

"She be right good at thinkin' on these things, and she figures out most things purrrtty good. Course now I don't think she has to be right ALL the time. . . . Still, chile, I believe you could do a heap worse than pay attention to that ol' woman."

I try and 'splain to him again how she sounds to me.

". . . No, you be purely mad with her now, chile. You best hold your tongue. Don't pay to be talkin' bad when you're mad like this. . . . Why, chile, I can see you're mad. Ain't I got eyes in my head? It don't be too easy 'round here when the two womens on the Place be havin' their disagreement. Course these things bound to happen. No way 'round it in this ol' world, chile. . . . But it do seem like a shame to let this go on, and you be a hurtin' so."

He's crazy. "I ain't hurting, Man. Honey never hit me."

"Yes, yes, you is, baby. Course she don't hit you, but you're still a hurtin'. Honey, too. She's hurt bad, too, 'bout this thing. Sure seems like you women got your hands full this time."

We stop a minute and he pitches a rock outa the yard. I look over at the house.

". . . Lord, seem like a shame, chile, how some things work out so bad for everybody. . . . Naw, chile. I can't tell you what to do 'bout this thing. You know I can't get in between you and that woman. Got enuff just to figure out my own self. Naw, I 'spec you be best off to think 'bout this and figure it out for yourself. . . . Well, maybe she be sorry, too, chile."

"I don't think so, Man. She says she make 'arrangements' about me . . ."

"She say that?"

"Yep, she say that to me, Man!"

"Well, I don't 'spec she means it, do you? 'Spec she was kinda sorry she talk like that to you."

"You think so? Honey alla time says she don't ever talk just to hear herself. You know that, don'tcha?"

"Well, yes. Still, all of us say things once in a while that we don't really mean when we calm down. Why, don'tcha think YOU ever say sumthin' once in a while that you don't mean? . . . Well, I reckon it be the same way with Honey. She probly be a thinkin' she like to have you in there helpin' her get that supper on the table."

"You think so, Man?"

"Well, I could be wrong . . . but don't 'spec be any harm iff'n you was to step in there and see. Course you don't wanta do that, be just fine. You best be doin' what YOU wanta do. You the best one to figure that out!"

I know Honey's mad at me. I don't wanta leave this Place, and I don't want her to be mad at me neither either. Ohhh, I don't like this.

". . . You gonna go without your supper, chile?" The Man turns to look at me. "You leavin' now? I be sorry to see you go so early. Sure you not stay till after suppertime? Smells pretty good, don't it?" He wiggles his nose and smells supper cooking.

What am I gonna do about this? I think I sure like to go in there, see how Honey's doing.

I go up the steps, just kinda slow. Honey's standing at the stove, and I go a little bit in the door.

I tell her I'm sorry. I tell her as pretty as you please. She's SO glad!

She says that's okay. "That's okay 'cause now you try not to throw them fits again. Okay, baby? We gonna forget 'bout that fit, and nobody gonna do like that again, okay?!"

Now it's all right. I won't do that no more. And I'm happy I come back. Honey's so glad, too.

The man grabs my arm. He is mad and getting madder all the time. Through his teeth he tells me that I'm going to deliver or he'll know the reason why!

He had thought he had it made, and here I am disappointing him. He doesn't like it one little bit either.

He grabs me. I pull away and tell him I hadn't promised him a thing. I say it in the kind of tough and smart-mouthed way I hear the others talk. "I promised you NOTHING, you hear me! And that's what you get. Nothing but NOTHING!!"

We look at each other. I'm scared, talking big like that, but I don't let on to him. It's like I do at home. I know not to let anybody see when I'm afraid. I can feel him, the soldier, and I know he is not a fighter. Not a bad one, anyway.

I try to calm him down and tell him it isn't too late for him to TRY AGAIN. He can try again with someone else if he goes now, I tell him. I see he is thinking about it.

"Try your luck again, soldier boy, with another girl," I say.

He slumps back a little against the booth. I have won. But only because he doesn't know what to do. He doesn't want trouble; he just wants a girl.

The soldier doesn't know where he's going to be sent to, or when, or if he'll be back ever. He's just a scared little boy. And he is sober. Flat sober. I know that makes a lot of difference. Any time or any place that makes a powerful lot of difference.

He looks at me and says, "Listen to me, girl. You better listen good if you got any sense."

His tone is not threatening, not like all the Foleys. He leans over toward me. "One of these days you're going to get your pretty ass caught in a crack and you'll be in a heap of trouble. You're playing with fire, you know. And someday you're going to get all burnt up. Yeah, you'll be in a bad fix, little girl. One you can't talk yourself out of as easy as this. A bad fix, girl, a real bad fix."

I listen to him. Something in his tone, some concern in his voice, I think, draws me into the words.

"One of these days," he tells me, "if you keep on like this, somebody is going to MAKE YOU PUT UP. Not me. No, there's too many willing ones around this joint for me to bother you. But somebody won't take 'No' for an answer one of these times. And then where will you be at, girl? Up to your backside in trouble, and you'll have asked for it, too!"

He tells me I better go home until I grow up. He puts some change on the table and starts to slide out of the booth. "Take my advice, girl, and stay out of here till you're full growed. You shouldn't be allowed in here to start with!"

Instead of just backing down, he looks right at me and tells me I'll get in big trouble if I don't watch out. He scares me, this young soldier, and I start to cry. I think I cry when he says that because he's saying the very thing I was already scared to death of: some day I wouldn't be able to get out of the fix I was in. And then where would I be? There wouldn't be any help out there, I knew that much. I sit there while huge, silent tears roll down out of my eyes.

The boy sees me crying as he's sliding out. He stops and looks at me. He leans down close to in front of me.

"Why, you're just a baby! What in the hell do them people think, letting you loose like this?"

It is the makeup and the clothes. They are too old for me, too grown up. He studies me from under a frown. "Girl, how old ARE you? And don't lie to me."

I don't answer. He takes a handkerchief out of his pocket. He says, "You listen to me now. I'll tell you something your mother ought to have told you. Don't you EVER do this again!! I'm telling you this like as if you were my own sister. You get your friends now and get yourself HOME. And you stay there!

"Ah, girl, girl, you got no idea what's going on, do you? You take yourself out of here and DON'T YOU EVER COME BACK. Not to this joint or any other one. This ain't no place for a decent girl, much less a baby. Do you hear me? You better never let me see your face here again. Goddammit, I mean what I say!"

He did, too. He was sickened to see a young girl painted up and dressed like a cheap whore. I can't quite picture him in my head now. I hadn't known him from before and I never knew his name. He was just a soldier boy being fed through the war machine at Fort Benson. But he was real and he told me the truth. I felt it then and still do. He had thought I was just playing hard to get. The tears did it. They scared him. He had looked in my eyes carefully and was scared for me.

"If you act like a tramp and dress like a tramp, you have to expect you'll be TREATED like a tramp." He looked at the way I was dressed, touched the sleeve I could tell he didn't like. "You're a GIRL and should DRESS LIKE A GIRL, in a decent girl's dress! Not in this rag," and he dropped the sleeve from his fingertips.

The soldier had handed me his handkerchief and told me to wipe the cheap makeup shit off my face. He'd warned me that I better stop advertising what I wasn't willing to sell.

"Well, that's my Boy Scout good deed for the day," he said with a half-laugh. "You get your ass home and wash that gook off your face. You don't need it no more. Put some decent girl's clothes on and act like a real little lady so men know what you are. Promise me now you'll do it."

He peeled some paper money off a few folded-over bills. "Take this and get the hell out of here. Don't come back, you hear, or else I'll make you sorry as hell you ever did!"

I hippy hop, hippy hop right along. I'm going to Honey's house. I gonna tell her I'm a bunny rabbit. Maybe I show her I'm a goose. I come outta the woods and stop. Something's not right; it's all changed. The door is shut! Suppose to be open but it's SHUT. It scares me.

The Place feels different and I don't know what it is. I don't see her. I DON'T SEE HER ANYWHERES!! What's wrong? I tighten up . . .

I'm so afraid, I bang on the door like as if the very devil hisself is after me. I scream, "Lemme in, LEMME IN!!"

I'm ascairt. Oh, oh I is losted. I'm locked out and she is gone and left me. She's gone.

Gone and left me!

Left me and gone to New York!!!

Grannie's full of cry-words again.

"Shut up, goddammit! Your Mama didn't want you, so now I'M stuck with you. . . . You want to know what happened? I'll TELL you what happened. The bitch took off and left you here, that's what happened. Left you for me to look after. Well, don't matter that she's gone 'cause she never did shit around here anyhow. You just better toe the line now or you'll be sorry as hell! You ain't mine, you know, and I don't have to put up with you. So just you remember that!"

Oh, she was mad. She had enough of her own to look after, to put up with, and she sure as hell didn't need to be stuck with me, she said. She was furious with Mama for dumping me on her, and I knew this time was different than when Mama just went out to have a little fun at night.

This time Mama had gone off to New York, to get a job and see the World's Fair. Grannie yelled at me, "YOU BETTER BEHAVE 'CAUSE I DON'T HAVE TO TAKE CARE OF YOU!"

It was a lie Mama told me. All of it was a lie. I'd heard them talk and had asked her, but Mama had said no, she wasn't leaving me.

She lied. I could tell, but I hoped I was wrong. I came home, walked in the house and asked Grannie, "Where's she at?"

"Don't ask me where she's at! SHE'S GONE! Your Mama left and she ain't never coming back. She's gone and forgot you, so you just better LEARN TO MIND ME, JOANNN!!! I ain't spoiling you like your Mama did! I ain't got time to be bothered with you." Grannie held a log pointed at me, a piece of wood cut for the stove. "You do like you're told around here or I'll knock the hell outta you. I ain't gonna take it easy on you like Hank and your Mama. It's about time somebody around here taught you a thing or two!"

I screamed and screamed and cried for Mama. Grannie couldn't get me to stop. I didn't understand all she was saying, but I think I knew it meant that now I had no one. Not even a mother who could barely stand to be around me.

Mama went up to work in New York in 1939, when the World's Fair was there. She lived with Grannie's sister in N.Y. and got a job there as a maid. I used to sit out by the mailbox and wait for a letter from her. After three months she came back because the job hadn't worked out. In one entire summer she never wrote or called me. She said she knew I was all right, and she didn't have time to bother with writing. Besides, she knew Grannie would take care of me. I was a fool, a pure fool, to sit by the mailbox and wait for a letter that wasn't ever going to come.

. . .

"Honey, open the DOORRRRR!!!"

I don't yell and scream. I feel it but I don't do it. Inside of me is a terrible scream, but all to show how I feel is I knock a little bit too hard.

She opens the door.

Honey says, "Good Lord, chile. You'se in a hurry, ain'tcha? You just 'bout scare me to death. . . . Why, no, I didn't hear you comin'. Didn't even hear you on the steps. . . . Ooowhee, you is cold, chile. Lord, your teeth is chatterin' sumthin' terrible."

It was too cool this morning, she says, and that's why she has the door closed. When she went out to milk the cow it was pretty cold. She was right glad to get back in the house, 'deed she was. Right chilly out there. Right chilly.

Honey tells me to go on up to the stove; be nice and warm right up beside the stove. She'll keep the fire up a little longer till I is all fixed. It'll be warm when the sun comes up good. But till then it's cool enough to have a fire in the stove of a morning now.

"We need to warm you up, chile. You is shakin' like a leaf. What's a matter with you, chile?"

I don't answer her 'cause I *can't* answer her. There just ain't any words that come out.

Honey says, "Come here, chile," and holds an arm out to me.

I can feel me close down. I don't go over there. I hold my hands out to the stove. Make her think I need to get warm. I shake and shake. Even my head starts to shake. My teeth make noise; I don't know it is chatter-noise, but it is. I shake all to pieces just like when Grannie or Mama grabs my shoulders to SHAKE SOME GODDAM SENSE INTO YOUR STUPID DUMMY HEAD!!

Honey didn't grab me or hit me. She just had the door closed for the first time since I'd started sneaking away to come see her and the Man. And she hadn't heard me come up on the porch and scream for her to open the door. Nobody could have heard my screams. I thought they were deafening, those sounds of panic, but they were so deep inside only I could hear them.

. . .

Don't Leave Me!

There it is. Since time began for me it has been there, this cry to not leave me.

Don't Touch Me!

And that's the other terrible but silent scream inside me, ignored by all in my family for as long as I lived with them.

Don't leave me! Don't touch me!

Which came first, I wonder? I'm not sure, but I think they came at almost the same moment.

18

THE PLOTS THICKEN

Stress, I've heard, is our response to the amount of change taking place in our lives within a fixed period of time. It doesn't matter if we experience the change as coming from the outer world or from inside, nor whether the change is perceived as negative or positive. Either one and either way necessitates making adjustments, causing stress.

While that definition impressed me enough to remember having deposited it in my shrinking memory bank almost twenty years ago, back then I recall thinking it sounded awfully mechanical and simplistic. Even though I marvel at someone's ability to explain an experience or complex function in a definitive sentence or two, I have a rampant, almost reflexive, urge to look for exceptions to any neat and quotable pronouncement. Of course there's plenty of spite in this on my part because, for me, things are rarely simple. A part of me is desirous of such simplicity, and I both envy and distrust those who find the world that way.

Despite my rebel stance at being told C always follows A and B, that definition of stress nevertheless kept returning to my mind as JoAnn and I wound our way through her therapy during a time when she again started to bear down on her past. Just prior to this period, though, there was a brief couple of months of a bit more reflection and a little less memory-saturation and writing. I'm not sure how she experienced the respite, but I welcomed it. I often urged her to ease up on the pace and intensity she brought to what she was doing since I thought time was needed to integrate the material and process the insights lighting up her psyche's switchboard. At least to *me* it felt needed.

So during this month or two JoAnn appeared to let up on the accelerator for a short while. We talked then about many things: how much more she was relying on her intuition, her bone-deep pleasure in understanding previously puzzling behavior and attitudes, what she was learning about her capabilities. We spent a few gentle hours exchanging our discoveries about the wondrous nature of the mind as we witnessed its powers from our respective vantage points. In stepping back to recognize and appreciate the distance she had traveled, JoAnn cautiously gave her first verbal gifts to me. Perhaps the sentiments were coolly abstract but the feedback was unmistakably supportive and encouraging.

Internal pressure built once more after she'd apparently rested and gathered her resources. Not surprisingly, JoAnn's pleasure with all the changes she could see in herself remained mostly in the cognitive realm. Since a good part of those changes had to do with an expanding capacity to experience sadness, actually *feeling* her ancient melancholia appropriately overshadowed her appreciation of now being *able* to feel it.

She began recalling still-opaque scenes about her separation from Honey and the Man. She knew she'd been told they couldn't see her anymore, that she wasn't supposed to go back there. For a while the images were ill-defined; she didn't want to, or wasn't ready to, remember. Tears, she said, would roll up to the edge but never quite fall. In addition, her present life was also resonating at the frequency of grieving. It would be hard to say exactly where the reverberations were first felt, but certainly her old and newly acknowledged losses served to amplify each other.

Peg continued to fail. And to rail against her fate with a vitriolic anger JoAnn had difficulty handling. If there was any contact between them, she was the one to initiate it until, over the months that followed, she slowly backed away. From co-workers she kept up with reports of Peg's condition; the women with the health bulletins visited Peg and then passed along the news at the office. That alliance surprised JoAnn at first. In the past she and Peg never had much to do with this group—they were people only made happy by talking about how miserable they were. Now Peg was inviting them to stop by her house after work, while continuing to avoid her old friend.

Rather than be hurt by this or feel rejected, JoAnn was curious. What had once been considered an asset of hers, she realized, was not valued in the current situation. She understood that Peg no longer wanted her bluntness, her view of the world, maybe instead feeling more comfortable around others convinced of life's unfairness. JoAnn spoke about all this with clear-eyed detachment, not a trace of emotion anywhere evident. Except she talked at great length about it, returning repeatedly to this subject of Peg's illness. There were things she still didn't understand about why her attention had been seized by an old friend's avoidance of her.

Also while Peg was withdrawing, a former neighbor died, an elderly woman who was once quite involved in JoAnn's life. She first mentioned her at a session, about a year into therapy, by saying Gladys had contacted her about coming back to the area for a visit (she had lived three houses down the street before moving to Florida five years earlier). JoAnn was anything but enthusiastic about the idea. But Gladys had been not well for a time and now wrote she was recently feeling strong enough to make the trip; there were some business matters to settle and she wanted to see a few people, Danny especially. At the time of the planned trip I think JoAnn saw the visit as an intrusion which would interfere with the psychological dig she longed to complete. And yet while her words might have dismissed someone as an inconvenience or annoyance, I already knew enough about her style back then to realize if she spent any of her session's time on a subject it was much more important than first met the eye. Or than probably she herself sometimes even knew.

Gladys had been an unhappy, dependent, and childlike woman for as long as JoAnn had known her. Never having had children of her own, she seemed to have come alive when Danny was born. Even though JoAnn hadn't cared much for Gladys, she could sense this lonely woman's delight in the new baby on the block. It came at a good time for both the baby and his mother for JoAnn was seriously depressed then, merely going through the motions of attending to Danny. In truth she was thoroughly without energy or interest in taking care of her baby. But Gladys was there, perhaps finally with a reason for being.

After JoAnn went to work a year or two later when Wesley said their budget insisted on the need for her to get a job, Gladys became the official baby-sitter. She was, JoAnn admitted, Danny's surrogate mother for several years. It was all he had for quite a while. When Gladys's husband died during this period, it may be that Danny was all she had, too. If there was any positive side for JoAnn in the situation, I think it was that at least she'd found someone who was devoted to her young son, who was able to give him what she couldn't at the time.

This arrangement continued until Danny was about five and JoAnn began feeling bothered by things she noticed in the interaction between her son and Gladys. She learned the energetic, curious child all too often couldn't go outside because he'd been told it was too hot, that he mustn't stay out with his little friends so long because it might rain or was too windy. She spoke of her concern with Dr. Cunningham, the psychiatrist she was then seeing. Based on her description of those interactions, Dr. Cunningham said it sounded like Danny's baby-sitter was continuing to relate to him as if he was still a baby, that maybe he was being infantilized. The picture took shape for JoAnn when she recognized that Gladys adored babies but had become uncomfortable with Danny's expressing his own personality and asserting his independence. The next day she found someone else to look after him.

Considering how emotionally shut down she was then, I doubt if the sudden transfer of Danny's care to an unfamiliar figure was handled with much sensitivity, at least with regard toward her son. Because she was more sensitive to good manners than personal feelings, she found a gracious way out of the arrangement with her neighbor. JoAnn reported the event as if there had been nothing more to it than correcting a mistake when an error was detected. Her response was completely typical: if something is wrong or doesn't work, you fix it.

Still Gladys continued to see Danny frequently and be involved in his life, though no longer as a primary caretaker. She moved away when he was ten years old, staying in touch through remembering his birthdays and special occasions. When JoAnn first brought up the story of Gladys and her impending visit, I had asked about Danny's feelings toward his former baby-sitter. She said he was fond of her, but didn't think he'd had any problems with her having moved away.

Perhaps she was right, although once again I wasn't very trusting of her reading of Danny's emotions—especially concerning someone to whom she had much more of an aversion than an attachment. Since his father had moved out of the house and his parents had gotten divorced after Gladys moved away, I told her to make sure Danny was given the chance to see Gladys and say good-bye before she returned to Florida. It was likely, I thought, this might be the last time they saw each other. I'm a believer in the importance of saying good-bye, if you can.

JoAnn made sure, during Gladys's visit, that Danny got to see her. He had wanted to, as it turned out, which surprised her. Years later she told me that she, too, had also made a point of saying good-bye to Gladys then. It was the first time she ever remembered actually saying good-bye to anyone.

Now, a little over a year later, she learned Gladys had died. She spoke at some length about her, trying to figure out—in yet another relationship—why it mattered. Why was she spending so much time on this woman? Consciously she didn't even like Gladys, never felt they had anything in common except caring about Danny, never had enjoyed being around her. On paper, though, her Unconscious was unveiling a written world of still-hazy impressions: of hearing Honey crying and looking frighteningly abject, eviscerated of spirit; of learning she herself had to go home to the Foleys, back home to her family. These memories raised questions about what the connection was between Gladys and Honey in all this, for the two women surely couldn't have been less similar.

Halfway through February I told my patients I'd be away for two weeks in the middle of March. JoAnn was one of the people I was seeing then who didn't react to this news. Since there were so many things she was dealing with, a week or two later I mentioned she could call Bev (who'd been her other group therapy leader) if she needed to talk while I was away. She had nothing to say about any of this until the last ten minutes of our last session before my vacation; she stated she'd decided to leave therapy, and this would be our last appointment. She was worn out from the work on herself, she explained, but thought she had enough understanding of the process to go ahead with it on her own now.

It's an understatement to say I was knocked off stride. The end of a therapy session is the perfect time for lobbing an emotional grenade; there's not enough time left to explore the motivation or clean up the mess. I tried for an abbreviated dialogue that didn't satisfy either of us, and had to settle for insisting on at least a final appointment when I got back. JoAnn was noncommittal. While I made a display of writing the appointment in my schedule as we talked, there was no indication from her that she intended to commit the time to memory. She thanked me for helping her, was glad to have had the chance to work with me, and thought it had greatly benefited her. Good-bye and have a good vacation.

I was stunned—which obviously even happens to people who've seen and heard just about everything. I'd thought we had more of a relationship than was warranted by that kind of ending. To her departing back as she walked down the hall, I thought, "Well, at least you're getting more practice saying good-bye."

And of course that's what this was about. Yet my knowing it to be the case still offered only a whisper of comfort. Within the therapy exchange, as in all relationships life offers, the trick is being able to separate personal responsibility from projection. It isn't always clear which part of an interaction hinges on one's own participation and what comes from the other person. I stewed off and on for the rest of the day, knew better than to take it personally but did for a while anyway.

Thankfully, when I'm on vacation I have the ability to *be* on vacation. I'm sure that uneasy ending trekked across my attention a few times over those two weeks but I had a wonderful visit with friends in Florida nevertheless. We went out shrimping in their boat on the Intracoastal Waterway almost every day for a week, catching enough shrimp to eat our fill, prepared in a variety of ways both simple and elegant. For someone raised in a landlocked region who's been trout fishing maybe a dozen times, I'd never thought much about shrimp outside their being in a restaurant or a market. They've always been a treat to me so, like making a salad of home-grown vegetables, being involved in actually catching what I ate meant this was something I enjoyed in taking personally; it provided a rare link in the customary food supply chain I usually didn't think about.

When I got back to the office one of the messages waiting for me amid memos and minutes of meetings was a confirmation from JoAnn stating she'd be at our appointment later that afternoon.

She started the session by saying the day after I left she knew her decision to leave treatment was premature. These had been diffi-cult days for her and she was worn down to the bottom of her reserve tank, stranded in memories of being abandoned. No, she didn't see that any of it had to do with me. Well, maybe she could *see* how there might be some connection but she didn't *feel* any. She'd never regarded me as other than a professional helper, and if she couldn't talk with me then she'd find someone else.

For the next several weeks she didn't go to work; instead she was assailed by waves of nausea, her whole body awash in pain. At the end of one of those weeks I got a call in West Virginia around noon on a Friday morning from the clinic saying JoAnn had just phoned and asked if a message could be forwarded to me. It wasn't an emergency but please call her if I could.

Reiterating, when I reached her, that it wasn't an emergency, she wanted to know if I'd be willing to keep all her notebooks and papers for a while. She denied feeling suicidal or self-destructive but just needed to know all her writing would be safe in case something happened to her.

"Something like what?" I asked.

"Nothing," she answered. "I'm sure nothing's going to happen. But just to be safe, would you?"

"Of course I would. Now tell me what's going on."

More of her recollections were slipping into focus, she said. Not only was she realizing that indeed her mother and aunts were all prostitutes but that she had been, too. Like them, she had "gone to work for the family" at about the age of eleven or twelve. What concerned her most was being unable to remember a huge chunk of time from those years.

"I think something awful must have happened," she said into the phone, "and I won't let myself know it. I think I'm afraid to know it."

Next Tuesday she brought to her session a brown paper grocery bag stacked to the top with all her papers. I said I'd take care of them until she wanted them back. We talked about her suspicion that during those still-blank years she'd done things at odds with her value system.

"I guess my Brain doesn't want to know what went on then, and the Child in me doesn't want to go through the pain of discovering any more."

"My hunch is if there's something important for you to know, you'll get to it when you're ready," I told her. "So far, that's always what's happened."

I believed that to be the case but I didn't know it for a fact. JoAnn was the only client I'd had up to then who had pushed this hard against the edge of the unknowns in her life. I believed she knew more about how it worked than I did, but I also realized when we're in the middle of something we often have no perspective on it. We all need reminding occasionally of what we know to be our truth. About all I could do was reflect back to her a central lesson her therapy was already disclosing.

During one of her sessions about a month later, JoAnn made a throwaway reference to being at the hospital—only it wasn't said with that much clarity. When I finally heard the comment, after it had passed by in the flow of her words, I stopped the conversation long enough to ask what she was talking about. This was an all too familiar and frustrating way I got information; sometimes we had sharply different ideas about what was important. I had to listen carefully to catch the thrown-aside lines which only functioned for JoAnn as the skeleton of two-by-fours over which she constructed each verbal edifice. No doubt I failed to pick up on many such comments over the years we worked together while I was listening attentively to what *she* believed to be relevant.

In this instance, though, I asked about the hospital reference. If I hadn't stopped her then, most likely I'd never have found out she went to the Emergency Room with chest pains while I was on vacation. Since the tests came back negative for a heart attack she didn't think the episode was worth recounting.

But I thought it was a statement, among other things, about the level of stress in her life. And maybe a commentary on the depth of her grieving. It certainly was another verification of the chasm between her emotions and her body. Although she still appeared quite self-contained when we talked, her writing was sounding as if her heart had indeed shattered. She kept speaking of "when Honey left me." Despite describing the reality of her family moving hastily away from their crowded house down the road from the old couple, she was unwavering in her perception of the situation having been that of ". . . when Honey left me."

Losing Honey and the Man and losing the refuge of their home meant JoAnn was left with nobody but her family. Yet being isolated with her family was worse than if she'd been left with nobody. She couldn't keep them away; there was no protection. To be pulled from the comforting arms of Honey and thrown into the grip of her family was to shift emotionally from having been deserted to being snared. Her sessions and notebooks were packed with sets of images that seemed to ride in tandem: seeing Honey sitting on the porch and sobbing into her apron as they said good-bye to each other— then being poked, touched by unfeeling hands, pushed aside; walking away from the Place after hearing she had to leave, afraid to look back—being powerless to get away from grabbing, probing fingers, growing nearly mute with rage, fearful of losing control; sneaking back, against the Man's directive, to watch a dispirited Honey from the edge of the woods—getting beaten, being forced, having a sense of her own dispiriting helplessness.

"Don't leave me! Don't touch me!" she had written several months earlier, voicing the conflicting feelings from her infancy. Now those cries once again caromed off fresh memories, this time not to do with her birth as much as with a sense of a part of her dying, of being unable to keep the vultures from carrying off her heart.

One afternoon Wesley angrily phoned JoAnn to say he had to go bring Danny home from Ocean City. Their son, while spending a weekend at the beach with a family from his old neighborhood, had been picked up by the police for possessing marijuana. Danny maintained his friend and the other boys with them had run off when they caught sight of the cops coming; they all got away and left him—quite literally—holding the bag. He said they'd stuffed the cigarettes in the pocket of his jacket just before hightailing it out of there. His friend's parents were furious and said he'd have to call his father. The police said if Danny's father came to get him they wouldn't press charges.

JoAnn couldn't believe it. Not the part about Danny getting picked up by the police; somehow that had suddenly shone light enough on a backward look to help her finally understand many of the changes in him. The part she found hard to believe, and one of the most troubling aspects of the whole business, was how skillfully Danny disavowed any responsibility and how eagerly his father denied the existence of any problem.

Now when I'd meet her in the waiting room before our sessions began, she'd most likely be reading a book from the library about drug abuse or addiction. She went again to some Al-Anon meetings. I didn't know until then that she had attended Al-Anon for nearly three years back when she found out her oldest child had a drinking problem and was probably an alcoholic.

During one of the last times she visited Peg, while they were catching up with news about each other's families, JoAnn shared how upsetting it was to realize, after his brush with the police in Ocean City, that Danny had been using drugs. Peg had no sympathy at all. In fact she thought he should've gone to jail. He was asking for it; as far as she was concerned if a kid breaks the law he should pay the price. Once again JoAnn said she could hardly believe her ears.

Peg went on to talk about how unfair it was that people like Danny, who bend the rules for years, eventually get away with breaking the law while other people who lead good lives and never do anything against society end up struck down through no fault of their own. She certainly didn't deserve the hand she'd been dealt, and couldn't accept how Danny ended up with the better cards.

JoAnn talked about all this with controlled intensity. It was unfathomable to her that Peg would speak of Danny with such anger. At first I thought this was a mother bear protecting her cub. And that may have been part of it. But later I understood she was primarily trying to cope with her own sadness that this fifteen-year-old was choosing to deal with his life by using drugs. It didn't take a Ph.D., she kept saying, to figure out there had to be reasons a child would do this. Couldn't Peg see that? Why condemn a child for his self-destructive behavior, she kept asking, and not look at the forces which shaped him? After the time spent studying her own history, she knew something about what had shaped him.

I'm not sure exactly when it was, in the course of her therapy, JoAnn began to talk about the time around and after Danny's birth. That pregnancy, she said, had been extremely difficult. It happened during a period when she was nearly drowning beneath the smooth surface and calm appearance of her days; she was miserably unhappy with her life and becoming ever more depressed. Wesley was unhappy with her life, too. He said she wasn't the way a wife should be anymore. She agreed with him, knowing she wasn't the way *anybody* should be.

They had been two lost children who found each other and got married, almost twenty years before. In the time since then they'd simply grown into two wraith-like adults. JoAnn still hadn't excavated her past, so she was literally lost in a marriage that existed above the overgrown and hidden ruins of her childhood.

Wesley was content with things as long as his authority remained unquestioned. For her part, she didn't know there was anything which warranted a question; she had slipped, completely unaware, from the house of one despot to another. The unimaginable happened when JoAnn finally acknowledged to herself an idea found scurrying around the seams of her activities that suggested she could possibly live apart from Wesley. She didn't speak of this to anyone at the time, though later wondered if she may have somehow communicated that things within her were changing. What she noticed was Wesley suddenly showing an interest in expanding their family. Just at the point of forming a plan to leave her husband, she became pregnant.

Situations of this sort happen with surprising frequency; perhaps they are one of life's quintessential expressions of ambivalence.

While we were working together during this first half of the 1980s, I became aware that another patient I saw at the clinic was a bit like a negative image of a photographic print of JoAnn. Ruth was a poised and soft-spoken, middle-aged black woman, a lovely person, married to a teacher and raising their ten-year-old adopted daughter. She was a member of another group I led for many years, made up of women who'd all had several previous psychiatric hospitalizations. Each had been referred for weekly group therapy by psychiatrists on our staff who provided follow-up care in order to monitor the need for psychotropic medication; all of the women had shown an interest and willingness to participate additionally in a talking approach to therapy, not just pick up their prescriptions during a fifteen-minute appointment once a month.

For quite a while Ruth didn't speak much in the group. When she did begin to talk about her history she used few words. She'd grown up in the South, one of many children, never knowing who her father was. Soon after she'd reached puberty, a well-to-do man who was influential in their community came by the house for a long talk with her mother. Ruth was later told anytime the man came back she was to go with him and do whatever he said. She did as she was instructed; the arrangement came to a stop a year or so later when she became pregnant and then had a miscarriage. Tensely holding back tears, she told the group the shoddy medical care she received back then had left her unable to have children.

None of us knew much about the dynamics of Ruth's relationship with her mother but we knew enough to understand she'd always tried to win her love and acceptance. She endeavored to be a good and dutiful daughter (even contributing toward her mother's upkeep) and managed to do well with her life despite the obvious hardships.

After missing the group one week, Ruth came to the following session quite shaken. She was just back from an emergency trip to

Louisiana and a visit with her mother, who'd suddenly become gravely ill. Most of her siblings had gathered at the hospital, figuring to be with their mother at the end. The family's matriarch, aware she was dying, asked that her children take their turn at her bedside so she could have a last, private conversation with each one. Ruth was the last child summoned.

In our group she could hardly talk about their encounter that final day. Her voice strained to make its way through the tension in her throat; her whole body was taut from an effort to keep her feelings corralled. She spoke so softly we were barely able to hear the words.

I could only imagine what hopes she must've held for their final communication, their deathbed intimacy. I wanted her mother to set things right between them, to tell Ruth she had never owed the debt she'd been paying on. This was the last chance.

She said her mother looked terribly weak and motioned her close. The older woman's voice was even weaker than her body. Still, her voice was clear, although whisperish, as she spoke the last two sentences to her daughter that fixed themselves forever in Ruth's mind.

"I wish," the dying woman said, "you'd never been born. I'm sorry I ever had you."

While telling of this, Ruth fought to keep herself, her attention and presence, there in the group. But she had sealed something of herself off from us. Not surprisingly. She hadn't had time to live with this revelation yet, much less to find a way of understanding it. Then again, how *could* she understand it? How does anyone accept learning such a thing?

JoAnn, I believe, had grown up with that kind of knowledge. The response of her mother and grandmother to her very existence never approached being maternal. They hadn't made any effort to disguise their feelings or to couch their attitudes in mixed messages. So knowing how they felt about her probably never came as a surprise because it was understood from the beginning, as much a fact of life as there not ever being quite enough food in the house. I think it's possible she never gave any thought to the matter. Most likely she simply sensed exactly where she stood in the household, not even attaching words or feelings to her knowing.

Hearing of Ruth's final encounter with her mother during the time I was also listening to JoAnn probe her reactions to Peg and examine her feelings about Gladys and Danny gave me a fuller perspective on this intrapsychic scene. I'm unsure now how many of my questions or ideas I shared with JoAnn then, but I certainly don't recall whatever thoughts I ventured producing any epiphany-like thundering cracks of recognition on her part. When a therapist offers an insight about a client's life and it's met with less than instant comprehension by the client, the office quickly fills up with the sound of one hand clapping. Regardless of how many blinding displays of a therapist's brilliance grace a session, if it's not helpful to the patient it's not helpful.

I *am* sure, though, that over this lengthy period of JoAnn's therapy, the idea of birth and the lives into which we are born increasingly intrigued me.

What if someone were physically connected, I wondered, to a mother who didn't want her or him there? What might be the effects of such a beginning on a person's life? In JoAnn's case, she heard a million times she'd never been wanted. Could she have known it before she was ever told it? In light of what she had remembered about her birth, and from which her quiet certainty would not be waylaid by my skepticism, I found myself considering the possibility of our being able to know things chemically, electromagnetically, cellularly, or in *some* other way that precedes our cognitive processes. If neurons and synapses aren't yet sufficiently formed in newborn infants to process thought or store memory, perhaps there's a more primitive intelligence at work not yet dependent on language.

It's widely accepted today that our thoughts affect our bodies, our health. Why wouldn't the thoughts and feelings a woman has about her pregnancy have an impact on the new life with whom she literally shares her internal space? Maybe something like that kind of communication led to JoAnn's trying *not* to be born. Could the sense or knowledge of how unwanted she was have instructed her to push against the contractions that would force her into a world offering no care from her caretakers?

I don't think JoAnn ever found these questions remotely as interesting as I did. For her there was not enough time to be fascinated with abstract notions about cause and effect when she could trace a thread of memory back to a particular event and connect it with a present-day value or a preference she currently held.

Once, for instance, she asked if I knew why she never liked to wear sundresses.

"No," I smiled. "Why?" At times she was like a child who finally managed to solve a riddle and couldn't wait to tell someone the answer. I don't think it occurred to her I never would have had a single thought on this subject.

"Especially the open-backed ones that used to be popular, made with a strap across the top at the shoulders. I never did like those kind, and you know why? I just figured it out."

The answer had come, unsought but not unnoticed, a day or two before when she grew uncomfortable wearing some blouse or jacket which was tight across the shoulders. The feeling of that pressure on her back and neck took her nearly forty-five years into the past; she was very small then because her waist barely came to the top of the mattress in the bedroom. Her Grandpa, she said, would push her forward across the edge of the bed, her feet dangling over the side, and hold her in place with his hand just below her neck as he sodomized her. She had never been able to stand any pressure of clothing or anything else there. And now she understood why.

So while JoAnn solved the very real puzzles of her life, I dealt with my own curiosity from the safety of the therapist's chair as I tried joining pieces together in a way that made some sense of things for me, even if not always being especially relevant for her. She remained busy making silken threads she then wove into a fabric which continued to reveal more of her history.

Peg, whom she'd come to care about over the years, was deserting her—even before she left in death. I think there was confusion for JoAnn far beyond the impending loss for she seemed to feel betrayed by Peg, who had for the first time failed to be consistent. Trust, never easily come by and always predicated on consistency, was being dealt a severe blow by the unfamiliar and unexpected bitterness in an old friend at the end of her life. Either Peg had changed into someone she no longer knew, or she'd never really known her in the first place. Whichever was the case, it caused a pain much closer to the bone because if she wasn't able to trust herself enough to know the difference, then her instincts—all she could truly count on—had betrayed her.

From my view of it, this was also the mirrored theme running through the recollections of being abandoned by Honey that were permeating JoAnn's writings and therapy sessions then. It was hurtful enough to remember having been deserted by the person who had saved her. But the most devastating thing, that sense of betrayal, came from realizing she'd held as immutable truth Honey's statements about never leaving her, of things working out. Promises like:

> That ol' Man and me, we ain't a goin' nowhere, chile. We always be right here. Now you know that, don'tcha?
> Iff'n you jest do the best you can, the Lord always give you a helpin' hand, chile. He's gonna make everthing okay.

JoAnn's emotional connection with Gladys, yet a different facet of this issue, gradually came to light. And, I think, it was another example of her responding to a deeper knowledge, much more searing, than consciousness provided. But once again I'm not sure how much of this was given a seat of honor at her banquet of awareness, or what simply came from my own hungry effort to understand, in a language I spoke. My notes from those sessions contain far more information about what JoAnn said and did than what I said or did. Since I've never had the degree of recall she had either, it's impossible to be certain about what I understood back then and what has slowly seeped into my comprehension over the years since her therapy.

While there were many and very obvious differences, I think Danny was to Gladys as JoAnn had been to Honey. I believe she may have sensed this in some way, and reacted to the death of Gladys more from an identification with Danny than out of her own relationship with the elderly neighbor she didn't even really like. In looking back, she thought Danny was well taken care of by Gladys —at least until he reached kindergarten—and there was no question but that he'd been attached to her. Probably he never experienced the attachment to Gladys which she'd felt for Honey (Gladys was a very different kind of person, after all), but that earlier connection was still her only positive frame of reference. Even though the death of Gladys wasn't an unsettling event from a personal standpoint, as was true with Peg's decline, it still touched the softening heart of the little girl who was not so hidden anymore in JoAnn's darkened past.

There was one more important figure in the Gladys-and-Danny and JoAnn-and-Honey pair of transferential equations, perhaps the pivotal one: JoAnn's mother, Marie. When you got right down to it, how much difference was there, underneath it all, between Danny's entry into the world and JoAnn's own? From the moment she stated she hadn't wanted to be pregnant with Danny, that admission became a filter through which I saw and heard almost everything she said and wrote about her youngest child.

I think it's quite possible that at the time of these disclosures I found them more upsetting than JoAnn did. For her the main thing was to bring the material into the light, to rob its covert grip of any more power over her. As usual, her intellectual understanding was miles ahead of her emotional recognition. And for me, the once upon a time Thanksgiving baby who had been the answer to years of hoping, I could hardly contemplate what it must feel like always to know one's life was maternally regarded as a cruel twist of fate, if not an outright horrible mistake.

JoAnn had experienced the situation from both sides. A year or so before, regarding a different matter, she'd written that it was more painful to think about what effect she'd had on her own children than to acknowledge what she herself had experienced. "Back then I was DONE TO," she wrote, "but in the lives of my children, I will be partly the DOER, one of those responsible for the lack of warmth and sufficient caring in their lives."

As much as she may have wanted not to get pregnant in 1966, when she later admitted her despair in that situation, I think she started forming an emotional connection to her son, a connection which had taken sixteen years to gel. It accounted for some of that mother bear protectiveness I saw in her reaction to Peg's angry, punitive stance. Regardless of the difficulties in parenting Danny over the years, despite an unfamiliarity with expressing affection, and despite her unemotional approach to limit setting and discipline, she was never able to dismiss his concerns. Even when she was distraught and at wit's end about his irresponsibility, his anger, and verbal abusiveness, she cared about what happened to him and sought help for him as well as for them both. As a result of discovering her childhood, the bottom line would always be that she could never throw him to the wolves as had been done to her. She had never wanted to be the mother in his life that she was finally identifying Marie as having been throughout her childhood. And very possibly it was only because of her brief experience of Honey's mothering that she was able to do it differently at all.

As for me and my place in this cast of psychic characters? I often wondered when I was going to show up on the Playbill or where my entrance would be noted. In fact I was probably the last person in a supporting role to be given a part, the last player receiving a review.

I knew my presence clearly had an impact on JoAnn's life, as was true of all the other people in orbit around her who were the occasional or frequent focus of her attention. It was evident to me she reacted to things I did and said; particularly obvious was the effect on her of my taking off time from work.

I thought it significant that, as the transference drama took place on center stage, I might as well have been an understudy. And yet, aside from the leading character, I was the only other live, flesh and blood player in the room. But she was not at the point of relating to me as other than an abstract function, a disembodied worker paid to help her. No doubt the very fact of my presence on the scene was exactly why I had to wait so long in the wings.

19

IN THE
BEGINNING . . .

The place was a bar we all went to, a bar Joint with a loud jukebox. It was deafening in there. Behind the bar were some little bitty rooms, with a cotlike bed in each one. You had to walk by the bar and go down the hall to the little closet rooms. It was the only way to get there. That's how they kept track of the money they should get from the girls who went to the rooms with the men.

The young soldier who handed me his handkerchief had said he didn't want to see my face in that Joint ever again. It was bad times for me then, and I could tell he was afraid for me when he saw how young I was. He didn't want anything to happen to me.

I never wanted to go with them, but I was afraid of the family's anger if I didn't go. The beatings were getting worse for me if I didn't do as I was told. Sometimes I tried to talk my way out of it, and sometimes I'd sneak off, but I knew I couldn't get around them forever. He said they weren't my friends. That's what he said, and I believed him.

I have to keep clear of that place any way I can. So mostly the only thing I can do is just close up and leave the world behind me. I go away inside so as not to be bothered with those Baddies that aren't my friends. I close up and tell them "No." I just keep saying "NO!

NO, I'M NOT GONNA GO!" And there is nothing they can do with me, not really. Just beat me.

I tell Mama, "NO, NO, No, no, no, no."

That is all I say to her. No. She's trying to make me get ready and go with them. She finally gets mad and stops the sweetness and the trying to fool me. She hits me in the head with her fist, which is stupid because it hurts her fist more than it hurts my head.

Mama screams at me that I am not even listening to her. She's yelling right in my face and spitting all over me, so of course I hear her. But I don't say a word except "No."

She is afraid of what Henry will do to her for not getting me ready by the time he comes to take us all to the Joint. He gets mad when he can't count on them to EVEN HANDLE A GODDAM KID, for Christ sake! They act like a bunch of damn babies around here, and think all he's got to do is baby-sit 'em. Well, if they don't watch out he'll just stop trying to HELP 'EM OUT. Then they'll see how long they can get by WITHOUT HIMMMM!!!

Oh yes, Henry is on his way to being a big shot. He wants us to know how well off he is and how great he's making it out there in the big world. Of course no one reminds him that HE isn't the one making the money! It's us girls bringing it in, the ones he is always calling "no account." I don't see HIM going in the rooms with any soldiers. No, we're the ones who make the money for his fine shirts. Us no good bitches, us two-bit whores. He used to joke that the only thing good about us was the money-making machine between our legs.

Mama whines that I won't do anything to help out. "You could do something to help out around here if you wanted to, you know! All you have to do is be nice to them. That's all." They all tell me that. Over and over I hear it. From all of them. They never say what it means to "be nice to them," or who "they" are.

I figure out what it means, though. "You could help out around here" means you can go and be a whore and GET MONEY!! When they say to BE NICE they mean you can get something extra out of them if you're a little nicer and do what the men say.

Mama says, "It wouldn't hurt you to be nice to them, would it? You don't really have to DO anything, JoAnn. Just let 'em THINK you're gonna do something!" This is the motherly advice I get.

"What's so damn hard about being nice to them for a few minutes, for God's sake? You'd think I was asking you to jump off a bridge!"

No, all she and the others want is for me to help out the family, to be a whore. They sell your body and soul out from under you for two bits, and don't see one thing wrong with it. Proudly they call it "helping out." As little as I am I know the only person we're helping out is Henry. Helping him be a big shot smart young fella by pimping for his sisters!

❋

I run away from them somehow and try to get to the Place.

Honey finds me by the tree near the garden, holding on tight as ever I can and sounding like some wild animal that's hurt bad. She hears me crying out there while taking care of the cow. She comes over to see what's wrong. Tells me to let go a that tree.

"LET GO A THERE right now, chile. LET GO, I SAID!! . . . Lord God in heaven, what they do to you? What happen to you, chile? Why, you can't hardly stand on your feets!"

Honey sees I is all beat up. All bloody and hurt. It's the baddest time ever. She gets my fingers to let go a that tree, and then she calls on Old Man God. Says for Him to LOOK HERE at this CHIIILE! She yells at Old Man God to listen to her.

"See what happen when YOU NOT PAY ATTENTION!!! Go and dump this baby down any ol' wheres and not watch her! Now you look a here, God. Just you look a here at what's happen to this baby! WHERE IS YOU AT?!! WHERE IS YOU AT, GOD, to let this here thing happen to this chile? To let my baby come to this?!"

Oh, Honey is so afraid for me.

"What's gonna happen to my little baby white chile?" She is rock and wail and cry; not make sounds but I hear and feel her.

Honey not wanta scare the baby, not scare me. But she is worry to death. She don't know what to do 'cept sit and wait till that Man gets to home.

When he comes hurrying in she tells him, "I'se 'bout run crazy with worry, Man. Not wanta scare this chile, but not know WHAT to do."

"You can let go now, Honey," the Man says. "Honey? Honey, you can let go now. Honey? You can let go a her now. I'm home now. Honey, do you hear me? For God's sake what's wrong, Honey?"

He feels different to me now. I'm half in and half out of it, I am. Can't stay awake, can't hold my head up. What'll we do? What will we do? Honey comes up out of herself and says, "What we do?"

He thinks something is bad wrong with her, the way she act. "I is worried 'bout YOU first, Honey. Is you all right? Is you?"

She's about to cry. "Looky here, Man. Looky here what they is done to MY BABY!"

Honey tells him she 'bout go outta her mind not knowin' what to do and him not here on the Place. She's scared to death, so she locks that door and sits and waits for him to come from town.

She's exhausted. I can feel it. She is OUT. Empty. She holds on long as she can till her man gets to home. She is shhush me in my sleep. When I make a noise she is shhush me 'fore anybody can hear us in here.

"Shhush, baby," Honey says, "you is all right. Honey is here with you now, baby," and she rocks us a little bit till I settle down again.

Honey is ascairt somebody might hear us in this house. She is ascairt of them DEVILS! Them's not human what do this to her baby!

"Ah well, ah well. What a mess. What a mess we've got."

It's a different voice I hear. I wake up when I hear somebody else talking. It's the Preacher man. He's saying What to do?

"Tell me. Tell me everything that's been going on, Sister."

He talks firm, the Preacher, and says tell him everything FROM THE VERY BEGINNING ABOUT HOW THEY GOT INTO THIS MESS.

"Start at the beginning and don't leave nothing out, Sister. Just tell me the story from the beginning."

I know the beginning. I settle down and I is snug as a bug in Honey's ol' arms. I don't worry about a thing.

She is talking . . .

. . . No, that's not right, Honey. Not right! It ain't the right

beginning, Honey! It ain't THAT STORY, Honey. In the beginning
God made the whole world, the WHOLE WIDE WORLD!! Honey is
telling the wrong story. I know the beginning story is when God
made it all. I can't talk. I'm mostly out of it and I can't talk for some
reason. I cry inside 'cause I wanta hear the right story, the right In
the Beginning story. The beautiful story about the pretty world what
God is made for us allll to enjoy: the flowers, the animals, the sun,
the rainbows. Honey is telling the wrong story! She is telling a bad,
bad story. About them baddie Foleys. I don't wanta hear Honey tell
it, but I can't talk and tell her to stop!

I stir around. Thoughts scare me. I'm just about asleep, and she
shhush me. "I is right here witcha, baby. You is all right now, baby."

She is telling the Preacher man the wrong beginning story.
What a mess. Dear Lord, what are we a gonna do?

I wake up again and hear Honey say she not can believe that her
God has let such things go on! Her heart is broked. "What kinda
God is us got, Man, to let such badness go on in this world? It ain't
right. You know it ain't right."

"What can we do, Honey?" the Man leans close and asks her.
"You tell me what we can do! Tell me, Honey, and we DO IT. You
tell me what we can do, and we'll do it or die tryin'. Find out a way
to keep this chile, and I be a doin' it right now, Honey! Don't you
know we do anything for this chile?"

I hear the Preacher man's voice: "What you think you can do
now, Sister? Nothing. Exactly nothing! We is the HAVE NOTS,
woman, and don't you forget it. They can CRUSH us! They can and
they would, with no more thought than if we was ants on the
ground. . . . Yes, they is TRASH! You're right about that, Sister,
and the proof of it is all beat up there in your lap. There's nothing to
argue about; they is plain ol' TRASH that ain't worth the time of day.
They is trash, BUT THEY IS WHITE! And don't you go forgetting it
either, woman. They is WHITE, and we can't touch 'em. Now there
it is, Sister, all laid out for you neat as you please. They is white and
that means they is RIGHT! They is right against a nigger any time or
any place!"

The Preacher says he don't know what is got into her. He tells
Honey that she oughta know Right and Wrong don't even begin to

count when it is black against white. What does she want them to do? he asks her. "Since you not wanting to let go of this child, just you tell us what we can do, Sister."

He tells Honey she could lose everthing, everything they have worked for. "They can take it away from you, woman! Take this Place and ruin you, just for the fun of it. You think I don't know about them folks? Why, I'd hate to tell you even half of what I've seen of their kind."

Oh, the things he has seen in the work with his people. If he thought for one minute there was a thing he could do that would make a difference to this child, then he would be out there doing it for her. "I'd do it for no other reason than what you claim, Sister: she's a child of God's."

But the Preacher can't think of one thing that would help. Black or white don't rightly matter to him. He wouldn't take it out on no little baby for what others is done, she knows him good enough to know that. He's trying to tell her there ain't no way to be a helping this child! There ain't no way for nothing good to come outta this thing what they is got into with this little white child.

Honey says he is thinkin' 'bout his own people and not 'bout this chile a HERS!

The Preacher looks sharp at her. "Ain't so, Sister. That just ain't so, and you know it, too. Sure, colored peoples is my own. But no, I got to help everybody that I can on this old road. Now, I know you don't need to be told that thing 'cause YOU is help teach me it, didn't you? But the thing is, you got to THINK, woman. Think before you do something you can't finish for yourself, 'cause when it come to black and white you won't get one speck of help, woman, and the TRUTH WON'T COUNT! In these parts, when your skin is black you won't even have a turn to open your mouth."

The Preacher keeps on talking to Honey but change his voice a little bit. " '. . . White Man, what's this here nigger got against you to be telling this story?' '. . . Nigger, who d'you think you are to speak out about this decent white man here? Don't you know your PLACE, nigger?' '. . . Sorry to have bothered you, Mr. White Man.' '. . . Get to hell outta here, nigger! Troublemaker. That there is a trouble-making nigger if I ever seen one. Where's he from? Might have to get rid of him if there's any more talk about this. Run him off, up North where them high-tone niggers belong. Think they can come in here and talk against a white man!'

"Them mans down here ain't sided with no nigger yet, woman," the Preacher goes on, "and they ain't gonna either. I tell you there ain't a thing in this world that you can do about this child."

Sounds to me like something gets caught in Honey's throat. The Preacher man sees his words get to her.

"It's bad. Bad in a lot of ways, Sister." He change his tone with her, not call her "Woman" no more. "Sometimes I get to thinking this place is the cross I got to bear. And it's hard, Sister, terrible hard to go around and see good and right trampled in the dirt. This here is a bad time and a bad place in a whole lot of ways . . ."

The Preacher is drifting off into his worries 'bout this place. I can feel it in him. He's 'bout to let go, but pulls hisself back to now. I can feel how hard for him to come back to this bad trouble what they is call him out for. He got to handle this the best way he can, got to talk some sense into her and forget the rest till later, after this is over. But right now he has to figure out the best thing for them all. The child, too.

The Preacher man tells Honey that she can hang on to that child if she decides to, but he wants to know what she thinks the girl's family gonna do when the child not come on home?

Honey tells him real quick, "They not want this chile. Never did. They don't care one thing 'bout this baby. Don't even care if she is took care of or not. Why, looky what them is done to her!"

She says them devils not miss this pore little thing. She gonna keep this baby with them, take care a this chile and love her all to pieces. This baby ain't no trouble at all!

The Preacher listens to Honey. He listens and she talks—'bout how she is alla time take care a this baby who ain't one bit a trouble in this world. She is a pure pleasure, she is. That family not even miss this chile, not even know this chile is gone from there. That's how much they care 'bout her baby. Them peoples not even WANT THIS BABY. And she does!! Honey is decide herself that she wants this baby. She thinks the Lord OWE her this here baby! This chile and her will be plum all right.

He listens, the Preacher, and lets her talk until she's talked out.

The Man don't like this kind of talk from Honey. He is still upset 'bout finding her, and her not being just right to him. He says, "Honey, stop it. We can't do it."

The Preacher raises his hand a little bit at the Man. Not much, not enough to bother Honey, but enough to stop the Man. I see him. He means for the Man to let her talk. She talks and talks. The Preacher looks at the Man and don't say a word. Not either one of them bother Honey. They let her talk.

We is all there, in the kitchen on the Place. She is talking about me and her and the Man. She talks on, then she rambles on. She tells about this chile what she done find inna GARDEN PATCH! Purely starving to death, this chile was. Chile follow that Man home, right up on to this Place like a scared puppy. She done find that chile out there in her own garden patch! Honey tells the Preacher this chile is smart, got more senses than a whole heap of growed ups what she is seen. This baby is just as good as gold, and she loves this baby to death.

She is find this chile and she ain't gonna let her go back to them wolves. Now that's all there is to it. They know she is right 'bout this thing, and she looks hard at that Preacher.

"You call yourself a Man of God, a Preacher of what's RIGHT?" Honey says to him. "Well then you know I is right 'bout this thing! You just better leave me alone. I ain't gonna let go a this baby!"

Honey says she fight them iff'n they try to take this chile from outta her arms. I can feel her. She kinda feels like the setty hen. She gonna take the broom and fight them devils, she says.

But she can't fight 'em. Honey can't win. I know more about them devils than she does. I look at the Man. I look at the Preacher who I don't like how he talks. I feel Honey; she is so sad and gone. She is lost, and I can't stay here 'cause I know them devils better'n Honey.

I have listen to them Baddies for years. I know the hateful talking Preacher man is right about them Foleys and what they do to hurt the Man and Honey. I know it even if she don't. They don't think that no-good nigger oughta have a wagon. Don't think that no-good nigger should have a Place. Don't think "that black son of a bitch oughtta live near decent white folks like us!"

I know I can't stay here. Them Baddies will hurt 'em. The

Preacher is right. I can tell he's right. I don't like to listen to his voice, but I know he's right. He lets her talk, lets her talk it all out. He waits. She rambles on, and they listen to her. I can feel it in the room, in all three of 'em. She knows it now, too. The words that keep coming out don't sound the same. They come out empty. Dead is what's left. All that's left of all them words is a dead cold WE CAN'T.

The Preacher starts to talk, so soft and low it's hard to hear what he says. But it don't matter. I know.

What? . . . what? I'm gone. Way far gone; tired and wore out from too much. The talk, the voices . . . off, off inna distance. There's a "want something" tone that pulls me back. He leans over to her chair and pulls up his chair closer. The Preacher talks soft, in a tone I hear alla time when somebody wants something! But, no, I ain't at home. I'm at Honey's, 'cept the tone's the same.

The Preacher man says she knows she has to let go this chile now. "Come on now, Sister. I know it is bad. I know it is hard. I know how it tears the heart from outta you!"

But he tells her they all know this is the way it's gotta be. Long time ago she had to let them other children a hers go when they growed up, and it was the best thing. Not easy to do, no, but it's the best thing. And then we have to go on, he says, and do what has to be done.

"You got to let go the child, Sister," he says real low. "Give her up to me. I'm not gonna hurt her, Sister. The Lord loves ALL the little children, and I do, too. Now you know that, Sister. You know I'd cut off my arm before I'd hurt a poor little child."

The Preacher keeps talking low and soft, but Honey's not getting much softer. I can tell. He is wanting something but she don't give it to him.

"We got to take that child back, Sister. You know we got to get her back up there to her own people. That ain't no more'n right, Sister. She belongs to them. She has a mother up there to watch out for her, don't she?"

Well, he might as well cut out his tongue when he says "Mother" to Honey. She ain't ever been happy with the kinda Mama I got. The Preacher man about lost alla ground he had made with

Honey right then. I can tell from the feel of her. He go right on talking easy to her, but he shoulda knowed better'n to say a word about my Mama 'cause me and Honey don't think much a that Mama!

They have to take the child back, the Preacher says, and they have to do it now. Right now before it's too late. He can see Honey is tired. She is drained from the day, too much on her ol' self. Her fingers is stiff from holding onto me all day long while she done wait for that man to come home and FIX IT.

The Preacher ease her fingers offa me. He just ease them ol' fat fingers right off, gentle like. Then she don't say nothing more to him. Honey don't talk no more when he picks me off her lap. He says he's gonna take the child now. The Preacher looks at the Man, tells him to take care of Sister now. They don't say a word. Just look at each other and know everything, without words.

He carries me onto the porch, the Preacher does, and tells the Man he got to take the child on along home. They is not to go in. He's gonna say they found the child and fixed her up before they brought her home. Didn't know right where she belonged, so it takes a while to place her. The Preacher thinks they tell it that the chile was at the church. Sound better, he says, if she was at the church. Leave you all out of it. Say it was one of his people who found her. It would be the truth. So they carried her here from the church. Look like something happen to her. They act like they don't know what it was happen to the child. Play dumb. Best thing is to play dumb alla time.

"Be best not to go in their place," the Preacher says. "I just take the child to the door, tell 'em I'm the Preacher and I found this child at the church. Figure they can take care of her now and watch out for her themselves."

He works up the story just right. The Preacher's gonna tell 'em that one of his people, a woman, had found this child a wandering in the woods, and she had been hurt bad. Something must have happened to the chile out in the woods. He ain't gonna blame 'em. Talk around it, not no hint of blame 'em in his voice. The woman belongs to his church, and she fixed the chile up. The child has BEEN ASLEEP all the time since then. That means the child hadn't told nothing, hadn't said anything to any of them. He say it took 'em most of the day to find out where the chile belonged at, so they don't even wake her up.

Honey is out of it. She just sits there and don't do a thing. I know she is gone away. Gone away inside. Like me sometimes.

"This is the best way. The truth is always the best way," the Preacher says. "I can just leave you and her out of the whole thing. Be the truth, but leave you and her altogether out of it. Don't need to ask for no trouble. . . . No, it won't matter what the child says. They won't listen to the child. . . . Because they just won't, and because they don't want no fuss. Child can tell what she wants to. They won't make no fuss as long as they can get out of it, long as they don't feel pushed in a corner."

The Preacher tells the Man this is too much on that ol' woman, just too much on Sister. He's worried about her.

"Children will come back," he says. "They come back easier than we do, Brother. They ain't beat out yet. It's your wife in there I'm worried about! I seen 'em like that before, Brother, and I tell you we is got our hands full tonight!"

The Preacher looks at me. His tone is a little bit like he just can't see how the Man let it happen.

The Man's asking, "Who'd a known it was gonna turn out like this? Who'd think all this happen over a little chile? Not never seen nothin' like it. Not seen nothin' like THEM, that family!"

How's he suppose to know the way it end up? Honey was so LONESOME. And him, too, if the truth was to be known. That little chile come out along the road for a ride on his wagon. Never think it cause no trouble. Like to have a nickel for ever little chile what ride a piece on that wagon. Never had no trouble before. No, them never seen no such people as this chile come from. Not like nobody he'd ever run up on.

Well, the Preacher could've told him. He knowed about their kind. Seen 'em far too much. The Man don't even listen to him. He just keeps on looking out over the porch and talking about how this chile eased 'em, she did. Eased their burden a lot, and they loved her. Hadn't got no way to know how it would end up. Thought they wasn't hurting a thing by playing with that chile.

"Brother, Brother," the Preacher man shakes his head, "where is you BEEN all your life? . . . Ah, Lord, don't do to rehash the past. Just got to take things as they are."

The Man goes to say something but the Preacher cuts him off with his worrying 'bout Sister. "Well, suppose you don't care about yourself over this child. What happens to HER if something happens to YOU?"

He is talking about our HONEY!! I don't like him, this Preacher man. I want him to hush up his mouth and leave us alone! Sometimes he sounds a little bit like Honey, but I don't like him!

"You'll lose everything you got, and it'll be all the excuse they need to take it and run you off this Place. Leave you with nothing but heartache and not think one thing about it. If you don't care about yourself, you'd BETTER THINK OF HER. What you think happen to her if they is to kill you? You be strung up and dead and outta your misery, but where would that good woman be? Better think again, Brother. You ain't got a leg to stand on once you open your mouth against their kind. You can't help that child, can't help nobody, not once you talk against a white man. Brother, you ain't got no other choice. I know you're hurting, but I know you can hear what I'm saying."

The Preacher man is winding up now, I can tell. They settle down a little, calm down some. He says for the Man to TAKE CARE OF HIS OWN now. Honey is in a bad way it looks to him like. He'll take the child and then get some womenfolk to come sit with Sister. He thinks she be all right if she could settle down and get some rest. She needs some womenfolk to sit with her, so the Man just have to hold on till he can get back.

"Take care of her, Brother, and we'll talk later. That woman needs you now. I'll take this child on home and pray for the best. That's about all we can do, pray for the best."

※

"I tell you chile, I just know you is gonna be a big woman someday. Ohhhh, and I know that you be GOOD, too!"

Honey is talking to me real serious 'cause this is a terrible time

we be going through. She says, "I wouldn't be one little bit surprised
to look up that ol' road one of these here days, and guess what?"

I not can guess what. I don't like this whole visit!

Honey bets one a these days she's gonna see me a comin' down
this road and she'll say to herself, "Can this be that little ol' white
chile what I took in? Why you be a great big woman now! Be sooo
pretty. I just know you gonna be so pretty, and be a real lady, too."

She think "real pretty" and "be a lady" just boil down to Pretty
Is as Pretty Does. "It not mean to be beautyful only on the outside.
The Lord do see right inside, past all that kind a pretty, chile. Not
nothin' wrong with your bein' pretty, but you has to 'do' pretty, too,
chile. Now I know you gonna be a real lady, ain'tcha, baby? You not
listen at them there Foleys, either, will you, baby? No, you not."

I ask her suppose the Lord reach down His hand and take her
and the Man away before I leave them Foleys, and before I come on
back down that ol' road? Then what?

Honey is about to cry. I ain't gonna cry. I want to, but I ain't
gonna do it. No. I feel tears run down my face, but I don't pay 'em
no mind.

She says iff'n the Lord do call 'em to His home place, she'll just
have to "sit down on the banks of the River Jordan and wait for you,
chile. I have to tell Him I can't go 'long to home yet awhiles. I gotta
wait on that little ol' chile what ain't here yet."

I ask if she is for SURE to wait right there for me and Lu Lu
Belle?

Honey tries to sound kinda cheery, but I see her eyes is getting'
shiny. "Yes, sir. Yes, sir-eee, I just stand at them Pearly Gates and tell
ol' St. Peter we better wait for that baby and Lu Lu Belle right now."

Ohhh, she starts to cry. Honey cries something awful; her
shoulders shake and she puts her face in her apron. Ah Lord, ah
Lord, she is heavy laden, mighty heavy laden. I can tell. I sit there
and cry big, big tears with no noise. Honey just sobs and cries right
out loud and don't even care.

I put my arm on her shoulder and lean on her and tell her,
"There, there, there, Honey. It'll be all right. The Lord fix it up real
soon, Honey. It'll be just as good as new, you'll see. Now don't you
cry, Honey, 'cause I love you. I love you all to pieces, Honey."

She looks at me through her big ol' wet eyes. Tells me I have to go on home now and stay there till I grow up big enough to leave that family a mine behind. Says I not can come back anymore but that won't stop them from lovin' me just like as if I was right there with her and that good ol' Man!

She cries more then. I don't know what to do.

※

I was under Honey's house and could hear her moving around inside. It was the last time I was there on the Place. I wasn't supposed to be there at all, but I had not gone home to where the Foleys lived. She had told me I had to be a good girl and go home. To be a "good girl" at home meant to be bad. To be a "good girl" at Honey's meant to do right, do the best you could. "Do right" from Honey and the Man wasn't like "Be a good girl for your Grandpa, now JoAnn!"

I'm hid under Honey's house 'cause she has tole me I gotta be a good girl and go home. I can't do right if I go home without my raggity baby who I am the mommy of. I know Honey don't think much of a mommy that don't look out for her baby. Honey don't come out for a while after I get under her house, but I know she will. She has to come out to milk the cow, and I can run quick as anything in the house and get my baby! I sure can't leave my baby just any ol' where.

When she does walk slooow out the door and down the steps, when she gets out of sight, I run in the kitchen and grab Lu Lu Belle! "I come to getcha, baby. Now don'tcha cry now, 'cause I not leave you," I coo soft and sweet to my sweet baby. Then I run quiet, quiet down the steps and cross the wagon tracks and into the weeds and into the woods.

I stay in the woods, away from the Place. I stay away from Honey's nice warm world, her nice warm kitchen, and her nice warm arms. At night I take my baby and hide up under Grannie's house. I tell Lu Lu Belle she has to hush up that noise now. Them devils are up there and they hear us! We have to be very quiet when they go to bed 'cause we don't want them to hear us. "If they find us, they gonna hurt us. They be mean and bad, y'know. We ain't ascairt one bit, huh baby? No, not us," and I hug her up tight.

"This ain't bad under here, is it, Lu Lu Belly ol' girl? Not bad at all. We make out just fine, won't we, baby? Course we will. My oh my, we gonna be just fine."

But I ain't really fine. Under this house I don't really feel happy and warm as toast. To tell the truth, I'm ascairt to death. I don't go in there with them Foleys. I stay right here with my baby that Honey knows I can take care of.

I was not even aware of time. I don't know how long we hid, but I never came out until they were moving. The family moved then because I'd gotten them in trouble. When the Preacher carried me home, it must've scared them that he knew stuff about the family that could cause problems for Grandpa and Grannie. I knew I had to stay with them. That lesson had been carved on my heart. Honey told me I couldn't come back to the Place, that I had to go home and stay with my family until I grew up and could leave on my own.

That was what brought me out from under the house. It's not that I was hungry or thirsty, because nothing mattered to me. I would just as soon have laid down there and died. I came out because if I didn't crawl out from under the house and go with the Foleys it would be bad for the Man and Honey.

It must have been Little Bobby or one of the other youngsters who first saw me, but it was Grannie's voice I remember. She was wild with hatred, shrieking at me.

"YOU'D BETTER GET OUT OF THERE, JOANNN, you goddam little bitch!! Just what in the hell do you think you're doing?!" Grannie leaned down beside the house and stared through the dark beneath the floor until she saw me. "Look what YOUUUU DIIIDD!!! Look at the TROUBLE YOU CAUSED!!"

When I crawled out Grannie grabbed Lu Lu Belle out of my arms. "Where'd you get this from?!" she yelled. "That ain't nothing but nigger trash!" Grannie's face was distorted with rage. Her face and her voice and everything about her was out of control.

She wanted to kill me—I knew she did—because of the trouble I'd caused. Instead she ripped Lu Lu Belle apart. I stood there and watched all my raggity baby's stuffing fall on the ground, and I couldn't do a thing.

I think until that moment I'd been barely floating in a big pot of gloom and sadness. I sunk under the surface when I saw Lu Lu Belle torn apart. That's where I stayed for a long, long time. My world was too much to bear anymore.

20

FENCES AND NEIGHBORS

JoAnn's world was sometimes more than I could bear, too. Hearing about it in my office seemed manageable; she was the kind of engaging and dedicated patient most therapists consider themselves fortunate to have. But there were many times as I read through her notebooks during long weekends in the country I'd wonder why I was taking all that horror and suffering along with me, outside the office.

One day as I shared with Bev something especially poignant JoAnn had written, she asked, "Do you read everything she writes?"

"Yeah, I do."

"How can you?" she wanted to know. "I looked through one of the notebooks you showed me. She tells the same story over and over a dozen times; it's so repetitious I don't see how you do it. But mainly, though, it's just really heartbreaking. That doesn't get to you?"

It did get to me, of course. And sometimes I wasn't sure why I kept at it, why I'd shove aside hours of free time to wind around me reams of those wrenching passages. I just knew I was transfixed; I became almost as obsessed with *reading* her material as she was about *writing* it. Yes, she did go over an incident many times, but each version held some new detail or a fresh nuance. Discovering those little nuggets made the panning worthwhile to me. Yes, there were plenty of heartbreaking sections, but there were also heart-warming ones I found precious and healing.

That whole process got me thinking quite a bit about boundaries. It was a subject often highlighted by the work JoAnn was doing in remembering her past, and in the awareness she was bringing to her present interactions. Many years ago she'd been unable to keep others out of her physical borders; we began investigating how that experience was playing itself out in her current life. And I had to keep checking on my own limits and boundaries, too, while trying to balance out a desire to know and understand the scope of her story with my desire and need to pay attention to the many other things going on in my life.

"Good fences make good neighbors," Robert Frost had the land-owner next door say in "Mending Wall." The fellow certainly understood something important about relationships. But I feel more of a kinship with the writer of the poem than his unwavering neighbor. The subject strikes me as so terribly complex I find myself blasting away again at a clear and simple notion. Or, at the very least, I notice the urge to insert an addendum.

All kinds of boundaries exist in the world, both real and metaphorical. The norms vary in different countries and even within different families in the same locality. Most Americans, for instance, can't conceive of twelve people from a family of three generations living in one or two small rooms as they do in many parts of the world. Psychic boundaries are no less real than the unseen survey lines which delineate one piece of property from another, and they're often constructed with dazzling creativity and impressive uniqueness. One's personal sense of boundaries may change over time and in various settings: what might've once been helpful as protection may come to feel imprisoning later on. I've begun to appreciate that we all have to deal with this issue in the grand array of our relationships, whether we like it or not. In fact I think it's one of life's greatest teachers, and my work with JoAnn in this area once more functioned as an important classroom in my schooling.

During these months in her therapy, JoAnn started gaining weight. It happened gradually but was quite noticeable after half a year or so. She stopped paying the careful kind of attention to her appearance as she had done when I first met her. This isn't to say

she was unkempt or wearing rags; the change, though, became pronounced. The energy and care she now invested in herself was just
about entirely directed to her inner life. Her focus was so far below
the surface of her appearance as to draw occasional comments from
some of my colleagues. A co-worker stopped me in the hall and said
something like, "JoAnn sure has put on some weight lately, hasn't
she? Do you know why?" Somebody else asked if I'd noticed the
difference in how she looked these days.

I was never sure how to respond to these comments. Perhaps it
should've been of more concern to me. I think I didn't judge the
importance of her appearance in the way others did because those
matters weren't very important to me, either. I've always hated
shopping, for instance, and only pay enough attention to what I
wear to get by. Also I knew, as no one else fully did, how much of
JoAnn's care and diligence was focused on her not-seen self. While I
really wasn't worried about it, I did have some moments of passing
doubt: maybe she was getting worse and I couldn't see it; perhaps
my own values about personal appearance placed me so far out of
the mainstream as to be naive and unhelpful in this situation. Although I didn't seriously believe that, it did occur to me.

One day JoAnn brought in an old copy of *Life* magazine, an
issue maybe twenty years old. She purchased it from a library selling
off wornout books and periodicals and wanted me to see the picture
she'd come across, the reason she'd bought the magazine. I don't
remember for sure but it was either a photograph of Hattie McDan-
iel or an advertisement for Aunt Jemima Pancake Flour, with a real
person in the picture—not the artist's rendering of subsequent ad
campaigns. Well, it must've been the latter because I recall our talking about the copy being for pancake *flour* not pancake mix, which
came into fashion afterward.

It was Show and Tell, and she was as excited as any youngster
about presenting her discovery. Pleased, too, with having found the
picture in such a fortuitous way.

"This is how Honey looked," she announced. "At least it's the
closest to anything I've seen like I remember her."

I studied the old black-and-white picture. "She was that big a
woman, huh?"

"Yes, she was." JoAnn let out a small laugh. "I think maybe unconsciously I've been gaining weight to be like her."

Throughout history people have adopted attitudes and mannerisms and the attire of others (including animals) they've longed to emulate. In primitive societies the practice has probably been more overt and conscious. People from "developed" countries, where rationality is highly prized, tend to be more unconscious in this regard. Still we see folks, especially children, do this all the time, and call it fantasy or identification with the aggressor. If this was happening with JoAnn, and she realized it related to her gaining weight, I couldn't see that as being harmful. She certainly hadn't wanted to identify with the people closest at hand when she was a small child. And then when she was seven and found the models she *did* want to be like, her family refused to accept her choice. She survived the later emotional cataclysm by simply repressing the whole trauma after she was banished from their home, the place which had become her own Garden of Eden.

Who and what we identify with is one of the mechanisms by which our identities get formed. In the march toward developing a sense of self, it's never too late to pick out worthy examples of decency to imitate. JoAnn had already done this on an unconscious level. Her value system was built on the shoulders of two people treasured for a brief time in childhood, even though her memory was denied access to them for over forty years. It's not surprising that when she finally recalled the fullness of their legacy she would choose to model herself after them.

I tended to view her gaining weight as one of many variations on the theme of boundaries, showing how it's possible for one's definition of self to expand or be permeable enough to incorporate the spirit of another—maybe even in a physical way.

An aside: in the years since working with JoAnn I've seen the issue of weight gain and obesity as particularly relevant for women who've survived incest and childhood sexual abuse. I also think it relates directly to this phenomenon of establishing one's personal boundaries. Naturally all kinds of people gain weight as they grow older; no group has a lease on that territory. But I've been struck with how many of my clients having a history of sexual abuse also have problems with their weight.

Often I ask people to bring in photographs of themselves at different ages. Time and again I've been astonished to see that an incredibly beautiful child, who was so generously open-faced in those pictures taken before the start of her abuse, is hardly recognizable in later photos. For many people I think this change is an unconscious, though heroic, effort toward self-protection. Extra weight can serve as more than a symbolic physical buffer and perhaps, at the very least, may be a desperate disguise. If such a remarkably lovely and vulnerable child becomes the target of an adult's violent attention, she might not want our prevailing standard of beauty to be part of her identity, sensing it was her physical attractiveness which got her noticed in the first place. And so a change in her physical appearance, the adding of mass and girth if not muscle, can be a redesigning of her perimeter, her body's boundary. It may or may not help her feel more safe in the world.

JoAnn came to one of her sessions distraught about Danny, who had, as usual, spent the previous weekend with her. She kept talking about how "out of it" he seemed the whole time, not really sick but lethargic and unresponsive. She grew quite concerned, even more so after learning he hadn't gone to school the week before.

"Do you think he's on drugs?" I asked.

"That's what I'm starting to wonder." She went on to say that earlier in the day she'd taken down the number of an area psychiatric hospital when an ad for their drug detoxification unit caught her eye. After getting back home she called the information line and spoke at length with a counselor from the program. JoAnn felt as if the woman had been living with them in their own home, so accurate and perceptive were her comments. She was puzzled to think about how a complete stranger could know her son better than she herself did. Based on the questions and concerns she heard the counselor express, JoAnn broke one of her deeply held taboos and searched Danny's room while he was at school. Taking the collection of bags and boxes and bottles of things found there, she had an interview with someone on the staff. Their analysis showed an assortment of illegal drugs in the various containers.

Out of these contacts they agreed on a strategy for getting Danny to the facility where he could be evaluated and, if necessary, treated. She did this on her own initiative, without any support from his father, and at the receiving end of Danny's fury when he was committed to the month-long program. The sigh of relief she heaved at his being in reach of help was short-lived: within a few weeks the staff discovered drugs hidden in Danny's room, smuggled in during a visit by his stepbrother. This breach in their contract caused a major crisis in the unit because a basic therapeutic tenet had been violated. Still, following a series of emergency administrative meetings, he was given another chance. When Danny completed the detox regimen JoAnn arranged for his admission to a residential treatment program for adolescent drug abusers where he didn't want to be, which his father thought he didn't need, and she believed was his best chance for getting the help he needed.

To meet the requirements of this program, over the next year she participated in weekly individual family therapy sessions and in a weekly family therapy group for all the residents of the facility and their families. Danny's father and stepmother also took part in this treatment plan, as did his much older siblings on occasion. It was an intensive and concerted effort designed to make an impact on young lives seriously out of control. Impressed with the concern and commitment of the staff, she attended every therapy session and function for the families of the residents throughout her son's stay.

And I think she hated every minute of it. Or rather, I think she was constantly disappointed the program wasn't all she believed it could've been. We talked about it during many sessions. She respected the staff and appreciated their treatment approach, and seemed quite sympathetic toward the adolescents themselves. Where she had no patience or tolerance, however, was with the parents of the kids, with the grown-ups she felt "should know better." She never heard any of the parents assume responsibility for the state of their marriages or the dysfunctional nature of their homes. Quite the contrary, as far as I gathered. The children alone were to blame for all the trouble they'd gotten into or caused (unless it was the crowd their kids had run with); the children all enjoyed advantages their parents never dreamed of having at that age; the parents had always done everything for them, given them whatever they wanted . . .

On and on it went. Really it almost made JoAnn sick. Sometimes she could barely stomach the denial and excuses she heard coming from adults who claimed to have absolutely no idea of why their sons had done what they did. And it was no different within Danny's own family group, either. She didn't like spending all those hours in the therapist's office with Danny's father and stepmother, and was fed up with their shock that all this had happened. Even Danny, himself, tried to tell them his stepbrother—there in his bedroom down the hall, practically under their noses—was using every drug in the book and they refused to see it. Sometimes it was almost more than JoAnn could stand. Especially, I think, because it drained away enormous energy from the project she felt she *could* do something about: reconstructing her own life.

Among the most difficult periods for her in this work was when she felt the pull from any of her children going through their own hard time. Frequently that seemed harder than shining light onto the nightmares of her own childhood because she had to figure out what she could and couldn't do for someone else. She may have appeared unperturbed to them, emotionally controlled as usual, but in our therapy sessions she studiously examined those borders separating her life from theirs. When could she appropriately offer what was being wanted or asked of her? When should she disengage and attend to her own needs? Psychologically it may be the least clear border there is, that one between a mother and her child.

There wasn't any question but that her own life, the one she felt such an urgent need to reconstruct, had been filled with people just like the ones she now heard complain about all the trouble their sons' drug problems had caused *them*. It was too much.

But she kept going to the sessions anyway. There was a vivid recollection, after all, which kept flying like a bat in and out of the cavern of her memory. It had to do with Honey's stern look and disapproving tone after finding JoAnn had left Lu Lu Belle in the garden during a rainstorm one afternoon.

"I just ain't got no use for a Mommy that'd leave her baby any ol' where," Honey had thundered. "Ain't nothin' worse than a Mommy that don't care about her baby."

With a longing to walk some of the countryside in England and Wales, I got excited about taking a fall vacation. After I told my patients of plans to be away for three weeks in October, JoAnn again decided to quit therapy. Before I actually left, though, while we talked about it, she reconsidered her decision, knowing she'd made it as a reaction to my leaving. Instead, she thought of perhaps seeing Bev while I was gone. She asked me to see whether it'd be possible.

Bev was more than happy to oblige if JoAnn was interested in an appointment. She didn't ask for one, I found out after coming back, but had been clear about her feelings on the matter. Bev showed me a letter she'd received from JoAnn.

Dear Beverly,
I believe this is going to be the worst time for me. I had terminated with Rose Mary, but when I got it all together for myself about how I still needed her I tried to hold it down until she got back. Well, I don't believe I will manage it so I should like to know that I can reach you anytime by calling your answering service and telling them it is an emergency.

I am not worried and I do not want to worry you but if I call you I want you to call me back as fast as you can, even if it's nighttime.

I'm not sure but I think this has to do with feelings of total isolation. The physical pain is nearly unbearable and the emotional pain is terrible. I haven't even let myself sink into all the emotional feelings yet . . . they're terrible, aw-ful beyond words.

I am near the end of this time and I suppose I'm afraid. It's different somehow from the times before. I really don't want to go through this because it's so painful. Still, I know it's live with it in my gut or go ahead and travel through it. For me the going through it is the only way.

Please call me back if I call you.

JoAnn

Returning from vacation, where I'd walked beside old, dark canals tunneling through the leafy, still-green canopy of broad-brimmed trees in Devon and Somerset, I found out JoAnn had taken her own trip, an inward one. On that journey she'd been alternately ambushed from cliffs of rage or mired in a swamp of sadness. The swampland was home to sinkholes of sorrow where she mourned lost time and wasted potential.

Chiefly, though, her life was overflowing with anger. Some of it was stirred up by having seen her internist while I was away. He diagnosed a leak in one of the valves of her heart, and recommended also getting tests to see if she had a thyroid condition. She was angry about having to spend so much time taking care of her body, especially since she believed the problem started with her getting the message long ago that she wasn't worth taking care of to begin with.

In an effort to express those inchoate feelings, part of which was probably anger from a preverbal age, she began to draw. Despite never having taken crayons in hand, she bought a roll of wrapping paper and filled it with huge pictures, made with large motions that involved putting the whole of her physical self into this act of expression.

JoAnn never brought in the drawing—her mural, I called it—for me to see so I can't give a firsthand impression of it. But she did describe her effort in some detail, even if that description was fairly emotionless in the telling. She drew her grandfather, she said, and other people who stalked her past. Using the roll of paper as backdrop she gave a visible shape to her rage. The mural was splattered with pictures of blood and bodies, knives and instruments of torture, pools of blood seeping from a variety of severed body parts. Especially penises.

Although I was curious to see how she had done this, I thought she seemed protective of her art work, and I didn't push her to bring it in. Possibly she wasn't hesitant at all about showing me the mural but simply didn't presume I'd really care to see it. That would've been her style. On the other hand, I didn't have much of a working knowledge about art therapy at that time and might very well have backed off out of a concern I'd get in over my head. I've certainly done that before. Nowadays, though, I frequently urge word-heavy patients to draw instead of talk, and I'm comfortable with later asking about the significance of their symbols.

In retrospect, such a rich source of wisdom, it's all too obvious I let a cache of valuable clues lay half buried at our feet. Yet, with some of that same hindsight, I can also now see this episode as an example of "the truth will out." If someone is working seriously toward self-understanding in her therapy, progress isn't going to be set back for long by a therapist's failure to pick up on a clue. The process itself is forgiving. The limitations of my knowledge may have slowed down JoAnn's forward momentum at times, but repeatedly the need to know led her back over the same ground until one of us would stumble decisively on that gem of truth nearly hidden at our feet.

We talked a good deal about her anger and, when I asked about how it showed up in our relationship, she didn't associate any of it with me or my going off and leaving her to stew in her fury. In fact, for all I could tell, she might have begun the first session we had after my return with a follow-up comment about the last topic we discussed three weeks earlier. I was just back from bed-and-breakfasting in three-hundred-year-old farmhouses, from hiking near Betws-y-coed and watching a slate-gray Dipper search for food by walking under the ecstatic waters around Swallow Falls, and JoAnn responded to me as if I'd never left the office. In her refusal to notice my absence, I definitely felt some of that anger land on me, although she wasn't saying anything about it.

There's an irony associated with taking vacations not altogether lost on me. I've always loved to travel. For me it's rejuvenating to throw routine aside, to be set upon suddenly by unexpected sights and sounds—smells, too—that leave me feeling a little off kilter, a bit more awake and alert. For some patients at a certain point in their therapy, however, those same breaks can mean something entirely different. In JoAnn's case, my going away kicked up issues for her of abandonment and feelings of withering loss. This isn't to suggest that a therapist's vacation is only a negative experience for the client. It may not always be an easy one, but it might prove to be a serendipitous route through material which needs mapping.

So my arranging for a while to be away from the histories of the patients I carry around in my head often led to those same people diving deeper into their therapy. The times before I left and just after my return were frequently periods of extra intensity in the work we were doing. The added attention asked of me then by that extra intensity was, in fact, caused by the vacation I took in the first place to get away from working so hard. Sometimes our lives are just a series of circular patterns . . .

Danny continued in the treatment program at Second Chance. And JoAnn continued to make the hour-long drive at least twice a week to attend family therapy sessions; sometimes, because of activities in which parents were expected to be involved, she'd be out there as many as five times a week. Gradually, she noticed Danny changing. He started doing better in his schoolwork and he even played on the basketball and softball teams, which he'd never done before. At one point she asked Larry, his counselor, if the reason Danny looked better than he had in years was that the drugs were finally out of his system.

"Partly that," Larry told her, "plus he's eating good food regularly, and he's getting lots of exercise and plenty of sleep. He doesn't have many distractions right now, and the expectations of him couldn't be more clear."

He was responding positively, she felt, to the discipline and order that formed the corridors through which he walked each day. Slowly he assumed more responsibility in the program; eventually he worked his way up to the position of a Senior, one of those responsible for looking after new residents.

While Danny was still at Second Chance his older brother got married. He was granted a pass to attend the springtime ceremony on the manicured grass of the spacious lawn at their father's house. The young couple had lived together for several years and decided to legalize their commitment to each other.

I don't believe I'd ever seen JoAnn become as anxious as when she spoke about the approaching wedding day. She probably had never really enjoyed family functions, beginning back in her childhood, but this occasion was more stressful than I'd have imagined. The bride and groom were handling everything to do with the event so nothing was being asked or expected of her except that she show up. It meant, though, that for the first time in over three years she would be seeing her mother. Actually she hadn't even talked on the phone with her mother in all those years—Marie had stopped calling after finally accepting the limit JoAnn had placed on their communication.

When she spoke about this meeting, forty-seven years fell away and she became like a little girl anticipating a scene overripe with danger. So now there was no getting around their meeting. She had to find a way through the tension between concern for her son and the hurtful history with her mother.

I suggested she take a friend with her. "It's a good opportunity to ask for support from someone who cares about you," I said. "And you'll know someone is there just for you. It'll also give your friend a chance to offer you something."

During the next session after the wedding I was surprised to hear how glad she'd been to have Lois with her.

"When you first suggested it, I thought it was the dumbest idea I'd ever heard. But I asked her to go with me anyhow. Then when we got there I heard myself saying, 'Lois, don't you dare leave me alone here! Not even for a minute.' "

JoAnn laughed at how she'd reacted that afternoon, and showed me a few Polaroid pictures taken at the ceremonies. I told her she didn't look any more uptight or anxious than anyone else. She smiled an easy and sudden smile, indicating the tightness of the last several weeks had vanished.

"My mother," she said, "is just a little old lady now."

It struck me how there are times when we brace ourselves to draw a firm boundary around our being, and then a moment arrives when there's absolutely no need to do so.

21

COUNTRY

"We have a lot to do today, chile," Honey says, "We sure do. Think I just rinse up these few dishes while you EAT UP. . . . No, no, we have plenty a time for you to eat. Can't go runnin' around without no food, chile! Has to EAT UP and put some meat on your bones. Need to fill you out some. You is just too thin, too thin. Time to put a little meat on them bones."

Honey don't think I need to be as skinny as a spring chicken.

"Don'tcha be a listenin' to her, chile," the Man says. "We is just 'bout right for us. The Lord don't mean for everbody to be all filled out!" and he looks at me like we know who is Everybody. The man is long and lean and tall. She is alla time calling him a Long Leggedy Man.

"Some peoples," and he gimme a wink, "just think everbody what the Lord makes should be round and plump like a ol' settin' hen. Well, ain't so. Room in this world for more of us long and lean peoples than there is for those round, FILLED-OUT folks. I just declare those round, filled-out people takes up a lot of room, chile. You ever notice that? Well, I'm not one to cast the first stone, but I have notice, chile, that those round, filled-out peoples do take up right much space."

He's going on now, our Mr. Man is. He asks me, "Have you notice that, chile? Well, I do believe if you just keep those big brown eyes wiiide open, first thing you know you might notice that."

Oh, I see that Man is getting ready now. He stands up, gets his knife outta his pocket. I jump up and get MY knife outta ITS place.

He's getting ready to GET THE LAST WORD. He tells me lotsa times, "The onlyest way to get in the last word with that ol' woman, chile, is to be a leavin' while we's talkin'!"

We is all ready now. He looks sideways at me, and that look says is us all ready, chile? I IS. I is all ready! I go to the door and he opens it to let me out. That's when the Man says, "I DOOO notice them round people take up a heap of room in the house, chile. Yep, sure do notice that. 'Specially in the BED!" and he closes the door quick, quick. We leave QUICK!

He tole me plenty a times "that be about the onlyest way to get in the last word with that woman, chile. Just gotta CUT AND RUN 'fore she preach your funeral!"

We did it! "We got out with the LAST WORD, didn't we, Man?" I laugh at how we do that ol' trick. I laugh inside and out loud, too.

The Man, he smiles like a shade tree. He says, "But she gonna be a waitin' to get us back, chile. Honey ain't gonna let us get off as easy as that. She just be a waitin' . . ."

He smiles at hisself and me 'cause we is Rascals!

There was a war overseas and lots of soldiers around town. They got trained on the Post a few miles away before being shipped out.

I remember a particular one, even though I never knew his name. He was young, a scared boy-man-soldier, and getting his pants on reluctantly. This was the last time he'd be "out." He was being shipped off the next day. He was a mere boy, and scared to death.

"Oh God, don't hurry," he said. "Don't go yet! Sit down here, please."

I knew how he felt, knew it exactly. Probably better than he did himself. I sat down on the shabby mattress while he talked. He wanted to be safe at home. Told me he wished he was back home on the farm. None of this fighting stuff was any of his fault, and it wasn't none of his business either. His family kept to themselves and minded their own business. And here this war came along and he had to go. He didn't even know why.

The training, all the soldiers' training, was enough to scare hell out of you, he said. All the fighting and killing just wasn't right. It went against all he ever was taught. It just wasn't right. He never wanted to fight anybody.

He was almost crying. The boy-soldier was nearly in tears thinking about "doing all that" to another man, doing the things they had been taught to do in the Army training. Even when he was a little kid he wouldn't fight.

"I just didn't want to. I wouldn't never fight anybody," he said, looking at his hands. "Didn't see no sense in it. You hit me; I turn 'round and hit you. What in the hell does that prove? I'd just like to know what in the hell that proves." The whole time he sat and talked he was twisting his hands.

The door rattled.

"Is there anybody in there?"

"GET THE HELL AWAY FROM THAT DOOR!!" the boy shouted.

There was a laugh in the hallway. Someone said, "We got a full house tonight. Have to try another door, old girl." I heard some girl's laugh trail off as they moved away.

Angry. He was plenty angry. "Duty? Hell! Let the damn big generals go fight overseas and I'll go home where I belong!"

He just simply didn't understand why there had to be this fighting and why he had to be part of it. He didn't tell anybody that. Didn't tell the other guys, didn't tell his father and mother. He couldn't tell anybody. And now it was time for him to ship out. He thought there'd be a hell of a lot less wars if the ones deciding to fight had to go and DO the fighting! He didn't see any of THEM going off to the battlefields!

I listened and watched him, this boy from a farm somewhere, with his shoulders slumped and hands that kept rubbing each other. I knew the scared look in his eyes, and I let them hold me there in that little room while people cussed outside the door about us taking too long.

"Too long, brothers. Toooo long have we been FORCED. Forced to crawl on our bellies!" When he said "toooo long, tooo long," I could feel how long it had been.

I used to sneak away from home when I was nine and ten and listen to the singing from the colored church that was in a field down from where we lived. I never went in but I always loved being underneath the floor—where I could crawl to—and hearing all "the fine singing we've enjoyed this morning. And I want to thank you all for joining in to make this joyful noise unto the Lord on this fine Sunday, brothers and sisters. Mighty fine! Don't believe we've ever sounded any better, do you?" and folks would say "Amen" all around.

Only *this* time when I was hidden under the church it was getting dark. And I hadn't seen any wives or children come in with the men. The Preacher was there, but a man they called the Night Rider was talking.

He said he was a man of peacefulness, a man of God, as peaceful as any of the Lord's shepherds. "But, brothers, there comes a time in every man's life when there is nothing to be gained by knuckling under. I am here to tell you there is a time for everything, and everything comes in its own time. The Good Book says that, now don't it, brothers?"

Some man said, "Amen, Preacher. Amen!" I felt like I knew there wasn't nothing to be gained, not one thing, by knuckling under.

"Even the lowest worm will turn!" the Night Rider went on. "Now that's a fact, brothers, and I know every single member of this congregation has seen it. Now ain't it the Lord's truth, brothers?

"Well? Well, what's it to be, brothers? Now's the time, for there is a mighty change a blowing in this country! Oh, I know," and I heard him take a couple of steps, "I know it, brothers, but I am standing here tonight to tell you THIS: there is a movement in this land that's stirring up the WINDS OF CHANGE. And there's no force, no force on the face of the earth, that can STOP IT!

"And I'll tell you why, brothers. Because God is on our side. We know that for sure because God didn't make any man for to crawl on his belly before another man! No, He didn't! No, God created allll mennn eeequal!! It is man, the WHITE MAN, who forces us to crawl on our bellies before him! There is nothing to keep us down unless we let them do it to us. Stand up, be prepared. BE PRE-PARED, brothers, and when the winds rise up and blow, then you be on call to STAND LIKE A MAN STANDS!

"The white man has ruled us tooo longgg, brothers. Listen to me now. Change is in the air. I can feel it and taste it wherever I go. And most of you know that I go about everywhere these days. As I stand witness to you tonight, brothers, we are on the move. We are!"

He called on them to stand together. As long as they stood together, there's nothing could stop them! That's all they had to do. That's all he was asking of them, to stand together as men. And he could tell them right now nothing would stop them. Together they would win.

That was all he was asking of those men: to "stand together when the time comes." He told them he knew they were tired and had already put in a hard day's work at their jobs. And he wanted them to know that he thanked them for coming out to hear him speak. He knew it wasn't easy to get up from the table and go back out on a workday night when they had to be up early again for another day of work the next morning.

He thanked them all for the effort, and said he wasn't going to talk all night. He knew they'd be glad of that! They laughed like he was right. He just begged them to work and listen to Brother Preacher here, and make ready. Make ready for the time that was coming. Make ready to stand together like men when the time comes, and IT IS COMING!!

"We ain't got a chance unless we stand together and knock their feet off of our necks. It's true, brothers, it's true. We've got to throw off their yokes! Got to, brothers. This ain't no way to live. You know the white man won't never let go on his own!

"Know why? 'Cause they're KINGS! And why? Only because they are WHIIIITE! That's why. They ain't no smarter, are they? Some of them are dumb as hell, in fact. No, they ain't any smarter, and not a bit braver, are they? But they got it all, and just because they're BORN WHITE! That's all they are, born white, and it makes them Kings! They won't hand it to you, brothers. You and I know they won't give you an inch, not one. Not even a quarter of an inch.

Did a white man ever give you a thing? Did he? No, nothing, except trouble! And then it's 'Yes, Sir' and 'No, Sir' and 'Thank you, mister. . . . !' I tell you it is time to STAND!!

"They ain't ever going to come up and say, 'Oh please, please stand up and be a MAN!' No, no indeed. That ain't the way of it, brothers. Ain't never happened and it never will, because the man what's on top don't care about you or you or me either! So it's up to us. It's up to us to care, and to be ready! You got to be ready to THROW OFF HIS YOKE! Stand like men on your own feet!"

When he was finished talking I just sat there, quiet, hunched down on the ground under the wood floor of the church. I didn't make a sound, but my heart was racing. He didn't know I was there, the Night Rider, but he could've been talking directly to me.

Grannie was mad. She said nobody cared but her. Nobody would clean up the mess but her. I knew the only reason she did it was because of being too afraid *not* to clean it up. Like everybody else, Grannie was afraid of making Henry mad.

The young girl in the bedroom was sick, could hardly move her head. She'd lie there as still as she could get, then suddenly the vomit would just gush up out of her mouth. She couldn't move. She hurt so bad she couldn't even move, so the vomiting just about tore her guts out.

She was a young country girl, maybe fourteen, only a couple of years older than me. From a farm somewhere in the mountains. I called her Country. I didn't understand what was funny when everybody in the house would laugh and say she was "fresh off the farm." Seemed like it was a joke to them but I couldn't figure it out at the time.

She was simple. Yes, Country was good-hearted but kind of dumb. She must've been lonesome the short while she stayed at our house because she talked to me some about her life, about her family. She was glad to get away from the farm, but you could tell she was lost.

I never paid much attention to her during the five or six months

she lived with us, but I do remember one night especially. I guess it
was a time she just needed to talk.

Only a few of us were still around and the fat man behind the
bar was counting the money. We were all dragged out from putting
in a long night's work in the stinking bar, dance hall, whorehouse
Joint. I got a bottle of beer, sat down at a booth, and slid my shoes
off under the table. The lights were turned up a little bit, enough to
see how dirty and smelly the place really was. The country girl
wandered over to where I was sitting.

"Is it okay if I sit here, JoAnn?" she asked softly.

I never heard of anything so stupid. "I don't own the goddam
place, you know. You can sit anywhere you want now they're all
gone back to camp!"

I thought it was funny for her to ask me that, then I realized she
was afraid. Afraid of Tom behind the bar, afraid of Henry. Scared of
everybody, really.

"I wish I could stand up to them like you do, JoAnn." Country
slid in across the table from me. "You just look 'em right in the eye
and say anything you want. I could never do like that. I don't know
what it is . . ."

She started talking, quietly, easy like. I wanted her to go away
and leave me alone, so I shut her out like I shut out everything.
There was some bluesy, sad song on the jukebox but it became a
hum in the background, like her voice.

I'm not sure what it was, but after a while something the girl
said snagged my mind. She said her mother never talked back either. But it was the tone and the mood that I finally heard, not her
words. What reached in to hook me was the feeling and voice of a
soul laid bare of all hope. Before I knew it I was listening.

She talked on and on that night, barely above a whisper, as they
straightened up around us. We could have been actors on a stage,
with the rest of the cast and crew moving dimly around the set while
a single spotlight fastened on the two of us in the booth. Only the
two of us existed then, as if all time had just fallen away. We were
two alone in the world, like marooned sailors. I suppose I was
hooked while she talked because we were so alike, both of us worn
down, our defenses low. While I clung with her that night to the
table which was our island, Country told this story:

I was the first one my mother had. And Maw was the first girl in *her* family, too. She told me they were poor, with too many mouths to feed. Maw said one day her daddy talked to a man with a farm in the next county about her going to work there for him. Next thing Maw knew was when the man drove up in a wagon to fetch her.

"Well, Mr. Slade," the man said to my mother's daddy, "I told you I'd be here before sundown to take one of 'em off your hands. I'm a man of my word, so here I am. Where's she at?"

I remember Maw told me the man didn't even get down and set foot on the place. He just sat up there like a stump till her daddy and the boys put her box on the wagon. Then my Maw's daddy handed her up. There wasn't nothing but a board for a seat, and since the man didn't move over, Maw said she wasn't sure what to do. "I ended up riding off from my folks like a sold cow," Maw told me, "in the wagon bed with my box."

Maw found out the man had had a wife who got sick and died. Left him with three or four younguns. So he'd just drove over and taken Maw, like a bag of potatoes. She begged not to go, but her daddy told her she'd be treated good, and fed, and be paid a dollar a week. She was to bring the money with her when she come to visit them.

So she went, my Maw did. Figured she might as well save her breath. Her daddy wasn't one to pass up a bargain, she told me. And this was a good deal for him. Her daddy would get a dollar a week out of it, and not have to feed her either. Be like double the money, he said, especially 'cause Maw ate so much. It was a good deal for both the men.

Well, the man drove Maw to his farm by the time it got dark, and unloaded her box. And you know what else she said? Maw said he went and took her to his dead wife's bed that very night since he wasn't paying a whole dollar a week for nothing.

Yeah, it wasn't hardly a year later till I come along. That man was my Paw, and I don't know if a meaner man ever walked on the earth. He never hardly talked to my Maw the whole time she lived, never took her anywhere or bought her anything.

The main thing with Paw was that he wanted sons. He planned to have a big place one day, and he needed lots of boys to work it. "Costs too much to hire on," my Paw used to say. Well, once Maw caught on how to have babies, she kept on having 'em until she just started wearing out. Oh, it was terrible hard on her.

When he wasn't working in the fields, Paw used to go to church all the time. He took us with him a few Sundays, but Maw figured it wasn't worth the trouble of getting the kids all cleaned up and making sure they sat still for the preaching. Paw'd be mad at her if they wasn't quiet. Maw didn't think much of church, to tell you the truth. Said it was just all hellfire and brimstone. No comfort there. But Paw went anyhow, every Sunday. Oh, he was such a good Christian, God-fearing, church-going man, my Paw. Ha! Well, he may have sat through a bunch of preaching, but I tell you folks used to spit on the ground after Paw went by! I remember once he beat up Maw real bad, then he climbed in his wagon and drove off to Sunday meeting!

I think Maw kind of got a breath of fresh air while he was at church. Later on, though, she was plenty upset when Paw started getting extra dressed up to spend time at church with the girl from the farm next to us. Maw was trying to get her strength back from having that last baby when Paw took to going to church even *more*.

Finally it was hurting Maw so bad, knowing he was running after somebody who wasn't no older'n me, that I went to the people at church to get help in pulling Paw away from the girl. You know what them church people told me? They couldn't do anything because Paw had never married my mother. All they could say was if he'd finally found somebody to marry in the church, well, they wouldn't stop him.

Paw got to fixing things up around the place after that. "I plan to take a proper wife," he told Maw, "so I don't need you here no more. Best thing to do now would be to take your kids and go on along. You ain't too old to get took on somewhere else, maybe closer to your home. Ain't you always saying how you miss your family? Well, here's a chance to go be closer."

I don't know why, but Maw didn't want to get out of there. She looked at him like he was gone crazy. He'd always been fair to Maw, he said, so he'd let her and her kids stay on if she wanted to keep working after he got married. He'd go on paying a dollar a week, too, he told her. Oh, he was so fair, my Paw! We were *her* kids now, not *his*. He meant the church didn't see us as belonging to him 'cause they hadn't never got married. So Paw said he'd fix up the shed out back for her and all of us since Maw didn't want to go live with her daddy again.

She was getting real bad off around then, from having the baby and being so weak, and she couldn't understand what Paw was telling her. He moved Maw's few little things out of their bedroom. Told her she couldn't sleep there no more since he was gonna wed in the church. The next day when he come in, Maw was curled up in their bed. Looked just like a child. Paw said if he ever caught her in there again he'd send her packing on the spot.

That night, after supper, Paw called us all outside. He was mad at one of his old dogs who wouldn't mind him anymore. The dog had got contrary and wouldn't mind. Paw made the whole family line up on the porch and told one of the boys to go fetch him a stick of firewood.

Right in front of us all Paw drug the old dog out of the pen and started beating him. Yeah, he made every one of us watch while he beat the poor old dog's head to mush using that stick of firewood. I tell you he looked at us the whole time. Made sure we didn't look away when he was beating the skin off his dog. Paw said it was the only Christian thing to do, to put the hound out of his misery. I took it to be a lesson about what to expect for not minding him.

My Maw lost the baby that night. It seemed like ever last little bit of strength left her when she came back inside. She sat all night without moving, even when I brought the baby to her to feed. Toward morning she started throwing up. I couldn't get her to stop; wet cool rags on her face and neck, nothing helped. She threw up when there wasn't nothing left to throw up! Then she doubled over her knees and started crying. I didn't know one dried-up woman could cry so long and throw up so much and hurt so bad! About then I knew the baby was lost. I saw how it was.

Still, I expected Maw to pull through and come around in a few days. She didn't though. She wasn't sick more'n a week before she died. She just plain quit. I think when she saw what Paw did to the dog she must've made up her mind to lose the baby and die herself. Anyway, that's what I figure happened.

And Paw? I reckon he was finally satisfied when they put my mother in the grave and out of his way. Oh, he thought he was just the most generous Christian man. He told me I could stay on there as long as I did right. Ha! Paw wouldn't know "right" if he fell in it!

"I'll take you on in your Maw's place," he said, "and let you keep them kids with you. I'll pay you a dollar a week just the same as I did your Maw before she died." He just hated to see them younguns sent off to the orphans' home, so he'd be willing to keep 'em and feed 'em if they'd help out a little bit.

Well, the girl from church started coming around before Maw had got cold in the ground, and right away she started talking me down to Paw. I could see the writing on the wall. Even though I'd been born and raised on that piece of ground I wasn't about to stay and watch somebody else sit in my mother's chair and sleep in her bed.

The day that girl from church came over the doorstep is the day I left. Figured things weren't going anywhere but down from there, so I might as well get out while I could. And I didn't see what good I'd do the other kids, either, being as mad as I was. To tell you the truth, I was afraid I'd kill the bastard if I stayed around another day!

I packed up the few clothes I had and set out walking

down the road, right under Paw's nose. He stood on the front porch, yelling about how I'd find out things wasn't no picnic out there. But I just kept on going.

Felt like I walked a thousand miles that afternoon. Still, when I looked up I'd only got as far as the church house. It wasn't quite dark yet and my feet just turned in at the graveyard, like I didn't even own 'em. It was the strangest thing. Then I saw Maw's grave and knew I'd better tell her I was going away.

"Don't know who's gonna come to clean off your grave, Maw," I told her. "I'd do it ever chance I got if I was to be here, you know that. But I just can't stay here anymore." I sat down and picked all the leaves and sticks off her grave, and cried the whole night. Seemed like it anyway. Except I remember waking up in the morning with the birds singing and all, so I reckon I fell asleep sometime before it got day.

It was real nice there. Quiet and nice, not anybody around. It was kinda pretty, too, in a way. I thought about how my Maw would like it there. Maybe it sounds odd but it seemed like to me it was just about the nicest place you'd ever want to see. I kinda wanted to stay there with her but of course they'd never of let me do it. You know lots of folks are scared of the dead, afraid of graveyards and stuff. Heck, I never did have no dead folks hurt me. That's a whole lot more'n I can say about the living ones.

I just hope my Maw knows why I ain't gone back to see her. I wouldn't want her to think I didn't care about her just 'cause I never been back to where she's buried. It ain't like I forgot about her. I couldn't ever forget my Maw, even for a minute.

Country was still for a while, remembering her Maw there in the quiet of the cemetery. It seemed like the night by her mother's grave was the most real thing in the world for the country girl right then. She was as unaware of me as she was oblivious to our miserable surroundings. I thought about what a godawful trail she'd been on. After being reassured that her Maw had a nice, quiet place to lay her head, Country walked out to the road and caught the first bus heading away from her Paw's farm.

When it dumped her out in town, why there was Henry Foley like a sleek and shiny vulture. Out searching for prey as usual, Henry spotted her before she was hardly off the bus. He must've known, when he swooped in, that she didn't have any money or a place to go.

The country girl had left her birthplace wanting only one thing: to find a different life than she'd had at her Paw's house. What she found instead was the same kind of life, only this time it was at Grandpa's house. Henry had brought her there to be one of his "girls." Oh, he could pick them. He could spot the ones who were so lost and abandoned they didn't stand a chance of making it.

She was afraid of everything, Country was. Never once in her young life had she felt safe or been protected, so she'd grown up scared of everything. She would do anything to please and be liked, anything to keep people from being mad at her. Henry zeroed in on this little desperate, stray thing, sweet-talked her without half trying and brought her home.

Country was big-boned and raw. She really didn't know anything except hard work. Soon after coming to our house she said, "I'll do anything you need done around here, Missus Foley."

Grannie was glad to have somebody helping out, but it didn't make her like the girl any. No, Grannie was just another in a string of folks who took advantage of the scared and defenseless. Like Henry did. Already Country was as beat down as her Paw's old dog, so Henry had no trouble keeping her in line. Just the threat of force was enough to get her to do as he wanted.

And she did whatever he wanted, too, everything he told her. Except for one thing. She got pregnant.

Henry was awful mad when he found out about it. "I don't know why she let herself get pregnant," he howled, thinking of how much money he was gonna lose because of her not working. "Jesus, she's so goddam stupid!"

Henry hated to be bothered by the girl "not feeling good." He liked to pull up front, beep his horn, and have everybody ready to file into the car so he wouldn't have to wait. He liked to get us to

The Joint and on our backs making money for him. Now this dumb
hick was slowing his business down. He told Grannie to take care of
the country girl until she was back on her feet. But it wasn't long
before I could see she wasn't gonna make it back to her feet.

In no time at all she got terrible feeble and sick, this backwoods
girl from a farm in the mountains. It was strange to watch her lay so
still and almost dead, and then to see such a violent gush of vomit
move up from her mouth like it was flying out with a life force all its
own.

It was just too much. You knew the life in the vomit was too
much for her, and you could feel it was the stronger force in her
body. Country was beyond caring, past hope really. The life force
was all in the sickness; there was no power and strength in the girl
herself. She was so weak she hardly moved anymore. And she was
hot enough you could feel the heat from her if you just looked into
the room.

Nobody wanted to be bothered with her. Mama and the other
girls didn't want to be kept awake by her sobbing and breathing.
Her very breath was a sound, and the sound bothered them from
their sleep, dammit, and they needed their sleep, didn't they? They
wanted her to be quiet.

She hardly moved. You could feel the stillness of death in her.
Then all of a sudden there was the violence of that vomit gushing
out with all the power in her. It was the strongest thing left in her
skinny little body. The only life left in her was the vomit and the
fever. Her body was empty and had given up. I could feel the "given
up" in her so keenly that it hurt me.

Yes, Country had let go. It was not an easy letting go either. It
was hard and bitter because she was just too tired anymore to keep
on when nothing was ever getting any better. How long can you live
on hope alone?

It had left her, the little bit of hope she brought with her when
she started in as one of Henry's girls. I think the hope died first in
her eyes. There was no more light in them.

What was left of her was blood. Lots of it. The blood was alive
and smelled strong. It ran out of her faster than you'd ever think
possible, soaking into the towels she held between her legs. When

one of the raggy old towels was filled up, Country would call out in a paper-thin voice to ask if it was too much trouble for somebody to bring another one. Hardly anyone went in there to see about her.

I wondered how someone so sick still had the power to throw up the way she did. It was like an explosion. She was so awfully sick and weak, like a near-to-death kitten. The girl needed to be nursed and petted and made as comfortable as possible in her pain and dying. At least when her Maw was dying she had a daughter to sit with her and put a cool rag on her forehead. Country had no one.

While Mama and her sisters dressed after supper Country sank into the sagging bed, her glassy eyes burning up from fever. Then, ever so slowly, she turned her head to the wall, away from them. She stayed like that all night and all the next day. That's when I knew she understood she was dying. Just like she'd known when her Maw quit trying to live.

Grannie whined and fussed and told Henry that the girl was running off at both ends. "She's bad off, Henry. You better do something goddam fast before you end up with a body on your hands!"

Grannie said this with no feelings about the girl who lay there dying by inches. No, there was not one ounce of concern for the girl; the emphasis was all on the "body" Henry would be left with.

Country just gave up and lay there bleeding while they walked around her that last day. Then later, as everybody came home and fell into bed half-looped, you could hear her breath come out in tiny gasps of pain when anyone jarred the bed that night.

The next day was when Grannie said, "You may as well face it, Henry. That girl is a goner. She ain't ever coming back. If you don't do something soon we could all land in trouble."

Grannie wanted Country out of the house right then but Henry had something else to do and didn't want to be sidetracked. She pushed him, though, because she knew the girl was near death and wouldn't last much longer. It was clear that Grannie didn't want to be stuck with a corpse.

Henry finally looked in on the sick girl, came back out in a hurry and told Grannie to pack up all of Country's stuff. Grannie couldn't see any point in packing all those clothes. The girl wasn't ever going to use them, that was for sure. So she kept out a few things for herself, as "payment" for all she'd done for the girl, and threw the rest in the sad suitcase Country had toted off the bus six months before.

Carrying the suitcase, the girl slung over his shoulder, Henry left the house mad that he got stuck with all this mess. He took her to the bus station and left her propped up in the corner on one of those long wooden benches. With her pitiful suitcase by her feet.

All anybody at home ever said was the country girl had just "gone on off." Nobody ever said anything about her going off to the bus station to die.

When someone found her there they first thought she was asleep, but she was dead. Because of all the traffic, people waiting and everything, Country had sat there for a long time before anybody noticed she had bled to death. The word was that no one had ever seen her around these parts. No one knew a thing about her.

In the dozen or so years she walked on the earth, life had given that poor girl a hundred years of pain. Why should she have fought to stay alive when there was nothing good behind her or in front of her? Country knew she didn't care to have any babies. The last thing she wanted was to end up like her mother, all dried out from having kids. So she had gone quietly off with Henry to meet the man he assured her would "get rid of the baby." It was right after Henry brought her back home that Country started getting sick.

For a while she believed she had broken away from the sorrowful life her Maw had led. When she left the farm she promised herself she wouldn't live the way her Maw had, with not having anything or anybody. For a short while she thought she had made it.

I remembered the time we sat huddled together in the booth at The Joint.

"You know, JoAnn," Country had said, "I reckon my Maw is better off now than she's ever been. At least now nobody can tell her she's got to move on. She'll always have that little plot of ground where she can rest her head, and that's a sight more'n she ever owned before. I guess the most that poor girls like us can hope for is at least a few laughs on the way to the grave." She laughed a not funny laugh at the idea. "That box in the ground is probably the only thing I'm sure of getting, you know? And once they turn me under I figure I'll stay planted. Won't nobody shove me around then."

Before she was even cold she had been forgotten. In our house the country girl was never mentioned afterward. The thin film that covered our lives closed over again as soon as she was gone, leaving no trace she'd ever been with us.

22

BORDER PATROLS

JoAnn never had her phone calls returned by Peg anymore. Or if she was in the area and just stopped by, there was always somebody at the house to say Peg was resting or not seeing anyone right then. The family finally asked people not to come visit, and there were days they put a note on the door conveying that message. During one of JoAnn's sessions the talk wound its way around to the last time she went over there.

She'd put together a small bouquet of flowers from her yard and called Peg's to say she'd come by and just drop them off on her way to run a few errands. Peg and Gerald's home was probably where JoAnn had felt the most at ease since she was seven and spent what time she could on the Place with Honey and Mr. Man. She had passed many hours there over the years, with different people and on many occasions. Always she'd been comfortable. This time when she got to their house Gerald was out in front fooling with the shrubs or some plantings. He was pale and looked drawn, she said.

Even before he had a chance to finish saying Peg was asleep, their twenty-year-old son pulled up in the driveway. That encounter between the son and his father wouldn't stray from JoAnn's thoughts. It was another example of her paying the closest attention of all to what was unspoken. As we talked about it afterward she recalled the feeling and mood of the moment rather than the words.

"I'll never forget the look that passed between them," she said. "Not for as long as I live."

Scott apparently had just gotten to the house for a weekend visit from wherever he went to college. Maybe he had been alerted by a telephone call which brought him there at that time, she didn't know. But she could tell he seemed worried, watchful, as he approached them.

"There was a look they exchanged . . ." she tried to explain. "I don't think I can describe it to you, but I knew right then they both understood she was dying. It wasn't anything they said. I'm not even sure they said anything, come to think of it. But the way they looked at each other, whatever it was in their eyes, said everything. You just knew it all at that moment, that she was dying."

This was not really a revelation to JoAnn. She'd known it was the case for some time now. At least cognitively she'd known it. But she'd never gotten any indication at all from Peg or her family that they knew it, too. None of them had really acknowledged how sick she was, and their denial had been going on for quite a long time. So this hit her in a different way, this act of being a witness to their knowing. I think it made her own understanding settle even deeper.

These things were mainly what she talked about regarding that last trip to their home while her friend was still alive. I believe Peg died about six months later.

Just a week or two before she died, though, she called JoAnn one morning. "I couldn't understand her. She didn't make any sense, and really she couldn't even talk. But I think it was her way of telling me good-bye." Later she learned from Peg's daughter that the call she received was one of four Peg made that day—they were her last contacts outside the family.

JoAnn didn't go to the funeral. She had already made plans to be out of town for most of that week and she went ahead with her plans. In truth, she also felt reluctant to see Peg at that point. She hadn't been let in to visit for so long by then and heard friends say Peg had wasted away to eighty pounds. She didn't want to have that last picture of Peg be the final print in the album forever in view behind her eyes.

Their last actual visit had been terribly painful for JoAnn. She said it felt like they didn't have anything to say to each other. Be-

cause we'd talked a lot in therapy about the importance of getting
closure with people, JoAnn was practicing the tying up of loose ends
whenever she could. Seeing Gladys during her last trip to the old
neighborhood had driven the lesson home. She wanted Peg to realize what their friendship had meant to her, so she began by saying,
"You and your family have been very important to me."

Peg cut her off, changed the subject. In fact she started talking
about one of their co-workers, a woman named Betsy, whom JoAnn
had never liked. It became completely idle chitchat, not the sort of
conversation she was used to having with her oldest and dearest
friend.

This was the last time they ever saw each other. And when that
day was followed up by total inaccessibility to Peg it caused more
pain than JoAnn could at first put into perspective. As we talked and
laid open the hurt, however, one of those shadowy lines to the past
reeled in its catch. Naturally, it wasn't just Peg she was grieving.

I remember once hearing that when someone close to us dies,
we mourn not only *that* loss but whoever's death preceded this last
one, that we're always also grieving the person who previously died.
In fact JoAnn was dealing with even more than the losses of Peg and
both Honey and the Man.

The experience with Peg hit a nerve she came to define as
helplessness; she could trace that awful sense of impotence directly
back to the Place. It had to do with being shut out, with being told
she must leave and couldn't come back. As a child, when she looked
into the eyes of the Long Leggedy Man and then sat on the steps by
their filled-out Honey, she had to listen to them sending her away.
She listened, unbelieving, as each one of them said she had to leave.

"You know what was the first thing that went through my mind
when they told me I had to go?" she asked. "I didn't know how
they'd be able to get along without me. I was afraid of what would
happen to them."

"What are you talking about?" I wanted to know. "They were
sending you back to your family and you were worried about *them*?"

"That's the first thing I thought. See, they talked all the time
about not knowing how they'd have gotten by if I hadn't come
along. I must have heard them say it a hundred times if I heard it
once. Honey would sit down on the porch when we got back from

the garden and say, 'Well, I just don't think I'd a got them peas picked today withoutcha, chile. Don't know what I'd a done 'bout that ol' Man's supper tonight.' And he told me, too. He was always saying things like, 'You're a mighty big help around here, you know. Reckon Honey'd have a right hard time on this Place if it wasn't for you, chile. Nope, I just don't know how we got along here 'fore you come on this Place and give us a hand.' "

They had loved her. They valued her and let her know their lives wouldn't have been the same without her. I'm sure they simply wanted her to know she was important and mattered, a message she hadn't heard before. They probably never guessed she'd take their words so to heart that she'd feel responsible for whatever might happen to them in her absence. But JoAnn had learned that if you loved someone you helped them out when they needed it.

Peg needed help, she knew that. Yet her friend wouldn't let her in, she wouldn't even let her get near. What JoAnn responded to once more was the being shut out. She didn't know any way of getting back to where she could be useful, where she could help out. There was nothing to do for her friend except stay away, as she was again being instructed. It was all too familiar.

Some days start out looking like any other. Everything goes according to expectation—with a predictability that's often not even conscious—until something doesn't fit and it derails the whole day. Or the entire week. Maybe even the rest of a lifetime.

I remember the end of a Washington's Birthday weekend in the country, during the winding-down days of winter. It was time to start loading up the car to make the drive back to the city and several days of work. Most likely the car hadn't been moved at all in the four days of the long weekend. Careful planning and thorough grocery shopping usually made it possible to stay put, if that was the most appealing thing, until time to head back for work. Since the nearest small grocery store was twelve miles away on the other side of Hedgesville and time was too dear to spend traveling, I used to joke about having moved to NoBudgesville, West Virginia. I thought it was manifest luxury not to have to budge if you didn't want to.

The going-back-to-the-city drill was well known: it didn't take us long to get everything loaded in the car and lock up the house. At the same moment the engine turned over on that chilly day, I noticed a piece of paper under the windshield wiper. The car was parked in a driveway at the end of a tiny lane which forked off a gravel road. All this in a small development of twenty-five homes spread over a hundred and twenty acres. It was about half a mile to the nearest hard-surfaced road, and that led to a one-room country church on a pretty hilltop three miles away. It's not as if the car was sitting on a city street or at a shopping mall where the odds are pretty good of finding a parking ticket or an advertisement for pizza under your wiper blade.

So, given the setting, I was more than surprised to find a note there on the windshield. When I got out and read it I was flabbergasted. The handwriting was almost as recognizable as my own. How in the world . . . ?

"Rose Mary," it said, "I tried to call you but there was no answer. This is not an emergency although I'd very much appreciate an earlier appointment if you have an extra opening this next week. Please call to let me know." The phone number was a local exchange. It was signed simply, "Thank you, JoAnn."

Dazed, I went back in the house to call. There was no date on the note so I didn't know how long ago it had been written and had been kept from blowing away by the windshield wiper. No answer to my call. After getting back to the Washington suburbs I managed to reach JoAnn there in town and we set up an appointment for late the next morning.

When she came into my office for that extra session, I'm sure she sat right down and started talking about whatever was troubling her. That's the way she did: no fanfare, not a greeting, just diving in. I have absolutely no idea what she began talking about that day or why she wanted an additional, earlier appointment. I think I was still trying to find my equilibrium.

After realizing she'd been going on and on for a while and I didn't have a clue about what she was saying, I cut into the middle of her sentence. "How in the world did you know where I lived?" I was still finding it hard to believe one of my patients had been to my house.

"I didn't," she replied. "Or at least I didn't before this last weekend. I wasn't happy about putting the note on your car but I couldn't reach you when I called. And I felt like I needed to see you . . ."

"But how did you know," I broke in again, "how did you know where to find me?"

She went on as if not hearing the question. "Gary told me to go ahead and write the note, and he walked down with me to your house. He thought I should knock on the door or just leave it inside the screen but I didn't feel right about interrupting your weekend." She must've noticed a look of bewilderment or frustration or whatever it was on my face because her voice changed and she said, "I'm sorry if that caused a problem."

I didn't know *what* it had caused but . . . "I still don't understand how you knew where I lived," I repeated. I was pretty sure I'd never said anything to her to that effect, or no more than maybe a mention of being at a place in the country, away from the city.

JoAnn went on to explain—at least it's what, in her case, passed for explanation—that her being there came about through a trip with a friend. Her explanations were typical of her regard for exposition. It's not that she wanted to conceal information or tried to mislead by omitting details. Rather, I think, she offered just the material she considered essential and relevant to the discussion at hand. Perhaps having grown up with almost no chance of being heard or getting her point across, she learned to speak in headlines; nobody in her family was ever interested enough to inquire about the rest of the story. In her speech there was a tendency for background and color to emerge only if the listener summoned those details. So her explanation about this event was typically terse. And right away I knew why I didn't seek out the fuller story at the time. I'm sure she would've willingly provided it if I had asked.

"You've heard me mention Shirley before," JoAnn stated. Yes, I remembered they had worked in the same office for a number of years and sometimes did things together socially. "Shirley's brother and his wife invited her to their cabin in the country over the holiday weekend. She asked if I wanted to come with her. That's how I ended up there."

"Ended up where?"

"At the Harkers. Gary and Barbara Harker are Shirley's brother and sister-in-law. That's where we were staying."

I felt dense; the words were like oatmeal trying to get through the sieve of my brain. "You mean the Harkers who live just a few houses down the road?"

JoAnn said yes, they were the people she happened to be spending the weekend with. When they were talking about the area she realized they knew me, and later on they pointed out to her where I lived.

I imagine the blood had to have drained from my face when she relayed all this. At least I can't picture there wasn't somehow a visible physical corollary to my state of emotional shock. And if thoughts or clusters of memories, feelings, and images were able to transcribe themselves to paper in the flash of their instant life, I think a couple of slender volumes might've sprung into existence during those few seconds of silence.

My mind was quickly flooded. I knew the Harkers—just minimally, but well enough—so I made a quick decision. Whether my voice came out as conversationally as I tried to make it sound I'll never be sure.

"I can't believe you know our neighbors. Why, they're not even half a mile up the road."

"I couldn't believe it either when I heard your name mentioned," she said matter-of-factly.

With as matter-of-fact a quality as I could muster, I went on. "Well, it's a small world, isn't it? Donna and I bought our place there in '73. I think our house was one of the first ones built, but seems like Gary and Barbara were also in that initial wave of homeowners."

I really don't know what I went on to say. Probably not a great deal since I was fairly reticent to talk about myself in those days. But no doubt I said a few more things about the area and the piece of it that was our neighborhood. The fact is we had quite a friendly, easygoing community which, with everyone's participation at our yearly Homeowner's Association meetings, ran smoothly with a minimal amount of hassle.

The only person in the whole development who was barely civil, who usually avoided eye contact altogether and sometimes didn't even speak if we passed each other out walking, was Barbara Harker. It didn't take much effort to imagine what kinds of things she had said about us.

So I went on talking for a little while about how lots of us city folks were flocking to places like that in those days, in the early seventies, trying to find a house on a little patch of land with some trees around. It had been a godsend, I told her, a retreat from work and a sanctuary from an oftentimes too-crazy world.

"It's funny how things work out," I said. "Donna and I had been wishing we could get a quiet place out of the city. Then one Sunday she saw an ad in the *Post* for property near the town of Hedgesville. We drove up that afternoon and found a place we loved. I think all of us loved our little piece of the country in those days. Seems like Gary and Barbara were there most every weekend as soon as their house was built, so I guess they've relished it, too. But then to think of all the things you could've done over the weekend and you ended up a few houses down the road, well, it really *is* a small world."

In reality I don't think I spent a lot of time on this subject although hours of dialogue were going through my mind. What talking I did was surely in an effort to right myself, to find my balance again. The issue of boundaries had come hurtling back into focus. My own boundary, this time. Our home in the woods *was* a sanctuary. It was my sanctuary, *our* sanctuary. It had come to be our refuge from a judging and often hostile world, a refuge from all the Barbara Harkers out there.

I had felt myself instantly become tense at hearing JoAnn's story, ready to do battle, I suppose, or at least defend myself and my lifestyle. And the thing was I didn't know whether I needed to or not. But it was a reflexive response honed on years of being alert to prejudice and signs of homophobia.

JoAnn appeared unfazed by our conversation, except for her concern about whether she'd caused me any distress in leaving that message. Mainly, though, there were other things she wanted to discuss. It was the reason she'd asked for an extra session in the first place, and so she got on with it. Knowing about her head-on, one-track approach, I'm amazed she put up with me talking as much as I did during that appointment. The posture I had immediately assumed to protect my personal life space was as unnecessary a stance as the one she had adopted in going to her son's wedding. But it had been a perfectly natural thing for both of us to do in our individual circumstances.

JoAnn's leaving the message on my car on a bleak February day, I've come to see, was a turning point in our work together. At least for *me* it was a turning point. On that day I couldn't possibly have known all the repercussions of going ahead and taking a step from shade into light. There were many ironies present in the situation that got my attention.

Before long, for instance, I realized how I'd been anchored in my work with JoAnn by the guiding principle that she was going to be better off discovering and bringing into the open all that had been hidden from her awareness. Yet here was something about myself which, though I'd become more comfortable acknowledging to my family, friends, and co-workers, I was still hiding from in my professional life. It had left me fearful that this one piece of information about just one aspect of my life might cost me credibility or perhaps even some clients. A secret, whether it's knowingly harbored or unconsciously held, affects us in ways we simply can't imagine until we've taken the risk of sharing it with someone else.

I'd probably never have done that with JoAnn if it had been left up to me. It hadn't taken a lot to convince myself over the years that therapists don't need to talk about themselves in therapy, and that patients don't really care to hear about the person in the other chair or on the other side of the desk. But I see now that it's one thing for a therapist to *choose* such an approach out of their therapeutic conviction and quite another for a therapist to slide into silence out of fearfulness or shame.

Actually, I think most of us have, or have had, something about ourselves we've wanted to keep away from others' notice (if not from our own recognition). Perhaps nothing more than trying to disguise some perceived inadequacy or failure. This incident with JoAnn let me see how much energy I'd been putting into monitoring what I said about myself, how I said it, what pronouns I used, and whether to say "I" or "we." I could stop wondering if I'd be questioned about who I'd gone with or done something with because suddenly I didn't have to pay attention to all that around her any more.

It was similar to when I quit smoking—back in the days when every place, public or otherwise, was a smoker's paradise. Until I stopped I had no idea of the amount of thought and planning I invested in smoking. Did I have enough cigarettes with me to last through the next meeting? Was there an ashtray in the group therapy room or should I take one along? Could I get by on what was left in this pack or did I need to buy another pack for tonight? It was the same kind of thing. A nearly obsessive awareness was needed in both instances to maintain a way of functioning I adapted to over the years. It was eye-opening in both cases to realize how much of my energy had unknowingly been bled away by those concerns.

On an important level I think this was an instance of our being funneled from different experiences onto a converging path. Just as JoAnn was learning how many aspects of herself remained unavailable for her benefit because of a forgotten past, so I started learning how much of myself had been hamstrung by a fear of exposure. In our therapy sessions after this encounter I might not have even shown much of a change in the way I worked, but as soon as I stopped scaring myself with imagined reactions, I noticed a change in my willingness to be more honest. Honesty, when you come down to it, is what therapy is all about—on both sides of the helping relationship. How effective can a therapist be at encouraging self-understanding and truthfulness if she's worried about being judged as unacceptable. In our different ways both JoAnn and I were coming out of our respective closets.

One of the paradoxes presenting itself to me with this boundary confrontation was especially poignant. It saddened me when I could admit to myself that the very thing which so generously sustained me had been kept the most hidden asset in my life. For instance, a look into practically any office of our clinic would show a clutch of sweetly framed pictures of smiling family members on therapists' desks. Even if those therapists didn't speak about their families, the photographs placed them in a supportive human context. So it's not that I necessarily would've shared more with my patients about my life had I been less afraid, but the absence of any personal touch like that was a complete denial of the relationship which nourished me and helped me do my work. Worse than that, though, more damaging than feeling the need to deny, was my fear of discovery. JoAnn had identified her painful experiences in being shut out; I worried most about being *found* out. Maybe they were the same thing in the end: if I were found out, I'd be shut out.

Until this time I couldn't have articulated that my greatest fear apparently had become that people who didn't know me might discover the wellspring of my greatest joy. In a world which increasingly comes across as cruel and hate-filled, something is terribly wrong when there's such passionate condemnation of *any* source of genuine caring and gentle love. It seemed another experience JoAnn and I shared was that of having become strengthened and enriched by the profound love we'd received from outside the mainstream. Once again I understood that in many ways we were more alike than not.

As it turned out, JoAnn wasn't the least bit interested in the goings-on in my life. So when my initial shock and worry about being "outed" (an old concept but a term not then in usage) had subsided and proven to be of no consequence, I was finally able to laugh about the whole privacy issue. If I thought about the lengths to which Donna and I had gone in order to protect our privacy, well, there was little to do but laugh. We had wound up traveling ninety miles away from our suburban apartment to find a place with a little acreage, the last house at the end of a lane, no neighbors in sight. And we didn't know a soul in the area when we set about settling onto our little swatch of land. Yet, over ten years later, here came a client one day walking up to the driveway. Obviously there was no external protection, no outward security, as much as I might've wanted to believe otherwise. You've either got it within or you don't have it. No amount of boundary maintenance or patrolling of one's borders can take the place of self-acceptance and the lessening of fear which accompanies it.

JoAnn's showing up practically at our doorstep was so farfetched I simply couldn't chalk it up to coincidence. When a situation arises that defies all odds of happening, I believe we'd best trust the wisdom of the universe and put ourselves into it. There are times we just have to jump in the raft and hold on, or we'll always wonder what it would've been like to ride down the rapids. I suppose I could've clammed up after JoAnn's shorthand account of walking to our place with Gary on that blustery, colorless day. A part of me instantly wanted to retreat into my familiar ways, but instead I deciphered the message of that moment as a wake-up call.

The best reason I can find for why these kinds of synchronistic events happen in our lives is that they help us awaken and move forward.

Perhaps the biggest irony of this entire affair was that I really hadn't been boxed into a corner at all and I wouldn't have had to say a word about my life with Donna. JoAnn hadn't really known *anything*! However, I didn't find out that was the case until seven or eight years after she'd finished treatment. We talked one day while I was reviewing my recollections of her therapy with the notion of writing about the experience. I asked about her memory of the note on the windshield incident. I guess I finally sought out those details I was too dumbstruck to solicit back when it all took place.

"Do you remember," she began, "when I was first coming to the Mental Health Center—I was in the group then—and there was a big snowstorm on a Monday night? I came to group the next morning and there was hardly anybody at the clinic yet. The receptionist was one of the few people there. She said Bev called to say she couldn't get in and so had the other group members. I asked Christine if she'd heard from you yet. I don't think she really thought about what she was saying but she just mentioned that you probably wouldn't be able to get here from West Virginia. 'From where?' I said, because it surprised me. I think that's when she must have said Hedgesville. I didn't know that was where you lived, and I didn't think about it anymore until my friend Shirley mentioned Hedgesville one day not too long after that. Seemed funny to me to hear a place talked about twice in a few weeks that I hadn't even known was on the map."

I sat back and listened as JoAnn laid out this story of amazing synchronicity. Although she'd never spoken of it to me, she'd actually been to Hedgesville a few times before. Well, rather to our little neighborhood. She'd gone for a couple of overnight visits with her friend whose brother had a weekend place there.

She went on to explain that the Washington's Birthday weekend was her third or fourth visit. While they sat around the breakfast table, Shirley talked to her brother and his wife about maybe looking to buy a house somewhere in the country. They told her a house was for sale right there in the neighborhood, and asked if she wanted to walk over and look at it. Shirley was eager to do so, and JoAnn went with them.

As they walked along the road in the development, JoAnn told me, Barbara pointed out the different houses they passed and said a few words about the owners. She supposed it was to give Shirley an idea of the kind of people living there. "As we turned around at the end of the road, she pointed to your place and said that two social workers—or two therapists, I don't remember which she said— lived there. We kept on walking and I wasn't paying any attention until I connected the word 'therapist' with remembering Christine saying you lived in Hedgesville. I must have asked if she knew who they were and she mentioned two names, one of them yours."

I shared with her then how upsetting that incident had at first been for me. That my head had buzzed with comments I was *sure* Barbara had made about the two women at the end of the lane. I could tell by her look JoAnn didn't understand what I was talking about.

Finally she replied, "Well, I knew she didn't like you."

"Oh, is that how she put it?" I asked, and the laugh that sprang out must've been tinged with sarcasm because she looked at me with a puzzled expression.

"No, she just said that two social workers lived there."

"You mean to tell me that's *all* she said?"

"That was all she said." She thought for a few seconds. "But you know how you can tell when someone isn't saying something they mean? She didn't say anything except your names and profession. Still I could tell she didn't like either of you. I don't know why she felt that way but it was pretty obvious she did."

When I heard her come out with this simple statement I had to laugh again. Then it was JoAnn's turn to be dumbfounded. (Sometimes she used to accuse me of being naive or slow-witted as I questioned or commented on the stories of her childhood—now I thought that shoe of naïveté was on the other foot.)

"You really don't know why Barbara had that reaction, do you?" I asked, though it was more a statement than a question.

"Well, I think she was not a happy person," she said seriously. "I know it kind of surprised me. I guess because she's a social worker, too, and is sort of in the same field as you. In fact, she's in the process of getting her doctorate." JoAnn shook her head a few times. "She's writing her paper—what do you call it? . . . her dissertation?—on guess what."

Totally perplexed, I said I couldn't even come up with a guess.

"We used to talk some about therapy," JoAnn continued, "because she knew I was seeing a therapist. So she'd tell me a little about her doctoral work. Said she was writing her dissertation on the subject of empathy."

Well, the ironies were flying. I gave a brief explanation of homophobia to this woman who had probably read more psychology and philosophy than I had and who was one of the most perceptive and insightful people I knew. And yet JoAnn was as surprised at the idea that someone might think less of me because of whom I loved and lived with as I had often been that teachers a long time ago only saw her as just another unwashed Foley, or that her grandmother had never been able to regard her with any feeling except hatred.

All through the course of treatment when JoAnn's memories returned, she caught sight of new features each time she circled a piece of her history. The same phenomenon happened when we would replay an interaction that occurred between us in therapy, even if years had piled up between those discussions. During an even later look back at that event which had been such a turning point for me in our work together, there were new things I still learned. She used to tease me for always talking about "levels of awareness" and "layers of understanding," but this conversation demonstrated the truth of those trite phrases.

It wasn't until we spoke further about the fallout from her holiday weekend in the country that we both began to realize how much she had known which she wasn't aware of knowing. The sequence was similar to the ways she would move from the surface of a newly found memory through all its shadings and then down to its full complexity. The more we talked, the more she put together. None of the signs she took in at the time had been enough of a curiosity for her to spend extra energy on, but some feelings and impressions had registered nevertheless. When I finally expressed an interest in understanding what had been her experience of my caution and secretiveness during a large part of the time she was in therapy, she unwrapped her mind's digging tools and went to work remembering.

"I hadn't thought of it before," she said, "until you asked just now, but I think I figured you were maybe seeing a married man. It had something to do with how careful you were in saying anything about your life outside the office. Actually, one time you mentioned plans to go away for a few weeks. I'm not sure why, because I don't usually care or figure it's any of my business, but I asked if you were going with your husband. I remember now you said you were going with friends. It wasn't what you said, though, that I noticed. No, there was something about the way you said it and moved off the subject that caught my attention."

I just looked at her and sadly shook my head.

"Another time you were illustrating a point you wanted to make by telling a story about a friend of yours. Donna, you said. The way you talked about her, even the way you said her name, I knew she was someone very special to you."

She watched while I took in her response. "It amazes me now," I told her, "to look back and remember how well I knew you then, and yet to have believed I could put something over on you. Or, that I felt I needed to."

Finally hearing her perceptions about a time when I thought I was being so careful . . . well, if it weren't so sad, it would've been comical. You can't hide who you are, I thought. At least not around someone who listens to you. And—more important, especially from my currently held, long-time-coming perspective—why would you even want to?

In the cusp between winter and spring I went for twelve days to a tiny island off the east coast of Puerto Rico. With a few patients my vacations never seemed to come at a good point, and JoAnn was still hard at work in her therapy this time, too. This time, though, I decided against playing out the usual scene. After announcing when I planned to be away, I told her I was a little tired of feeling like a piece of interchangeable scenery on the set of her life. As far as I could tell she'd be perfectly content as long as another warm body sat in an office with her while I was away. Looked like it didn't matter to her *who* was there to listen. It seemed to me that I didn't matter at all as a person; I could just as well have been a stone column with ears.

I sounded fed up, even to myself. If nothing else, it got her attention. And I doubt if I'd have taken that tack with her if she hadn't stumbled into the middle of my personal life a bit earlier. Tired of feeling so cautious and fearful, I was committed to being honest with her now, determined to be as real as possible.

JoAnn was quite floored by these assertions, and for a week or two struggled to grasp what I was talking about. Before I left on my trip, however, there was a shift in the way she dealt with my going. She may not have been fully connected with the feelings involved, but she was able to acknowledge that she wished I wasn't leaving ("even though you're certainly entitled to your vacation . . .") and thought she'd probably miss me over the next several weeks. She didn't like the feeling of needing me, she said; in fact she had never let herself have those feelings before.

She had, of course, a long, long time ago—and now she permit- ted a dash of those same sentiments to register in her inner world. Our exchanges before and after my trip to the perfect beaches of Culebra, to suspended afternoons snorkeling at an end of the island we could only get to by boat, were a milepost in our work together. I'm sure it wasn't simply my imagination that something significant had taken place in our relationship, something important for both of us.

Danny completed his year of drug treatment and graduated from the program at Second Chance. JoAnn said he seemed like a different person in his appearance and behavior; she couldn't recall that he ever looked so healthy or acted with such maturity. In accord with the program's treatment policy, the whole family was involved in his discharge planning.

Options were discussed and, where they existed, he had the responsibility for figuring out what he wanted and deciding what would be best for him. He chose to move back to his mother's house and finish his senior year of high school. Danny didn't want to return to his father's, JoAnn told me; she sensed there was much more associated with that decision than was ever spoken about in their sessions. She picked up the unstated message that it wasn't really an option for him, although his father didn't seem opposed to the idea. Maybe the specter of his being around again, she thought, had touched off some conflict between his father and stepmother.

JoAnn and Danny met with Larry, his primary counselor, and another staff member to draw up a contract between them for this new stage of their living together. Each talked about the expectations held of the other and both signed the document spelling out their mutually agreed upon terms. JoAnn, over many hard lessons from hard years, had learned not to let herself get either too discouraged or too hopeful. Still, I think, she was more encouraged about Danny during this period than I'd ever seen.

Within a month, maybe even less, he had broken all the conditions he'd agreed to meet.

She was heartsick. The treatment staff always cautioned new graduates and their families about the first few months after discharge being so critical in the recovery process. Everybody in the family continued meeting with Larry for follow-up sessions; deciding on the next step became their focus.

Danny's father rented a room for him not far from where he'd be going to high school. Wesley made the arrangements with a friend of the family who, five years earlier, had turned his home into a kind of halfway house. Victor himself was a recovering alcoholic and quite invested in helping those with drug and alcohol problems. So Danny moved to a room in Victor's house. He agreed to follow the rules laid down by a man who had been about to self-destruct until he joined AA ten or twelve years before. Wesley paid six months rent in advance, with the understanding there would be no refunds for any reason, even if Danny decided to move out or Victor asked him to leave before that time was up.

At the same time JoAnn was trying to let go of the notion about having any real control in Danny's life, she started getting hold of some memories vaguely sensed but heretofore always beyond reach. For nearly six months she'd been pursued by questions about what had happened to her during the years she was eleven and twelve.

Going back in time to those days was a ragpicker's task. As the weight of it on her grew heavier, intuitively she knew the job was going to be difficult and exhausting. She seemed to dread the under-taking. Or maybe that was my own projection because I knew I'd be right up behind her on the two-seater she was steering, pedaling with her through whatever lay ahead.

"I think this will be the worst time for me," JoAnn said. "But when I get through it then I'll finally be done." She had said the same thing before, at least two or three times along the way that I knew of. I don't know whether she remembered it or not, but I didn't have the heart to point it out.

This may, in fact, have been another one of those times I tried to tell her she had a choice about what she did. If she didn't want to dig into that period, or at least not right then, I assured her, she didn't have to. I should've known better; she put no more stock in my view on the subject at this time than she had before. As was previously the case, she truly felt she *didn't* have a choice when it came to facing something that seemed to be holding her back. For her there was simply no option.

(This was hard for me to comprehend or accept; personally I'd always believed I could either do or not do whatever I wanted. I was finally disabused of this idea, however, some ten or twelve years after we had this particular discussion and long after her therapy had ended. It was at a time when I found myself being bludgeoned by the stubborn certainty I had to write about my experience with JoAnn, if only so I could figure out what had happened to me. I must say she got an enormous kick out of hearing me admit to feeling I had no real choice in this matter. No doubt she felt vindi-cated at last!)

So, JoAnn gave herself over to the job at hand, collecting the rags and tattered remnants of memories thrown aside in painful piles nearly forty years earlier. When I realized I was becoming a bit apprehensive in the face of this endeavor, I spoke with Donna one day about the client I had who kept insisting she had no choice about her direction in therapy. Occasionally we consulted with each other about difficult cases; this time we were having tea out on the deck late on a summer morning. Two wood thrushes, the flautists of our forest, called back and forth to each other while we talked.

Donna seemed to completely understand JoAnn's conviction.

"I'm starting to think," she summed it up, "that free will is just giving consent."

Before long JoAnn appeared to be merely weathered flotsam caught in the undertow of her recollections. The tide took over; there was no reprieve to be had. Dark images from the mural she'd once drawn came floating to her psyche's surface, revealing some old ocean-floor clues that had foreshadowed this leg of her voyage.

23

THE FOX IS GOT

"My, my, my," Honey says when she opens the door. She smiles at me but I don't hardly look. I walk on past her and into the kitchen.

"Howdy-do to you, too, chile," she says in her "nice" tone. Like she uses all the times when she reminds me about good manners.

She tips her skirt up and bends her knees a little bit. "Iff'n you curtsy nice like this and say, 'Howdy-do. How are you?' I think you gonna find out that be the best way. Yep, best thing is to be nice to people."

Honey is just talking on and on. I sit down, don't say a word. All at once she stops and turns around to look at me.

"Why, you just a little storm cloud today, ain'tcha? C'mon over here, chile, and tell me what ails you." She holds a big ol' arm out for me to come to.

Soon as she says how I look I know it is all inside me. There is some terrible feeling, like a violent storm, raging inside me with nowhere to go. I don't have any way to get rid of all the feelings swirling in me. I don't have any words for them.

The storm had come up in full force that morning while it was still dark outside. I'd been asleep in my bed and woke up with someone doing bad things to me. Some Foley thing was happening, and the hurt of it woke me up. I was afraid, too, as I tried to come up from the darkness. It was like waking from a nightmare that's only barely remembered but you're still dead afraid of it.

Being scared to death wasn't the worst thing though. The worse thing was knowing I couldn't do anything about it, that the badness was beyond my control. The hurtful things would go on and on, and nothing at all would be done to stop them. That's what hurt the most. Already the terror of helplessness was something I knew about, knew and was used to. I knew there was nothing I could do to stop those things from happening to me. I had to stay there, so I *had* to get used to it.

In the kind of house where I grew up no one ever asked you if you wanted something done to you. They just told you what *they* wanted and then did it to you. No word was ever mentioned about what I wanted so I never even thought about it. It's just the way things were in my world.

Being forced out of a heavy sleep, knowing how helpless I was to stop the mean handling, had brought fierce, dark clouds to my morning.

This is the mood I'm in when I get to Honey's house; anger swirls and churns me into a thick, dark batter. There is no place for the feelings to go but round and round inside of me, as if molasses was being stirred with flour in a bowl.

Honey knows something is ailing me almost as soon as I come in the door. I go in and walk on by her. Don't talk to her or even look at her. Just sit down in the chair that I always sit in.

I can't tell her, though, 'cause I don't know the feelings or the words. But something comes through to me about how she changed from all sunshiny to quiet. The one thing I feel is her being sad to see me so unhappy.

". . . Oh, I just don't like to see you hurtin', chile," she says in a voice that wraps around me like a soft blanket.

Her sad sound pulls me out a ways from the pit I waked up in.

Henry Foley is talking dirty and leering at everything in skirts. Another man is sitting in the front seat of the car with him. I'm in the back corner of the backseat.

There's lots of money in the front seat. A roll of money, not folded but rolled. I don't know for sure who has the money because

I'm not really paying attention to what's going on. At least not until the man in the front seat turns around to look at me. Then I tighten up. I've seen him before and he gives me the creeps.

"If he takes a shine to you," I'd been hearing them say, "you've got a ticket to EASY STREET."

Mama tells me again and again how much money the man has. "He can have any girl in town. All he's got to do is snap his fingers, JoAnn. Like that," she says with a snap of her fingers and a little twist of her hand.

Oh, everybody brightens up trying to look as pretty as they can so he'll fall for them. It's all they can talk about, his coming back to The Joint sometime soon. I think to hell with them. I think he's got eyes like a dead lizard. Everybody is telling me he's a BIG SHOT!

Just before we got in the backseat of the car where the men were talking someone said, "At least smile, JoAnn. Won't hurt to smile, will it? He can do things for you if he likes you. Oh, if he likes you, JoAnn, you could have EVERYTHING YOU WANT. Every single thing!"

✳

"Sit still, dammit. Don't you move again. You're messing this up faster than I can fix it."

Mama yells at me as she paints my fingernails. "I GOT TO GET MYSELF READY, TOO, you know! I got better things to do than bother with you!"

She puts the top on the nail polish. Blood red. I look at it and don't feel a thing. I just remember all the hateful times I've spent sitting in The Joint watching the red fingernails and the red, red mouths. Blood red lipstick on so many mouths, all opening and closing. Blood red lips chewing and talking, drinking and smoking while I feel nothing.

It is very important to me that I not feel or think. Nothing. Nothing at all. Or else I'll die. I'll come apart or go crazy. All surrounded by blood red lipstick and bright red fingernails.

Nights at The Joint are all the same. I know the patterns. Why wouldn't I? I've sat there for hours and hours, night after night. I hate it. Always did hate it. I hate the drinking and smoking, eating, the dirty talk, the noise of it all. You can't hear many actual words because the room is so jammed with noise. The air is never clean, never "aired out." The sickening smells of old, stale beer and cigarette smoke are locked like paneling in those walls.

Mama is getting herself ready now, finally ready for the big night. She selects her best blouse and combs her hair while "talking" to me. Tonight of all nights, she doesn't want me to make them mad.

"For God's sake don't start any of your shit tonight, JoAnn. I promise you Henry ain't gonna put up with it. D'you hear me? You just better not mess this up for him, and I mean it."

She says Henry has told them to be ready on time. He doesn't want to wait, so we'd better be ready to go when he gets here. "Now don't let him down tonight, JoAnn," Mama warns me, "or he'll KILL YOU!" She lets me know this is Henry's big chance to "make it."

It's *my* chance, too, to hear Mama and the others tell it. I'm sooo lucky. So lucky to have been noticed by this big shot man. My God, how some girls would sell their souls for this chance! Why, plenty of girls would do anything for a break like this. I'm sick of hearing how lucky I am; it's all any of them can talk about.

After going through the whole list of things I better do, and the other things I better *not* do tonight, Mama changes her tune. The syrupy talk and bribe tone start. She has gotten me a "present." Some kind of trinket for me to wear to make me pretty for Mr. Big Shot. I know it isn't a present, because "presents" don't exist in the Foleys' world. It's an out and out bribe for good behavior on my part, payment toward my being still, being quiet, being good and doing like I'm told.

She shows me the trinket with such excitement. It's so beautiful and I'm just the one who can "set it off." Mama can't help herself; she is so PROUD! Her little JoAnn is sooo pretty! She keeps on about how pretty I will look tonight, how I'll be the prettiest one, how Mr. Big Shot will take to me and make me one of HIS girls!

Every word Mama says is a sharp, red hot poker jabbing me. I'm starting to sink under her promise of the future. The trinket in my hand is like a rock pulling me down, and so I yank it apart and throw it on the floor because I don't know what else to do.

Mama lets out a little gasp and grabs my shoulder. Very quietly, without even looking at her, I say "Don't."

She pulls back as if hit. She is shocked and upset, but I know she won't do anything. It would be too risky to let them hear she's having trouble with me tonight.

So Mama lets go of my shoulder and turns back to the mirror for a last check of how she looks. I put on the greasy, blood red lipstick that I hate, that gets so smeared and messy after a little while at work. But it's what Henry likes his girls to wear, so I put it on.

※

I think his name was Floyd.

Yes, Floyd Callahan. He was a boy I knew when I worked at the custard place out on Fort Benson Boulevard. He was a young tall high school boy with red hair, and he'd just started to drive.

I remember standing with the other carhops and seeing his car pull into the drive-in. I recognized the car, and was really pleased to see it and know the car was his and he was in it. I went right over to see him.

There was a girl in the car next to him. I didn't know her but she was sitting close to him, and the eager, pleased-to-see-you feeling in me died dead. I thought she had probably made him bring her over to the drive-in to let me know who was his girl.

All these years I have remembered that feeling, though none of the circumstances, nor how hurtful it was to me. I would not know now except that when I first woke up today the name Floyd Callahan popped into my mind.

It was the staking out of a claim on someone, like kids do. She wanted to teach me a lesson.

Or else he did . . .

Yes, it was the boy; I am sure it was the boy. He was getting back at me through the girl. I am not positive but I think it was because I said no about sex.

There was a falling out, and it was over sex. He didn't like being told no by any drive-in trash, and so he showed me.

We'd been parked in his car. Everything was comfortable and fine. We were just sitting there talking when it got out of hand.

Back then I had no conscious memory of the past, of The Joint and having been a two-bit whore. All that had happened to me was buried way out of reach. So when the feelings came up that night I think I went crazy and it scared him.

All of a sudden everything in the car changed. It changed and I didn't like it anymore. When I suddenly felt the difference I just couldn't keep holding the stirred-up hornet's nest. I think I would have gone along with the sex to keep some kind of connection, but I didn't have a say in the matter. I simply did not.

Unaware, I'd been, of sliding into the sex. And then it was there, BAMMMM! All the feelings came up in an explosion, and I came up fighting like a crazed tiger.

STOP IT! STOP IT!! I had to GET OUT! I started running. I didn't even know he was there.

He was all of them. All of the people from my life who had grabbed me and made me do what they wanted. All the Foleys and all the men from The Joint. I was terror-stricken, scratching and pushing to get out . . . out . . . out . . . a way from there.

The child self went crazy and had to get the hell out of there. Ruined. You be ruined if you do like that, chile. She put them ribbons in the fire, hell fire. Flames jumped up, burned 'em up! Not do that no more. One of these days you be able to get outta there, get away from them folks what don't Do Right. And all the time the Lord be right witcha, chile. Don't matter at all atall where you is. Ol' Man God, He's everywheres. He is all over the place, with us all the time, see everything we do, chile. The Lord do watch over all us, all the time!

I had to GET OUT OF THERE! I didn't know where I was, where we had parked, or how to get home. All I know is I came up fighting and clawing to get out and away from there.

Lost to the present time, I was back in The Joint, back on Pine Ridge Road, back in a ball on the sandy path and I had to get out. The poor boy never knew what hit him as I shoved and scratched to get out of the car. I walked off in a state that was long familiar to me: hurt, frightened, scared to death, and no place to go.

No place in this old world to go to get away from the Baddies. I was losted. Lost and in blind, black panic. So I walked. I walked and left that poor boy frightened out of his wits.

I wasn't looking or seeing, but I knew he came after me. He tried to get me in the car. "I can't leave you here," he shouted.

He kept it up but I just kept on walking. I couldn't listen. First thing you know they pull you down, way down with 'em to hell. They be bad! Don't care 'bout nothin'. I never seen the like. She wail and wail. Like to see 'em dead, Man, for what they done to that chile! Never think I say that 'bout anybody, but I be glad to see 'em dead and in their graves. I go dance on their graves!

He was driving and leaning out the window, talking and trying to get me into the car. I would never have gotten in there, not for all the tea in China. He didn't want to leave me "way out here." He couldn't leave me there, but he didn't know what else to do. So he parked the car, got out, and tried to talk sense to me.

I just walked right over, around, through him, off the dirt road where we had parked, and onto a highway. I didn't know where we were; it seemed I walked forever. If you kept on going, I figured, you would get somewhere where you knew you were.

The boy yelled from the other side of the road, "Wrong way. WRONG WAY! You're going the wrong way!"

I turned around and went the other way. Toward town. He drove off fast. Up ahead he waited . . . and drove on . . . and waited . . . until he led me all the way home like that. Poor boy.

And overnight I forgot the entire incident. It was so horrible, so scary for me that I forgot every bit of it overnight. I didn't even remember it when he came driving into the custard place with the girl. To get back at me.

I can recall the feeling of warmth to see his car, and then SHOCK!! when I saw the girl in there with him. I had absolutely no memory of the fight. Seeing her in the car was like a sudden ice bath, as if I'd been plunged into Arctic waters. Shock was all I registered, and I never understood what it was all about. Poor boy. He was unprepared to be involved in such a mess.

We wait together in the front room for Henry to pick us up. Mama and her sisters have been told to keep an eye on me to make sure I'm ready when he gets here.

I may as well have been in a trance; I don't think or feel anything. The little windup doll that is me has only a sense of heaviness. It seems I move in weighted slow motion. I mumble that I have to go pee.

Passing the kitchen door on the way to the outhouse, a tiny glint of light on metal catches the edge of my eye. Grannie's big old butcher knife is lying by the sink full of dirty dishes. I pick it up and take it with me.

Since then I've wondered what was going on in my mind at that moment. The answer was buried so far inside, back then, I had no idea as to what motivated me. I was responding to messages I didn't even hear. With today's awareness, though, I can trace an invisible and undiscerned thread back to Honey. "Watch out around that knife, 'cause it could hurt you sumthin' awful," she had once told me. And somewhere, still barricaded away with the awful pain of losing them: "They can make you do terrible things, chile, but they can't make you be bad!"

The butcher knife has a hole in the handle with a loop of string through it. In the outhouse I tuck the knife under my skirt, nestle it in the folds of a stiff petticoat, and tie the loop of string around my belt.

Back in the living room, then in the car, and later in the booth at The Joint I maneuver with it hanging under my skirt. No one notices a thing out of the ordinary.

I didn't have a conscious plan or thought about what to do with the knife. It never crossed my mind that I could use it on myself, to siphon away the despair overtaking me. Or even that I could turn it on somebody else if I was cornered. All I knew is that I had it with me. And I was the only one who knew it.

Mama has been somewhere else, across the little dance floor, and now comes back over to the booth where I'm sitting. She leans over, saying something, but I can't hear the words. I see the blood red lips moving and talking but I can't hear any of the words. I don't care. Let her talk; it doesn't mean anything to me. We never "talk" anyway. Even when our lips move and we are in the same room, never do we talk to each other.

But she is busy talking now, her blood red lips moving. She seems charged up, and I think she's pointing to someone across the room. I know she's talking but I don't care. I know I am just a piece of meat. I know I have to do like they say. I don't even need to know what the red mouth is saying. I just have to move where they tell me, do what they say. I don't have to understand what they say, all I have to do is do like I'm told.

Someone says the man at the table by the bar wants to buy me a drink. This flunky is telling me the man wants me to come over to where he's sitting. You can feel he's a big shot; it's a feeling in the place.

"Can't he walk? . . . Oh, he can? Well, usually the men come over here and ask me themselves, see. So of course I figured he couldn't walk or something was wrong with him if he had to send you over instead."

The errand boy is stunned. "I don't think YOU KNOW WHO HE IS, GIRL!" he sputters.

"You know what, buddy? I don't even care."

So terribly odd it seems to me now to think back and realize that I cut his throat. I know it as sure as I know my own name. I cut his throat like they killed the hog when we lived on Pine Ridge Road. My mind says it's impossible. Where would a twelve-year-old girl get strength enough to kill a full-grown man? But I know I did it. I held him down and slit his throat.

Fury and rage and hatred must carry with them tremendous strength and power. Certainly all emotion translates into energy. I suppose I found physical power in being nearly drowned in desperation.

The knife was a dull knife. It had to be because Grandpa would never have sharpened it for Grannie. But it mattered not to me for I would have torn his throat open with my fingers if that was the only thing available. I would have torn into his flesh with my long, blood red finger-nails, just like Grandpa and the others had slit open the hog's throat.

"What in the hell's going on in here? OH, JESUS CHRIST. OH, SHIT!"

Tom had come out from behind the bar, run down the hall and pushed his way through the people standing in the doorway. "OH,

GODDAMMIT TO HELL! WE DON'T HAVE ENOUGH TROUBLE
WITHOUT THIS GODDAM MESS, HENRY?" he shouted. "Shit,
Henry, what are we going to do?"

Tom stepped over to where Henry, speechless, stood at the foot
of the bed. ". . . She did this? SHE did it? Henry, you brought her
back here!"

The tone was "it's your fault, Henry." He wanted to hit Henry, I
could tell. I was glad and hoped he would, but I knew he wouldn't.
No one ever did. "After all the trouble that girl caused, YOU
BROUGHT HER BACK HERE AND DIDN'T WATCH HER!! Goddammit, you stupid half-breed."

Henry shook himself, pulling his eyes away from the bed to
glare at Tom. "Don't start trouble now, d'you hear me? It's your fat
ass, too, you know!"

No, no. The man said it wasn't HIS trouble! What in the hell
was Henry talking about? His ass in the crack, too? Oh no, he didn't
have a thing to do with it.

"She ain't MY trouble, Henry. She's yours. Yours and nobody
else's. You know she ain't right. Why didn't you WATCH HER, for
Christ sake? . . . You did? Well, if you did such a good job watching her, then how'd THIS happen? . . . You left her with THEM?
Jesus Damn Christ, Henry. They couldn't watch shit, and you know
it! We got to call the cops."

"The cops? What for?" Henry wanted to know. "He's dead, ain't
he? Things ain't bad enough, now you start with the COPS, for
Christ sake."

"We can't cover this up. We got to call the cops, Henry. . . .
Oh God, that's all we need, the cops in here with their goddam
hands out!"

The man kept saying the shit had hit the fan now. The shit had
hit the fan just as sure as hell.

Henry was thinking. He said they had to cover up this mess,
they had to get him out of here. Tom was sick from the sight. He
wanted to know how and where, that's what he'd like to know. He
said that Henry was crazy.

"Jesus, we got to get him out of here, that's all." Henry made it
sound so easy, to just GET HIM OUT OF HERE. He said to give him
time to think. "Shut your mouth, I said. Don't forget it's your ass,

too. You're in this up to your balls, you damn fool. It's your place, ain't it? Well then, how do you think you're gonna get out of this? I oughta just walk out and leave you with it all to do! How'd you like that?"

The man backed down some. Henry told him not to forget who owned this Joint.

"But you brought them here. Don't forget who brought them here, Henry!"

"And you didn't want them here, I guess."

"No no, Henry, but they're YOUR girls. You brought them here and they're yours, not mine. It's your trouble. Hell, I've got nothing to do with this mess!"

Henry reached out and grabbed him with both hands, grabbed his shirt and the bar apron. The man was sick from the sight and looked weak in the knees.

"YOU'D BETTER SHUT YOUR MOUTH, GODDAMMIT. YOU'RE UP TO YOUR NECK IN THIS SHIT, AND DON'T YOU FORGET IT FOR ONE MINUTE. Not one! Don't you EVER forget it for one minute, or it's your ass. One way or the other, it's YOUR ASS!"

Henry threatened him with the cops, or if they didn't get his ass, it'd be Henry who would fix him so he'd wish he was dead.

They said the first thing to do was get rid of THAT, and they talked about how to do it. What used to have been such a Big Shot, just an hour or so ago, now was a THAT.

They talked and argued about the filthy old piece of a mattress on the bed. If they rolled THAT up in the mattress to get rid of it, Tom wanted to know, who would pay for the goddam mattress? After all, he wasn't in business for his health, was he? Who was gonna pay for it if they threw the mattress out?

It was soaked in blood. Soaked in THAT'S blood.

The best thing, Henry said, was to get rid of it all, just roll up the mattress with the body in it and dump it somewhere. Get rid of it all. The sweating, fat man wanted to know where and how. Henry didn't know. He'd have to find a place, but for right now they had to get rid of THAT before somebody else came in here.

The man asked who in the hell did Henry think was coming in here this time of the night? Henry said he goddam well wasn't taking any chances, so they'd just have to get rid of all this mess right now.

". . . MY car?" Tom couldn't believe he heard right. "Oh no! Shit no! I don't want no part of it."

"YOU'VE GOT A PART OF IT, and if you don't shut up I'll walk out that door and see how you like it."

They argued. They rolled up the cot mattress, rolled IT up in the covers and the thin cheap cot mattress. Henry wouldn't let the mess be put in his car.

I was slumped on the floor in the corner. I had collapsed there, like a puppet would land if all its strings were suddenly cut. I don't think anybody really noticed me until then.

"Jesus Christ, it looks like a damn slaughterhouse in here. Get her out of here, Henry! GET THAT GODDAM BITCH OUTTA HERE! Jesus, she gives me the creeps, the way she looks at you. I wish I'd never seen her."

He wished he'd never seen Henry either. Henry and all that easy money. It had sounded so damn easy at the time, and now look! He didn't sign up for nothing like this. He'd wanted the easy money, but hadn't bargained for this. Oh God, the shit had really hit the fan!

"I DO NOT THINK YOU BETTER DO THAT AGAIN, HENRY FO-LEY!"

He was so surprised. No one ever talked back to Henry Foley. No one. He took a kind of pride in that. It was all part of being a little Big Shot, I suppose. I had talked back to him. He'd been furious at that and had slapped me so hard I don't know why it didn't snap my head off. He hit me across my face as hard as he could swing without hurting his hand.

I looked at him level in his eyes, and talked in a calm and quiet voice. "You're mad now, Henry. You oughtta know it doesn't pay to get so mad that you stop thinking ABOUT YOURSELF!"

He stopped. He wasn't used to being talked back to, so he stopped and looked at me, not in the eyes, but around my face. My pretty little face. He had threatened to change my pretty little face often enough. Tales had it that he had changed quite a few pretty little faces, and I believed them. He would have loved the pain and suffering it would cause a pretty woman who had bothered him in some way. And besides, it would have set an example and helped to keep his girls in line.

Henry finally got over his surprise and got his mouth to working again. I didn't even listen to him. I managed to get the car door open; I was so weary, so terribly weary. I just wanted to lie down right there in the filthy dirt driveway and go off to never-never land. But I stood up the tallest I was able to stretch, and spoke to the great and wonderful son who liked to brag about all his important connections in town and at the courthouse.

"Do not ever in all you born days even act like you are THINKING about slapping me! I hope you hear me, Henry. For your sake I hope you are listening. DO you hear me HENRY CHARLES FOLEY . . ." and I raised my voice just one little bit when I said ". . . JUNIOR? Answer me. Answer me so I know you hear me and will remember this. You'd better listen, Henry, because I wouldn't like to see you lying dead with your handsome face all cut up."

Oooh, I knew that would get him, to think of his handsome face cut up. "I WOULDN'T LIKE TO SEE YOUR THROAT CUT FROM EAR TO EAR AND YOUR PECKER LYING COLD ON THE FLOOR BY YOUR BED."

I waited. Waited for him to soak it in like the blood soaked into the filthy cot. He wasn't too quick to take things in, and I knew it. He liked to be called a smart fellow, but he wasn't quick to think. "I wouldn't like to see you allll cuuutt uuup, HENRY CHARLES FOLEY, JUNIOR!"

We were quiet. Very quiet. And then I spoke, still and low. It was like some teacher I had had. She never raised her voice, but she could control the students better than most of the other teachers. You would have to be quiet to hear what she was saying. It was most effective.

I waited for Henry to get his head in gear and hear me. "You do know that could happen to you, Henry," and I sounded so sad to think of his handsome face cut to shreds, and his throat letting no more air into his lungs, and his ice cold pecker thing just lying useless on the floor. It was all of his worst nightmares right there in one thought.

It took him a while to realize what this dummy was saying and how she was talking to him. Him, who nobody talked back to! Instead of him being able to threaten me like always, I was coldly and cruelly threatening *him* and his goddam face and goddam THING. I believe it may have been too much for his little bitty brain. I slammed the car door.

Even though on the inside I was scared, there was nothing to do except get out of the car and dare him. In spite of just having witnessed how I had butchered the Big Shot, I think it may have been the unexpected that stopped Henry. They all understood rage and anger; that was how they talked and how they behaved. What he wasn't used to was the stony dead calm in my voice. I had stood up tall and said each word clear as a bell, like the teacher had done. I wasn't going to be pushed around anymore.

I had served notice. And it worked. It stopped Henry and all the rest of them, it did.

There are always threads back to root causes. It may be forty or more years later, if you're looking, before you see a thread.

I get to Honey's house after school. She gives me a plateful of pancakes she done made to fatten me up. I have my little legs wrapped 'round the chair legs, taking nice little bites, and just talking and telling her things. Then she tells me the fox is got. She says the Man done got Ol' Mr. Fox last night. Mr. Fox, he was a "right smart fella," but the Man be smarter'n that fox!

I can't hardly wait to see Ol' Mr. Fox. I been hearing 'bout him for a long time. The Man tole me how that ol' fox looks, how his nose is pointy so he can out-smell them chickens, how he just lies out there inna field till he gets his chance. Then, quickasaflash, he'd have hisself some chickens!

I remember alla things they has tole me 'bout that fox. I tell Honey, "Why, iff'n he was to get in that henhouse, then all that hard work me and you has put in on them chickens be GONE! Gone just as quick as anything, did you know that, Honey?"

"Well, yes, yes. I do know it ain't no sense tryin' to mix chickens

316 CHILDHOOD'S THIEF

with no fox! Now I may not know as much as SOME FOLKS around
here . . . (I know Honey means me and the Man! I don't look at
her or my raggity baby 'cause I'm sure Lu Lu Belle is trying not to
laugh!) . . . but I do know if ol' fox gets in there with them chickens there's liable to be a whole lot less chickens than there is fox
when he gets done!"

And now here is ol' Mr. Fox got! He's around behind the barn,
and I'm gonna see him. I finish them good ol' pancakes and take the
plate to her. I tell her I be back after me and Lu Lu Belle see Ol' Mr.
Foxy. I fold Lu Lu over my arm and we go hoppity right across the
yard and around the BARN.

Soon's I see him I know SOMETHING IS TERRIBLE WRONG.

I start yelling and screaming. Everything in me stops moving
'cept these screams that keep coming out . . . until I realize that
the fox is DEAD. Now he's just a bundle of fur with a long bushy
tail, hanging up against the barn wall.

When Honey said the Man done "got" Mr. Fox, I don't really
know he's dead! He's always been part of a story, a Tall Story they
tole me. I never knowed Ol' Mr. Fox is a animal who can be DEAD!

For a little bit the onlyest part of me that works is the screaming
part. Then I run, run fast to Honey, who comes rushing out on the
porch when she hears me yelling. She thinks maybe a bee done
sting me since she ain't seen any snakes around lately. It takes her a
while to settle me down. All I can get out is a lot of sounds that ain't
words. I'm shaking so hard she wraps me in a quilt and holds me
tight. She rock us both till I fall asleep.

Honey tells the Man how I let out a yell that like to scare her to
death. Thinked I be kilt back there, but she not find a thing the
matter with me that she can see.

"That chile come in after school and eat a pile a flapjacks. Just a
yammerin' on, then lick the plate as clean as that ol' cat do. Chile be
just fine, Man, till she get outta my sight. Then, first thing I know,
she come a runnin' back and screamin' like somebody what taked
leave a their senses!"

"Well, why you not get her to calm down, Honey?"

"Couldn't. Don't you think I TRY to hush her up? Course I did!

I quick wrap the chile 'round and 'round with the quilt, and hold onto her real tight. That chile shake so hard, why, she was a shakin' ME, Man!"

The Man says he not want to do it like that. Just the way it is.

He done have to catch that ol' fox somehow, and the onlyest way be to kill him. Says he has to make sure that fox not get in the chicken house again.

"Wasn't no way I be wantin' to do like that, chile. No sireee. Can't think a no time I just take it into my head to go out and KILL sumthin'! No, no, no. Tell you the truth, chile, I be feelin' pretty bad to see sumthin' what was once alive and runnin' free all messed up, and with the life gone outa him."

He talks slow and thinks 'bout what he says. "Now I sure do hope you can understand that I ain't the kind a man who kills a thing just to be doin' sumthin'. But sometimes we gotta do a right many things we don't want to do, chile. Some a them things be right hard to do, matter a fact. Still we can't always go 'round sumthin' just 'cause it's the hardest thing. Have to do what we have to do. Whatever we think be the right thing. And that's all there is to it! Now I just tell you, chile, I can't put very much dependency in no person who don't do what has to be done. Can you, chile?"

I shake my pretty little head NO 'cause I agree with him for sure 'bout that thing!

Ah, the fox . . .
Such a lesson for me that was forgotten for so long.
I guess there wasn't much difference in my mind between a fox that had to be killed to save the hens, and a Big Shot who had to be killed to save the soul of a twelve-year-old.

24

SAFE PASSAGE

JoAnn was right. Opening her memory to those last times at The Joint had been a horrendous, exhausting task. But the way she went about it had the effect of lancing a boil or removing a painfully infected splinter.

Once again she'd taken some leave from her job in order to devote herself to the personal work that superseded everything else in her life at that time. And her no-holds-barred pace kept the words racing across her notebooks. When she stopped to catch a breath in my office it seemed some of the horrors of what she was writing about finally ran her aground. Even though she could barely wrap her mind around the idea of those things happening to a child, she knew with stone-cold certainty it was all true.

By this time I had started to get a bead on another feature of JoAnn's personality having to do with control. I saw it as another of those vibrant threads in the extensive tapestry on the theme of boundaries that continued to occupy so much of our attention.

JoAnn, like others I later worked with who endured physical and sexual violence as children, survived by deadening herself to the pain inflicted, numbing herself where a boundary had been violated by someone older or bigger. A child's boundaries are basic building blocks in structuring a sense of self. They are an avowal that the child is a separate being, an individual deserving of respect and with a right to have some influence in the world. When this vision is lost by adults bent on meeting only their own needs, not those of the child's, the embryonic definition of self is painfully damaged.

When one's boundaries have been ignored, the ability to say no, to make choices, and to exert control over one's life can become major issues. It seems the coping skills which result from these assaults frequently land along a continuum between chaotic, irresponsible functioning and a rigid, overly controlled effort to gain feelings of mastery. Surely the most natural defense mechanism for JoAnn and other such survivors is to separate the body, which has been violated and hurt, from the mind, which remains in control of thought. Feelings then split off from intellect. How else are children to tolerate the unbearable things done to them over which they have no say and even less understanding?

JoAnn, remembering the little girl she had been long ago, once wrote:

> With no difficulty I can recall my terror when Grannie stamped to the closet where she'd locked me away all day. If you could know the fear I felt then, as a toddler, you would understand how it was necessary to find some way to protect myself from such hatred and violence. And how can helpless humans protect themselves? With the mind. Only the mind. As a powerless child you can't do anything or make anything happen in your world. You have to find some way to block out feelings or you would simply die of exposure. Exposure to pain. Just as if you were exposed to a blistering sun had you been set adrift in a tiny rowboat in the middle of the ocean. There must be some mechanism in us that flips over to begin the shutting down process when life is too cruel to face. There must be some defense like that which saves us.

A little further on, in the same bunch of loose-leaf notebook papers held together through the top hole with a green twist tie from the produce section of her grocery store, were these additional sentences. "I was so afraid of touching and being hurt," she wrote, "that I had to draw away from the skin shell of myself. I could not stand being touched because it meant only more hurt. I simply could not stand it. Even worse, I could not bear the sensation of touching my own skin from the *inside*."

It isn't hard to picture the effect this had: human contact was unbearable because of its inevitable painfulness in her life, nor could she risk exposing her own feelings to herself—much less to the world around her. I heard just such a survival technique sharply summed up in a wide-ranging discussion during a 1989 workshop in Durham, North Carolina, on "Conscious Living and Conscious Dying." Stephen Levine, the workshop leader and speaker, said simply, "For a sexually abused woman, to be in the body is to be in the target."

There isn't any doubt, for people like this, that feelings are a certain kind of annihilation. "I'd be shut down," JoAnn wrote one time, "like a little Mom and Pop store where a sign hangs in the window. One side says OPEN and the other says CLOSED. I was inside, CLOSED." She often spoke of how like the "living dead" she was during her childhood, of how much time she spent completely "powered down." Children in these situations simply can't survive by admitting they hurt or need care when the chances of getting cared for are down to zero.

In my experience with her it was obvious to me JoAnn had landed toward the rigid and overly controlled end of the coping spectrum. Unlike many abuse survivors, she was far more controlled than she was controlling. People resort to different methods of getting through their days. So while she didn't try to manage others, control of herself was the fulcrum on which her behavior balanced. (In reality, I imagine that unconsciously keeping herself in check *did* result in having some control over others. Those closest to her couldn't possibly know what was happening in her life when she herself either didn't know or didn't express it.)

For quite a time, however, I regarded her as one of the more adjustable, adaptable people I'd come across. In fact she was extraordinarily adaptable, and there was a period when I thought of her as being almost Zen-like in how she lived. If, say, the plans she made a month ago were canceled by a friend at the last moment, she'd be perfectly content to switch directions and head toward something else of interest, maybe to read the last chapter of a book she hadn't finished. She didn't seem to need or be attached to anything, particularly on a material plane.

Actually, I thought JoAnn was too adjustable. Over the following years I began to see this trait more frequently in my patients. What had once been a useful survival tool, like adaptability, eventually becomes discordant, an impediment to growth by virtue of being about the only note the psyche's orchestra has learned to play. There are moments, particularly in adulthood, when a greater harm is done by accommodating oneself to something that is simply unacceptable.

While it might've been terribly unperceptive of me, I think it took my being with her a while to recognize the difference between nonattachment and not feeling. She had grown up with an absolute sense of having no power in the world, so she didn't expect or ask anything of it. Since all she'd ever had was herself, control of her inner world was all she could count on. Later I found out what I'd first thought of in her as a rather spiritually evolved attitude of being nonattached to things and events was more accurately a matter of having learned not to feel, not to want or need.

Nothing helped me as much in making this distinction as seeing the changes in JoAnn as we worked together. A difference in the way she related to me was the first and most obvious change I noticed.

For several years in therapy, by this time, she had been trusting me with her most precious possession, the memories of her childhood. And gradually, as she also began having them, with her *feelings*. But almost always she reported on interactions or events in the past tense, confrontations already dealt with, rather than alive and present happenings between us.

Ever so cautiously JoAnn started engaging more often with me about the emotions she was working to define even as she was having them. She began to let go of some of the control that came with presenting a finished state rather than something still evolving—a feeling, for instance, or an insight not yet understood.

To my surprise the next time I spoke with my clients about going on vacation, a verbal bon voyage gift came my way from JoAnn. She stated, with lots of intensity if not much readily apparent emotion, she didn't want to respond again in such a cold or distant manner to my going away. She didn't want to treat me as impersonally as I told her I'd felt she was doing when I confronted her before my last trip. But she didn't know how to do it differently, she admitted, and would need my help to find another way. It wasn't easy for her to identify something she wanted, and it was even harder to ask for help with it. Somehow I knew this risky request was momentous, like a quiet explosion that could cause a chain reaction among the emotional atoms in her subsequent encounters.

Control and Trust are tightly interwoven. One doesn't let go of a piece of control without feeling some measure, however lightly sensed, of trust. In the mind-set of beleaguered children, such as JoAnn once was, everyone is a potential threat to storm the walls of the fragile self. Therefore trust, because it requires in all of us some safe spot to establish a toehold, has poor odds of developing. Unless a safe place is found *somewhere* along the way, many once-small sentinels will grow up learning to wear fear and caution like an extra layer of skin. A dreadful cycle ensues where it becomes ever more difficult to take a chance. JoAnn's saying she needed my help with learning how to be truly engaged in a personal exchange was, paradoxically, an example of actually doing what she claimed she didn't know how to do. Someone who's terribly afraid and yet tells you, "I don't really feel very safe talking about this right now," has thrown herself at total darkness in a supreme act of trust.

JoAnn had once written of seeing herself as a huge, unshed tear. And she wondered why she couldn't release that held-in-mid-fall, quivering tear she'd become. During this period of her therapy she dismantled sections of the ramparts previously erected around her tender and vulnerable feelings. By allowing me nearer her emotional den I discovered even deeper aspects of her than I'd come across in my wandering among her most intimate writings. Occasionally now she would weep in our sessions. Not much but some. It was a far cry from those situations, always so unbearable to me, when the only sobs I heard from her were released into a tape recorder.

In retrospect, I think JoAnn's willingness to be more trusting and to risk being in less control was another chicken-and-egg kind of proposition. More often than not, human relationships resist our best attempts to describe their development along a linear track. It was also throughout this time I found myself more trusting and willing to be in less control. (Of course any notion of believing I could decide how close she got to *my* emotional den had been shot down when she ricocheted into my driveway.) How do we figure out what statement or action begat which response or behavioral change? Whose reaction was first to affect the other's? It's a Gordian knot with no lack of challenge for the unraveling.

Seeing this determined woman start to venture into new areas, try different ways of interacting, and finally experience some unfamiliar calm, gave me greater confidence in my work with her. I grew more trusting of myself (and her) as she seemed to be more trusting of herself (and me). Or maybe it was the other way around . . .

The last portion of her treatment slipped into gear shortly after JoAnn excised the memory of what would've been a life of certain enslavement if her family had gotten its way when she met the Big Shot. The ending to that critical night was thoroughly covered up by the stunned parties at hand. She's sure none of them ever worried about a Missing Persons investigation being launched into the whereabouts of the man who bought and sold women in a bustling, boom-time Army town. Besides, everyone involved in those activities had too much to lose for any of them to talk, especially since the commodity in question had been a twelve-year-old girl.

The youngest in her family was still in JoAnn's field of concern all during these months. With about the best spin one could put on it, Danny managed to get through high school. After some trouble in the final weeks he found a way to pull out of his nosedive at the last minute and graduate. Even that accomplishment might not have been predicted a year earlier.

Soon, though, he failed to meet his side of the contract with Victor and was kicked out of the self-styled halfway house which had seemed his only option when told he had to leave his mother's home. He moved back to his father's. JoAnn didn't see that as much of a solution, but before long she realized Danny rarely stayed at his father's house anyway. He kept his things there, however, while holding a series of jobs and living with a girlfriend. JoAnn spoke again about walking that fine line that separates *helping* out your child and *bailing* out your child. Having learned it was painfully fruitless to get involved in the choices her youngest son made, she could only hope he was somehow finding his way in the world.

One of the hardest things faced by those who make major changes in their lives is locating the support to do so among family and friends. Alcoholics, for instance, routinely encounter this problem: rarely are the friends at the bar very supportive of their drinking buddy's efforts to become sober. That's why having a ready-made band of struggling fellow travelers only a meeting or a phone call away is a significant part of the phenomenal success of Alcoholics Anonymous.

JoAnn realized the need for new input in her life, for people who understood the wish to grow and change instead of settling into a long and comfortable groove. Clearly she needed some different experiences. Many of the friends who had known her the longest were not altogether pleased or understanding about what she wanted these days. And so she came up against the same dilemma that catches almost everybody who is suddenly alone or feels mired in outworn relationships: how do you meet new people?

Since she'd finished the lion's share of the work on herself and now had the time and energy for considering what she wanted to do, JoAnn gave thought to other passions she'd left waiting in the green room while her therapy occupied center stage. Despite working part-time and living on an income below the poverty line, she began a two-year stint as a volunteer office worker in the Planned Parenthood clinic nearest her home. She believed, as did Honey, that every child should be a wanted child; helping address that goal seemed a worthy undertaking.

Later on she answered the call for volunteers to work with the Literacy Council. A life without the books which introduced her to history's great minds, ideas, and literature, she felt, would've left her impoverished indeed. And so she taught a mother and her teenage daughter how to read.

These endeavors may not have provided the new friendships JoAnn hoped for but the experiences were unlike any others that had come her way. Even more significant was getting to meet different kinds of people in the process. Her explorations into new settings, activities, and interactions supplied plenty of grist for our therapy mill. She continued to notice, and be puzzled by, the difference between her own perceptions and attitudes and those of other people. What delighted me was to see the budding of a sense of humor in her, or rather, I expect, a reemergence of the lightheartedness she'd once known with Mr. Man and Honey.

Off and on for maybe three or four months, between serious concerns, we were a bit like free range chickens in a fenceless farmyard of words, stories, observations, ideas, reflections. Together we roamed around this wide-open landscape, rooting out tasty tidbits, turning over whatever looked interesting. I knew she'd never talked about these things, or shared these parts of herself, with anyone before. Also I'd never engaged in such seemingly unfocused discussions with a client before this. But I knew I was seeing another aspect of JoAnn defining herself, watching as she painted a more vibrant self-portrait with a palette of stunning colors. Whether or not she ever regarded them as helpful, I hoped these conversations might show her how she could talk and relate to the friends I felt sure she was bound to find.

At one point in this ending-up section of therapy, JoAnn made a trip to her hometown to see if she could find any trace of Honey and the Man. On several occasions in the past I had asked if she'd thought of looking them up, aware that it's what I would've wanted to do if they'd been in *my* life. She hadn't, though, I think figuring they'd probably died long ago. And she didn't carry any interest or energy for it, I realized later, until having finished all that essential life-in-the-balance work on herself. But now, with the strength, time, and curiosity available, she went back down to Georgia to look up property deeds, census information, or any document which might hold something of value probably only to her. Since she didn't know their names, all she could track was the land itself. However nothing on those records fit together with what was familiar in her memory.

The only useful thing she found there was a woman in the courthouse doing research for a book on how to locate deeds of properties and titles no longer held by current landowners. The woman agreed to take up JoAnn's search if she should someday decide to employ her services.

A trip out to the place where Honey and Mr. Man had lived was equally disappointing. Their house didn't exist anymore, she said. A small business had been built on the same spot; looked like some sort of a feed and grain store, something local farmers patronized. But, laughing at herself, she admitted to half-expecting that when she drove there Honey would come out on the front porch and greet her with a huge smile. Never mind that nearly fifty years had passed and Honey was already an old woman way back then. Maybe sometime she'd pick up on the search again, she said. Maybe one day contact the woman she'd met in the courthouse.

Despite her life being calmer and fuller, JoAnn was still writing during this period. I don't think it was only habit, either. She seemed drawn to focus on remembering everything not yet resurrected from her short time with the old couple who "raised" her. As if to become infused with the abundance of their affirming and healing love, she let herself steep—like a teabag—in those precious recollections. Among the memories which surfaced then were yet more incidents and conversations having to do with the Preacher's message and with saying good-bye to Honey and the Man. This came as no surprise to either of us. Since recently we'd begun talking of ending therapy, we both knew that her experience of endings and leavings typically carried with it an echo of having been exiled from the Place. So it was no wonder stacks of paper were still ending up on my desk each week, and the writings in them now made another, deeper, foray into that pivotal separation.

What *did* come as a surprise to me during the start of this same period was becoming aware of a difference in me, something changing in my outlook. Because the change was subtle and quite gradual over the space of several years, at first I don't think I connected it to my work with JoAnn. Before long, though, I knew she'd also had an impact in still another area of my life.

As the winding down began, the two of us spent a good bit of time considering how we'd arrived at this end stage of her treatment after such an ordinary, even inauspicious, beginning. These discussions usually contained about an equal amount of amazement at what had happened in the process and knowledge of work well done. In spite of her interest in almost everything, JoAnn seemed far more content than I was to simply notice and accept the fact she'd reached her present vantage point. She'd had years of practice paying careful attention to her world and then lots of experience in accepting the reality of it. But I could neither stop nor silence a slew of insistent questions which increasingly tugged at me throughout this period.

My training did not sit especially well with me at this juncture, in this case. I'm not the first person to think psychotherapy has been regarded by "hard" scientists as a poor relative of the medical profession. For almost a century its practitioners have worked impressively, and with plenty of decent results, to corral the scientific features in this approach to better health. Much of that effort withstands critical examination, too, principally in the study of brain chemistry and medications. But in my mind there have been more than a few areas in our field, particularly as I came across them in working with JoAnn, that fell short of the science and certainties I had imagined encountering.

For me, JoAnn's story begged more questions than it answered. I was fascinated by how she had become the woman sitting in my office. Of course the lessons she'd learned from Honey and the Man were recognizable, traceable. That they gave birth to her character is as clear to me as that she was physically born to a mother who never wanted her. But even with giving due credit to the influence of her one year on the Place, I stayed puzzled over what was the core ingredient which differentiated her from the rest of the Foleys.

Why was she repeatedly drawn to the old couple down the road, I wondered, while nobody else in the family was? Why weren't Bobby and Francie, who'd also been present when the Man drove by, as interested in being around his gentle presence? There's no reason to believe they, too, weren't abused in all the ways so commonplace among that family. In fact, JoAnn has early memories of Grannie fondling Little Bobby on her lap and getting excited over his young erection.

Most assuredly she was raised with the same prejudice and hatreds that fed everyone in the household; she knew and used all the same violent language fueling their every encounter. So why did *she* keep seeking out a vilified, elderly black couple, and continue to

stay around when they disciplined her, while Bobby chose banish-
ment rather than change his behavior? What was that resolve which
made her risk going another direction, and many times at great
peril, from everyone else at home? If, indeed—and we'll never know
for sure—she *was* born of the twisted union between a narcissistic
mother and her mother's tyrannical father, then how in the world
was she not warped beyond recognition? If, genetically, she'd gotten
a double dose of such psychopathology, what was there to start with
that could've possibly given rise to any impetus to be different?

These were the questions which kept tripping me up. Searching
for answers that might make sense of it kept leading me further
afield of my profession's main current.

We talked at some length about all these unknowns through the
quieter days approaching the end of therapy. JoAnn was no more
able to explain the drive that initially led her back to the people who
then changed her life than I was able to account for why or how
things had happened as they did. But these conversations, resonating in me with something internal already shifting, helped me
appreciate, and even honor, all this unknowing. Maybe, in the long
run, JoAnn's attitude was the more appropriate. For someone whose
intellect had been her lantern against the darkness, now she simply
remained attuned to herself in the present moment instead of forcing words and ideas into an interpretation or explanation of it all.

Each one of us lent a quality of herself to the other in this
passage. Her response helped me pay sharper attention to that
which actually existed than the "how come?" of it. My response, I
think, helped her key into some of the emotion inherent in our
having been aboard as this mighty ship finally sailed through a deep
channel and into a safe harbor. I came to see that both wonder and
amazement, such significant features of my childhood, were two
qualities I'd later pushed aside in order to conform in my maturing,
academic years. Now I was once more filled with that old sense of
awe, and it manifested in the coalescing of a spiritual aspect to my
world view.

This inner realignment didn't appear epiphany-like in my life
but had actually been quite some time in the making. In 1978 or
1979, soon after its publication, Donna and I spent many winter

evenings by the fireplace reading aloud to each other M. Scott Peck's *The Road Less Traveled*. It had had a seismic effect on the psychotherapy community back then, in large part by letting the helpers know it was safe to come out of the closet spiritually.

So I'd been slowly moving for several years in the direction of therapeutic explorations that weren't just intra- or interpersonal. But, perhaps because there were so many things I couldn't account for in JoAnn's life, she was one of the first clients with whom I allowed my questions and thoughts to stray from the well-worn paths of my profession. I wanted to know her ideas about why and how she'd survived, what she believed was her reason for being here, and being here at this particular time. It seemed to me that in her story there was more involved than someone simply surviving, more even than transcending the limits of one's background.

We talked and talked. I believe she started to appreciate the awesomeness of the journey she'd made thus far. And I really began to enjoy the mystery of it all, of feeling okay about not knowing the answers (although I tended to believe someday it just might be made clear to me). The fact was that out of our whole Community Mental Health Center staff of maybe twenty therapists, our director had referred JoAnn to *me*. Also the fact was that I, with curiosity and the gift of time at hand, had been assigned to *her*. That she once ended up at my house in another state, more than 115 miles away from the only place I'd ever seen her, contained as much mystery and surprise as any of the other astonishing things that had happened to me.

At this point in the proceedings we both acknowledged how little each of us had known along the way. I told her how, from the very beginning, all I knew was that I believed her; I couldn't recall ever doubting her honesty or sincerity. And JoAnn admitted how her earlier comment about knowing she'd have done the work on herself someday, even if we'd never met, hadn't conveyed the entire scope of her truth. "There was an animal sense I had back then," she now told me, "that therapy was okay, that *you* were okay. It wasn't a thought or feeling. It was a sense, like an animal has about there being something dangerous ahead. I didn't have any feelings back then, but I could sense things."

.   .   .

With little more than a month to go before the date we'd set for our last session, I took in to the office the stack of notebooks and piles of papers JoAnn had left with me during the years of her therapy. It was a staggering amount: to think she'd written all that! To think I'd read all that!

"Well, I still believe this is a pure treasure," I said to her, nodding in the direction of the box and shopping bags I'd piled in a chair nearest the door. "I believe there's stuff in there somebody would publish if you could figure out what to do with it."

She just looked at me and smiled.

"What is it?" I asked.

"Same thing I said to you before. If you think it's good, or it could maybe help somebody, then I think you should do something with it."

I'm sure I must've cut my eyes at her. "Why me?" I groaned. Yes, she'd said the same thing before when I'd broached the subject, and my reaction now was the same as then. "JoAnn, I can't even imagine trying to deal with all that material . . ."

"Well, I don't really care to do any more with it." She leveled her gaze at me again. "But if you ever do decide to write anything about all this, I'd be interested in reading it." That was all she said.

Quickly, before she moved on to another topic, I added, "Just don't throw it away, okay? At least not without letting me know before you do."

"Maybe one of these days," she thought, "after I do some other things, I'll type it all up. In case you or somebody else wants to look at it."

Returning JoAnn's papers was a sizable part of what was hard for me about saying good-bye to her. I hadn't fully appreciated how attached I'd become to all that material, perhaps because of the many times I just wanted to get away from its heaviness. I knew very well I was going to miss *her,* and I told her so, but I was surprised with my feeling of loss at the idea of not having any more of her meandering recollections and poignant prose to read.

Those notebooks were priceless, I felt, and I'd always guarded them with great care. Although I'd read and studied the entire collection, I hadn't put a single mark on a single page; I was returning it just as I'd been given it. Whenever I'd had a question or comment to bring up in a session, I flagged the page with a paper clip or sheet from a self-stick notepad. My attitude toward them, I realized, had been one of utter reverence. In handing the whole mass of material back to its owner, I told her I felt it had been my good fortune to have had access to it.

The time for tying off loose ends was at hand. In the doing of this we added a few other threads to the creation we'd woven over the years on the loom my office had become. JoAnn spoke about how fortunate she felt, too. In fact, she considered herself to be one of the most blessed people she knew. This was typical of her, I thought: after having nearly drowned in the pit of sewage which she once described as passing for her childhood, she was still able to draw a deep breath of clean air from the experience. Not many people, she said, have had a Honey and the Man in their lives. And since she personally didn't know anyone who'd been exposed to that kind of influence, it still terrified her to think of what would've become of her had she not met them.

We talked some more about good-byes, as we'd done many times before when the issue had come up—for instance around my vacations, or when Peg died. Many new recollections pounded their way into JoAnn's consciousness:

In spite of knowing she wasn't supposed to go back there, she recalled how defeated Honey had looked when she returned for a final visit. She recognized the look of Honey's having "gone away" inside.

She remembered overhearing the Preacher, anticipating the effects of this separation on Honey, quietly tell the Man that he thought it "might've been easier on Honey if the child had just died of that beating instead of her having to go back home."

When the Preacher carried her into the Foley's house she was barely conscious. Yet she spoke, with remarkable detail, of his handing her over to her mother. "Soon as the Preacher left," she went on to say, "Grandpa rushed toward me in a rage with his huge arm drawn back, cocked like a shotgun. Mama, who was sitting there with me on her lap, jumped up out of the chair as quick as a cat.

Dumped me right out on the floor. She didn't want to get hit, too, when her papa beat me up again—this time for causing them so much trouble."

These were the kinds of memories still so easily tapped by another ending in her life. With my hopes that we could lay down some less devastating and less violent associations, we set out to cover as thoroughly as possible what this present relationship had meant, had provided, had taught us. Both of us.

JoAnn looked to be pretty well in control throughout all this, I thought; far more than I felt myself sometimes to be. In several sessions tears came to my eyes or my voice choked. At one point she stated, with her usual perceptiveness and searing self-awareness, "I think this is harder for you than me."

For a moment I was embarrassed. I thought maybe it wasn't right to be feeling all this about a patient leaving therapy. I felt exposed, that I'd not only been caught being sadder than was appropriate for a therapist to feel, but that I was obviously more affected by our leave-taking than she was. Then I looked at her and replayed the words again; there was no judgment in her eyes or her voice. The comment, as was so often the case, had been more an assessment of herself than a statement about the other: she didn't feel what I was saying and showing because she *couldn't* feel to that extent. In fact, I think she later went on to say something about hoping one day she'd be able to experience that degree of emotion.

I brought up again the subject of the notebooks JoAnn had written during her therapy, the remembrances at the heart of our work together. Although feeling her purpose in writing them had been served, she appreciated the fact I valued the material and believed it just might be instructive for other people. Even so, I knew I wasn't ready to do anything about it at that point. It seemed far too early to me to make such a commitment; besides, we hadn't yet ended the one we *had* made.

And there was another consideration involved. If, in the future we were to collaborate in some way around this material, it would mean a redefining of our relationship. Never having done that before with a client, I wasn't sure how, or if, it would work. I didn't want to take advantage of the situation or of my position, so I suggested waiting at least a year after our last appointment before making any contact. And I would not be the one to initiate it, I told her. I felt strongly that the move should come from her, if it came at all. A year would allow some time to think about whether she still wanted anything done with the writings, or if she still wanted me involved in it (assuming I'd be interested then).

JoAnn listened closely to everything I said; she didn't comment or raise questions. While she didn't actually say so, I nevertheless felt she believed I was making too much of all this, that I was being overly scrupulous. But, as I sat for a second with this notion, it was clear to me that whenever she disagreed or wanted to go in her own direction, she was perfectly capable of making her views known. Perhaps, I thought, she'd already gained that sense of parity which is the best indication of someone having finished their work in therapy, or at least being done with it for the present time. When a patient and therapist finally start to talk as just two people, and there's some interest being shown in the life of the person who'd previously asked the questions, then you know the original therapeutic imbalance has been righted. That's when it's time to bring the curtain down on the final act.

The last sessions we had were difficult for me. Sitting there with JoAnn, I knew something momentous and full of mystery had happened over the space of the last six years. There was no question but that I'd been changed in the process. When an awareness like this hits, often it's on the heels of trauma, as after a potentially fatal illness. But this had come at the end of a long march, as inexorably as a tidal wave approaching in slow motion from the other side of the earth. I knew with certainty that being the therapist in this case had forced my awareness to expand. I was beginning to see there were connections in all things, leading to purposes we could scarcely envision. I also realized this was possibly the last time I'd see or talk with the woman who almost never wore black and white prints anymore, whose hair had become far more salt than pepper.

And of course I knew JoAnn had been changed, too, in ways I imagine she may never have dreamed possible. On one of our last appointments she told me how important I'd been to her, despite my occasionally feeling baffled or unsure of what she needed. "I know," she added, "it wasn't always easy for you." She wanted me to especially understand that she had valued me for being myself during these years, that transference had not overtaken her.

"During this whole time we've been here, I always knew you weren't Honey," she said with characteristic earnestness. "It's been very important to me not to confuse one person with another; that's how I try and be clear about who is really who. I know you've helped me, and I know you did it as you, not as Honey."

Her comment fit snugly with one of the turns our ending sessions had taken. I'd been doing a lot of thinking then about what set JoAnn's situation apart from other stories I was starting to hear. Over the past few months we'd talked even more about Honey and the Man having provided all the crucial lessons she'd carried through her life. But now we both considered that maybe an equally critical function each one of them had served, perhaps every bit as important as being a teacher, was of having been a witness. So, when her last pages and our last conversations were placed there in my office, some of them touched poignantly on this subject.

It rekindled JoAnn's abiding fascination with the idea of perspective. If Honey and the Man hadn't broadened her field of vision by offering a different view, and hadn't outwardly validated what was her inner experience . . . well, she shuddered anew to think about it.

"They saw in me how I was affected by the Foleys because of the way I got treated. They noticed," she said, "and they talked to me about it, just like they talked to each other about it. I guess really that's what you did, too, in a different way. You were here and paid attention to all the things I was remembering. They saw it while it was happening. You saw the same things, too, but later on, when it was finally time to dig them all out of the pit where I'd buried them."

She was fortunate, she said again, to have had three of us as witnesses in those times where nothing else existed for comparison, when she didn't know what she thought or felt, when it was hard to believe her memories. The reactions of Mr. Man and Honey confirmed what she instinctively sensed was hurtful about her upbringing; they were passionate about their beliefs and what they valued. I let her know, too, in my own way (less passionate, I expect, and more within the confines of "professionalism"), that her family's treatment of her was aberrant as well as abhorrent.

JoAnn had been a witness for me as well, I told her; a dedicated and faithful one throughout this undertaking. Just as she said, it had not been easy for me at many points along the way. What amazed me was that, despite staying so focused on her own issues, I knew she was aware of the difficulty I was having even as we went on. Yet somehow—with her fragile trust, or in her desperation, or whatever it was—she supported me venturing alongside her. I knew she realized my world had widened, too. She had seen, and indeed *helped,* me grow stronger and more trusting of myself.

We had given those gifts to each other.

And so, consistent with JoAnn's approach to everything, we found our way through what I felt to be the kind of uncovered and thorough leave-taking which easily remains as important as any aspect of psychotherapy. The good-byes were exquisite, I thought: feelings of liberation tinged with a sense of loss.

25

. . . A BLESSING ON MY HEAD

"Oh, Lord have mercy on myyyy soul!" Honey says. She rolls her eyes and tells me she is just gonna wait. "I not like to hear them made-up stories come outcha mouth, chile. No, I don't."

I hush up. When she do me like that I know it's time to hush up. I know I ain't got a leg to stand on.

"Now I listen to you, chile, iff'n you got sumthin' to say," and she stretch her eyes and folds her arms over her apron front and just stands there and looks at me. "But not when you talk thataways."

I has got caught in one a them bad made-uppities. Honey don't like to hear "nothin' but the trooth," and she is put out with me.

When the Man comes home and me and him give Ol' Horsey his supper I tell him all about how Honey done me.

"I know it be the best thing if I just go ahead and 'fess up, but I was not wanting to do it!" I explain to him.

"Yep," he looks over at me, "I hear you, but sometimes you gotta take your medicine like a man, you know."

But I tell him sometimes I don't wanna 'fess up and take my medicine like a man. Besides, I tell him, I'm a child!!!

He stops what he's doing to get the strap things off the horse, and he talks to me in a quiet-like tone. "Well, I guess it don't rightly matter, chile. Seems like you done been set down in the lion's den.

You is gonna have to grow up mighty fast over there with them people—or else they eat you alive."

The Man says he has seen it hisself, he has. I can tell he is thinking before he talks. "I ain't given to talkin' like this to no little chile. Little children should be talked to like little children," he says. "But the thing is that in this world things ain't just like they oughtta be. No matter what the Bible says, or no matter what you think about it, chile, things ain't nowhere near being like they oughtta be." He tells me this in a did-you-know-that tone, and he looks to see is I getting the drift of his words. He always used to say, "Ain't one bit a sense in me a talkin' and you a listenin' unless you can take my meanin', chile."

He comes over to where I'm petting Ol' Horsey's back leg. The Man gives the horse a good rub on his rump; then he stops and looks down at me. "When somebody is done been set down in the lion's den? Well, that feller had just better watch out for hisself. Now that's the truth, chile, and it don't make a bit of difference if the feller is a little tadpole like you is or iff'n he's a growed-up man."

The Man leans a little against Ol' Horsey, like maybe he's tired. I think maybe he's tired a having to talk this way to me. "The thing is," he says, "you can't count on nobody when you is in a fix like you is in up there, chile." He means up there with them Foleys what he don't think much of. "Them folks ain't fittin' to have no sweet little chile like you! Now that's just the way I see it."

He says he is bound and declarin' that he is not ever in his life "seen no chile no brighter than you is." Says he is seen a lot of little childrens in all his borned days and he knows what he is talkin' about. His words all come out calm and serious-like while he looks right at me.

"Has you seen a hundred, Mr. Man?" I ask him.

"What? What's that, chile?"

"Has you seen a hundred sweet little childrens?" I know a hundred from the blackboard at school. It has a one and then two oh's. He tole me he done seen a lot of children in his borned days, so I wanta know if a lot means a hundred.

"Oh Lord, chile. A hundred ain't nothin' to the childrens I has seen. Why, if this town was plum full to overflowin' with little childrens . . . ? Well, I know for a sure thing that there not be a one could hold a candle to youuu, chile!"

He don't think he is ever seen no little chile what is "catch on like you do. I be pretty sure if Honey don't watch out, you gonna be takin' over that biscuit makin' business one a these days. Now that's just how quick your little ol' mind catches on to a thing when somebody stop and explain it to you." He looks at me and asks if I has took notice a that already?

I feel snug and warm. I think I *has* start to notice that very thing myself . . .

The Man he lets out a big sigh. He says, "The thing is, JoAnn, you done been set down in just 'bout as bad a place as you can be in. So you got to watch out for yourself, even if you ain't hardly knee high to a grasshopper. I reckon, though, if any little feller was to ever be able to look out for theirself, why that'd be you, chile. . . . Why? 'Cause, you is one smart Little Missy. And 'cause you is on the side a the Angels, that's why."

�֎

I've lately felt an inability to settle down and rest or sleep. Tired and weary, and still I need to sit here pushing myself to write this crap out!

Distressing that it never ends!!

So that's life, isn't it? Peck summed it all up: Life is hard, he said. I was up early after a pain-filled night with only a couple of hours' sleep; had to get up at six to be at the doctor by seven. Did not want to get up so early, but went just the same.

All my life, *all my life,* I have been the only one in my family who has consistently done the hard-to-do things! It is not fair, and is making me pissed offfff!! Why should I be the only one who has to do the hard things? Why in the hell should I be the only goddam Foley who does what's right? Goddammit!

Why, huh? Because of the Place. Oh Lord, I know the answer to that question well and good. Well and good, indeed.

I know how my life would have been different if I had not gone on THE PLACE. Believe me I know what it would have been like without them and their teachings. Oh, how well do I know—because I still see it today in all the Foleys, the way they live such low-level, disgusting, less-than-human lives.

"Not for you. That way ain't for you, chile."

They told me time and again *that* way was not for me. I was tuned in to the gut-grabbing intensity of the telling. They always spoke the truth. I had not ever known anyone who told the truth before. Not ever.

In our life truth did not exist. It was a given that truth did not exist. It's like the word RME came across, "widdershin," I think she said it was. Means against the natural way things flow. That's how it was with my family. Everything was upside down. Truth that went with what they said, and feelings to match the spoken word, were just not part of our life in the Foleys' house. And they *still* don't flow in the same direction there, even today.

But on the Place, ah my, on the Place it matched and was real. I think that was a part of the attraction for me. You could count on them; you could count on what they said being the way they said. And I could make sense of my world there. Not so with the Foleys, though. There was no structure, no predictability, no nothing to depend on in that world! An insane asylum is what I was raised in, a goddam fucking crazy house!

And the wonder of it all is that IIIII knew it!!

I had the great good fortune to be one of the few who found a witness to share my view of the world. I think it made a difference for me. I think that is what made all the difference. It made me believe my own view somehow, even when it was all repressed for so long. Without having a witness to the truth, could I ever have been planted in truth? Not to this degree, I don't imagine. It was the fact that they did not "think much a them folks down there what you got stuck with."

That was such a revelation for me, knowing they did not think much of my family. A rock; it gave me a rock on which to build my house. Just like in the story she told me from back in the Bible days, about building your house on a rock. Honey did not like it when ". . . a Mama don't teach her chile what she oughta!"

Oh, you could feel it in her, so strong a conviction. She was like a rock placed in the earth of her beliefs. She, and the Man, too, made it so clear to me that where I came from was not the way it ought to be. I will forever be grateful to them for being a reality check for me, a witness to the awfulness of the only ways I had known.

I guess what happened is that they became my touchstone, the means by which I learned to tell if something was real, if the truth was being told.

❋

"It ain't nothing, JoAnn. You're okay," Mama said. "Go on now, you'll be all right. It really ain't nothing."

I was little, but it WAS something. It was my female organs, rubbed and bleeding just a bit. Not lots of blood, but I was raw and a little bloody, too. I knew from her tone and the feeling in the air that she was lying when she said it was nothing. She hardly even looked. She never paid attention to anything about me.

Honey looks real close when I come running in from playing in the yard. "Lemme see now, chile. Hold still. Lemme see is it all right," and she looks real good to see is I okay or is I gonna DIE?!

She says, "Don't look like to me there's too much there. Think maybe a bug done bite you, chile, 'cause I just can't see too much. . . . Yeah, it hurts. I know it hurts you!" She gonna fix it up; rub it and fix it up with a nice clean rag.

I show the Man the nice rag she put on me. "It's not so clean now 'cause I been playing with it on my arm, Man. Probably won't be able to see a thing there, but it sting me like the very devil. . . . Well, we don't know for sure. Honey thinks maybe a little buggie done bite me, and she fix it right uppity up for me real good, Man. Feels just fine now. Don't hurt me a bit now."

We look close and decide it looks Pretty Good now. We take the rag off now he is seen it. He thinks Honey do a "mighty fine job a fixin' that ol' hurt place up!"

No pain touched the Foleys except their own. They felt not a twinge for anyone else's pain, just their own. You could be dying a bloody death at their feet, and they'd only be upset by the awful realization their shoes were getting stained.

Mama's fingernails were a frequent cause of pain for her. She would HURT so bad if she "snagged a fingernail." She acted like it was unbearably painful. I guess she didn't know fingernails don't "feel" because they don't have any nerves. But she would cry flowing tears over a snagged or broken fingernail. Lord, could she cry over that!

Honey, though, she'd look at every little bite or cut I got. She'd blow on it or wash the sore place good and clean. Wrap a nice bandage around where it hurt.

I remember going one time out to meet the Man where he and the Horsey turn in off the road onto the little track to their house. I get up on the seat beside him for the last little way home. "Owww," I say when I sit down. "It hurts me, Man."

"What's that, chile? What's hurtin' you?"

I watch him and wonder if it's okay to tell him. When I think it's all right, I say, "My hiney hurts."

He asks do I want him to look at my backside and see if mebbe I done sat myself down on a splinter?

"No, Man. That ain't where it hurts." I 'splain to him, "It's my FRONT hiney."

He just looks at me for a second or two. "Oh well, then I reckon that's sumthin' Honey gonna know how to take care of for you, chile. No, I don't think I be the best feller to help you out there. Honey, she be just the one to take a look-see, fix you right up good as new. Let's get you in there so she can see what's ailin' you, chile. You gonna be just fine, I think."

"Lookit me. Lookit me, Honey!"

I is naked as a jaybird and I spin and dance 'round all over the place. Honey laughs till she's 'bout to cry. I is a mess. She wraps that towel 'round me and hugs me snug in the middle of it.

"Lordamercy, I don't know why inna world I waste my time on you for, Chile What Acts Like a Jaybird. Wonder what somebody think who go by here and see you a runnin' 'round this here yard like that!?"

I laugh and I tell her they think Miss Honey is got a jaybird a runnin' 'round her place today, that's all.

Honey rubs me good, dries me off good, starts to comb my hair while it's wet and not all tangled up. She says, "You is just too much, chile. I dunno what in the world to do witcha!"

"Why, I 'specs you have to KEEP ME, Honey. You done had me so long I don't reckon as how you could get rid a me now! Ain't nobody'd take me." Oh, we laugh and laugh 'cause we know how she's alla time talkin' 'bout bein' stuck with That Man and That Chile!

Honey says she can't get rid a us. No, no, no, she never would. She never would send me away, not if she could help it, and she rubs my hair around. "You is a blessin' on my head, chile. Yes, you is."

She feels strange to me now; it don't scare me but it's kinda different. Like when she tells me 'bout how sometimes everthing look awful dark and cloudy, with a sky full a black clouds, but one a these days everthing be all bright and gay.

"Be blue skies then," Honey says, "and you know what, chile? You be a great big growed-up lady one a these days and you sit yourself down, look up into that blue blue sky, and do you know whatcha see up in them clouds?"

I don't know. I don't know a thing about it 'cause this is a new one. She never tole it to me before, this one.

She never tole it to me again, either, 'cause that was one of the last days I was on that Place.

She says that someday I'm gonna look up and see the Lord God Almighty a standin' there, and she'd be right there with Him. She and her ol' knotty head! Sure would. She sure would be there a waitin' for me to come along the road after her and that Man.

"So when you look up inna sky you'll see your ol' Honey and the Man a wavin' at you, chile. Hear that?"

"Yessume, I do hear that."

"And even if we don't be together, we ain't gonna worry a bit about you, chile, 'cause you is the Lord's own lamb what He loves more'n anything!"

· · ·

Sometimes I wonder if I go outside and look up will I see them peeking over the edge of a big white puffy cloud, just checking to see how I'm doing these days.

✖

The Man whittles his stick. Me and him walk around a little bit and talk.

"I believe you grow pretty big one a these days, chile. 'Deed so. Appears to me that you done growed a whole lot this summer. I don't believe you gonna be a fittin' into your coat, you done got so big!" He slows down and he looks at me REAL GOOD. "Yep, appears to me that you've done growed CONsiderable!"

"He did? He did say that, did he?" She laughs out loud. "Chile, chile, you be the death a me yet! One a these fine days I just laugh myself to pieces over you!"

Honey do like to laugh. She says it do make her day to HAVE A GOOD LAUGH.

"Chile, you is better'n a picture show, you is!"

I tell her about the Man. "He did say that, Honey, he did. He say I grow up to be *SMART*LIKE*YOU*!" I think how he has a warm feeling when he says that to me.

"I be just like you, Honey. I be big like you! Why, I be sooo big," and I spread my arms wide as I can to show her how big. "I pick myself up and I walk right off and I leave them people so fast it make your head swim!!! 'Deed I will!"

I sit up there at the table just as nice as ever you please. I talk and take little, little nice bites. ". . . When am I gonna leave? Soon's I get my growth, Honey! The Man says soon's I get my growth about me."

I think of "get my growth about me" kind of like it's a coat or a sweater that I just gonna put around me. Just put it on and I'll be big all over.

Oh, I is such a Somebody a sitting at that table and talking. I say, "You'll see, Honey. You'll see. Yep, I hope to tell you that you gonna see that thing! Sure as the world. They ain't a gonna GET ME!

They ain't 'cause I say so, and you know when I say a thing I MEAN THAT THING, don'tcha?"

I look at her to see does she know that thing. I ain't gonna waste my time saying something if I don't mean it! I think she's 'bout to bust loose a laughing 'cause I sound so much like her.

❈

"Come on in here. I'm awful glad to see you; glad you able to get here. Sister is feeling mighty bad." The Preacher holds the door open for the women who come here from the church. They all come in off the porch where he went when he heard the wagon pull up in the yard.

They come in now to see how is Sister doing. Each one of 'em nods to Brother. They all know each other, I can tell. These are women of the church who the Preacher knows can be trusted with his life. They come when he sent out the word he needed help. He tole the Man these good sisters was doers and not talkers. "Less talk the better, when it comes to things like this," he says. "Let talk start and you double your trouble, Brother. It's for sure talk will kill you quick as a bullet or a rope."

The Preacher man tells the Man why he sent for these women to come and take care of Sister while they go do "what has to be done to save us all. Now, I hope you do what has to be done, Brother, not just for this child here but for all of us."

It is so important to him, and he is dead certain of what needs to be done. Not an ounce of doubt in him, the Preacher man, that this is the thing they got to do to save the most they can out of this here mess that oughta not been in the first place. But even now, at the end of the long night of trouble in this place, he don't demand it be done his way. He talks soft to the Man, I think maybe 'cause he knows the Man's gotta make the decision, but still he kinda push him a little bit with his words.

I am scared now for them. I feel it now for the first time. I am convinced by the Preacher, even if the Man ain't quite certain.

What he has done actually is preach. He has preached with all the courage and conviction in his soul to this Brother and Sister

from the church. He's gonna tell them the truth, is all. And the truth
is they have to turn their back on this here child! His voice rings as
he says "this here child." This little girl, he tells 'em, could drag
them all down. "This child was put here by the Lord and that's
where she's been set to do her work!!! It just don't do to question
His ways. No, we may not like it but we got to do it, the Lord's
work, wherever at the Lord puts us, don't we? Well, He set this here
child out where He wants her to be at, and she has her work to do
right where He done put her down. We may not think much of all
this, but He knows more'n we can see. It don't do to take it on
ourselves to question the ways of the Lord."

But I know he does. He questions the way of the Lord sometimes hisself and I know it. I feel him not telling it all.

The Preacher man is one who believes in live and learn. He hopes to
learn something every day, every day. He talks to me as him and the
Man take me back to the Foleys in the wagon. He don't know what
it is he's supposed to learn from out of this here mess, though, but
guess he's gonna find out someday.

"I just hope you be able to make it, child. I don't like to throw
you to the wolves; I'd do anything else I could see my way clear to
do instead of this. But the thing is I got to deal with what I got, and I
ain't got much in this hand. A man's got to know when the cards
ain't on his side and it's time to cut his losses. That's all there is to
do when you already lost. Be a fool to stay in and keep on getting
deeper and deeper in trouble. Now that don't mean I like it. But I
sure hope and pray you be able to make it, child. Pray to the Lord
you will. It's gonna be right hard on you, down there with them
folks."

He's seen them before, he tells me, those folks I got stuck with.
They look like trash to him, and he ain't ever seen trash do a thing
you could put the name Good to! They out to beat you any way they
can, is all he ever seen out of that kind. And drag you down with
'em, too.

He says, "Lord, you have to hold this child up from the badness
going on around here. Don't know why in this world you seen fit to
set this child down in that place, but I guess you got your reasons. I

ain't quarreling with that. But I tell you this thing, Lord, tell you to hold on to this here child's arm and not let her go. Don't let her slip down into the filth of how them folks of hers live."

The Preacher man gets quiet; he's tired. Mr. Man don't talk at all, just looks off up ahead. The Preacher glances over and says to him that he ain't a mean man who wants to deliver a sweet little child into the hands of those bad people. It's hard for him but it is the lesser of two evils, and he is responsible for his flock. Got to think of more than just one or two; got to think of allll his people. He says them folks I got don't think about nobody but themselves, and they just look for any excuse to take what they can get and hurt anybody who's unlucky enough to be around. Seems like they just go out of their way to make trouble, is what he says.

The Man is driving the Preacher and me in the wagon. Mr. Man don't say nothing. He can barely hold hisself up on the seat. The Preacher calls me A Child of God. Says I am one of God's Own. "You got to do for yourself, child," he nods his head at me, "and not count on nooobody! This is a terrible thing to tell a little child like you, but the truth is the truth and you do a heap better if you see a thing for what it is and not play like it's the way you'd like it to be. Now that's a fact, child. Man be a plum fool to stare the truth in the face and call it something else. Don't you listen to none of them in your family 'cause they never gonna tell you a good or true word. Keep yourself to yourself and don't go and mix in with none of them. Hold your tongue and first chance you get, child, you cut and run. Just get out of that hell hole fast as you can!"

He was so convinced, so sure about what he'd seen and what he knows about those people. It's as if he was cutting the feeling into my soul with a chisel. I think he was saying what I wanted to hear about that no good, bad family of mine 'cause I thought the same way myself!!

The Preacher man was a witness to my hatred, giving confirmation to how I felt. I did indeed hate them, and still do hate that style of life.

He told me to bide my time with them and one day I'd know when to break out of there. He said, "I've seen a heap of meanness in my time, child, but this takes the prize. I think that Brother there," and he looks over at Mr. Man, "is thinking bad of me. But the fact is that it's on me, on my shoulders, to do what's best for the most of us, child. Lord knows I don't like it, but this ain't the first time I got to do something I don't want to do. Looks like that's true for all of us here. It may take some time but I think Brother and Sister get over this one of these days. Yes, and I hope you do, too, child. You, too."

I'm always wantin' to get done with whatever work we has to do so me and Honey can both go set a spell. We rest up and she tells me stories and talks to me 'bout all of them things. She has happy, happy memories, but she is lonesome now that alla her chicky chicks has growed up and flown the coop.

"That's the way it supposa be, chile. That's how the Lord intend it to be," Honey tells me.

They wouldn't want it no other way. Still, it was kinda lonesome for them with no little children left on the place. And I know just what she's gonna say now. I feel all warm 'cause I sure do know what's comin' next. And I is plum happy 'bout that thing, too.

Yes, they was right lonesome, and her 'specs the Lord look down here and He figured that out. 'Cause the very next thing she knowed—DO YOU KNOW WHAT, CHILE?—she's a minding her own business and looks up one day, and whatcha think that OLD MAN come a draggin' in to this place on his WAGON SEATTT?

I don't know. I don't know a thing what her is a talkin' about! I can't even guess what that man would do! Him is liable to do any ol' thing. I agree with her that it ain't no tellin' what him is liable to drag onto this Place. I hear this a hundred times and I still do like to hear it again. I just feel all warm and tickled to death.

Honey says she didn't rightly know just what in the world it was him come a draggin' in on that wagon seat. Look like a little skinny half-starved dirty old baby kitten! Now that's what she first was a thinkin'. Then she looks again and wants to know where did he find THAT CHILE AT?

He said he find her along the way from town, and think she be a right much company for Honey. Once she gets that little 'un all clean and fixed up, he thinks it be a right nice little girl chile in there. He knows Honey can fix her up. He knows Honey is just the one to FIX THAT CHILE UP AND TAKE CARE OF HER!

Well, Honey tells him she ain't a gonna start takin' in no little stray chilluns! She done taked in alla them cats and dogs what he drug onto the place, but she didn't never 'spect him to take to draggin' in no little dirty white chile!! Where did he FIND her? Honey thinks that man is take leave of his senses a comin' on this place with a CHILE. But she reckon she have to take care of that little dragged-in thing after all.

"And do you know what, chile?" She looks at me.

"I just can't even guess 'bout this thing now, Honey. It do seem just too much for me to guess."

"Well now, IT WAS YOUUU, CHIIILE. IT WAS YOU! Here you come along to us!" She pokes my little nose, and says she thinks that old Lordy is done seen them was a little bit lonesome without no chick nor kin. So He send this little scared rabbit of a chile to 'em, and now, "We is have such good times round here 'cause of youuu, you little stringbean."

I hear all about her happy times with THAT MAN. She thinks the world and all of that man! She not take a share in the railroad for him. And she smiles a great big smile at me on account of I already knowed we not take a share in the railroad for him! "We's real glad to have that good man, ain't we, Honey?"

"Lord yes, Chile. Tell you the truth, we be right hard put to get along without HIM, wouldn't we?"

She tells me all about how her and the Man COURTED. Yes, yes they was a sight to see when them was courtin', and she tells me all of the things what they did when they was a Goin' Courtin'. She says they is "just keeped on a courtin' all of these years, too, Chile." And we fall over each other and laugh and laugh.

"Lord, we was a sight to behold in them days. I don't think my feets has touched the ground yet. . . . Why? 'Cause him is sweep me *offa* my feets, that's why. Just come along and 'bout take my breath away with his ol' self."

She thinks maybe he was a little sure of hisself, she did. He come a steppin' up there like as if he owned the place. She laughs and tells me that he was scared to death! "It was all SHOW, Chile, all show."

The Man says he was scared to death she would laugh at him. Says he had to get up alla his nerve to even speak to her. Honey thinks he is teasin' her, but he says no, he ain't. He say she was SOOO PRETTY that he was scared to death a her.

". . . And her DADDY! Lord, woman, that daddy of yours be enough to scare a young man into his grave!"

He talks in a deep voice and says, "Young man, I want to know just what are your intentions when you come around this house to see my daughter?"

And she laughs, and I laugh, and the Man laughs to think that he sounds just like her ol' daddy.

"He was quite a man, quite a man. But he sure put the fear of God in me 'bout courtin' his girl! Lord amercy, chile, it's a wonder I didn't turn tail and run like a yellow dog!"

Honey says she don't think it was THAT bad. He tells her she just don't know. She just don't know what he had to go through to get her!

Another time we is settin' under the shade tree and he tells me she is a wise ol' woman, and he says that it was a blessin' on his head when SHE IS CATCHED HIM.

Honey looks sideways at him, Hummppp is all she has to say 'bout that. To tell the truth, SHE the one got plum tired a runnin' away from HIM! And she declare he shouldn't oughta be telling this chile no such other story as that.

He keeped on though. "That woman turn her hand to catching me, and she did it, chile. Naw, I wasn't looking to marry up with that woman."

He says he was dead set against marryin' one of them pretty girls. Oh, them pretty girls can be a heap a trouble to a husband. He thought he'd just have a right good time with some of them pretty girls and then go on off and find a right ugly one to marry. Save hisself a heap of trouble that comes with having a pretty wife. Why, he be willing to bet she was the prettiest girl in three counties, iff'n not the WHOLE STATE! She run him plum bowlegged, and then took him right to the church just as soon as she catched him.

Oh, Honey rolls her eyes at him, to think he'd say that's the truth! "That man couldn't tell the truth if it jumped on him! Why, how can he lie to a chile like that and go on livin' with hisself?!" she says to me.

The Man winks at me. "Tell you the truth, chile, it did work out pretty good."

Course it wasn't exactly his IDEA, but seem like it's workin' out right well for him. He don't know 'bout HER, seein' as how she had to work so hard to get him into that church. But HE is right pleased with how it all turned out. "Cause," he tells me, "she is purely a blessin' on my head!"

"Where you heading to, Preacher?"

The man, walking by in his dark suit, answered Grandpa's question right away. "I'm off a preaching the word of the Lord, Mr. Foley."

That's what his voice said, but it was his tone that got my attention. I was sitting beside the house, hunched up so nobody could see me or get me. It was not as hot there—almost under the house—because that was the only place it was shady. As the sun started setting the shade strip was getting smaller, but it still was big enough to hold me.

I could feel the man's passion, his raging belief, when he said "the word of the Lord." But underlying those few words was the plain, somehow insultingly disrespectful way he said "Mr. Foley" to Grandpa. It reached in and got my attention; it was kind of like my mind tripped on its own shoelace when I heard that tone.

And Grandpa didn't even know it.

The reason the man walking by got my attention is very plain now, but I didn't know it at the time. Preacher Sawyer was "doing" Mr. Foley, just like the Man had showed me how to do it so the white folks didn't even know they were being "done."

The Man showed me so many important things in the short

while I knew him. The things he told me to remember, well, I have remembered them and I have followed his teachings just like a vine follows the pathway along a wire. He would recognize his teachings in my behavior today if he could see me go about my daily life.

It's as if an operation was performed on me long ago, all unknown and unfelt. Even though every memory of his influence was lost in some dark sub-basement of my soul, it still managed to control my life with a powerful force. That my every unknown thought and emotion should have been so hidden from me for so many years is just mind-shattering.

I recall once seeing a picture of a huge, full-grown old tree that was rich with grand limbs and branches. But the most wonderful thing was the root system which was shown as it existed under the ground; it was every bit as full and magnificent as the tree everyone could see above the earth.

That picture is what my life is like. Only I have not grown as my original roots would have dictated; instead I feel I was grafted from different stock onto those old, sickly, early roots. The Man and Honey have been that grafted-on tree. Now I've explored and mapped all of that structure below the ground. I've watered and tended the new roots their kindness prompted me to set, and pruned and cared for all the luxuriant growth they encouraged in me those many long-forgotten years ago.

I am with her, with Honey. She ain't right. I don't know what is wrong but I can see she ain't right. I am trying to get her in the house. It's a long time we just been staying right out there on the sandy ground.

". . . get myself together, chile. Just rest here a little bit longer till I can pull myself all together. Then we go on. Just have to stay right here a while is all. Now don'tcha worry none, okay? My legs got kinda weak, that's all. I gonna pull myself together and then go on in the house, mebbe start fixin' supper soon. . . . No, no, not now, chile," she says in a hush-hush-don't-worry-none kind of tone. "Not quite ready to go in just yet." She says we just wait right here is all. No need to worry.

I know something is not right with her. Never see her like this before. I have gone back there when I know not to, 'cause I got to see for myself one more time is Honey okay. I hide in the trees and watch. I can tell she ain't okay. I run out from where I'm hiding to help her 'cause I see her stagger around and almost fall down.

She is really out of her head, I know it now. I'm not sure what I thought at the time except she looked different and sounded a little different. But she was plain out of her head with grief, with fear for me. She kept trying to get me not to worry or be afraid for her.

The Man says she is sick. "Honey's sick, chile. Bad sick. I don't know what's gonna happen but I tell you right now I am mighty uneasy 'bout her." He tells me how she is been. No, he don't think it do much good to doctor her up. "Think her heart is broken, chile. Think there ain't no medicine for no such thing as a broken heart."

He is disturbed, and picking his words carefully. I know the feeling in him when he is thinking hard to pick out what he wants to say so I get his meaning. I can see he is so worried about her. The Man tells me I done the right thing. "Reckon I'm beholden to you for it, chile. I know it wasn't easy for you to get her up, but I sure hate to think 'bout her being out here all this time till I got to home." He rubs his ear, rubs his face.

It is not a familiar gesture to me, I think. It is tears. He moves his hand somehow to wipe tears off his face. He tells me how ". . . I know you can do it, chile. Know you be all right. Won't be easy, bein' by yourself and all. But I think you gonna be all right, chile, just as longs you hold on to the Lord."

In my mind "hold on to the Lord" means like I hold on to the Man's hand to get over the bad places. He always says maybe he can give me a little hand over this here hard place. "Just give me your hand right here and I help you get across the log, chile. Like this, see there! Whooowee, why YOU [what-a-smart-girl-you-is! tone] can do it just as good as anything, now can'tcha?" Oh, he beams and shines on me. Says, "Just hold on to my hand and I help you over the bad places, chile."

That is what I think is the bad places: the big puddles, the big logs across the path that I can't get over by myself. I think the Lord is gonna hold me just like the Man or Honey holds my hand over the hard places. The Lord do me just like they do iff'n I hold on to Him real tight.

The Man don't like doing this way but he says it's time for us to talk turkey. "I don't like saying this, chile, but you is in one mess. Now you know that, don'tcha?" His tone is like he's sure I get his meaning 'cause he tole me lotsa times I'm about as sharp as a brand-new tack.

"Comes a time in every man's life, chile, when he finds out he can't do nothin'. Kinda like a feller finds out he done been runnin' round and around thinkin' he's gettin' somewhere only to find out, when push come to shove, he ain't got nowhere. Ever which way I try and go, chile, I just run into a wall. Now, I done the best I could for you—me and Honey both is done the best we could—and I sure hope you can see that."

I can see he's hurt; I can feel his hurting. He is picking his words. The Man says, "I'd just as soon cut off my arm at the shoulder as tell you this, JoAnn." I know he means it. I can feel he's in bad pain. Says we just got to face the truth and go on. He'd as soon do anything else in the world, he tells me, than be having this talk.

"The truth is I can't do nothin'." He is about to cry. His shoulders shake some. I can feel him try and get aholt of hisself. "It's easy to do the right thing when things go along good, chile. Don't take much of a man to keep goin' along in easy times. You know that, now don'tcha. But comes the wicked times?" He is crying a little bit. "Come the wicked times, chile, and then a man got to just hold on and do the best he can till times get better. That's 'bout all we can do when things turn against us. Just hitch up our pants and go on along."

He looks at me, the Man does, as we walk out to the road that goes a ways on down to where my family lives. This is a man who is suffering, there is no doubt about it. Even a child can feel it. He is doing something harder for him, in some ways, than facing death would be.

". . . 'bout to kill her." I can't hear all he says 'cause his voice is quiet; I only catch a few of his words. I feel like he's trying to smile, but he don't smile at all. He tells me, "I'm afraid this is 'bout to kill Honey. And I don't reckon it do me any good either, chile."

The Man stops and looks close at me. His eyes are like wet

glass. "Lord God, chile. Lord God," he says. Then he reaches up his arms. I think is he gonna talk to the Lord? But no, he don't. He just says "Lord God" and raises his arms like a toddler waiting to be lifted up. "Lord God," is all he says.

I suppose that is a prayer in itself.

❋

I never looked back at the Man. Not that day, the last day. I turned around and waved bye bye but I knew there was no "see you tomorrow" this time. Not ever again after I waved.

I had barely glanced up to see him for one last time. It was an unclear view of a tall, too thin man (he was "too thin," Honey said, but she done give out on tryin' to fattenin' him up), waving one hand, his arm held about halfway up. I was so terribly sad. It was as if I'd been treading water in a swamp for all the days of my life and, when I heard those two loved people say good-bye, I wasn't able anymore to keep the alligators from pulling me down into the thick, murky waters.

He was indistinct when I'd turned around to wave, only a tall figure of a man. I did not cry. I never cried those tears of sorrow and loss. Never until this week, almost fifty years later. Imagine carrying around all those tears for fifty years!

She didn't know, but she reckoned one of these days to see that little chile be a big growed-up Somebody! Oh, how they sustained me all this time, all these years. Unremembered and unrecalled, they kept some tiny part of me alive, some small part they claimed that wasn't even as big as a penny. I had two pennies once upon a time; he gave them to me.

Once upon a long ago time I played in paradise. Through the ages people have written and spoken of a place called Paradise. Well, I lived there for a while. I may have been a dirty little white trash child, one of the ignorant Foleys, neglected and wild, but for a year I dwelt in a haven right there on the southern red clay and sandy soil of a ninety-nine-acre slave grant farm.

Between heaven and hell I found a pathway. I traveled it every day after I found the Man, until the day Bobby and Grannie snatched Lu Lu Belle from me as we hurried to move away. It was a path I made, a way I found to escape my family.

It wasn't a path to start with. It couldn't look like a path or else they'd catch on that I was using it to go somewhere. TO THAT GODDAM SMART ASS UPPITY NIGGER THAT HAD THE NERVE TO TELL BOBBY TO KEEP OFFA HIS PLACE! But he hadn't. The Man had told Bobby to get off of his property. I'm sure I had never heard the word "property" before, but right now I can see and hear, I can smell and feel that moment in my life when he calmly told Little Bobby to go away.

Some while later, when Little Bobby and I were playing Hide and Seek, I tricked him as soon as he gave me a turn to hide. I just ran right on, picking my way through the woods. There wasn't any path then, and I was worried over the way to go.

I can remember so clearly knowing that I couldn't let them catch me. I'd go off in the opposite direction across the fields for a good ways, then cut over to the railway tracks and double back toward the Place. Honey and the Man's Place. I knew I wouldn't leave any tracks on the railroad ties.

If they had caught sight of me anywhere near the old couple's house, I'd have gotten an awful beating. Grandpa had said he'd beat the shit out of any of us who he caught near that Old Nigger's farm. So I carved out a secret path that took me daily all the way from death to life's abundance.

Now, once again, I can hold Honey and the too-tall Man close to me in the full remembrance of their love and goodness. I may have lost them for a while, and thought I'd never again rise from the depths of the swamp, but memory has given me back that time when I learned something about paradise.

26

FOLLOW-UP:
A WORK STILL
IN PROGRESS

In March 1989 I found myself driving along a back road in Georgia on a journey I never imagined. I had joined JoAnn on a trip to her hometown to take up a search she'd abandoned a few years earlier when her leads ran out.

What we can't imagine ourselves doing, and undertake anyway, probably says more about us than realizing our long held dreams. I'd never socialized with a patient before; I'd never wanted to. In fact all the standard proscriptions against it made perfect sense to me. I wasn't sure how either therapist or client could get free of the accepted roles and expectations they'd both assumed as an essential element of their therapeutic relationship. Always such an honored trust, that relationship deserves protection from any possibility of misuse.

Yet there I was, ethical considerations and personal rules of conduct notwithstanding, on a trip with a former client. Being there said less about my doing something out of the ordinary than it showed how limited was my vision. Soon after my first appointment with JoAnn I started leaving the beaten trail behind and ending up in new territory. This outing wasn't so very different, except there were actual wheels under us this time.

It had been three years since her final therapy session—and that followed the six previous years of letting me accompany her on a breath-taking trip through the memories of her early days. Now here the two of us were again, this time heading into the actual landscape she had described with such keen detail in my office.

Not long before this JoAnn had given back to me all the writings I'd returned to her at the end of our work together. She'd lately been cleaning house, she told me then, and was determined to get rid of things from the past she no longer needed. What she *did* need was to make room for a future she now wanted. If I was interested in those notebooks, she'd be glad for me to have them all; they had already served their purpose for her. So, by the time we set out on this trip together, those same papers had come to be a considerable part of my present life. For about the last year I'd been reading through them again, captivated with the idea of seeing whether a coherent story might be drawn from the recollections they contained. If a way could be found, it would clearly be the result of a joint effort.

When JoAnn asked if I'd like to go with her back to her hometown, I leaped at the chance. I was most eager to be part of the search for Honey and the Man. I felt I'd learned a lot from them and—if we did find them—wanted to express my appreciation, much the way one returns to campus years later to thank a favorite professor for the lessons learned there. Also I thought the trip would be a chance to get a feel for the place where she grew up, with the principal character as guide.

We'd certainly come a long way together, the two of us, in making it to the city limits of a childhood she had exhumed in therapy. The miles driven in her car were the least of it. Now I was once again in the midst, this time quite literally, of JoAnn's seemingly infinite capacity to discover all she could know about herself. It was this combination of perseverance and curiosity, hers as well as my own, overlaying her previously buried past that finally propelled us toward her hometown in Georgia.

The particular part of the state she's from is pretty flat, boringly flat if you grew up near mountains. Oh, there's a little rolling to the landscape, but nothing that gives the eyes a workout if you're look-

ing to see how sky meets up with earth. As is true with many rural
areas, there are tiny outcroppings of houses clustered around most
crossroads. There are lots of crossroads in this part of the country,
apparent intersections of old wagon tracks, long since paved, connecting the many farms that lie about in all directions: peanut crops,
I guess, and some tobacco.

JoAnn's hometown strayed from its boundaries in the last few
decades. Shopping malls have popped up all around like mushrooms in a pasture after a summer rain. It looked like a valiant
attempt was made to revitalize the downtown business area. City
planners even tried the now-familiar practice of closing off a main
artery to traffic and bricking over the sidewalk and street for pedes-
trians to shop unimpeded. The idea didn't seem to have taken off
here, though; the malls had won the battle for commerce. Having
gone downtown for lunch when we arrived, we were alone in the
restaurant at noon and saw only a smattering of folks walking by the
boarded-up storefronts.

At the end of the bricked-over street, in the center of the city,
the famed Marketplace House sat at the hub of a decaying wheel. It's
a proud example of historic preservation. The irony of this handsome structure surviving in the midst of economic devastation is not
lost on the visitor who learns that the market in question was once
where slaves were bought and sold.

It was fitting that JoAnn and I began our visit to her past here in
the shadow of an institution that regarded some people as property
and others as having dominion over them. For me the Marketplace
House symbolized the heart of a web that was woven of her childhood. One of the strands certainly related to the abuse of power.
Another to the immorality and corruption of the spirit in those with
such awesome and absolute power. Still another thread reached out
to grasp thorny racial issues that reflected life then as it still does
today. And yet another stretched far beyond the city center to a
military presence that affected JoAnn's adolescence as surely as it
had left terrible scars on our young country over a century ago.

To reconstruct and locate ourselves in this fifty-six-year-old
web, we first went to the public library. There we examined old city
directories and studied colorful, intricate maps that let you know
such things as whether a particular house on a given street was built

of wood or cement block, was owned or rented by the occupant. Her grandfather, as "head of household," left a trail on those pages of the various houses she remembered with no fondness. But, try as we might, we couldn't find any evidence of Mr. Man and Honey. Nobody in her family had remembered their names, so the papers we were chasing kept leading us up blind alleys and out dead-end streets.

Interestingly enough, the two maps we found for the years she remembered most vividly showed neither of the houses the family rented then. You could see the area all right, but the little color-coded squares and dots only went as far as the other side of the street where they'd lived. In both cases, on both maps, the city limits ran down the middle of the streets that encompassed JoAnn's world, and her family was indisputably beyond what got counted. It had been one thing to hear her verbal picture of their life on the margins of society, quite another to see the reality on official documents.

After several hours of absorbing these relationships between time and place in her life, we left the library and JoAnn drove me through her former neighborhoods. What amazed her most was seeing how tiny had been the world her family inhabited: the various houses they'd occupied were within a mile or so of each other, largely on one end of town. In her child's memory, the distances between one place and another had been immense, surely because the emotional travels were so far-reaching for her at the time.

Wade Street, about which she wrote voluminously, was considerably changed since the early 1940s. There had been only a smattering of houses along a narrow and unpaved road in those days. Now, many small homes—mostly clapboard—lined the street, filling in the fields and empty lots of a less-crowded era. Railroad tracks ran hard by the back door of the house her family had jammed itself into. The place had been deserted for some time, just barely standing. No vestige remained of the outhouse she'd feared and hated. Because the railroad tracks splayed out right there, I imagined a freight yard close at hand being well fed through the ten or twelve pairs of tracks that suddenly materialized. Nothing else nearby looked well fed.

I was not surprised by anything JoAnn showed me on our drive, though I was shaken by much of it. Years before, while reading through her notebooks, I recall asking repeatedly, "How could that have happened?" "How was this possible?" It wasn't that I'd doubted her truthfulness, but it was difficult for me to believe people actually lived the way her family did. Maybe, come to think of it, I *had* been touched by some nethermost doubt back then because, now, taking in the setting where all those lives played out their parts, I was both saddened and relieved by what we found. I think perhaps there was relief in knowing that JoAnn had not convinced herself—and therefore me—of a reality at odds with the world around her. And I know I was profoundly saddened to realize that that *was* her reality after all.

For the better part of a whole day we wandered around, talking to the men and women on Wade Street who, it always turned out, had only moved there five or ten years before. We asked questions of people who didn't seem to relish talking with two middle-aged women whose accents were from another part of the country. A few weeks earlier, JoAnn had called the woman she met at the court-house and commissioned her to find out who once lived on the property where the feed and grain store now stood. Mrs. Sheridan had done her homework: the McDowell property had belonged to a prominent family from the area, and the deed had listed a total of seventy-five heirs. No one, however, according to all the informa-tion she came across, had lived there. JoAnn looked puzzled when she came back from making the call to Mrs. Sheridan; I was crest-fallen.

Finally, having grown tired of hearing that no one could help us, we looked up JoAnn's school records at the Board of Education. Copies of old report cards showed her grades were barely passing for those ten years, and the attendance figures were abysmal. During the year she lived on Wade Street, just down the road from the Place, she was absent more than a third of the school year. Most all absences were ascribed either to sickness or truancy.

Once more, conferring in the car, we went over what we'd learned so far. I didn't seem able to drop my disappointment about the information Mrs. Sheridan gave JoAnn over the phone. How could it be there was no record of anyone living there?

"You *did* tell her the people you were looking for were black, didn't you?"

"No," she answered, surprised at the question. "Should I have? I didn't think it was important."

"Well, I don't know if it's important or not, but I suppose it *might* matter in where you'd go to look up things down here, especially about that era. I think we should call her back."

JoAnn said she'd run out of steam, so I made the call this time. After telling Mrs. Sheridan who I was, I explained that the people we wanted to find were a black family.

"Oh, goodness," she replied after a short silence, "nobody told me. She never said anything about them being black." She apologized over and over about not knowing that, and again stated all the records she found indicated nobody lived on the McDowell property.

We must've spoken with thirty or forty people during those few days, putting quarters into pay phones as if they were slot machines. Among the most helpful group we came across was the assistant pastor of the Metropolitan AME Zion Church and several parishioners who kept suggesting names of people for us to question. Somebody with deep roots in the community remembered a man with a horse and wagon who sold vegetables in town. In spite of finally having a name to go on, it didn't show up on any records we could locate. Culled from several conversations, though, the one name which continued to surface was that of a man who'd been an administrator with the city school system. It was thought his father had a horse-drawn wagon back in those days.

As we tried to find the link to JoAnn's past, I thought often of my grandmother. She'd had a long-standing interest in genealogy, and apparently enjoyed searching along the branches of our family tree. I remember once hearing about her locating a document while on a trip to England in the late 1930s, a deed for some property around Stratford-upon-Avon sold by one of her ancestors to a chap named Wm. Shakespeare. Obviously Grandma's genes for this kind of cleverness hadn't made their way into my DNA in a sufficient amount to help our cause. If any trace of them had been present in me on this mission to Georgia, I'd surely have understood what must be a cardinal rule of genealogical research: never assume you know how a name is spelled.

We could've easily saved two days of phone calls and library time if I'd thought a name like Fisk might be spelled with a "Ph." A belated look in the phone book, after listings for the Phelps and Phillips, testified to the city being heartily stocked by Phisks.

Late in the afternoon of the last day we were going to be in town, JoAnn met the son of Honey and the Man. She had phoned him a few hours earlier, said who she was and what she was interested in learning, and asked if he'd meet with us before we left the area. When he came into the room she rushed over with tears in her eyes and threw her arms around him, something I'd never seen her do. He was a tall, handsome man; seventy-five years old, he told us later, and retired after a career in education of more than forty years.

She explained that his parents had been a godsend to her when she was a very young child. They were good people, he stated. His father took things pretty easily and liked to joke around, which was probably why he lived to be 102. The only time he ever went to the hospital was after being robbed and beaten over the head in his own home—and he was 95 years old then! He remembered his mother as being a very hard worker and having strong convictions, quite a bit more serious than her husband. She died in 1958, he went on to say.

An inaudible, except to me, long sigh came automatically from some deep and worried place in me. I'd wondered—for many years, I think—whether Honey had survived JoAnn's being taken from them and returned to her family. I realized I'd been hoping we weren't going to be told she had died soon after the Preacher carried JoAnn off the Place.

This distinguished gentleman, who'd come to meet us on an uncharacteristically cold early spring day wearing a gray fedora and a gray-black overcoat, told us he was one of seven children; only he and his youngest sister were still living. I don't know whether it was JoAnn or me who asked if he ever heard his parents mention a little white girl who lived not far from them in 1940.

No, he replied, maybe because he'd already left home by then, in 1934 it was, to work and put himself through college. He met his wife there, they soon got married, and there was never cause to move back in with his parents. In answer to our questions—mostly mine, really—about why their names hadn't shown up on any deeds or census information, he said his father had been the caretaker of the McDowell property for many years. Before that he'd lived on his father's hundred-acre farm in a nearby county.

So, I gathered, if you didn't own land or rent a house you didn't get counted in the census figures. Was that why Mrs. Sheridan wasn't able to find evidence of them? Or, in assuming JoAnn was looking for a white family, had she overlooked other sources of information? Even though many of our questions had been answered on this trip, since we'd run out of time and had to leave the next morning, it looked like others would have to go unaddressed.

I soaked up the bantering and reminiscing going on between JoAnn and the thoughtful man sitting across from her. He mentioned he and his wife had a large house with plenty of extra room (their children were gone and had families of their own now) and she would be welcome to come stay with them if she ever came back to visit. I don't know quite how she regarded it—she wasn't much given to flights of fancy, after all—but it appeared to me this encounter was a good deal more than two people simply talking about mutual acquaintances. I felt like I was witnessing a reunion between JoAnn and the family she never got to have, a meeting at last with a long-lost brother.

Soon after getting back home from our trip south, JoAnn decided to channel some of her newly freed energy into an issue about which she'd grown understandably more interested. Once again she chose to volunteer, this time to spend a day each week helping out in the office of the county hospital's overworked and under-staffed Sexual Assault Center. The first such facility in the region when it opened in 1975 (then as a rape crisis center), it often functioned as a proto-type for programs in other hospitals addressing problems of sexual violence in the community. As was her way, JoAnn made herself available for whatever the professional staff needed done: filing papers, typing, answering the phone. She even served as baby-sitter if a child's mother had an appointment with one of the counselors and either hadn't been able to get, or couldn't pay for, child care.

Before long another opportunity presented itself. A therapist at the nearby Community Mental Health Center, who was launching for the first time a one-year educational group for sexually abused clients, asked JoAnn to participate as a volunteer co-facilitator in the group. Not coincidentally, I'm sure, this same therapist had led the parenting group JoAnn attended almost ten years earlier.

After thinking about it for a couple of months, JoAnn decided to sign on. And she went about the job as if she'd been hired at a hefty salary. She read and studied, even more than before, the literature from this burgeoning field; she had regular conferences with the group's leader; she kept her own account of group meetings in order to understand process and how the group functioned. Always she was careful to be clear about her limits, and not to promise more than she felt qualified or was appropriate to deliver. She viewed her commitment to this program with the same degree of seriousness she'd held for her own therapy years earlier. At the very center of this enterprise, it seemed to me, JoAnn was moving from having been a consumer of services to being an adjunctive provider of them. In the setting where she'd once been a patient, she was now sharing what she'd learned with those needing help.

After the Georgia trip, while JoAnn was involving herself in new activities, I knew I needed to settle several things within myself if there was going to be any progress in my efforts to write about her story and the work we did in therapy. An old bugaboo of mine since I'd become a therapist, especially shadowing me in times of ease or abundance or joy, had again shown up in the form of some ambushing questions: Why did *I* have it so good? Why had *I* been so fortunate all my life? How come *I* got delivered to kind and caring parents while others were unwanted or hated or worse? For years, as I read of JoAnn's hardships, I would sometimes feel apologetic about how comfortable and agreeable my life had been. Now I was noticing a variation on this theme, becoming more menacing in proportion to my increasing preoccupation with the idea of giving voice to my recent experiences.

I was realizing that before I even got out of the blocks, the "starter" in me had quit aiming the starting gun skyward and instead was shooting me in the foot. I'd been in therapy with Celia for six months or so by that time, and I talked with her about how I was doing myself in.

It wasn't enough I was overwhelmed by the fact I'd never written anything before, or that I had close to five thousand typed pages to winnow down to something readably manageable. No, what I kept stumbling over—as maybe many do who scribble themselves onto paper—was the certain knowledge that I didn't know what I was talking about. I wasn't an expert on sexual abuse through any training and I didn't know anything about it firsthand from personal experience. I was concerned, in the end, about not having any credibility. Who would listen to me?

Celia let me talk on about the relative ease with which I'd moved through the years and the guilt I seemed to have about that. She told me I didn't need to apologize for not having had it as hard as my patients. "In fact," she said, "you have a valuable viewpoint because you know what it's like to grow up *without* abuse coloring everything you see. You can bring a clarity of vision to your work since those personal ghosts won't be haunting you."

I felt immeasurably lightened by her comments; they gave validity to the very circumstances of my life I'd frequently considered irrelevant, if not a drawback, to the work I did. The effect this had on me was reminiscent of a conversation with my mother four years earlier. I was telling her about my difficulty in accepting a bequest I'd received after the death of a relative. On and on I went about it: I didn't deserve such generosity because I hadn't done anything to earn it; it should more appropriately have gone to others who'd been more sensitive and loving to my benefactor.

I remember I was driving us somewhere in my parents' car; it was the first time I'd used cruise control.

"She wanted you to have it," Mom stated.

"Yes, but how can I accept it? It's only come to me through an accident of birth. I don't know what I should do . . ."

Peripherally I saw her turn toward me. I took my eyes off the road to look over at her; she was quiet for only a second or two.

"Do? Just be grateful, that's all," she said and turned back to look again at the highway ahead of us.

. . .

JoAnn was ready to move beyond her past. She had once summed up that feeling in a notebook finished during the last weeks of therapy. "The past," she wrote, "has been used as a potter's kiln, an oven, to form my being. But now the past has served its usefulness for me. It can, and shall, be sealed away. Sealed behind a crystal door, where it's clearly seen and remembered, though now set apart."

For a good while this seemed to be the case. She had more energy and was enjoying learning from her new work experiences. Then one day, or within the span of a week, a couple of crowns popped out of her mouth. The dentist who'd put them there said they were perfectly okay and, since there was no reason he could see for why this had happened, he reglued them. She thought he sounded defensive, as if he felt accused of having done a poor job many years ago. She became frustrated when he wouldn't hear that she wasn't blaming at all but simply saying something wasn't right.

What had happened, what it came down to, was that she *hadn't* been entirely able to seal off the past from her present. Perhaps she was no longer unconsciously governed by all those yesterdays, yet there were still aspects of the past with which she had to deal.

My father, the middle of seven children, grew up in a three-room house on Wolf Branch in Lee County, in the Appalachian tip of southwestern Virginia. His father had a small country store and the family worked a hillside farm which—along with chickens, cows, and pigs—yielded enough to sustain them. His mother was especially proud that none of her five sons had to work in the coal mines.

JoAnn, at least metaphorically, wasn't so lucky. For years she'd been mining the rich vein of her childhood, following the mother lode as deep as she could see it go. But now, with her crowns suddenly coming loose, she learned the work on herself wasn't done. Going about it the only way she knew how, she took herself back down in the mines, equipped with nothing but the pick of her interest and the shovel of her will.

Serendipitously, she found her way to Dr. McClure, a head pain and TMJ specialist. After the examination, he said that her temporomandibular joint was badly degenerated, her jaw was structurally misaligned, and the muscles around the entire area were extremely tight. He couldn't understand how she wasn't in excruciating pain.

Thus began a two-and-a-half-year project to reclaim her body. I thought she'd done that already in psychotherapy, but not in this way or to this extent. As was her style, JoAnn read all the literature on TMJ Dr. McClure shared with her, including fairly technical publications. He later stated she was the epitome of the kind of client who becomes a helpful and active participant in her treatment.

Before six months passed she was in unceasing pain; what began in her jaw and neck spread to every part of her body. She was hurting all over, in every muscle. McClure fashioned an appliance which fit over her lower teeth, kind of like a night guard worn by people who grind their teeth as they sleep. She wore it in order to maintain some measure of comfort in her jaw, head, and neck. Eventually she had to wear it so she could eat. Without it in place, her teeth met in front but there was almost an eighth of an inch space between the upper and lower chewing surfaces of her rear teeth. The bones and muscles in her head seemed to have thawed and were constantly shifting. She might finally feel relief in his office after having the appliance adjusted to her present bite, only to have her jaw move to a different place by the time she got back to her house. The pain was terrible, and once in a while she took medication to relieve it.

Just about as difficult to cope with as the pain JoAnn endured, was the kindness shown to her by Dr. McClure and his staff. I gather that he hadn't seen a situation quite like hers, in such flux for so long, and was eager to learn along with her. Even though he was sometimes perplexed about what was happening physically, she never sensed any annoyance with her for the time her appointments required. In agony late one night, she overcame her tendency to keep quiet and phoned the office's emergency number. He called back and arranged to see her first thing the next morning. She was worried he'd be angry with her, as her family always was when her needs were a bother to them.

As a measure of her growing trust, she told him how scary and hard it had been to ask for an emergency appointment. She described to me how he just looked at her and said with the utmost sincerity, "I would come in for you, JoAnn, anytime you called." While speaking of this encounter over the telephone, I could hear her softly crying about his show of concern. Realizing that someone cared about her was still not easy to accept.

One of the ironies of all this was that in order to help with her treatment she had to focus as much attention on her physical self as she once had given to her inner life. McClure relied on her body's awareness of pain to inform him of the areas needing attention. In identifying the place below her left ear from which the pain always seemed to radiate, she remembered the genesis of the entire problem; never was she beset by a moment's doubt about it. JoAnn recalled, as an eight- or nine-year-old, trying to run away from her grandfather by getting out of the house. He grabbed the twobyfour ("He always said it like it was just one word.") he kept by the door and slammed it against the side of her head. It knocked her out and she never felt a thing. Not then, not later, until just now.

As with the memories buried in her unconscious, she went from having no physical feelings to being adept at pinpointing a specific muscle, for instance, loosening in her hip when he worked on an acupuncture point in her shoulder. She was even able to feel the plates in her skull shift! I didn't know there were bones in the head which did that sort of thing, and couldn't imagine being that attuned. McClure, a holistic dentist, counseled her about diet and exercise; he also suggested massage and referred her to a chiropractor to realign her spine. "The head bone's connected to the neck bone, the neck bone's connected to the shoulder bone . . ." weren't just words from an old gospel song to her anymore. She could truly *feel* all those connections, each piece to all the others.

Trysh, her massage therapist, said that initially working with JoAnn was like trying to soften a plank. Over the years, in effect, she'd become physically encased in a full-length suit of armor. Her body was apparently still holding much of what her unconscious had already released. The feelings she'd had while shifting painfully in my office chair—having recalled being kicked as a child—had impressed me then with their inbuilt sense of timing. Now they seemed little more troublesome than a paper cut compared to the crushing of cartilage and bone, the tearing of muscle, she currently felt was happening in the somatic earthquake engulfing her and from which she couldn't escape.

JoAnn kept going deeper into her numbed body. Trysh went along with her, sometimes leading the way, sometimes following. To keep apace of the tone set by her client, she took additional training in structural integration work and working with sexual abuse survivors. She encouraged JoAnn's using yoga for stretching and balancing exercises. I suppose the body, since it can be touched and felt, is a bit easier to measure or assess than the psyche. Trysh told JoAnn her muscles and tissue needed time to respond to the workout they were getting. Because they're unable to release tension overnight, she said places of extreme tightness require a period of rest to adjust to the softening and loosening that's part of the healing process.

It was much the same message I used to deliver about the mind needing time to assimilate newly uncovered emotional material. Trysh didn't feel she was any more effective than I'd been in trying to influence her client's driven nature, her headlong pace. Still she did her best to encourage JoAnn to lighten up, do some other things, have some fun.

For JoAnn, I expect, the "fun" came in seeing the first joints of her fingers, bent for years by what had been diagnosed as arthritis, straighten out after kneading and massaging them over countless free moments. The payoff was in being able to move in ways never before even attempted, of feeling muscle where there was once just a solid, unyielding mass. Trysh was pleased one day to hear JoAnn finally tell her she was applying too much pressure to several areas being massaged, places where she'd worked at a deep level and never gotten any feedback. It was a great illustration—hurtful, but happily so—of how dramatically her body had changed. Seeing the effects of the various treatments JoAnn was receiving confirmed for me the importance of attending to the whole person.

As she continued her work toward being more integrated, and I was well into writing about it, it struck me quite often that we were on parallel tracks. I became as obsessive about remembering what happened during the years we worked together as she was back then about recalling her childhood. Where I used to urge her to take a break, to relax, now I found myself unable to ease up. I felt newly

driven and without any real choice about this project, just as she
used to argue was true for her regarding therapy. But lately her
journey had taken a decidedly outward turn while my trip on this
section of track was heading in the other direction.

JoAnn had become much more involved with people. Even
while not feeling well, she kept reaching out to others and was
forming new relationships. Five and six years after ending therapy
she could see how her already-known inner experience was now
being manifested in the pain felt in her outer, physical self.

For me, though, the turn was inward. I'd left my job with the
Outpatient Mental Health Clinic, after twenty years, so I could
devote more energy to writing. In the process I became almost reclu-
sive, seeing friends infrequently and only occasionally doing things
socially. With the intention of creating some balance in my life, I
maintained a small private practice that offered both stimulation and
a different sort of challenge from the solitary experience of sitting at
my computer. Courageous and earnest clients helped keep me
grounded during this introspective period.

Once, after rereading and working on some of her material for
many months without any let up, it hit me that I was feeling as grim
and humorless as JoAnn used to be. I couldn't even access the
carefree and spontaneous parts of myself anymore. Despite realizing
it was probably a natural response to my present circumstance, it
still felt kind of spooky. I got so I could write just like her. If some
descriptive passages were needed to clarify one of her pieces, the
inclusion of my words into her story was a seamless one. The border
between us faded; at least from my perspective it did.

I guess in a way similar to the accounts of actors becoming
enmeshed in their roles, that boundary separating me from my subject had dissolved, sometimes eerily so. Over a couple of stretches,
my jaw would suddenly and unaccountably start to ache—to such
an extent I couldn't sleep at night without taking aspirin. After some
of these incidents I later found out JoAnn had suffered particularly
painful episodes during those same times, and had seen Dr. Mc-
Clure several days in a row to have her bite adjusted. On a weekend
in May she called, puzzled and curious, to say she was having a
sense of moving backward through time: "I've been feeling like, in

an *emotional* way, I'm somehow going back to the beginning." The weekend of her call, I was in the middle of writing about her birth, her memories of being unwanted and pushed aside as soon as she was born.

And then there was the most upsetting time a while afterward, when I finally ended a chapter it took a month to finish. In a rare release of exuberance, I jumped up to hoop and holler and applaud my effort. A minute later it was all gone. The mistake was a fluky one, but I was careless in saving the material and wiped it out of my computer with an inattentive key stroke. What had vanished was chapter 20, my first extensive attempt to write about boundaries. Yeah, I thought, fluky, eh? A shift from the reality of my text on the monitor to its sudden nonexistence was a completely unexpected take for me on the subject of boundaries. Then, when my disbelief and anger subsided, I invoked the spirit of JoAnn to help me. If she could retrieve verbatim conversations repressed for fifty years, I certainly ought to be able to recall material that surely was still present in the less-than-month-old section of my memory. I did it, too, largely by slipping over into her consciousness.

There were many other effects the material and the experience were having on me. One such example happened on a raw and overcast March afternoon, fairly early in this project. I'd buried myself in the batch of JoAnn's papers that told of the incident about Hank Foley's ordering her into the bedroom one evening. When she didn't budge, he beat her up, then demanded somebody else service him. After managing to distill a three-page story from those unstructured recollections, I had just about brought the thing to a close when a knocking at the door finally registered with me. I was oblivious to the noise, but now that I heard it, I knew it had been going on for a minute or so.

I'd let Muffin out a few hours earlier and, truthfully, forgotten about her. She's our fourteen-year-old dog, and lots of times would lie around for half a day on the front porch. Obviously wanting in, she made herself heard by bumping against the screen door with her hip, the well-known signal for having had enough time alone. I was pissed off about being interrupted, out of all proportion to her request. Because I was so deep in the material, I think her insistent knocking was like shaking me awake from a dream I didn't want to give up.

So I clomped across the living room to let her in, neither taking time to think of a file name for the piece or entering the SAVE command. I whipped open the door and just stared because I hardly recognized her. There was no more lush black coat, no white collar and white-tipped tail that were her border collie markings. She was a mess, completely caked in mud. Only her size and stance looked familiar. That's when I saw it had been raining, in fact was still drizzling. And that's when I realized she'd been visiting our local groundhog. We'd seen him lumbering into his den a few days before; she tried to catch him then but he ducked into his hole ahead of her. She'd dug at the entrance like a puppy, stopping only when I gave a serious yell for her to come away.

In spite of the rain, she must've caught whiff or sight of him again, while I was busy in JoAnn's world. Apparently she'd had a field day digging at his hole, unbothered by any human reproach. The towel I gathered from the hall to dry her off with was worthless. So I grabbed her brush and snagged her by the collar. Before knowing what was going on, I began savagely to brush the clumps of dirt and mud from the fine hair of her legs and belly. Muttering, cursing, gasping for air, I raked the brush over and under her, harder than I'm sure she'd ever felt.

It was then I noticed her eyes. They were filled with shock and fear. I didn't even care. In fact, an ugly and joyful feeling shot through me when I saw how frightened of me she was, and it finally stopped in my clenched teeth: I could absolutely terrorize her. And I could do it so easily!

It was an awful moment of truth for me. Hank Foley wasn't a figure somewhere out there I could sit back and write about with contempt and righteous judgment. In my mind, while putting together JoAnn's story shortly before, I'd cursed at his inhumanity, his total self-absorption and disregard for anyone else. Yet here I was, in effect, beating up a dog for simply being a dog and instinctively doing a doglike thing.

JoAnn, with the skills of a survivalist, came through a childhood of almost constant cruelty. On the other hand, for too long I've felt somehow sorry about having had loving, supportive parents and innumerable advantages. Whereas she recalled and released the darkness that once imprisoned her, as I wrote up JoAnn's story and our story, I've become more acquainted with the characters in myself that I helped her rail against during those years in my office.

The Baddies were certainly obvious in her world. My struggle has been, and still is, to identify and claim as part of myself those darkling forms that hounded her and have stalked the lives of my other clients, but which I never encountered externally as a child. I am becoming conversant with a self-centered, angry, and cynical me I imagine my parents would have trouble recognizing. The real danger for us comes in refusing to acknowledge the existence of parts of ourselves we don't like or which we judge as bad. So it seems that after helping JoAnn feel safe enough to write out her childhood demons, I've typed them into a more whole me. In this shared process, we have helped each other become more of who we are.

Three months after she turned sixty years old, JoAnn took a women's self-defense class. All the previous and extensive work done on herself, including the recent treatment for TMJ, had brought her an increasing awareness of her feelings. She was able, for example, to register and name anxiety when driving somewhere she didn't want to be going. To know anxiety and ambivalence, on a deeper level yet, were mileposts for her. But even so, she knew there were still feelings that remained inaccessible. When she got a sense that maybe anger was stuck in her emotional passageway, blocking the flow of other feelings, she enrolled in an IMPACT class.

It was an intensive, twenty-five-hour course designed to help women protect themselves from physical violence. Great emphasis and sensitivity to the emotional component of the students' experience was built into the training. During the first five-hour class, each participant spoke about her greatest fear in taking the course. Quite a few mentioned being afraid of hurting someone, of being overwhelmed by their unfathomable anger. JoAnn was most afraid of *not* letting herself feel her anger.

The instructors taught moves and techniques applicable to a variety of assaultive situations. Two men, trained to be merciless and realistically fierce, functioned as the attackers. Both were encased in fifty pounds of padding, with virtually none of their bodies exposed. After being assured it was impossible to hurt their attackers, students were encouraged to use full force, to pull no punches or stay any kicks, in defending themselves or subduing their "muggers."

Laura, the main instructor, said it was probably the most intense class she'd ever led. She described JoAnn as not asking much of the experience, although she was extremely eager to learn and to get as much as she could from the course. "Everybody has a governor on their actions," she stated, "but JoAnn seemed to put her brain functions aside more than most others do."

The centerpiece of the class, toward which it all progressed, was the session in which every student was charged with creating her own custom scenario. The guidelines were simple: select, write up, and then present an incident in which you were assaulted, frightened, threatened, or otherwise in danger, and for which you want to construct a different ending this time.

JoAnn picked a quintessential scene for her exhibition. As usual, she cut to the core of it by telling the group about having killed a man when she was twelve years old. All she knew back then, which she never could've articulated, was that she'd have died and gone to hell if she hadn't done it. She never felt anything at the time, though, didn't even remember it until forty years later, she went on to say, and still hadn't felt the emotions of that act.

So she gave herself over to the most intense role-playing scene imaginable. Her attacker, expressing all of the Big Shot's status, power, outright threats, and slimy manipulations, played his part to perfection. With full consciousness this time, and to the sound of cheers and encouragement from her classmates, JoAnn unleashed the force of a survival instinct she had never owned. And then she didn't hear the whistle being blown. The whistle served to indicate the end of the exercise, when the attacker signaled that—without his padding—he'd have been immobilized by his "victim." In this case, Laura had to move the sixty-year-old, gray-haired student off and away from him.

She was pleased with all she did and what she got from the class. She felt it had been one of the best decisions she'd made, well worth the time and money spent. "JoAnn was always open to new experiences in the program," Laura mentioned, "and was most courageous about facing her issues."

Every once in a while we may be lucky enough to meet someone who brings out the best in us. They do it by their example more than anything else, by giving us the best of themselves.

A large part of why I've wanted to write of my experience with JoAnn is because I sense she has done that with me. Just by being who she is, she's offered a mark I've found myself stretching to meet. I don't believe she ever designed it as a kind of challenge, like a long jumper might lay down for the rest of the field. In fact, a lot of what has made her mark so appealing is the total lack of self-consciousness involved on her part. Somehow because of her determination to do better, because of a dedication and commitment to her own growth, similar qualities seem to have set their roots in me as I've tilled the loamy soil of our relationship.

If she had lived in a time and place where the ways of the people ran deeper and along a more natural path, I think JoAnn would've been regarded as a tribal elder, one who held the wisdom of the ancestors. I believe she might very well have been the village shaman, a crone or wise woman sought out for her valued counsel. People would've sat around the fire she tended. In those times and places, they'd have gone for help to the person who was herself, or himself, often the wounded healer of the community.

Thankfully, that's still frequently true today; the healing professions are home to many who've prevailed against the terrible odds of a hurtful and inhospitable childhood. Even without earning a degree that hinged on years spent in a classroom, JoAnn has become such a healer. It's been my blessing to have been touched by her.

I know as well that she, too, has been touched by me and my devotion to this process. I've always been amazed how people from profoundly different backgrounds and worlds manage to establish a connection or define a common purpose. Yet, with life so full of mystery and magic, JoAnn and I have done just that.

Throughout the years she has remained a model for me. Today she still moves back and forth along the spiral of her life, sometimes winding in toward the center, now more often sweeping further outward. Although I wouldn't say JoAnn has triumphed over her past, I think of her as triumphant. For all of us the victory comes in continuing our efforts to claim and integrate the forgotten, lost, or unacknowledged parts of ourselves. It's a job never finished.

Sometimes now I think of the Preacher's comments to the Man about the little white trash girl they were taking back to her awful home. "This child was put there by the Lord," is what the Preacher said, "and that's where she's been set down to do her work."

Of course I can't help but wonder if remembering and writing of those long-ago days has been some of the reason she was set down here for. Since she was always convinced of not having had an option about doing the work her therapy required, I imagine that perhaps she was indeed chosen instead of getting a chance to choose.

And yes, while the years have gone by I've grown more convinced that I was meant to do a section of this work with her. So, the element of choice has felt absent for me, too, as I've tried to keep faith with my half of the bargain we made many years ago during her first session in my office. There is a gift to the self that comes of doing what you must. The exchange between us has formed a pure and simple circle.

ABOUT THE AUTHOR

Rose Mary Evans is a clinical social worker in private practice in the Maryland suburbs of Washington, D.C. She lives in the countryside of West Virginia, where she gardens and raises shiitake mushrooms.